LIBRARY OF HEBREW BIBLE/
OLD TESTAMENT STUDIES

680

Formerly Journal for the Study of the Old Testament Supplement Series

Editors
Claudia V. Camp, Texas Christian University, USA
Andrew Mein, University of Durham, UK

Founding Editors
David J. A. Clines, Philip R. Davies and David M. Gunn

Editorial Board
Alan Cooper, Susan Gillingham, John Goldingay, Norman K. Gottwald,
James E. Harding, John Jarick, Carol Meyers,
Daniel L. Smith-Christopher, Francesca Stavrakopoulou,
James W. Watts

BIBLICAL NARRATIVES, ARCHAEOLOGY AND HISTORICITY

Essays in Honour of Thomas L. Thompson

Edited by

Łukasz Niesiołowski-Spanò

and

Emanuel Pfoh

t&tclark

LONDON • NEW YORK • OXFORD • NEW DELHI • SYDNEY

T&T CLARK
Bloomsbury Publishing Plc
50 Bedford Square, London, WC1B 3DP, UK
1385 Broadway, New York, NY 10018, USA
29 Earlsfort Terrace, Dublin 2, Ireland

BLOOMSBURY, T&T CLARK and the T&T Clark logo
are trademarks of Bloomsbury Publishing Plc

First published in Great Britain 2020
Paperback edition first published 2021

Copyright © Łukasz Niesiołowski-Spanò, Emanuel Pfoh and contributors, 2020#

Łukasz Niesiołowski-Spanò and Emanuel Pfoh have asserted their right under the Copyright,
Designs and Patents Act, 1988, to be identified as Editors of this work.

All rights reserved. No part of this publication may be reproduced or
transmitted in any form or by any means, electronic or mechanical,
including photocopying, recording, or any information storage or retrieval
system, without prior permission in writing from the publishers.

Bloomsbury Publishing Plc does not have any control over, or responsibility for,
any third-party websites referred to or in this book. All internet addresses given
in this book were correct at the time of going to press. The author and publisher
regret any inconvenience caused if addresses have changed or sites have
ceased to exist, but can accept no responsibility for any such changes.

A catalogue record for this book is available from the British Library.

A catalog record for this book is available from the Library of Congress.

ISBN: HB: 978-0-5676-8656-5
PB: 978-0-5677-0177-0
ePDF: 978-0-5676-8657-2

Series: Library of Hebrew Bible/Old Testament Studies, ISSN 2513-8758, volume 680

Typeset by Forthcoming Publications (www.forthpub.com)

To find out more about our authors and books visit
www.bloomsbury.com and sign up for our newsletters.

Thomas L. Thompson

Contents

List of Figures	xi
List of Contributors	xiii
List of Abbreviations	xv
Introduction	
Łukasz Niesiołowski-Spanò and Emanuel Pfoh	xix
The Publications of Thomas L. Thompson	xxiii

Part 1
Method

THE CITY OF DAVID AS A PALIMPSEST	
Margreet L. Steiner	3
LIVING IN THE PAST? KEEPING UP-TO-DATE IN ANCIENT NEAR EASTERN STUDIES	
Raz Kletter	10
WHAT PEOPLE WANT TO BELIEVE: OR FIGHTING AGAINST 'CULTURAL MEMORY'	
Niels Peter Lemche	22
THE NEED FOR A COMPREHENSIVE SOCIOLOGY OF KNOWLEDGE OF BIBLICAL AND ARCHAEOLOGICAL STUDIES OF THE SOUTHERN LEVANT	
Emanuel Pfoh	35

Part 2
History, Historiography and Archaeology

THE ABRAHAM AND ESAU-JACOB STORIES IN THE CONTEXT OF THE MACCABEAN PERIOD	
Łukasz Niesiołowski-Spanò	49

TELL BALATA (SHECHEM):
AN ARCHAEOLOGICAL AND HISTORICAL REASSESSMENT
    Hamdan Taha and Gerrit van der Kooij   62

'SOLOMON' (SHALMANESER III) AND THE EMERGENCE OF JUDAH
AS AN INDEPENDENT KINGDOM
    Russell Gmirkin   76

ON THE PRE-EXILIC GAP BETWEEN ISRAEL AND JUDAH
    Étienne Nodet   91

PERCEPTIONS OF ISRAEL'S PAST IN QUMRAN WRITINGS:
BETWEEN MYTH AND HISTORIOGRAPHY
    Jesper Høgenhaven   101

IS JOSEPHUS'S JOHN THE BAPTIST PASSAGE A CHRONOLOGICALLY
DISLOCATED STORY OF THE DEATH OF HYRCANUS II?
    Gregory L. Doudna   119

THOMPSON'S JESUS: STARING DOWN THE WISHING WELL
    Jim West   138

THE QUR'AN AS BIBLICAL REWRITING
    Mogens Müller   145

Part 3
BIBLICAL NARRATIVES

THE FOOD OF LIFE AND THE FOOD OF DEATH IN TEXTS FROM
THE OLD TESTAMENT AND THE ANCIENT NEAR EAST
    Ingrid Hjelm   159

A GATE IN GAZA: AN ESSAY ON THE RECEPTION OF TALL TALES
    Jack M. Sasson   176

DEBORAH'S TOPICAL SONG: REMARKS ON THE *GATTUNG* OF JUDGES 5
    Bob Becking   190

HOW JERUSALEM'S TEMPLE WAS ALIGNED TO MOSES' TABERNACLE:
ABOUT THE HISTORICAL POWER OF AN INVENTED MYTH
    Rainer Albertz   198

CAN THE BOOK OF NEHEMIAH BE USED AS AN HISTORICAL SOURCE,
AND IF SO, OF WHAT?
    Lisbeth S. Fried   210

CHRONICLES' RESHAPING OF MEMORIES OF ANCESTORS
POPULATING GENESIS
    Ehud Ben Zvi   225

THE BOOK OF PROVERBS AND HESIOD'S *WORKS AND DAYS*
    Philippe Wajdenbaum   248

THE VILLAIN 'SAMARITAN':
THE SĀMIRĪ AS THE OTHER MOSES IN QUR'ANIC EXEGESIS
    Joshua Sabih   258

Index of References   274
Index of Authors   284

Figures

Figure 0.1   Thomas L. Thompson, photo by Ingrid Hjelm.
Figure 6.1   Tell Balata in its recent urban setting, after clearance in 2010, view to south (courtesy Tell Balata Archaeological Park). Photo taken by Hamdan Taha and Gerrit van der Kooij.
Figure 6.2   Tell Balata plan showing the excavated parts with numbered areas of special attention. It also shows the location of the new entrance and the 'Interpretation Center' for visitors (courtesy Tell Balata Archaeological Park, drawing based on G. R. H. Wright 2002: Ill. 2). Photo taken by Hamdan Taha and Gerrit van der Kooij.

Contributors

Rainer Albertz, *University of Münster, Germany*

Bob Becking, *Utrecht University, the Netherlands*

Ehud Ben Zvi, *University of Alberta, Canada*

Greg Doudna, *Independent Scholar, USA*

Lisbeth S. Fried, *University of Michigan, USA*

Russell Gmirkin, *Independent Scholar, USA*

Ingrid Hjelm, *University of Copenhagen, Denmark*

Jesper Høgenhaven, *University of Copenhagen, Denmark*

Raz Kletter, *University of Helsinki, Finland*

Niels Peter Lemche, *University of Copenhagen, Denmark*

Mogens Müller, *University of Copenhagen, Denmark*

Łukasz Niesiołowski-Spanò, *University of Warsaw, Poland*

Etienne Nodet, *École biblique et archéologique française de Jérusalem, Israel*

Emanuel Pfoh, *National Research Council (CONICET) / National University of La Plata, Argentina*

Joshua Sabih, *University of Copenhagen, Denmark*

Jack Sasson, *Vanderbilt University, USA*

Margreet Steiner, *Independent Scholar, the Netherlands*

Hamdan Taha, *former Deputy Minister of the Ministry of Tourism and Antiquities, Palestine*

Gerrit van der Kooij, *University of Leiden, the Netherlands*

Philippe Wajdenbaum, *Independent Scholar, Belgium*

Jim West, *Ming Hua Theological College, Hong Kong*

ABBREVIATIONS

AAR	American Academy of Religion
ÄAT	Ägypten und Altes Testament
ABRL	Anchor Bible Reference Library
ABS	Archaeological and Biblical Studies – Society of Biblical Literature
ACR	*Archaeological Review from Cambridge*
ADAJ	*Annual of the Department of Antiquities of Jordan*
AfO	*Archiv für Orientforschung*
AMI	Archäologische Mitteilungen aus Iran
*ANET*³	*Ancient Near Eastern Texts Relating to the Old Testament.* Edited by James B. Pritchard. 3rd ed. Princeton: Princeton University Press, 1969
AOAT	Alter Orient und Altes Testament
ARM	Archives Royales de Mari
ArOr	*Archiv Orientální*
ASOR	American Schools of Oriental Research
ASORAR	American Schools of Oriental Research, Archaeological Reports
AuOr	*Aula Orientalis*
BA	*Biblical Archaeologist*
BAR	*Biblical Archaeology Review*
BASOR	*Bulletin of the American Schools of Oriental Research*
BEATAJ	Beträge zur Erforschung des Alten Testaments und des antiken Judentums
BEThL	Bibliotheca Ephemeridum Theologicarum Lovaniensium
BI	Biblical Intersections
Bib	*Biblica*
BJS	Brown Judaic Studies
BJSUCSD	Biblical and Judaic Studies
BK	Biblischer Kommentar
BN	*Biblische Notizen*
BTAVO	Beihefte zum Tübinger Atlas des Vorderer Orients
BTB	*Biblical Theology Bulletin*
BZAW	Beihefte zur Zeitschrift für die alttestamentliche Wissenschaft
CBÅ	*Collegium Biblicum Årskrift*
CBET	Contributions to Biblical Exegesis and Theology
CBQ	*Catholic Biblical Quarterly*
CIS	Copenhagen International Seminar series

CRAIBL	*Comptes-rendus de l'Académie des inscriptions et belles-lettres*
DJD	Discoveries in the Judaean Desert
DSD	*Dead Sea Discoveries*
DTT	*Dansk Teologisk Tidsskrift*
EdF	Erträge der Forschung
EI	*Eretz Israel*
EncJud	*Encyclopaedia Judaica*
ESHM	European Seminar in Historical Methodology
FAT	Forschungen zum Alten Testament
FBE	Forum for Bibelsk Eksegese
FRLANT	Forschungen zur Religion und Literatur des Alten und Neuen Testaments
HAT	Handbuch zum Alten Testament
HLS	*Holy Land Studies. A Multidisciplinary Journal*
HThKAT	Herders Theologischer Kommentar zum AT
HTR	*Harvard Theological Review*
IAA	The International Association for Assyriology
IEJ	*Israel Exploration Journal*
IES	Israel Exploration Society
INR	*Israel Numismatic Research*
JANES	*Journal of the Ancient Near Eastern Society*
JAOS	*Journal of the American Oriental Society*
JBL	*Journal of Biblical Literature*
JBS	*Journal of Biblical Studies*
JBTh	Jahrbuch für Biblische Theologie
JES	*Journal of Ecumenical Studies*
JESHO	*Journal for the Economic and Social History of the Orient*
JETS	*Journal of the Evangelical Theological Society*
JJS	*Journal of Jewish Studies*
JQR	*The Jewish Quarterly Review*
JR	*The Journal of Religion*
JRA	*Journal of Roman Archaeology*
JSHJ	*Journal for the Study of the Historical Jesus*
JSJ	*Journal for the Study of Judaism*
JSJSup	Journal for the Study of Judaism Supplement Series
JSOT	*Journal for the Study of the Old Testament*
JSOTSup	Journal for the Study of the Old Testament Supplement Series
JSS	*Journal of Semitic Studies*
JTS	*The Journal of Theological Studies*
LAI	Library of Ancient Israel
LAR	D. D. Luckenbill, *Ancient Records of Assyrian and Babylonia*, 2 vols, Chicago: University of Chicago Press, 1926
LHBOTS	Library of Hebrew Bible and Old Testament Studies
NEB	Neue Echter Bibel
NTT	*Norsk Teologisk Tidsskrift*
OA	*Oriens Antiquus*
OBO	Orbis Biblicus et Orientalis

OTL	Old Testament Library
OTR	Old Testament Readings
OTS	Oudtestamentische studiën
PEQ	*Palestine Exploration Quarterly*
RB	*Revue Biblique*
RBL	*Revue of Biblical Literature*
REA	*Revue des Études Anciennes*
RevQ	*Revue de Qumrân*
RIHAO	*Revista del Instituto de Historia Antigua Oriental 'Dr Abraham Rosenvasser'*
SBL	Society of Biblical Literature
SBTS	Sources for Biblical and Theological Study
SHANE	Studies in the History of the Ancient Near East
SHCANE	Studies in the History and Civilizations of the Ancient Near East
SJOT	*Scandinavian Journal of the Old Testament*
SPB	Studia Post Biblica
STDJ	Studies on the Texts of the Desert of Judah
StTh	*Studia Theologica*
SWABS	The Social World of Biblical Antiquity, Second Series
TA	*Tel Aviv*
TSAJ	Texts and Studies in Ancient Judaism
UF	*Ugarit Forschungen*
VT	*Vetus Testamentum*
VTSup	Supplements to Vetus Testamentum
WBC	Word Biblical Commentary
WHJP	*World History of the Jewish People*
WMANT	Wissenschaftliche Monographien zum Alten und Neuen Testament
WUNT	Wissenschaftliche Untersuchungen zum Neuen Testament
ZAR	*Zeitschrift für Altorientalische und Biblische Rechtsgeschichte*
ZAW	*Zeitschrift für die alttestamentliche Wissenschaft*
ZBK.AT	Zürcher Bibel Kommentar – Altes Testament
ZDPV	Zeitschrift des Deutschen Palästina-Vereins
ZEP	Zeitschrift für Papyrologie und Epigraphik

Introduction

Łukasz Niesiołowski-Spanò and Emanuel Pfoh

Thomas L. Thompson has been, for the past five decades, behind some of the – if not all – major changes in Old Testament historiography, if we consider that his criticism of the patriarchal narratives, the exodus and settlement and the United Monarchy were each at their own time forerunners of what later on would become accepted in the field (Thompson 1974, 1987, 1992, 1999). His work from the 1970s through the 1990s was certainly decisive in crafting a critical understanding of that now infamous creature 'ancient Israel' – a task he, along with Philip R. Davies, Niels Peter Lemche and Keith W. Whitelam, deconstructed in different ways within the field of Old Testament studies. The grouping of these four scholars is not innocent, of course, as already during the 1990s they were thrown together under the tag of 'biblical minimalists' by scholarly adversaries (the so-called, by opposition, 'maximalists'). As has been noted elsewhere (Whitelam 2002), understanding these four scholars under this epithet is not only misinformed but eventually wrong, since they did not agree on every point nor were they addressing the same issues from the same perspective. However, on many issues they agreed, if not on the results, certainly on the methodology and the ways in which to conduct historical research in Old Testament studies. And the arrival at such a situation in the 1990s has a lot to do with Thomas's career.

Thomas was born on 7 January 1939 in Detroit (Michigan, United States); however, some fifty years later he ended up becoming a European citizen. This latter event resulted not only from the objective aspects of academia's international movements of scholars in the field of biblical studies, but also reflects a historiographical declaration by Thompson: an appreciation of the European academic tradition and the European way of conducting scholarly debates. Thomas's early experiences in Europe were not typical. Initially, after his early university studies at Duquesne

University in Pittsburgh, he continued his education in Oxford and Tübingen. The period spent in Tübingen was paramount in his scholarly training as it was precisely there that he worked on his doctoral dissertation and became involved in the collective efforts of the 'Tübinger Bibelatlas'.

Between 1967 and 1971, Thompson prepared his PhD thesis on the historicity of the patriarchal narratives, and his fate in relation to this work is now well known in the scholarly field (something evocated in one of his own books, in which Thompson narrates his scholarly odyssey much better than we do here: Thompson 1999: xi–xix). The dissertation was not accepted in the Faculty of Catholic Theology of the University of Tübingen, and he would end up earning his doctorate with a *summa cum laude* across the Atlantic, in Temple University in 1976. Nonetheless, Thompson had by then already published the undefended dissertation in 1974 as *The Historicity of the Patriarchal Narratives: The Quest for the Historical Abraham*, and the book now constitutes a pivotal event in Old Testament studies regarding discussions on the historicity of the biblical narratives while also aiming to develop the critical methodologies of the 1990s. But this is the perspective we have now after more than four decades! In the context of the academia of the 1970s, Thompson's thesis was – apart from a few exceptions – generally rejected as standard knowledge and results, and he started a period of his life in which he would find himself, in his own words, 'unemployed and unemployable for ten years'.

Thomas's second scholarly life started in the mid-1980s, with a visiting professorship at the École Biblique et Archéologique in Jerusalem. His next few years would have been typical of an early-stage-career post-doc employment structure. Paradoxically, the author of an already groundbreaking and by then widely quoted work was offered only short-term rather than tenure-track positions, and when finally in 1992 he was about to get tenure at Marquette University, the publication of his *Early History of the Israelite Peoples* caused controversy within the university's religious establishment and once again academia reacted against his challenging ideas by expelling one of the trouble-makers. But Thomas's story did not end there; quite the contrary, it was about to have another new beginning. Supported by Niels Peter Lemche, in 1993 he was awarded a chair as Professor of Old Testament at the Faculty of Theology of the University of Copenhagen. At 54 years old, Thompson had found his stable place for good. He was employed at the University of Copenhagen for sixteen years, and retired in 2009, becoming a professor emeritus thereon.

The fact that Thomas had to start his academic career twice (or three times!) made his profile unique in the best of ways. In spite of all the years that have passed since his early involvement in academia, he continues to be a young scholar in thought and enthusiasm. Thomas's research also continues to be uncompromising in a very particular way: he resists the influence of routine and avoids falling into academic ruts – a danger that lurks at the door of every professor sitting comfortably in his or her chair and enjoying academic stability.

Another characteristic of Thomas is that he has always sympathised with the rejected ones and the 'weaker' in academia. As noted above, he himself had a varied experience with rejection by the scholarly establishment in spite of being correct in many of his insights, as time was sure to prove. The current, should we say, undisputed impact of his PhD thesis on the ahistoricity of the patriarchal narratives in biblical scholarship, in the light of its initial opposition, illustrates the triumph of a resolute ethics of research. The fate of Thomas's doctorate also shows the prevalence of integrity in scholarship, against the submission to the demands of academic authority and the expectations of the scholarly majority. Giovanni Garbini – another uncompromising ally of Thomas's – used to say that his early teachers would tell him that it was better to agree with the scholarly environment than to be right. Unsurprisingly, Garbini added that he always acted in opposition to this advice. This attitude also characterises Thomas's scholarship. He does not intend to please his readers and side with the mainstream. His work is often set against the *communis opinio* and never goes uncritically with the flow.

Thomas is also an engaging person, a protective friend and a true believer in peaceful resolutions. Even during the harshest moments of the debate between the so-called biblical maximalists and minimalists, Thomas served as an emissary of dialogue. While some of his colleagues were irritated by absurd and sometimes painful accusations, Thomas was able to sit over a glass of wine or a cup of coffee with the adversaries and talk. Thomas always separates – something not common enough – scholarly polemics from personal relationships.

We wish to honour this eminent scholar in the year of his 80th birthday by paying homage to his scholarly achievements with a set of studies dealing with the archaeology of the Levant, questions of history and historiography and themes related to the biblical narratives (in plural, from the Old Testament to Qumran to the New Testament and the Qur'an), all topics that have been of interest to Thomas during the more than five decades of his career.[1] We hope that this volume serves as a fitting tribute in honour of a great scholar who is also a great and a most generous person.

References

Thompson, T. L. (1974), *The Historicity of the Patriarchal Narratives: The Quest for the Historical Abraham*, BZAW 133, Berlin: de Gruyter.

Thompson, T. L. (1987), *The Origin Tradition of Ancient Israel, I: The Literary Formation of Genesis and Exodus 1–23*, JSOTSup 55, Sheffield: JSOT Press.

Thompson, T. L. (1992), *Early History of the Israelite People: From the Written and Archaeological Sources*, SHANE 4, Leiden: E. J. Brill.

Thompson, T. L. (1999), *The Bible in History: How Writers Create a Past*, London: Jonathan Cape = *The Mythic Past: Biblical Archaeology and the Myth of Israel*, New York: Basic Books.

Whitelam, K. W. (2002), 'Representing Minimalism: The Rhetoric and Reality of Revisionism', in *Sense and Sensitivity: Essays on Reading the Bible in Memory of Robert Carroll*, ed. A. G. Hunter and P. R. Davies, JSOTSup 348, 194–223, Sheffield: Sheffield Academic Press.

---

1. While this volume was in preparation, we learned of the untimely death of Philip R. Davies, who was to contribute with a paper on 'Genesis to Kings as a "Primary History"', a topic very close to Thomas's interests.

The Publications of Thomas L. Thompson*

Books

1. *The Historicity of the Patriarchal Narratives: The Quest for the Historical Abraham*, BZAW 133, Berlin: de Gruyter, 1974. Repr. Harrisburg, PA: Trinity Press International, 2002, 392 pp.
2. *The Settlement of Sinai and the Negev in the Bronze Age*, BTAVO 8, Wiesbaden: Dr. Ludwig Reichert Verlag, 1975, xi + 210 pp.
3. *The Settlement of Palestine in the Bronze Age* (with technical assistance from Maniragaba Balibutsa and Margaret M. Clarkson), BTAVO 34, Wiesbaden: Dr. Ludwig Reichert Verlag, 1979, xiv + 495 pp.
4. *The Origin Tradition of Ancient Israel: I. The Literary Formation of Genesis and Exodus 1–23*, JSOTSup 55, Sheffield: Sheffield Academic Press, 1987, 221 pp.
5. (with F. J. Gonçalves and J. M. van Cangh) *Toponymie Palestinienne: Plaine de St Jean D'Acre et Corridor de Jérusalem*, Publications de L'Institut Orientaliste Louvain, 37, Louvain La Neuve: Université Catholique de Louvain, 1988, 132 pp.
6. *Early History of the Israelite People. From the Written and Archaeological Sources*, SHANE 4, Leiden: E. J. Brill, 1992, 1994, 2000, xv + 482 pp.
7. (with Niels Hyldahl [eds]) *Dødehavsteksterne og Bibelen*, FBE 8, Copenhagen: Museum Tusculanums Forlag, 1996, 159 pp.
8. (with Fred H. Cryer [eds]) *Qumran Between the Old and New Testaments*, CIS 6, Sheffield: Sheffield Academic Press, 1998, 398 pp.
9. *The Mythic Past: Biblical Archaeology and the Myth of Israel*, New York: Basic Books, 1999, 2000; published also as *The Bible in History: How Writers Create a Past*, London: Jonathan Cape, 1999; London: Pimlico, 2000, 431 pp. Arabic translation: Damascus: Cadmus Press, 2001, 620 pp.
10. (ed.) *Jerusalem in Ancient History and Tradition*, CIS, London: T&T Clark International, 2003, xxii + 301 pp. Arabic translation: T. L. Thompson and S. K. Jayyusi (eds), *Al-Quds, Urūshalīm al-'adūr al-qadīma bīn altūrāh wa al-tārīkh* [Al-Quds, The Ancient City of Jerusalem Between Tradition and History], Beirut: Centre for Arab Unity Studies, 2003, 381 pp.
11. (with Henrik Tronier [eds]) *Frelsens biografisering*, FBE 13, Copenhagen: Museum Tusculanums Forlag, 2004, 307 pp.

* This bibliographical list builds upon the one compiled by Ingrid Hjelm in *SJOT*, 23 (1) (2009): 149–59, and updates the data to December 2018.

12. (with Keith Whitelam, Niels Peter Lemche, Ingrid Hjelm and Ziad Muna), *Al Iadīd fī tārīkh filasīīn alqadīmah rīkh filasīīn alqadīmah* [New Information about the History of Ancient Palestine], Damascus and Beirut: Cadmus Press, 2004, 249 pp.
13. (with Mogens Müller [eds]) *Historie og konstruktion. Festskrift til Niels Peter Lemche i anledning af 60 års fødselsdagen den 6. september 2005*, FBE 14; Copenhagen: Museum Tusculanum Forlag, 2005, 444 pp.
14. *The Messiah Myth: The Near Eastern Roots of Jesus and David*, New York: Basic Books, 2005; London: Jonathan Cape, 2006; London: Pimlico, 2007; Damascus and Beirut: Cadmus Press. 2006 (in Arabic), 414 pp.
15. (with Thomas S. Verenna [eds]) *'Is This Not the Carpenter?' The Question of the Historicity of the Figure of Jesus*, CIS, Sheffield: Equinox, 2012, viii + 280 pp.
16. *Biblical Narrative and Palestine's History: Changing Perspectives 2*, CIS, Sheffield: Equinox, 2013, xv + 352 pp.
17. (with Philippe Wajdenbaum [eds]) *The Bible and Hellenism: Greek Influence on Jewish and Early Christian Literature*, CIS, Durham: Acumen, 2014, x + 297 pp.
18. (with Ingrid Hjelm [eds]) *History, Archaeology and the Bible Forty Years after 'Historicity': Changing Perspectives 6*, CIS, London: Routledge, 2016, xvi + 229 pp.
19. (with Ingrid Hjelm [eds]) *Biblical Interpretation Beyond Historicity: Changing Perspectives 7*, CIS, London: Routledge, 2016, xiv + 208 pp.

Articles

1. 'Notes Toward a Theology of Existence', *Philosophy Today*, 6 (2) (1962): 125–32.
2. (with Dorothy Irvin) 'Some Legal Problems in the Book of Ruth', *VT*, 18 (1968): 79–99.
3. 'A Catholic View on Divorce (Mt 19,9; 1 C 7)', *JES*, 6 (1969): 53–67.
4. 'The Dating of the Megiddo Temples in Strata XV-XIV', *ZDPV*, 86 (1970): 38–49.
5. 'The Settlement of Early Bronze IV-Middle Bronze I in Jordan', *ADAJ* (1974): 57–71.
6. 'Corrections to the Coordinates in Glueck's Negev Surveys', *ZDPV*, 91 (1975): 77–84.
7. (with Dorothy Irvin) 'The Joseph and Moses Narratives', in J. H. Hayes and J. M. Miller (eds), *Israelite and Judaean History*, 147–212, London: SCM Press, 1977.
8. 'The Divine Plan of Creation: 1 Cor 11:7 and Gen 2:18–24', in L. Swidler (ed.), *Woman Priests: A Catholic Commentary on the Vatican Declaration*, 209–11, New York: Paulist, 1977.
9. 'A New Attempt to Date the Patriarchal Narratives', *JAOS*, 98 (1978): 76–84.
10. 'Historical Notes on "Israel's Conquest of Palestine: A Peasants' Rebellion?"', *JSOT*, 7 (1978): 20–7.
11. 'The Background of the Patriarchs: A Reply to William Dever and Malcolm Clark', *JSOT*, 9 (1978): 2–43.
12. 'Palästina in der Frühbronzezeit', *Tübinger Atlas des Vorderen Orients*, map B II 11a, Wiesbaden: Dr. Reichert Verlag, 1978.
13. 'Palästina in der Übergangszeit der Frühbronze/Mittelbronzezeit', *Tübinger Atlas des Vorderen Orients*, map B II 11b, Wiesbaden: Dr. Reichert Verlag, 1978.
14. 'Conflict Themes in the Jacob Narratives', *Semeia*, 15 (1979): 5–26.

15. 'Palästina in der Spätbronzezeit', *Tübinger Atlas des Vorderen Orients*, map B II 11d, Wiesbaden: Dr. Reichert Verlag, 1980.
16. 'Palästina in der Mittelbronzezeit', *Tübinger Atlas des Vorderen Orients*, map B II 11c, Wiesbaden: Dr. Reichert Verlag, 1980.
17. 'History and Tradition: A Response to J.B. Geyer', *JSOT*, 15 (1980): 57–61.
18. 'Sinai und Negev in der Übergangszeit der Frühbronze-Mittelbronzezeit', *Tübinger Atlas des Vorderen Orients*, map B II 10b, Wiesbaden: Dr. Reichert Verlag, 1982.
19. 'Sinai und Negev in der Spätbronzezeit', *Tübinger Atlas des Vorderen Orients*, map B II 10c, Wiesbaden: Dr. Reichert Verlag, 1982.
20. 'Sinai und Negev in der Frühbronzezeit', *Tübinger Atlas des Vorderen Orients*, map B II 10e, Wiesbaden: Dr. Reichert Verlag, 1982.
21. 'Text, Context and Referent in Israelite History', in D. V. Edelman (ed.), *The Fabric of History: Text, Artifact and Israel's Past*, 65–92, JSOTSup 127, Sheffield: JSOT Press, 1991.
22. 'Palestinian Pastoralism and Israel's Origins', *SJOT*, 6 (1) (1992): 1–13.
23. 'From the Stone Age to Israel', *Proceedings of the Eastern Great Lakes and Midwest Bible Societies*, 11 (1991): 9–32.
24. 'Martin Noth and the History of Israel', in S. L. McKenzie and M. P. Graham (eds), *The History of Israel's Traditions: The Heritage of Martin Noth*, 80–91, JSOTSup 182, Sheffield: Sheffield Academic Press, 1994.
25. 'Some Exegetical and Theological Implications of Understanding Exodus as a Collected Tradition', in N. P. Lemche and M. Müller (eds), *Fra dybet. Festskrift til John Strange i anledning af 60 års fødselsdagen den 20. juli 1994*, 233–42, FBE 5, Copenhagen: Museum Tusculanums Forlag, 1994.
26. 'Hvorledes Jahve blev Gud. Exodus 3 og 6 og Pentateukens Centrum', *DTT*, 57 (1) (1994): 1–19.
27. 'Det gamle Testamente som teologisk disciplin', *DTT*, 57 (3) (1994): 177–98.
28. (with Niels Peter Lemche) 'Did Biran Kill David? The Bible in the Light of Archaeology', *JSOT*, 64 (1994): 3–21.
29. 'A Neo-Albrightean School in History and Biblical Scholarship', *JBL* 114 (4) (1995): 683–705.
30. 'Gösta Ahlström's History of Palestine', in S. W. Holloway and L. K. Handy (eds), *The Pitcher is Broken: Memorial Essays for Gösta W. Ahlström*, 420–34, JSOTSup 190, Sheffield: Sheffield Academic Press, 1995.
31. 'Dissonance and Disconnections: Notes on the BYTDWD and HMLK, HDD Fragments from Tel Dan', *SJOT*, 9 (1995): 236–40.
32. 'Das alte Testament als theologische Disziplin', in B. Janowski and N. Lohfink (eds), *Religionsgeschichte Israels oder Theologie des alten Testaments*, 157–73, JBTh 10, Neukirchen–Vluyn: Neukirchener Verlag, 1995.
33. 'How Yahweh Became God: Exodus 3 and 6 and the Heart of the Pentateuch', *JSOT*, 68 (1995): 57–74.
34. 'House of David: An Eponymic Referent to Yahweh as Godfather', *SJOT*, 9 (1995): 59–74.
35. 'Offing the Establishment: DBAT 38 [*sic*] and the Politics of Radicalism', *BN*, 79 (1995): 71–87.
36. 'The Intellectual Matrix of Early Biblical Narrative: Inclusive Monotheism in Persian Period Palestine', in D. V. Edelman (ed.), *The Triumph of Elohim: From Yahwisms to Judaisms*, 107–26, CBET 13, Kampen: Kok Pharos, 1995.

37. '4 Q Testimonia og Bibelens affattelse. En Københavnsk lego-hypotese', in N. Hyldahl and T. L. Thompson (eds), *Dødehavsteksterne og Bibelen*, 112–28, FBE 8, Copenhagen: Museum Tusculanums Forlag, 1996.
38. '"He is Yahweh; He Does What is Right in his own Eyes": The Old Testament as Theological Discipline, II', in L. Fatum and M. Müller (eds), *Tro og Historie: Festskrift til Niels Hyldahl*, 246–63, FBE 7, Copenhagen: Museum Tusculanums Forlag, 1996.
39. 'Historiography of Ancient Palestine and Early Jewish Historiography: W. G. Dever and the Not So New Biblical Archaeology', in V. Fritz and P. R. Davies (eds), *The Origins of the Ancient Israelite States*, 26–43, JSOTSup 228, Sheffield: Sheffield Academic Press, 1996.
40. 'Defining History and Ethnicity in the South Levant', in L. L. Grabbe (ed.), *Can a 'History of Israel' Be Written?*, 166–87, ESHM 1 / JSOTSup 245, Sheffield: Sheffield Academic Press, 1997.
41. 'Historie og teologi i overskrifterne til Davids salmer', in O. Davidsen (ed.), *Den poetiske litteratur i Gammel og Ny Testamente*, 88–102, Collegium Biblicum Årsskrift, Århus: Collegium Biblicum, 1997.
42. 'The Background of the Patriarchs: A Reply to William Dever and Malcolm Clark', in J. W. Rogerson (ed.), *The Pentateuch: A Sheffield Reader*, 33–74, The Biblical Seminar 39, Sheffield: Sheffield Academic Press, 1997.
43. '4Q Testimonia and Bible Composition: A Copenhagen Lego Hypothesis', in F. H. Cryer and T. L. Thompson (eds), *Qumran Between the Old and New Testaments*, 261–76, CIS, Sheffield: Sheffield Academic Press, 1998.
44. 'Creating the Past: Biblical Narrative as Interpretive Discourse', *CBÅ* (1998): 7–23.
45. 'The Exile in History and Myth: A Response to Hans Barstad', in L. L. Grabbe (ed.), *Leading Captivity Captive: The Exile as History and Ideology*, 101–19, ESHM 2 / JSOTSup 278, Sheffield: Sheffield Academic Press, 1998.
46. 'Salmernes bogs'enten-eller' spørgsmål', in T. Jørgensen and P. K. Westergaard (eds), *Teologien i samfundet. Festskrift til Jens Glebe-Møller*, 289–308, Frederiksberg: Anis, 1998.
47. 'Kritiske synspunkter på religion – også vor egen. Eller: Hvordan man studerer islam i Jordan', *Chaos: Dansk-Norsk Tidsskrift for religionshistoriske studier*, 30 (1998): 111–30.
48. 'Hidden Histories and the Problem of Ethnicity in Palestine', in M. Prior (ed.), *Western Scholarship and the History of Palestine*, 23–39, London: Melisende, 1998.
49. 'Etnicitet og Bibel: Flere "jødedomme" og Det nye Israel', in N. P. Lemche and H. Tronier (eds), *Etnicitet i Bibelen*, 23–42, FBE 9, Copenhagen: Museum Tusculanum Forlag.
50. 'Yahweh as Godfather', *Biblicon*, 1 (1) (1999): 7–17.
51. 'The Bible in History: How Writers Create a Past', *Religious Studies News* (Nov. 1999).
52. 'Historical and Christian Faith', in V. P. Long (ed.), *Israel's Past in Recent Research: Essays on Ancient Israelite Historiography*, 354–59, SBTS 7, Winona Lake, IN: Eisenbrauns, 1999.
53. 'Historical Notes: The Bible Has No Need of Archaeology', *The Independent*, London 15.2.1999, p. 9.
54. 'Historiography in the Pentateuch: Twenty-Five Years after "Historicity"', *SJOT*, 13 (2) (1999): 258–83.

55. 'Historieskrivning i Pentateuken: 25 år efter "Historicity"', in G. Hallbäck and J. Strange (eds), *Bibel og historieskrivning*, 67–82, FBE 10, Copenhagen: Museum Tusculanums Forlag, 1999.
56. 'Eksilet i historien og i historier', *Bibliana* 1. årg. Nr. 1 (1999): 19–30.
57. 'The Search for History in the Bible', *BAR*, 26 (2) (2000): 36–7.
58. 'Tradition and History: The Scholarship of John Van Seters,' in S. L. McKenzie and T. Römer (eds), *Rethinking the Foundations: Historiography in the Ancient World and in the Bible. Essays in Honour of John Van Seters*, 9–21, BZAW 294, Berlin/ New York: de Gruyter, 2000.
59. 'Reply from Thompson', in C. D. Isbell (ed.), *God's Scribes: How the Bible Became the Bible*, 260–2, Warren Center Pennsylvania: Shangri La Publications, 2000.
60. 'Lester Grabbe and Historiography: An Apologia', *SJOT* 14, no. 1 (2000): 140–61.
61. 'Problems of Sense and Historicity with Palestine's Inscriptions', in A. Lemaire and M. Sæbø (eds), *Congress Volume – Oslo 1998*, 321–6, Leiden: E. J. Brill, 2000.
62. 'If David Had Not Climbed the Mount of Olives', in J. C. Exum (ed.), *Virtual History and the Bible*, 42–58, Biblical Interpretation 8/1–2, Leiden: E. J. Brill, 1999.
63. 'A View from Copenhagen: Israel and the History of Palestine', *Bible and Interpretation*, 3 (2001): 8 pp.
64. 'The Messiah Epithet in the Bible', *SJOT*, 15 (1) (2001): 57–82.
65. 'Methods and Results: A Review of Two Recent Publications', *SJOT*, 15 (2) (2001): 306–25.
66. 'The Bible and Hellenism: A Response', in L. L. Grabbe (ed.), *Did Moses Speak Attic? Jewish Historiography and Scripture in the Hellenistic Period*, 274–86, ESHM 3 / JSOTSup 317, Sheffield: Sheffield Academic Press, 2001.
67. 'On Reading the Bible for History', *JBS*, 1 (3) (2001), 6 pp.
68. 'Kongedømme og Guds vrede eller at lære ydmyghed', in G. Hallbäck and N. P. Lemche (eds), *'Tiden' i bibelsk belysning*, 65–100, FBE 11, Copenhagen: Museum Tusculanum Forlag, 2001.
69. 'Jerusalem as the City of God's Kingdom: Common Tropes in the Bible and the Ancient Near East', *Islamic Studies*, 40 (3) (2001): 631–47.
70. 'Hal nistati'a kitabat tarikh falastin al-qadim?', *Al Karmel*, 14 (2) (2001): 27–39.
71. 'A History of Palestine: The Debate', *The Journal of Palestinian Archaeology*, 2 (2002): 18–24.
72. 'La guerra santa al centro della teologica biblica. "Shalom" e la purificazione di Gerusalemme', *Studi Storici*, 3 (2002): 663–92.
73. 'Kingship and the Wrath of God, or Teaching Humility', *RB*, 109 (2002): 161–96.
74. 'From the Mouth of Babes, Strength: Psalm 8 and the Book of Isaiah', *SJOT*, 16 (2) (2002): 226–45.
75. 'Bibelens relevans for the moderne verdenssamfund', *TEOL-information*, 25 (2002): 19–23.
76. 'At sætte det guddommelige i verden', *Bibliana* 3. årg. nr. 2 (2002): 45–59.
77. (with Ingrid Hjelm) 'The Victory Song of Merneptah: Israel and the People of Palestine', *JSOT*, 27 (2002): 3–18.
78. 'An Introduction: Can a History of Ancient Jerusalem and Palestine Be Written?', in T. L. Thompson (ed.), *Jerusalem in Ancient History and Tradition*, 1–15, CIS, London: T&T Clark International, 2003.
79. 'Holy War at the Center of Biblical Theology: Shalom and the Cleansing of Jerusalem', in T. L. Thompson (ed.), *Jerusalem in Ancient History and Tradition*, 223–57, CIS, London: T&T Clark International, 2003.

80. 'The Bible's Context as a Problem of Knowledge', *CBÅ*, 7 (2003): 7–13.
81. 'An Introduction: Can a History of Ancient Jerusalem and Palestine Be Written?' [in Arabic], in T. L. Thompson and S. K. Jayyusi (eds), *Al-Quds, Urūshalīm al-'adūr al-qadīma bīn altūrāh wa al-tārīkh* [Al-Quds, The Ancient City of Jerusalem Between Tradition and History], 23–42, Beirut: Centre for Arab Unity Studies, 2003.
82. 'Shalom and the Cleansing of Jerusalem' [in Arabic], in T. L. Thompson and S. K. Jayyusi (eds), *Al-Quds, Urūshalīm al-'adūr al-qadīma bīn altūrāh wa al-tārīkh* [Al-Quds, The Ancient City of Jerusalem Between Tradition and History], 307–29, Beirut: Centre for Arab Unity Studies, 2003.
83. 'Should We Leave History to the Archaeologists?' [in Arabic], in K. W. Whitelam, T. L. Thompson, N. P. Lemche, I. Hjelm and Z. Muna, *Al Ìadīd fī tārīkh filasiīn alqadīmah rīkh filasiīn alqadīmah* [New Information about the History of Ancient Palestine], 47–71, Damascus and Beirut: Cadmus Press, 2004.
84. 'From the Stone Age to Israel' [in Arabic], in K. W. Whitelam, T. L. Thompson, N. P. Lemche, I. Hjelm and Z. Muna, *Al Ìadīd fī tārīkh filasiīn alqadīmah rīkh filasiīn alqadīmah* [New Information about the History of Ancient Palestine], 73–102, Damascus and Beirut: Cadmus Press, 2004.
85. (with Ingrid Hjelm) 'The Victory Song of Merneptah: Israel and the People of Palestine' [in Arabic], in K. W. Whitelam, T. L. Thompson, N. P. Lemche, I. Hjelm and Z. Muna, *Al Ìadīd fī tārīkh filasiīn alqadīmah rīkh filasiīn alqadīmah* [New Information about the History of Ancient Palestine], 163–77, Damascus and Beirut: Cadmus Press, 2004.
86. 'Is the Bible Historical? The Challenge of "Minimalism" for Biblical Scholars and Historians', *HLS*, 3 (1) (2004): 1–27.
87. 'Job 29: Biography or Parable?', in T. L. Thompson and H. Tronier (eds), *Frelsens biografisering*, 115–34, FBE 13, Copenhagen: Museum Tusculanums Forlag, 2004.
88. 'A Problem in Historical Method: Reiterative Narrative as Supersessionist Historiography', in M. Liverani and G. Garbini (eds), *Recenti tendenze nella ricostruzione della storia antica d'Israele (Roma, 6–7 marzo 2003)* (Rome: Accademia Nazionale dei Lincei, 2005): 183–96.
89. 'At skabe bibelske figurer', *Teol-information*, 32 (2005): 45–9.
90. 'The Role of Faith in Historical Research', *SJOT*, 19 (1) (2005): 111–34.
91. 'How the Heroes Have Fallen!', in M. Müller and T. L. Thompson (eds), *Historie og konstruktion. Festskrift til Niels Peter Lemche i anledning af 60 års fødselsdagen den 6. september 2005*, 374–86, FBE 14, Copenhagen: Museum Tusculanum, 2005.
92. 'Bibliography of Niels Peter Lemche', in M. Müller and T. L. Thompson (eds), *Historie og konstruktion. Festskrift til Niels Peter Lemche i anledning af 60 års fødselsdagen den 6. september 2005*, 421–38, FBE 14, Copenhagen: Museum Tusculanum, 2005.
93. '"Minimalism" and the Context of Scripture: Reassessing Methods and Assumptions – A Review and Reply', *Review of Biblical Literature*, 04 (2006).
94. 'Archaeology and the Bible Revisited: A Review Article', *SJOT*, 20 (2) (2006): 286–313.
95. 'The Comparative Method: Canon and the Interpretive Context', in T. Engberg-Pedersen, N. P. Lemche and H. Tronier (eds), *Kanon. Bibelens tilblivelse og normative status. Festskrift til Mogens Müller i anledning af 60 års fødselsdagen den 25. januar 2006*, 212–28, FBE 15, Copenhagen: Museum Tusculanum Forlag, 2006.

96. 'Mesha and Questions of Historicity', *SJOT*, 21 (2) (2007): 241–60.
97. 'La arqueologia y la Biblia reconsideradas: Un artículo de reseña', *RIHAO*, Tercera Serie, 14 (2007): 179–216.
98. 'A Testimony of the Good King: Reading the Mesha Stele', in L. L. Grabbe (ed.), *The Rise and Fall of the Omri Dynasty*, 236–92, ESHM 6 / JSOTSup 421, London: T&T Clark, 2007.
99. 'The Politics of Reading the Bible in Israel', *HLS*, 7 (1) (2008): 1–15.
100. 'Imago Dei: A Problem in Pentateuchal Discourse', *SJOT*, 23 (2) (2009): 137–52.
101. 'Clarel, Jonah, and the Whale: A Question Concerning Rachel's Missing Children', *Leviathan: A Journal of Melville Studies* 12 (2010): 53–65.
102. 'Reiterative Narratives of Exile and Return: Virtual Memories of Abraham in the Persian and Hellenistic Periods', in P. R. Davies and D. V. Edelman (eds), *The Historian and the Bible: Essays in Honour of Lester L. Grabbe*, 46–54, LHBOTS 530, London: T&T Clark, 2010.
103. 'Genesis 4 and the Pentateuch's Reiterative Discourse: Some Samaritan Themes', in J. Zsengellér (ed.), *Samaria, Samarians, Samaritans: Studies on Bible, History and Linguistics*, 9–22, Berlin: de Gruyter, 2011.
104. 'The Bible, Zionism and the Heritage of an Empty Land', *HLS*, 10 (1) (2011): 97–108.
105. 'Memories of Esau and Narrative Reiteration: Themes of Conflict and Reconciliation', *SJOT*, 25 (2) (2011): 174–200.
106. 'Introduction', in J. Van Seters, *Studies in the History, Literature and Religion of Biblical Israel: Changing Perspectives 1*, 1–14, CIS, London: Equinox, 2011.
107. 'Memories of Return and the Historicity of the "Post-Exilic" Period', in P. Carstens and N. P. Lemche (eds), *The Reception and Remembrance of Abraham*, 103–30, Perspectives on Hebrew Scriptures and its Contexts, Piscataway, NJ: Gorgias Press, 2011.
108. (with Thomas S. Verenna) 'Introduction', in T. L. Thompson and T. S. Verenna (eds), *'Is This Not the Carpenter?' The Question of the Historicity of the Figure of Jesus*, 1–23, CIS, Sheffield: Equinox, 2012. Also online: also online in: 'Is This Not the Carpenter's Son?', *The Bible and Interpretation* (July 6, 2012), www.bibleinterp.com/articles/tho368005.shtml.
109. 'Psalm 72 and Mark 1:12–13: Mythic Evocation in Narratives of the Good King', T. L. Thompson and T. S. Verenna (eds), *'Is This Not the Carpenter?' The Question of the Historicity of the Figure of Jesus*, 185–201, CIS, Sheffield: Equinox, 2012.
110. 'Without Evidence or Method', in D. Burns and J. W. Rogerson (eds), *Far from Minimal: Celebrating the Work and Influence of Philip R. Davies*, 429–58, LHBOTS 484, London: T&T Clark, 2012.
111. 'An Allegorical Discourse on the "Fear of God": The Bible's Contemporary Theology', in T. Davidovich (ed.), *Plogbillar & svärd: En festskrift till Stig Norin*, Uppsala: Molin & Sorgenfrei, 2012.
112. 'Response to Diana Edelman's "Writing a History of Yehud in the Persian Period"', in A. Hunt (ed.), *Second Temple Studies IV: Historiography and History*, 46–9, LHBOTS 550, London: T&T Clark, 2012.
113. 'Palestine's Pre-Islamic History and Cultural Heritage: A Proposal for Palestinian High-School Curriculum Revision', *HLS*, 12 (2) (2013): 207–33.
114. 'Your Mother Was a Hittite and Your Father and Amorite: Ethnicity, Judaism and Palestine's Cultural Heritage', *SJOT*, 27 (1) (2013): 76–95.

115. 'What We Do and Do Not Know about Pre-Hellenistic Al-Quds', in E. Pfoh and K. W. Whitelam (eds), *The Politics of Israel's Past: The Bible, Archaeology and Nation-Building*, 49–60, SWBAS 2/8, Sheffield: Sheffield Phoenix Press, 2013.
116. 'The Faithful Remnant and Religious Identity: The Literary Trope of Return – A Reply to Firas Sawah', in E. Pfoh and K. W. Whitelam (eds), *The Politics of Israel's Past: The Bible, Archaeology and Nation-Building*, 77–88, SWBAS 2/8, Sheffield: Sheffield Phoenix Press, 2013.
117. 'Reflections of a Stranger in the Land (Lev 19:34): Celebrating Temple University's Department of Religion's 50th Anniversary', *Bible and Interpretation* (December 12, 2013), www.bibleinterp.com/articles/2013/12/tho378011.shtml.
118. 'Why Talk About the Past? The Bible, Epic and Historiography', *The Bible and Interpretation* (March 2013), www.bibleinterp.com/articles/2013/tho378004.shtml.
119. 'Politics and the Bible', *HLS*, 13 (2) (2014): 223–7.
120. (with Philippe Wajdenbaum) 'Introduction: Making Room for Japhet', in T. L. Thompson and P. Wajdenbaum (eds), *The Bible and Hellenism: Greek Influence on Jewish and Early Christian Literature*, 1–15, CIS, Durham: Acumen, 2014. Also online: *The Bible and Interpretation* (15 May 2014), www.bibleinterp.com/articles/2014/05waj388014.shtml.
121. 'Narrative Reiteration and Comparative Literature: Problems in Defining Dependence', in T. L. Thompson and P. Wajdenbaum (eds), *The Bible and Hellenism: Greek Influence on Jewish and Early Christian Literature*, 102–13, CIS, Durham: Acumen, 2014.
122. 'Biblical Archaeology: The Hydra of Palestine's History', *DTT*, 78 (2015): 243–60.
123. 'Sheep without a Shepherd. Genesis' Discourse on Justice and Reconciliation as Exile's raison d'être', in A. K. de Hemmer Gudme and I. Hjelm (eds), *Myths of Exile: History and Metaphor in the Hebrew Bible*, 101–24, CIS, London: Routledge, 2015.
124. 'Giovanni Garbini and Minimalism', in Ł. Niesiołowski-Spanò, C. Peri and J. E. West (eds), *Finding Myth and History in the Bible: Scholarship, Scholars and Errors*, 1–14, Sheffield: Equinox, 2016.
125. 'Ethnicity and the Bible: Multiple Judaisms', in Ł. Niesiołowski-Spanò, C. Peri and J. E. West (eds), *Finding Myth and History in the Bible: Scholarship, Scholars and Errors*, 223–32, Sheffield: Equinox, 2016.
126. (with Ingrid Hjelm) 'Introduction', in I. Hjelm and T. L. Thompson (eds), *History, Archaeology and the Bible Forty Years after 'Historicity': Changing Perspectives 6*, 1–14, CIS, London: Routledge, 2016.
127. 'Ethnicity and a Regional History of Palestine', in I. Hjelm and T. L. Thompson (eds), *History, Archaeology and the Bible Forty Years after 'Historicity': Changing Perspectives 6*, 159–73, CIS, London: Routledge, 2016.
128. (with Ingrid Hjelm) 'Introduction', in I. Hjelm and T. L. Thompson (eds), *Biblical Interpretation beyond Historicity: Changing Perspectives 7*, 1–12, CIS, London: Routledge, 2016.
129. 'The Problem of Israel in the History of the South Levant', in L. L. Grabbe (ed.), *'Even God Cannot Change the Past': Reflections on Seventeen Years of the European Seminar in Historical Methodology*, 70–87, LHBOTS 663 / ESHM 11, London: T&T Clark, 2018.

130. '"Rewritten Bible" or Reiterative Rhetoric: Examples from Yahweh's Garden', in J. Høgenhaven, J. Tang Nielsen and H. Omerzu (eds), *Rewriting and Reception in and of the Bible*, 49–63, Tübingen: Mohr Siebeck, 2018.

Book Reviews

1. H. Schwager, *Schriften der Bibel literaturgeschichtlich geordnet. Band I: Vom Thronfolgebuch bis zur Priesterschrift* (Stuttgart: Calwer Verlag & Munich: Kösel-Verlag, 1968), *CBQ*, 31 (1969): 134–5.
2. H. Schmid, *Mose: Überlieferung und Geschichte* (BZAW 110; Berlin: de Gruyter, 1968), *CBQ*, 31 (1969): 607f.
3. W. F. Albright, *Yahweh and the Gods of Canaan: A Historical Analysis of Two Contrasting Faiths* (London: Athlone Press, 1968), *CBQ*, 32 (1970): 251f.
4. P. R. Miroschedji, *L'époque Pré-Urbaine en Palestine* (Paris: Gabalda, 1971), *ZDPV*, 90 (1974): 60f.
5. J. Mallet, *Tell el-Far'ah (Region de Naplouse): L'installation du Moyen Bronze antérieure au rempart* (Cahiers de la Revue Biblique 14. Paris: J. Gabalda, 1973), *Die Welt des Orients*, 8 (2) (1976): 328–9.
6. Ilona Skupinska-Løvset, *The Ustinov Collection: The Palestinian Pottery* (Oslo: Oslo Universitetsforlag, 1976), *JAOS*, 98 (3) (1978): 344.
7. Stig L. Norin, *Er spaltete das Meer: die Auszugzüberlieferung in Psalmen und Kult des alten Israel* (Coniectanea Biblica: Old Testament Series 9; Lund: C.W.K. Gleerup, 1977), *JAOS*, 100 (1) (1980): 65.
8. John J. Bimson, *Redating the Exodus and Conquest* (JSOTSup 5; Sheffield: Almond Press, 1981), *JAOS*, 100 (1) (1980): 66–7.
9. Frank S. Frick, *The City in Ancient Israel* (SBL Dissertation Series 36; Missoula: Scholars Press, 1977), *JSOT*, 5 (1980): 66–7.
10. Paul Maiberger, *Topographische und historische Untersuchungen zum Sinaiproblem: Worauf beruht die Identifizierung des Gebel Musa mit dem Sinai?*, Orbis Biblicus et Orientalis 54, Göttingen: Vandenhoeck & Ruprecht 1984), *JAOS*, 109 (1) (1989): 117–18.
11. Hans J. Nissen with Elizabeth Lutzeier and Kenneth J. Northcutt, *The Early History of the Ancient Near East, 9000–2000 B. C.* (Chicago: University of Chicago Press, 1988), *JR*, 70 (1990): 82f.
12. Matthias Köckert, *Vatergott und Väterverheissungen: eine Auseinandersetzung mit Albrecht Alt und seinen Erben* (Göttingen: Vandenhoeck & Ruprecht, 1988), *JBL*, 109 (1990): 320–2.
13. Israel Finkelstein, *The Archaeology of the Israelite Settlement* (Jerusalem: Israel Exploration Society, 1988), *JBL*, 109 (1990): 322–4.
14. Niels Peter Lemche, *Ancient Israel: A New History of Israelite Society* (The Biblical Seminar; Sheffield: JSOT Press, 1988), *Bib*, 71 (1990): 559–61.
15. Hallvard Hagelia, *Numbering the Stars: A Phraseological Analysis of Gen 15* (Coniectanea Biblica: Old Testament Series 39; Lund: C.W.K. Gleerup, 1977), *SJOT*, 8 (2) (1994): 311–13.
16. John van Seters, *Prologue to History: The Yahwist as Historian in Genesis* (Louisville, KY: Westminster/John Knox Press, 1992), *CBQ*, 57 (1995): 579–80.

17. Hans Barstad, *The Myth of the Empty Land: A Study of the History and Archaeology of Judah during the 'Exilic' Period* (Oslo: Scandinavian University Press, 1996), *NTT*, 101 (1996): 150–1.
18. Gary N. Knoppers, *Two Nations under God: The Deuteronomistic History of Solomon and the Dual Monarchies* (Harvard Semitic Monographs 52; 2 vols, Atlanta: Scholars Press, 1993), *JNES*, 57 (2) (1998): 141–3.
19. Philip R. Davies, *The Origins of Biblical Israel* (Library of Hebrew Bible/Old Testament Studies 485; London: T&T Clark, 2007), *SJOT*, 22 (2) (2008): 304–8.

Lexicon Articles

1. *Biblisches Wörterbuch*, ed. H. Haag, Freiburg: Herder, 1972: Abraham, Ächtungstexten, Esau, Isaak, Ismael, Jakob, Lea, Mari, Nuzi, Patriarchen, Rakel, Rebekka, Sara
2. *Biblisches Reallexikon*, ed. K. Galling, Tübingen: J. C. B. Mohr, 1977: Beth-Sean, Jerusalem, Megiddo, Samaria, Shechem, Thaanach.
3. *Anchor Bible Dictionary*, ed. D. N. Freedman, Garden City: Doubleday, 1992: Historiography: Israelite.
4. *Gads Bibelleksikon*, ed. G. Hallbäck and H.-J. Lundager Jensen, Copenhagen: G. E. C. Gads, 1998: Edom, Edomitter, Fønikien, Hyksos, Jemen, Megiddo, Mesopotamien, Saba, Sabæere, Smed, Tanis, Tyrus, Østjordanlandet.
5. *Dictionary of Biblical Interpretation*, ed. J. H. Hayes, Nashville: Abingdon Press, 1999: Elliger, Karl, Galling, Kurt.
6. *Den Store Danske Encyklopedi: Danmarks Nationalleksikon*, 21 vols, Copenhagen: Gyldendahl, 1994–2003: Moses, Pentateuk.

Part 1

METHOD

THE CITY OF DAVID AS A PALIMPSEST

Margreet L. Steiner

In Jerusalem the south-eastern hill, now called the City of David, contains the oldest part of the ancient settlement. It is here that the earliest inhabitants built their houses and fortifications, worshipped their gods and buried their dead, from the Early Bronze Age onwards. It is here that the City of David Archaeological Park attracts thousands of visitors each month who flock to the place to admire the biblical city and celebrate their religious and nationalistic inclinations. As the Goldstein family from France wrote on the park's website: *'We visited City of David and it felt like we were taken back 3000 years'*.[1]

In the Hebrew Bible the phrase 'City of David' occurs about 45 times, predominantly in the books 2 Samuel, 1 and 2 Kings and 1 and 2 Chronicles. Most of these texts are connected with King David, who captured the settlement and went to live there, and with King Solomon who built the palace and temple in Jerusalem. The other verses concern kings that 'were buried with their ancestors in the City of David'. In these texts, City of David is obviously a reference to the settlement as a whole, which was confined to the south-eastern hill in the Bronze and most of the Iron Ages and in the Persian period.

In archaeological research the name was not often used. Early explorers who tackled the hill, from Charles Warren in 1867 to Kathleen Kenyon in 1960–67, did not call the area they were excavating the City of David. Warren published his findings in *Underground Jerusalem* (1876), Bliss and Dickie in *Excavations at Jerusalem* (1898), Macalister and Duncan in *Excavations at the Hill of Ophel* (1926), Crowfoot and Fitzgerald in *Excavation in the Tyropoeon Valley* (1929), while Kenyon's excavations have been reported in the series *Excavations in Jerusalem (by Kathleen Kenyon) 1961–67* (Tushingham 1985; Franken and Steiner 1990; Steiner

---

1. http://www.cityofdavid.org.il.

2001; Prag and Eshel 1995; Prag 2008, 2017). Only Raymond Weill mentioned the phrase 'City of David' in the title of his report, possibly because he headed a 'Jewish expedition', according to the Jewish Telegraph Agency of 20 November 1923 (Weill 1920/1947).[2]

It was only after excavations were resumed on the south-eastern hill in the 1970s that is was called City of David in all publications and public discourses (Shiloh 1984; Ariel 1990, 2000a, 2000b; de Groot and Ariel 1992; Ariel and de Groot 1996; de Groot and Bernick-Greenberg 2012a, 2012b). Of course, this label is an archaeological interpretation as well as a financially viable move. Connect an excavation or even a single find with the (in)famous king, and attention, money, volunteers and tourists pour in. It is notable that publications of the most recent work on the site refer to it as the south-eastern hill again, thereby sidestepping the ideological connotations (Gadot and Uziel 2017).

However, there is more to the City of David than imposing ruins taking visitors back to the time of King David. Both under and above the ancient walls so proudly presented are remains that are now invisible, or barely visible because of neglect. Some walls look ancient but are actually very recent. Some buildings are imagined, others obliterated. Many remains are deemed not important enough to be shown in the park, others too politically charged. There is conflict and dispute over land, money and interpretation, not immediately discernible. Besides overt triumph there is hidden oppression. Yes, there is much more to the City of David than meets the eye.

Visible and to Be Admired

What is visible for tourist and scholars alike is but a small part of what has been excavated since the second half of the nineteenth century. Walking from the south end of the hill to the northern tip the visitor can gaze at the Siloam Pool, the so-called 'tombs of the Judean kings', the entrance to Warren's Shaft and finally the 'Royal Quarter', showing the stepped stone structure with a series of houses built on top of it, all hugging the slope, while on the top of the hill King David's palace is located, next to the small Persian tower and the large tower and city wall dating from the Hellenistic period. A Herodian road leads from the Siloam Pool to the Temple Mount.

All impressive constructions, showing glorious Jerusalem, the Jerusalem that was the capital of the Judean kingdom, that was restored after the Exile and again functioned as a capital, this time of the Maccabean kings, and that eventually became the beautiful city of Roman times. To

2. https://www.jta.org/1923/11/20/archive/jews-to-excavate-davids-city.

the north lies the Temple Mount, once crowned with a temple central to the Judean and Jewish religion.

Here is tangible what is so eloquently described in the Bible and by the classical writers: King David took the city through the 'sinnor' and constructed a palace there, Nehemiah rebuilt the walls of Jerusalem, the Maccabeans restored the ancient kingdom and once again fortified the town, and King Herod built roads to access his beautiful new temple. This is what the park is all about.

Visible but Imagined

Some remains, however, though prominently visible and visitable and constituting the main attraction of the park, do not really exist: the walls of the palace of David (Mazar 2006, 2009). You can walk over them, you can admire them, but, quoting a recent president of the USA, 'What you're seeing and what you're reading is not what's happening'.

The so-called palace of David is not a palace, it is not even a building, as many archaeologists have noted (see for instance Finkelstein et al. 2007; Steiner 2009). It consists of a series of walls and some floors, not belonging together and dating to various periods. However, archaeological evidence is not what is at stake. Imagination, religion, nationalism and emotion set the tone here.

Visible but Not Ancient

Some clearly visible remains are not as ancient as they seem to be. Parts of the stepped stone structure and of the terraces underneath it were excavated by Macalister and Duncan in 1923–25 and were afterwards restored and cemented by the then Department of Antiquities. On visual inspection it seems they have been re-restored recently by the City of David Archaeological Park organisation. Thus, although ancient remains once existed at that same spot, what you see now is not ancient, and it is unclear how accurate the restorations are.

Hardly Visible and Neglected

Walk from the glorified edifices on top of the hill down, down, down, and you will find the MB II town wall that surrounded the settlement in the eighteenth century BCE. The place is a dump, with bushes growing between the stones of the wall and litter all around it, and it has been so for the last sixty years. This part of the wall was uncovered by Kenyon and although it is near the archaeological park, it is not part of it and thus is not maintained. I have heard many times that it is just a matter of time before this small piece of land will be added to the park, but so far this has not happened.

Larger parts of the same wall were excavated by Shiloh further south, and these are invisible too. To be fair, a more recently excavated MB II structure has been kept and restored, and attracts many visitors. Located at the end of Warren's Shaft and covering the entrance to the spring, two large towers have been excavated, made of gigantic blocks of stone. They still stand up to 5 meters high and mark the end of what may have been a covered procession way leading down from the town to the spring. The buildings are dated to the MB II period, although new evidence led some scholars to believe the complex was only built at the end of the ninth century BCE (Regev et al. 2017).

Hidden from Sight

The earliest inhabitants of Jerusalem lived in the area in the centuries just before the third millennium BCE, in the Early Bronze I period. Traces of their presence, such as pottery, have been found in caves and cavities in bedrock, deep under the remains of later periods (Steiner 2001: 7; Macalister and Duncan 1926: 177; Shiloh 1984: 25). Parker in his ill-fated excavation found a grave with multiple burials accompanied by EB I pottery (Vincent 1911: pls. IX, X). In Shiloh's area E1 a small EB I building was uncovered (Shiloh 1984: 11–12; de Groot and Bernick-Greenberg 2012a). Stone benches lined the walls, which led to it being interpreted as a (possible) shrine.

The pottery found by Kenyon in several caves proved to come from various regions in Palestine, while only a small part was made from local clays (Franken 2005: 19–21). This suggests a semi-nomadic population that roamed the wider area, occasionally visiting the site to bury their dead and pay homage to the deities that were worshipped in the local sanctuary. None of this is visible in the park, nor is it mentioned in the park's leaflet or on the Time Line on its website.[3]

Not Visible

What is not visible may be the most interesting part of the area. When the Babylonians took the city in 586 BCE, they destroyed city walls and houses in a thorough manner. Wherever archaeologists dug on the slope of

---

3. http://www.cityofdavid.org.il/en/virtual-tours/city-david-time-line.

the south-eastern hill, they encountered thick layers of destruction rubble. The houses were completely filled in with stones from their walls and with broken objects that had fallen from upper stories and houses above. This was the utmost and final destruction that ended the occupation of the eastern slope of the hill.

The destruction of Jerusalem at the end of the Iron Age plays a major role in the history of the city and gave rise to some of the most beautiful verses of the Hebrew Bible, such as Psalm 137. However, none of this is visible in the archaeological park.

Of course, excavators tend to clean out the rubble in a building and then try to reconstruct the building as it was originally used, if only on paper. Nevertheless, when telling the history of this small part of Jerusalem, it seems contradictory to neglect the event that shaped the identity of the Judahite people and plays such a vital role in Jewish thought and religion.

Invisible but oh so Present: The War on Jerusalem

The City of David Archaeological Park was established and developed by the Ir David Foundation, an organisation 'committed to continuing King David's legacy as well as revealing and connecting people to Ancient Jerusalem's glorious past', according to its own website.[4] All recent excavations in the City of David, such as those of David's Palace, the Givati Parking Lot, the Spring House and the Herodian Road, are sponsored by the Foundation.

These excavations, the website makes clear, are part of a plan to develop and extend the area for 'tourism development, educational programming and residential revitalization'. Harmless as these words sound, the plan includes the appropriation of Palestinian land and the relocation of its Palestinian inhabitants; the building of the Kedem Center, which is so large it will transform the city's skyline and is meant to house a visitor's centre and a museum; the development of a cable car linking the area with West Jerusalem; and the construction of parking areas and a synagogue in the neighbourhood of Silwan.[5]

All this to 'continue King David's legacy', focussing on the remains of a (supposedly grandiose) Israelite and Jewish past, while the Palestinian population of East Jerusalem and Silwan is not considered to have any

---

4. http://www.cityofdavid.org.il/en/The-Ir-David-Foundation.

5. For in-depth information, see the websites of Wadi Hilweh Alternative Information Center: http://www.silwanic.net/?page_id=684; and Emek Shaveh: https://alt-arch.org/en/; as well as Meiron Rappoport's report *Shady Dealings in Silwan*: http://www.ir-amim.org.il/sites/default/files/Silwanreporteng.pdf.

connection with the site. Resistance to this colonial enterprise is put up by Palestinian and Israeli organisations, such as the Wadi Hilweh Alternative Information Center and Emek Shaveh, but nothing of this 'war' is visible in the Archaeological Park.

A Palimpsest

The Merriam-Webster Dictionary gives a down-to-earth definition of the term palimpsest: 'Something having usually diverse layers or aspects apparent beneath the surface'. In the City of David the term refers to the multi-layered character of the remains at the site and the nature of their cultural transmission. What is visible as well as what is invisible gives testament to the many cultures that inhabit(ed) the south-eastern hill and to the wars that were and are being fought over the city, both materially and ideologically. For those with eyes to see, there is much to discover.

Bibliography

Ariel, D. T., ed. (1990), *Excavations at the City of David 1978–1985, Vol. II. Imported Stamped Amphora Handles, Coins, Worked Bone and Ivory, and Glass*, Jerusalem: The Institute of Archaeology, The Hebrew University of Jerusalem.

Ariel, D. T., ed. (2000a), *Excavations in the City of David 1978–1985 Directed by Yigal Shiloh, Vol. V: Extramural Areas*, Jerusalem: The Institute of Archaeology, The Hebrew University of Jerusalem.

Ariel, D. T., ed. (2000b), *Excavations in the City of David 1978–1985 Directed by Yigal Shiloh, Vol. VI: Inscriptions*, Jerusalem: The Institute of Archaeology, The Hebrew University of Jerusalem.

Ariel, D. T. and A. de Groot (1996), *Excavations at the City of David 1978–1985, Vol. IV: Various Report*, Jerusalem: The Institute of Archaeology, The Hebrew University of Jerusalem.

Bliss, F. J. and A. C. Dickie (1898), *Excavations at Jerusalem 1894–1897*, London: Committee of the Palestine Exploration Fund.

Crowfoot, J. W. and G. M. Fitzgerald (1929), *Excavations in the Tyropoeon Valley 1927*, London: Annual of the Palestine Exploration Fund.

Finkelstein, I., L. Singer-Avitz, D. Ussishkin and Z. Herzog (2007), 'Has King David's Palace in Jerusalem been found?', *TA*, 34 (2): 142–64.

Franken, H. J. (2005), *A History of Potters and Pottery in Ancient Jerusalem: Excavations by K. M. Kenyon in Jerusalem 1961–1967*, London: Equinox.

Franken, H. J. and M. L. Steiner (1990), *Excavations in Jerusalem 1961–1967, Vol. II: The Iron Age Extramural Quarter on the South-east Hill*, Oxford: Oxford University Press.

Gadot, Y. and J. Uziel (2017), 'The Monumentality of Iron Age Jerusalem Prior to the 8th Century BCE', *TA*, 44: 123–40.

de Groot, A. and D. T. Ariel, eds. (1992), *Excavations at the City of David 1978–1985, Vol. III: Stratigraphical, Environmental, and Other Reports*, Jerusalem: The Institute of Archaeology, The Hebrew University of Jerusalem.

de Groot. A. and H. Bernick-Greenberg (2012a), *Excavations at the City of David 1978–1985 Directed by Yigal Shiloh, Vol. VIIA: Area E: Stratigraphy and Architecture*, Jerusalem: The Institute of Archaeology, The Hebrew University of Jerusalem.

de Groot, A. and H. Bernick-Greenberg (2012b), *Excavations at the City of David 1978–1985 Directed by Yigal Shiloh, Vol. VIIB: Area E: The Finds*, Jerusalem: The Institute of Archaeology, The Hebrew University of Jerusalem.

Macalister, R. A. S. and J. Garrow Duncan (1926), *Excavations on the Hill of Ophel, Jerusalem, 1923–1925*, London: Palestine Exploration Fund Annual.

Mazar E. (2006), 'Did I Find King David's Palace?', *BAR*, 32: 16–27, 70.

Mazar, E. (2009), *The Palace of King David: Excavations at the Summit of the City of David. Preliminary Report of Seasons 2005–2007*, Jerusalem and New York: Shoham Academic Research and Publication.

Prag, K. (2008), *Excavations by K. M. Kenyon in Jerusalem 1961–1967, Vol. V: Discoveries in Hellenistic to Ottoman Jerusalem Centenary volume: Kathleen M. Kenyon 1906–1978*, Oxford: Council for British Research in the Levant and Oxbow Books.

Prag, K. (2017), *Excavations by K. M. Kenyon in Jerusalem 1961–1967, Vol. VI: Sites on the Edge of the Ophel*, Oxford: Council for British Research in the Levant and Oxbow Books.

Prag, K. and I. Eshel, eds. (1995), *Excavations by K. M. Kenyon in Jerusalem 1961–1967, Vol. VI: The Iron Age Cave Deposits on the South-East Hill and Isolated Burials and Cemeteries Elsewhere*, Oxford: Oxford University Press.

Regev, J., J. Uziel, N. Szanton and E. Boaretto (2017), 'Absolute Dating of the Gihon Spring Fortifications, Jerusalem', *Radiocarbon*, 59 (4): 1–23.

Shiloh, Y. (1984), 'Excavations at the City of David I, 1978–1982', Interim report of the First Five Seasons, Jerusalem: The Institute of Archaeology, The Hebrew University of Jerusalem.

Steiner, M. L. (2001), *Excavations in Jerusalem by K. M. Kenyon 1961–67, Vol. III: The Settlement in the Bronze and Iron Ages*, London: Sheffield Academic Press.

Steiner, M. L. (2009), 'The "Palace of David" Reconsidered in the Light of Earlier Excavations', *Bible and Interpretation*, http://www.bibleinterp.com/articles/palace_2468.shtml.

Tushingham, A. D. (1985), *Excavations in Jerusalem 1961–1967, Vol. I*, Toronto: Royal Ontario Museum.

Vincent, L.-H. (1911), *Jerusalem sous Terre – Les recentes fouilles d'Ophel*, London: Horace Cox.

Warren, Ch. E. (1876), *Underground Jerusalem: An Account of Some of the Principal Difficulties Encountered in Its Exploration and the Results Obtained. With a Narrative of an Expedition through the Jordan Valley and a Visit to the Samaritans*, London: R. Bentley & Son.

Weill, R. (1920/1947), *La Cité de David: Compte-rendu des Fouilles à Jérusalem sur la Site de la Ville Primitive*, Paris: Geuthner.

Living in the Past?
Keeping Up-To-Date
in Ancient Near Eastern Studies

Raz Kletter

The Information Overload

Scholars agree that keeping up with the literature is crucial (Pontis et al. 2017: 23; Tenopir et al. 2009: 18–21; 2011: 11–12) – in some fields, such as medical care, it can be a matter of life or death (Alper et al. 2004). Studies have found a correlation between reading more and academic success (Tenopir, Mays and Wu 2011: 7; Tenopir, Volentine and King 2012: 132), but reading is a demanding task.

An estimated 2.5 million scientific articles are now published every year in c. 34,500 journals (Ware and Mabe 2015: 6, 27; Plume and van Weijen 2014). The explosion of data preceded the digital age (Bush 1964; Edmunds and Morris 2000: 20; Blair 2010).[1] Formerly, the library was the domain for keeping up with the literature. Today it is the web, and we create private libraries on our PCs (Dalton and Charnigo 2004; Tenopir et al. 2009: 18; Pontis et al. 2017: 28).[2] Yet while our ability to locate bibliographic items has improved, our reading capacity remains limited. Epidemiologists would need 627.5 hours to read the 8,265 articles

---

1. Some doubt that there is an information overload; but it exists (Tindale 1999; Pijpers 2010: 20–5). After being criticized once for not reading a nineteenth-century book, which – in the eyes of the critic – was a 'must', I tried to explain that reading recent literature is a more pressing task (cf. Tenopir et al. 2009: 21–2). Reading nineteenth-century scientific literature is a luxury – except for scholars of that period.

2. In a large recent survey, 93.5% of the scholars reported interacting with the library electronically and only 1.7% reading in it physically (Tenopir, Volentine and King 2012: 133). For keeping up to date with literature in the ancient Near East, see Crown (1974).

published in 341 relevant journals in just one month (June 2002) – or even 6,000 articles per day if a broader frame is considered (Alper et al. 2004; Ford 2010). Complaints about the burden are common:

> Trying to stay up to date with the literature is tremendously difficult... My job is to not only do research but also to teach, obtain funding, do professional service including peer review, give talks, attend committee meetings, and more.
>
> I find that keeping up with the literature always comes with a trade-off: Do I spend more time on my research projects, or do I read the latest papers? (quotes from Paine 2016)

The first complaint seems typical of established scholars; but suppose that professors are freed of all other duties, and even that family, friends, and vacations are sacrificed on the altar of science – would it solve the problem? Nobody can read 'everything'. The issue is not reading 'everything', but finding and reading what is important (Edmunds and Morris 2000: 22; Pontis et al. 2017: 22–3).

The literature (if you have the time to read it) does not lack advice as to how to cope with information overload (Lively 1996; Edmunds and Morris 2000; Barr 2006; Cullis and Webster 2010; Haapoja 2013; Landhius 2016; Paine 2016). Many studies (often by librarians) define and discuss the information requirements and seeking behaviors of scholars (Ellis 1993; Wilson 1996; Meho and Tibbo 2003; Dalton and Charnigo 2004: 403; Palmer, Teffeau and Pirmann 2009; Pontis et al. 2017), including those in the humanities and social sciences (Stone 1982; Benardou et al. 2010).

Students perhaps roam freely through the literature, but on the path to becoming an established professional writing receives preference over reading. Reading narrows: one leafs through many items, looking for relevant bits, trying to 'assess and exploit content with as little actual reading as possible' (Renear and Palmer 2009: 829). Publishers' logs indicate that users are 'bouncing, flicking, or skittering: they move rapidly along the digital surface', performing 'lite' reading (Nicholas and Clark 2012: 55–6). We 'skim' and 'monitor' and 'scan' tables of content, abstracts, reviews, publishers' alerts, etc. (Runnels 1994; Dalton and Charnigo 2004; Palmer, Teffeau and Pirmann 2009; Nicholas and Clark 2012; Morgan and Winters 2015).

Scientists have practiced 'lite' reading since long before the digital age, although some worry that it erodes 'deep' reading (Nicholas and Clark 2012). It is likely that 'deep' reading is not reflected in publishers' logs, because it is done separately. 'Lite' reading is a necessary, unavoidable part of keeping up with the literature. The issue is not 'lite' reading *per se*, but the balance between 'lite' and 'deep' reading. Due to the 'publish or perish' reality and the difficulty of assessing quality (as opposed to quantity), scholars might reduce 'deep' reading in order to increase the quantity of publications – at the expense of quality. 'Lite' readers produce 'lite' papers. There are no easy remedies.

Surveys from the US suggest that scholars now read more articles than ever before – numbers grew from 150 articles per year in 1977 to 280 in 2005. Yet the time spent on each article decreased from c. 47 to 31 minutes (Renear and Palmer 2009: 829; Tenopir et al. 2009: 12; 2011: 7; Davis 2014).[3] This despite the average length of US scientific articles increasing by 85% from 1975 to 2007 (Tenopir, Mays and Wu 2011: 6). Recent surveys from England indicate that, on average, an academic staff member reads for 37 hours per month (18 hours dedicated to articles, 12 to books and 7 to other publications). This equates to 448 hours every year, that is, 56 working days (Tenopir, Volentine and King 2012: 132). Adding the considerable time spent on finding, downloading, and sorting, an average staff member spends an impressive 600 hours per year keeping up with the literature, or 76 working days (Tenopir, Volentine and King 2012: 134).

We can now answer, perhaps, the second complaint (cited above): both 'lite' and 'deep' reading are required, in different proportions. A research project requires more 'deep reading' than just keeping up with the literature. Finding a correct balance between 'lite' and 'deep' reading is one key to integrity in scholarly life.

A quote in Paine (2016) claims that 'it is of no use going through a bunch of papers if you are unable to remember what you read in them'. Yet scholars forget vast amount of data when moving from a completed study to a new one. One does not have to remember every detail. Remembering the author's name and the subject, and sorting the file so that it can be retrieved by subject/period (etc.), would enable re-finding it when needed.

Some suggest that the transition to the digital world in History has been slower than in other disciplines, because of the importance of primary sources and books (Dalton and Charnigo 2004; Holden 2016). Holden (2016: 4) suggests that serendipity – 'stumbling' by chance on useful information, for example, by looking in surrounding shelves in a

3. In a large survey from 2008, scholars reported citing one article for every 24 read (Tenopir, Mays and Wu 2011: 13). There are significant differences between disciplines. For example, in 2005 the average reading of a medical faculty was 414 articles per year, but 'only' 233 in social sciences (Tenopir et al. 2009: 12–13; Tenopir, Mays and Wu 2011: 6).

library – is a peculiar habit of historians. However, this practice is neither unique to historians, nor lost in the digital world (Solomon and Bronstein 2016). Holden suggests that:

> Information seeking behaviours of classical scholars will vary vastly from that of Cold War scholars where born-digital and digital archives provide abundant resources. (Holden 2016: 8)

Yet digitisation of primary sources (e.g., the Dead Sea Scrolls) affects all periods. Notice that in Holden's (2016) own paper, only one out of 25 bibliographic items lacks a digital link. '*Nolens volens*, we are all "DH-ers", Digital Humanists' (Clivaz and Gregory 2014: 8).[4]

Information seeking by archaeologists has rarely been discussed. The studies that do exist are small in scope or not quantitative (e.g., Lönnqvist 2007; Huvila 2008, 2014). Other studies treat specific aspects, such as the use of archives, information practices of excavators or improving online resources (e.g., Borchardt 2009; Sufian 2009; Olsson 2016; Power et al. 2017). Much attention is given to digitization of archaeological materials (e.g., Vlachidis and Tudhope 2015; Averett, Gordon and Counts 2016; for biblical studies see Clivaz and Gregory 2014).

In tandem with the explosion of data/literature, disciplines (cf. Menken and Keestra 2015: 27–8) have been divided into ever smaller segments. A hundred years ago one scholar could 'cover' the Archaeology of the Levant as a whole. Fifty years ago, even for a small area like Palestine/Israel, there were Prehistorian, 'Biblical' (Bronze-Iron), Classical, and a few 'Post-Classical' archaeologists. Today the Early Bronze Age is drifting away from the Iron Age; although one can still find a rare scholar that deals with both, this can be at the expense of periods in between, or else there is a focus on specific aspects within periods (figurines, architecture, pottery, etc.).

Gaps of Updating

We are hopefully fluent in the literature of our discipline, or rather, the limited segments of it that form our expertise. Some news reaches us fast via web-based networks and media. Newsletters and journals carry preliminary publications and articles, and these come to our knowledge fairly quickly. For example, the journal *Excavations and Surveys in Israel* (*ESI*) allows us to 'cover' almost all the new excavations carried out in

---

4. Holden (2016) reports little change in historians' information habits in recent years (but see Blevins 2016).

Israel, though there can be a hiatus of a year or two between excavation and publication of reports (more in the case of large excavations). Social media generates 'breaking news', but not necessarily important news, or all the important news. We use conferences, emails, publishers' alerts, database searches – and a lot of reading. This takes time, so even in our own discipline we lag behind 'real time', although perhaps not much (especially concerning 'dramatic' discoveries).

Sorting out 'important' literature is a delicate art. It is hard to define 'important' (one's garbage is another's treasure). We have powerful searching tools, but the immense scope of the literature is challenging.[5] One cannot be certain about the quality of an article without reading it.

When it comes to 'news' or theories from other disciplines, the gaps are wider. In theory, we may join the social media networks of another discipline and start reading a few of its leading journals. Yet if we are unfamiliar with the other discipline – its history, theories and methods – we cannot judge if an article is important or just aspires to be so. If keeping up with the literature of one discipline is a burden, adding another discipline means doubling that burden.

The discourse on interdisciplinarity (for definitions see Klein 2010; Menken and Keestra 2015: 31) assumes that one can feel at home in more than one discipline (e.g., Wilson 1996: 196; Ivakhiv 2004). Yet studies on the information-seeking requirements of interdisciplinary scholars suggest that they are particularly 'plagued by problems' (Bates 1996: 157). Such studies analyze the scatter of literature used from each discipline, and advise scholars and librarians (Bates 1996; White 1996; Spanner 2001; Palmer et al. 2002; Jamali and Nicholas 2010; Lyall 2011). However, new 'interdisciplinary' disciplines tend at some point to become established disciplines. While it is not unusual to find interdisciplinary undergraduate students (e.g., in the US, undergraduate archaeology is subsumed within anthropology), higher up the roads bifurcate. Aspiring to be interdisciplinary also means adding to the burden.

---

5. Suppose that one comes up with the (absurd) idea that 2 Samuel 6 shows three different arks of God. To check if this idea is 'new', and find relevant literature, both specific and general searches are necessary. A search of 'three arks in 2 Samuel 6' might bring zero relevant results, or thousands of irrelevant results, depending on the search engines and their databases (Google Scholar, PubMed, Academia.edu, etc.), search options (e.g., full text or titles), and terms (e.g., II Samuel, 2 Sam. – performing various searches maintains serendipity). In Google Chrome this search proudly yielded 142,000 results in 0.50 seconds, which included everything from the 'Raiders of the Lost Ark' to 'Piglets for sale Kent'. A search in Helsinki University Library resources (books) yielded zero results.

The best solution to this situation is cooperation with scholars from other disciplines (Wilson 1996; Landhuis 2016; Green et al. 2017). It should be meaningful cooperation, not merely adding together sections in articles (or the recent habit of writing the names of entire teams on articles in the humanities, Plume and van Weijen 2014). Until recently, at least, scholars in the humanities tended to work alone (Wilson 1996), drawing on models from other disciplines (Stone 1982; Benardou et al. 2010: 20).

While quantitative data is missing, the following examples suggest that gaps of 20–30 years in 'adapting' new theories and methods from another discipline are not unusual:

1. *Ethnicity*. Anthropologist Fredrik Barth (1969) and sociologists like Anthony Smith (1981) turned the common consensus on ethnicity upside-down, leading to the near abandonment of 'primordial' definitions of ethnicity in favor of those that stress feelings and awareness. In Biblical Studies and Archaeology of the Southern Levant, however, this was first noticed twenty-three years later, by Skjeggestad (1992). Wishing to preserve an early Iron Age 'ethnic Israel', some scholars still hold pre-Barthian, primordial views, even if they cite Barth (Kletter 2014).

2. *Nationalism and Nations*. Since the 1960s Ernest Gellner (1983) and others (Smith 1971, 1986) have shown that nationalism and nations are a recent phenomenon. This knowledge only reached archaeologists of the Southern Levant in the 1990s, but some scholars continue using 'nations' as if their existence in ancient periods is a natural given (Kletter 2006: 573 n. 5).

3. *The 'Neo-Evolutionary Model'*. Scholars introduced this model to anthropology in the 1960s–70s (Fried 1967; Service 1962, 1975; Claessen and Skalník 1978). According to this model societies climb a linear ladder of evolution/complexity from bands to tribes, chiefdoms and states. Adapted for biblical studies, archaeology, history – and various other fields of study – this model became widely used. Yet anthropologists could not find stable definitions for 'tribe', 'chiefdom' or 'state'. They modified the model time and again, but reality refused to conform: the assumed 'steps' slotted together a wide variety of societies that had little in common with each other. Other societies ('tribal kingdoms') crossed the ladder from bottom to top. By the late 1980s it became clear that this model was popular only because it was easy to use: it allowed finding whatever one wanted to find (Yoffee 1993). Even Claessen

(2000) 'repented' and criticised sharply the simplistic uses of the original model. Still, in biblical studies and archaeology, scholars continue using this model. Some use it to show that Saul funded a 'chiefdom' and David a 'state', while others prove that David was a 'chief' and Omri a 'statesman'. Scholars also abused the model, replacing aspects of it with imaginary creations like 'full-blown states' in order to 'prove' their pre-conceptions (Kletter 2004: 16–28).

Probably for every successful or influential 'adoption' from one discipline to another there are many that fail. Failures usually make no 'buzz', leaving few traces in the literature. An example concerns the 'riverine' or 'upstream–downstream' model developed by Bronson (1977) for areas in Asia where human occupation and transportation (before airplanes) were limited to narrow river gorges divided by steep, high mountains. Bronson warned that this model would not be applicable to other geographical areas. Nevertheless, almost 25 years later, Stager (2001) imported this model to Ashkelon under the name 'Port Power model' (see also Schloen 2009: 7, 43–4, 449). The model is inapplicable to Palestine: some 'rivers' are dry for most of year and even in winter access by boat is limited to a short distance inland. There are no steep mountain ranges that limit passage in any direction. Agriculture is not limited to river valleys (add to this that Ashkelon is located far from any river) (Kletter 2010).

Twenty- or thirty-years gaps in keeping up with the literature can occur even within the same discipline, especially when it comes to complex theories/methods in areas or sub-disciplines with limited contacts. For example, 'New Archaeology' caused a revolution in 1960s' USA and England. It took 20 years for it to reach the Levant (Dever 1981; Bunimovitz 2000: 28–32), where its influence remained limited. Another example is the Wheeler-Kenyon method of excavation, invented in 1920s' India. It was first employed in Palestine in 1938, and by British archaeologists in 1950s' Jordan. Awareness of it grew in the 1960s, thanks to debates between British and American excavators (the latter were using the 'Locus to Stratum' method). Following this debate, Aharoni (1973) wrote a polemic against the Wheeler-Kenyon method, claiming that there existed an equal or even superior 'Israeli method of excavation'. This myth persisted for a long time; the replacement of the Locus to Stratum method by the Wheeler-Kenyon method was presented as an amalgamation of two equal methods: the Israeli and the Wheeler-Kenyon ones (Kletter 2015).

One reason for these gaps is that it usually takes time for a new theory to make an impact in its original discipline. A discourse must be formed about it, as followers carry the message forward and try to win over the unconvinced. Several 'rounds' of publications may be necessary, forming ever-widening ripples. It is only at this point that signals can be easily noticed in other disciplines.

Quantitative studies are lacking, so it is difficult to say if the above-mentioned examples are typical. Examples of gaps of 20–30 years are still related to the pre-digital world. Would such gaps disappear in the faster digital world, where the pace of publication is accelerated and in some fields articles more than a couple of years old are considered ancient (Pontis et al. 2017: 28)? In the humanities paradigms may live side by side and articles maintain their relevance for longer. If the gaps discussed above indicate inherent limitations in the human ability to read, one doubts that they can be solved by digital tools.

In sum, when a family member tells you next time that 'you live in the past', she/he may be right. In terms of keeping up with the literature, we all live in the past.

Acknowledgment

It is an honor to be invited to contribute to this book. I wish to warmly thank Łukasz Niesiołowski-Spanò and Emanuel Pfoh for their assistance and for the invitation to participate in this volume. I have benefitted from comments on a lecture given at the Annual Meeting of the Centre of excellence ANEE of Helsinki University in October 2018.

Bibliography

Aharoni, Y. (1973), 'Remarks on the "Israeli" Method of Excavation', *EI*, 11: 48–53 (Hebrew).
Alper, B. S. et al. (2004), 'How Much Effort is Needed to Keep Up with the Literature Relevant to Primary Care?', *Journal of the Medical Library Association*, 94 (4): 429–37, https://www.ncbi.nlm.nih.gov/pubmed/15494758.
Averett, E. W., J. M. Gordon and D. B. Counts, eds. (2016), *Mobilizing the Past for a Digital Future: The Potential of Digital Archaeology*, Grand Forks: University of North Dakota, https://thedigitalpress.org/mobilizing-the-past-for-a-digital-future/.
Barr, D. (2006), 'Staying Alert', *C&RL News:* 14–17.
Barth, F., ed. (1969), *Ethnic Groups and Boundaries: The Social Organization of Culture Difference*, Boston: Little & Brown.
Bates, M. J. (1996), 'Learning About the information Seeking of Interdisciplinary Scholars and Students', *Library Trends*, 45 (2): 155–64.

Benardou, A. et al. (2010), 'Understanding the information Requirements of Arts and Humanities Scholarship', *The International Journal of Digital Curation*, 1 (5): 18–33.
Blair, A. (2010), *Too Much to Know: Managing Scholarly Information before the Modern Age*, New Haven: Yale University Press.
Blevins, C. (2016), 'Digital History's Perpetual Future Tense: Debates in the Digital Humanities', http://dhdebates.gc.cuny.edu/debates/text/77.
Borchardt, E. A. (2009), 'Historical Archaeologists' Utilization of Archives: An Exploratory Study', MA thesis, San José State University, CA, http://scholarworks.sjsu.edu/etd_theses/3648.
Bronson, B. (1977), 'Exchange at the Upstream and Downstream Ends: Notes Towards a Functional Model of the Coastal State in Southwestern Asia', in K. L. Hutterer (ed.), *Economic Exchange and Social Interaction in Southwest Asia*, 39–52, Ann Arbor: University of Michigan Press.
Bunimovitz, S. (2000), 'Cultural Interpretation and the Bible: Biblical Archaeology in the Postmodern Era', *Cathedra*, 100: 27–46 (Hebrew).
Bush, K. H. (1964), 'In My Opinion: Keeping up with the Times', *The American Biology Teacher*, 26 (5): 324.
Claessen, H. J. M. (2000), *Structural Change, Evolution and Evolutionism in Cultural Anthropology*, Leiden: Leiden University.
Claessen, H. J. M. and P. Skalník, eds. (1978), *The Early States*, The Hague: Mouton.
Clivaz, C. and A. Gregory, eds. (2014), *Digital Humanities in Biblical, Early Jewish and Early Christian Studies*, Leiden: E. J. Brill.
Crown, A. D. (1974), 'Tidings and Instructions: How News Travelled in the Ancient Near East', *JESHO*, 17 (3): 244–71.
Cullis, J. and A. C. Webster (2010), 'How to Get the Most from the Medical Literature: Keeping Up to Date in Nephrology', *Nephrology*, 15: 269–76.
Dalton, M. S. and L. Charnigo (2004), 'Historians and Their Information Sources', *College and Research Libraries*, 65 (5): 400–425.
Davis, P. (2014), 'Are Scientists Reading Less? Apparently, Scientists Didn't Read this Paper. The Scholarly Kitchen', https://scholarlykitchen.sspnet.org/2014/02/07/are-scientists-reading-less-apparently-scientists-didnt-read-this-paper/.
Dever, W. G. (1981), 'The Impact of the "New Archaeology" on Syro-Palestinian Archaeology', *BASOR*, 242: 15–29.
Edmunds, A. and A. Morris (2000), 'The Problem of Information Overload in Business Organisations: A Review of the Literature', *International Journal of Information Management*, 20: 17–28.
Ellis, D. (1993), 'Modeling the Information-Seeking Patterns of Academic Researchers: A Grounded Theory Approach', *The Library Quarterly*, 63 (4): 469–86.
Ford, M. (2010), 'Hidden Treasure', *Nature*, 464 (8): 826–7.
Fried, M. H. (1967), *The Evolution of Political Society: An Essay in Political Anthropology*, New York: Random House.
Gellner, E. (1983), *Nations and Nationalism*, Ithaca: Cornell University Press.
Green, H. et al. (2017), 'Humanities Collaborations and Research Practices', in D. M. Mueller (ed.), *At the Helm: Leading Transformation. ACRL 2017 Conference Proceedings*, 292–304, Chicago: Association of College and Research Libraries.
Haapoja, J. (2013), '"I want to see what others have found Interesting": Online Social Filtering of News and Magazine Articles, MA Thesis, University of Helsinki.

Holden, C. (2016), 'Information Seeking Behaviour of the Historian: Serendipity Remains', *Navigating History*, www.csjholden.com/articles.

Huvila, I. (2008), 'The Information Condition: Information Use by Archaeologists in Labour, Work and Action', *Information Research*, 13 (4), http://www.informationr.net/ir/13-4/paper369.html.

Huvila, I. (2014), 'Archaeologists and their Information Sources', in *Perspectives to Archaeological Information in the Digital Society*, 25–54, Uppsala: Uppsala University, http://uu.diva-portal.org/smash/record.jsf?pid=diva2%3A776286.

Ivakhiv, A. (2014), 'The Discipline of Interdiscipline', *RCC Perspectives* 2 (Minding the Gap: Working Across Disciplines in Environmental Studies): 11–14.

Jamali, H. R. and D. Nicholas (2010), 'Interdisciplinarity and the Information-seeking Behavior of Scientists', *Information Processing and Management*, 46: 233–43.

Klein, J. T. (2010), 'A Taxonomy of Interdisciplinarity', in R. Frodeman (ed.), *The Oxford Handbook of Interdisciplinarity*, 15–30, Oxford: Oxford University Press.

Kletter, R. (2004), 'Chronology and United Monarchy: A Methodological Review', *ZDPV*, 120: 13–54.

Kletter, R. (2006), 'Can a Proto-Israelite Please Stand Up? Notes on the Ethnicity of Iron Age Israel and Judah', in A. Maeir and P. de-Miroschedji (eds), *I will speak the Riddle of Ancient Time: Archaeological and Historical Studies in Honor of Amihai Mazar*, 573–86, Winona Lake, IN: Eisenbrauns.

Kletter, R. (2010), 'Review of Schloen, D. (ed.), *Exploring the longue Durée: Essays in Honor of Lawrence E. Stager*', *RBL*, 9, https://www.bookreviews.org/bookdetail.asp?TitleId=7114&CodePage=7114.

Kletter, R. (2014), 'In the Footsteps of Bagira: Ethnicity, Archaeology, and "Iron Age I Ethnic Israel"', *Approaching Religion*, 4: 2–15.

Kletter, R. (2015), 'In Search of the "Israeli Method of Excavation"', *PEQ*, 147 (2): 146–59.

Landhuis, E. (2016), 'Information Overload: How to Manage the Research-Paper Deluge?' *Nature*, 535: 457–8.

Lively, L. (1996), *Managing Information Overload*, New York: Amacom.

Lönnqvist, H. (2007), 'The Research Processes of Humanities Scholars: Advances in Library Administration and Organization', *Advances in Library Administration and Organization*, 25: 175–202.

Lyall, C. (2011), *Interdisciplinary Research Journeys: Practical Strategies for Capturing Creativity*, London – New York: Bloomsbury.

Meho, L. I. and H. R. Tibbo (2003), 'Modeling the Information-Seeking Behavior of Social Scientists: Ellis's Study Revisited', *Journal of the American Society for Information Science and Technology*, 54 (6): 570–87.

Menken, S. and M. Keestra (2015), *An Introduction to Interdisciplinary Research: Theory and Practice*, Amsterdam: Amsterdam University Press.

Morgan, C. L. and J. Winters (2015), 'Critical Blogging in Archaeology', *Internet Archaeology*, 39, http://eprints.whiterose.ac.uk/90793/.

Nicholas, D. and D. Clark (2012), 'Reading in the digital Environment', *Learned Publishing*, 21 (2): 51–6.

Olsson, M. (2016), 'Making Sense of the Past: The Embodied Information Practices of Field Archaeologists', *Journal of Information Science*, 42 (3): 410–19.

Paine, E. (2016), *How to Keep Up with the Scientific Literature*, http://www.sciencemag.org/careers/2016/11/how-keep-scientific-literature.

Palmer, C. L. et al. (2002), 'The Information Work of Interdisciplinary Humanities Scholars: Exploration and Translation', *The Library Quarterly*, 72 (1): 85–117.

Palmer, C. L., L. C. Teffeau and C. M. Pirmann (2009), *Scholarly Information Practices in the Online Environment*, Dublin, OH: OCLC, www.oclc.org/programs/publications/reports/2009-02.pdf.

Pijpers, G. (2010), *Information Overload: A System for Better Managing Everyday Data*, Hoboken NJ: John Wiley & Sons.

Plume, A. and D. van Weijen (2014), 'Publish or Perish? The Rise of the Fractional Author', *Research Trends*, https://www.researchtrends.com/issue-38-september-2014/publish-or-perish-the-rise-of-the-fractional-author/.

Power, C. D. et al. (2017), 'Improving Archaeologists' Online Archive Experiences through User-Centred Design', *ACM Journal on Computing and Cultural Heritage*, 10 (1): Article 3, https://doi.org/10.1145/2983917.

Pontis, S. et al. (2017), 'Keeping Up to Date: An Academic Researcher's Information Journey', *Journal of the Association for Information Science and Technology*, 68: 22–35, https://doi.org/10.1002/asi.23623.

Renear, A. H. and C. L. Palmer (2009), 'Strategic Reading, Ontologies, and the Future of Scientific Publishing', *Science*, 325 (5942): 828–32, https://doi.org/10.1126/science.1157784.

Runnels, C. (1994), 'The Place of Book Reviews in the Professional Literature', *Journal of Field Archaeology*, 21 (3): 357–60.

Schloen, J. D., ed. (2009), *Exploring the Longue Durée: Essays in Honor of Lawrence E. Stager*, Winona Lake, IN: Eisenbrauns.

Service, E. R. (1962), *Primitive Social Organization*, New York: Random House.

Service, E. R. (1975), *Origins of the State and Civilization: The Process of Cultural Evolution*, New York: W. W. Norton.

Skjeggestad, M. (1992), 'Ethnic Groups in Early Iron Age Palestine: Some Remarks on the Use of the Term Israelite in Recent Research', *SJOT*, 6: 159–86.

Smith, A. D. (1971), *Theories of Nationalism*, London: Duckworth.

Smith, A. D. (1981), *The Ethnic Revival in the Modern World*, Cambridge: Cambridge University Press.

Smith, A. D. (1986), *The Ethnic Origin of Nations*, Oxford: Blackwell.

Solomon, Y. and J. Bronstein (2016), 'Serendipity in Legal Information Seeking Behavior: Chance Encounters of Family-Law Advocates with Court Rulings', *Aslib Journal of Information Management*, 68 (1): 112–34.

Spanner, D. (2001), 'Border Crossings: Understanding the Cultural and Informational Dilemmas of Interdisciplinary Scholars', *Journal of Academic Librarianship*, 27 (5): 352–60.

Stager, L. (2001), 'Port Power in the Early and Middle Bronze Age: The Organization of Maritime Trade and Hinterland Production', in S. R. Wolff (ed.), *Studies in the Archaeology of Israel and Neighboring Lands in Memory of Douglas L. Esse*, 625–38, Chicago: University of Chicago Press.

Stone, S. (1982), 'Humanities Scholars: Information Needs and Uses', *Journal of Documentation*, 38 (4): 292–313.

Sufian, A. (2009), 'Information Seeking Behaviour of Archaeology and Heritage Management Professionals of Delhi: A Study', *Pearl: A Journal of Library and Information Science*, 3 (4): 68–73.

Tenopir, C., D. W. King, S. Edwards and L. Wu (2009), 'Electronic Journals and Changes in Scholarly Article Seeking and Reading Patterns', *Aslib Proceedings*, 61 (1): 5–32.

Tenopir, C., R. Mays, and L. Wu (2011), 'Journal Article Growth and Reading Patterns', *New Review of Information Networking*, 16 (1): 4–22.

Tenopir, C., R. Volentine and D. W. King (2012), 'Scholarly Reading and the Value of Academic Library Collections: Results of a Study in Six UK Universities', *Insights: The UKSG Journal*, 25 (2): 130–49.

Tindale, T. J. (1999), 'The Mythology of Information Overload', *Library Trends*, 47 (3): 485–506.

Vlachidis, A. and D. Tudhope (2015), 'A Knowledge-Based Approach to Information Extraction for Semantic Interoperability in the Archaeology Domain', *JASIST*, 67 (5): 1138–52.

Ware, M. and M. Mabe (2015), *The STM Report: An Overview of Scientific and Scholarly Journal Publishing*, 4th Edition, March 2015, https://www.stm-assoc.org/2015_02_20_STM_Report_2015.pdf.

White, H. D. (1996), 'Literature Retrieval for Interdisciplinary Syntheses', *Library Trends*, 45 (2): 239–64.

Wilson, P. (1996), 'Interdisciplinary Research and Information Overload', *Library Trends*, 45 (2): 192–203.

Yoffee, N. (1993), 'Too Many Chiefs?', in N. Yoffee and A. Sherratt (eds), *Archaeological Theory: Who Sets the Agenda?*, 60–78, Cambridge: Cambridge University Press.

WHAT PEOPLE WANT TO BELIEVE:
OR FIGHTING AGAINST 'CULTURAL MEMORY'

Niels Peter Lemche

In his address at the celebrations marking 400 years of the University of Copenhagen in 1879, the vice-chancellor demanded from the members of the Theological Faculty the same scholarly critical methods that were common to all faculties – apart from theology, or so it seemed. The dean of the Theological Faculty, who of course was present, became so upset with the chancellor's attack on theology that he threatened to withdraw the faculty from the university and establish an independent school. Happily his threat did not materialize and the faculty still has its place among the other faculties of the university (the story can be found in Müller 2013: 3). But of course the dean was right. It was impossible to demand that the same scholarly standards be used in theology as in, for example, medicine or natural science. It was not that the dean was defending scholarship as such – he was not – but he knew that theological scholarship had to accommodate the demands of its public, the faithful members of the Church of Denmark. In the theology of his day, scholarly criteria were very different from the ones used elsewhere in academia. It was not so much the subject itself that enforced the methods to be employed by theological scholars, but the expectations of the public.

It goes without saying that at that time the Theological Faculty at the University of Copenhagen was not exactly among the frontrunners of scholarly progression; it was basically a very conservative theological establishment with a view on scripture almost bordering on fundamentalism. Of course it was still accused by the leader of the Inner Mission, Wilhelm Beck, of destroying the word of God with critical studies of the texts of the Old and New Testament. 'On your knees in front of the Bible, professors' he shouted from the pulpit, but he was wrong: the professors were not kneeling in front of the Bible, they were already lying prostrate in front of it.[1] Wilhelm Beck, however, understood very well that his appeal to the professors would find a public, not at the university but among his own followers. These were people who were not the least interested in critical scholarship; on the contrary, they instinctively reacted against anything that could be interpreted as a threat to their accepted beliefs and ideas.

Conservative Scholarship – Critical Scholarship

After almost 150 years of intensive critical scholarship, we have to accept that the negative view of critical biblical studies has not really changed among traditionally minded spectators. It is as if the hostile reaction to biblical criticism only intensifies rather than diminishes whenever criticism of the historicity of biblical events and personalities attracts attention from the public. It is also obvious that it is a common praxis in certain parts of biblical studies to appeal to this general hostility to critical scholarship through attacks on critical scholars, such as we witnessed during the so-called minimalist–maximalist controversy some twenty to fifteen years ago, even if none of the parties involved in that discussion would accept being counted among the most conservative propagators of biblical truth.

In this connection we may distinguish between different reactions to critical scholarship. We have, for example, an almost totally isolated discourse among the most conservative elements of biblical scholarship, between scholars who will accept nothing that is in disaccord with the words of the Bible itself. It is not really worth giving such discourse much attention, although the personal experience of this writer says that it is definitely possible to entertain an interesting and rewarding dialogue about biblical theology as long as historical questions are left out of the

---

1. The faculty was not involved in a scandal of the kind that hit the Scottish Old Testament scholar W. Robertson Smith, whose career was cut short because of his too liberal ideas and his support of Wellhausen, whose *Prolegomena* he translated into English. Yet a similar fate hit the well-known Danish biblical scholar Frantz Buhl, who as a lecturer in Copenhagen took up a position as professor in Leipzig. When Buhl returned to Copenhagen, he was not admitted to the Faculty of Theology but instead became professor of Semitic Philology. Here he could do less harm, or at least this seemed to be the reason for his rejection (on this, Lindhardt 1970). Buhl is generally regarded as the scholar who introduced historical-critical methodology to the study of the Old Testament in Denmark. In New Testament studies, it took another generation before the same level of methodology became generally accepted.

conversation.² The attitude of scholars like Kenneth A. Kitchen to critical scholarship says everything: Kitchen has never been interested in any discussion with the critical part of scholarship but has often expressed his absolute contempt of his opponents. From his first book on biblical history (1966) to his last one (2003), he has made it abundantly clear that we have nothing to learn from critical analyses of biblical texts, and this he does in a fashion that was claimed by the late James Barr (1977: 130–1) to be a hundred percent fundamentalist.

Kitchen has never tried to endear himself to critical biblical scholarship. Whatever you think of his attitude, he never falters in his contempt for critical analysis. Accordingly, he is not a problem to critical scholars: they know where to find him. Another trend in conservative scholarship is a much more serious problem to critical scholarship. This is a fairly recent type of conservative scholarship that tries to present itself as an alternative to critical scholarship by using the same kind of language as critical scholars, thereby pretending to be critical scholars. Scholars of this category present themselves as critical alternatives to mainstream historical-critical scholars by employing a strange combination of fake arguments and methodological refinement in order to persuade the general public to believe that they have a legitimate scholarly case. Any critical student of their methodology would have to dismiss their arguments as based on an illegitimate reasoning, flawed logic and twisted presentations of facts. Several years ago I dealt extensively with this trend (2005), which among other things had resulted in a major 'history' of Biblical Israel, and several seemingly critical discussions with accepted methodology and its advocates (Provan, Long and Longman III 2003).³

It is obvious that this group of conservative biblical scholars are presenting themselves as an alternative to critical scholarship at large. Their position is, however, not really far away from that of Kitchen and his evangelical supporters. They only differ from Kitchen in that they seemingly accept the presence of critical scholarship in order to present the general public with two alternative scholarly positions to choose between – but it is only a screen. In fact their position is more or less the same as those of the evangelical scholars of the category of Kitchen.

---

2. In this way it has been possible to entertain a fruitful theological conversation with members of staff of the Danish Bible Institute (Dansk Bibelinstitut). It is my experience that a meaningful discussion will always have to begin where contacts are to be found. Matters of dispute will pop up soon enough.

3. This writer wrote a review of the first edition (2003b). Studies within this category include Long, Baker and Wenham (2002) reviewed by this writer (2003a) and Kofoed (2005); cf. also my discussion (2011).

It would therefore be correct to dismiss their position as false: evangelical endeavours masquerading as critical scholarship.

Such scholars can, or could until recently, rely on the cultural memory of ordinary people brought up with Bible history from Sunday schools and primary school in religious communities. Their viewpoint is based on the messages presented to them by the lay preachers visiting their home towns – though nowadays more likely from preachers on religious television channels or even on the internet. One could say that they have been brainwashed since early childhood. This is something conservative scholars have always been well aware of, and no matter what arguments critical scholars put forward, the conservative mind is extremely difficult to penetrate.

A full-scale attack on traditional biblical scholarship based on the memory, i.e. indoctrination of evangelical groups, was published some ten years ago by Hector Avalos (2007). Avalos failed to make much of an impression, at least among biblical scholars, simply because he overstated his case and presented an almost total rejection of biblical scholarship that showed too little awareness of the dividing lines in existence between different congregations of biblical scholars. He was, however, correct in stressing the importance of the religious background of most scholars, and how decisive it has been for their attitude to a critical discourse within biblical studies.

The conservative impetus is still very much in evidence, and is continuously producing textbooks and collections presented as alternatives to critical scholarship (cf. recently Arnold and Hess 2014). Conservative scholars certainly know to tell their audience what it wants to hear. In parts of the Western establishment, the blind acceptance of biblical truth may recede but this development does not change much, since both critical studies and conservative tracts are under the influence of the diminishing importance of accepted religion today in the Western world. It could be said that the conservative idea about how to understand the Bible will probably survive indefinitely but it will at the same time lose its importance as an alternative to other types of religious speculation. Therefore the general situation remains the same. Critical scholarship is not in any way victorious. Conservative scholarship is still around and intends to stay, but its importance is increasingly marginal and limited to specific religious groups. Conservative scholars know this all too well, and their tactics have increasingly been to cover up for the deficiencies as far as method goes by directing their activity directly to the public through the media, knowing very well that the majority of the laity will not be able to distinguish between proper scholarship and religious propaganda presented as 'scholarship'.

W. G. Dever and His Repeated Showdowns with Modern Biblical Scholarship

A special case of scholarship originating in conservative circles but liberating itself more and more from this background is presented by the well-known North American archaeologist William G. Dever. Dever comes as he himself admits it from a fundamentalist environment (his father was a lay preacher) but nowadays presents himself as the scion of critical scholarship.

His background sometimes becomes very clear in his various clashes with critical scholarship, where he frequently employs a vocabulary more suited to street fighting than to proper academic exchange. A reading of Dever will tell you that he has no interest in engaging in a serious discussion with critical scholars, an attitude that definitely has its background in his religious upbringing. Instead of exchanging arguments with his opponents, he rhetorically often presents his case only in order to obtain approval for his position from the lay community, which will not normally be in the position to differentiate between critical positions and religiously inspired propaganda.[4]

Dever evidently borrowed his style of 'argumentation' from his father, a lay preacher, visiting various conservative communities and never bothering to present a balanced view on his opponents, the not so pious part of the community. Inspired by his background, taking on critical scholarship became a personal matter for Dever. Examples of the Dever method of argument became legion during the so-called minimalist–maximalist controversy, which raged for about fifteen years, running roughly from c. 1992 to 2007 or 2008 – although in some ways it has never ended. Dever's approach somehow appeared to be a continuation of the way that the students of William Foxwell Albright handled their opponents, who, doubtlessly inspired by their master, had no qualms in dubbing German scholars of the Noth–Alt circle 'nihilist', if not worse. Albright himself had called Martin Noth a nihilist, which shows where the language of his

---

4. The problem is simply that the lay person who has never been trained to participate in a debate among scholars/scientists does not have the logical tools that would enable them to distinguish between postulates and arguments. The lay person will simply not be able to initiate a falsification process of the assertions presented to them. This is of course not a phenomenon restricted to theology and biblical studies; it is a general problem made painfully obvious by modern discussions about fake news, where messages are hammered into among a defenceless public left without guidance.

students originated.[5] Dever once described the difference between North American scholars and their German colleagues in this way: The North Americans are maximalists, the Germans minimalists (Dever 1977: 77)!

It is, however, characteristic the way that Dever, after an initial outburst of anger because of his opponents 'nihilistic' positions, has adjusted to the ideas of those same scholars, probably too often without acknowledging it himself. Thus in his contribution to John H. Hays and Maxwell Miller's *Israelite and Judaean History* (Dever 1977), Dever defends the basic historicity of the patriarchs, although accepting – or so it seems – the reservations of Thomas L. Thompson (1974), a study he may have read but only partially understood. In more recent times he has given up the idea of seeing the patriarchs as historical persons, echoing almost exactly Thompson's position from more than forty years ago.

When Dever launched his campaign against the minimalists, he had already adopted the essential positions of the German 'minimalists', especially the positions of Albrecht Alt and Martin Noth, at least as far as the exodus and the conquest of Canaan are concerned (Dever 1990).[6] However, when the minimalists questioned the historicity of the united monarchy of David and Solomon, he bolted and began his campaign with an atrocious volley of accusations. He has never been satisfied with pointing out that the other party is wrong on single issues, but instead keeps stating that we so-called minimalists have no case, or even that we have a counter-cultural agenda. In this way the minimalists become:

- Philologians – with no pertinent texts
- Historians – with no history
- Theologians – with no empathy to religion
- Ethnographers – with no recognizable 'ethnic groups', no training and no field experience
- Anthropologists – with no theory of culture and cultural change
- Literary critics – with little coherent concept of literary production
- Archaeologists – with no independent knowledge or appreciation of material cultural remains. (Dever 2001: 40)

5. On this cf. the trenchant discussion of the politics of the Baltimore School of Albright and his students, notably G. Ernest Wright and John Bright (Thompson 1974: 5–7). Burke O. Long (1997) also made the politics of the Albright circle very clear; on Albright's view of the German scholars see Long (1997: 53–9).

6. In many ways the most balanced work by Dever. Here Alt is introduced as 'Europe's Albright' (Dever 1990: 53); Noth's history, denounced by Albright and John Bright, is called 'great' (Dever 1990: 53), evaluations that would hardly have endeared Dever to his mentors.

There is no reason to discuss any of these accusations in detail. However, when he describes himself as a non-maximalist he sounds rather hollow:

> My view all along – and especially in the recent books – is first that the biblical narratives are indeed 'stories', often fictional and almost always propagandistic, but that here and there they contain *some* valid historical information. That hardly makes me a 'maximalist'. (Dever 2003)

He is basically saying here exactly the same as the people he opposes. This writer would thus never say 'there is no history in the Old Testament, only that what there may be has to be confirmed by external evidence, including archaeological evidence. That hardly makes me a maximalist!' Thomas Thompson has written extensively on history. Thompson's 'sin' is that he is not writing in the same style as Dever.

The most aggravating part of this discussion, and the reason I have wasted too much space on it here, has to do with the way Dever on one side misrepresents his opponents, while on the other appropriates their ideas and positions. Coming from the school of Albright through his mentor, G. Ernest Wright, he inherited the habits of that school, but has since then adopted practically all the ideas nourished by the first German scholars of the mid-twentieth century, and toward the end of that century the ideas of the very people whom he attacks. For obvious reasons some may be in doubt as to the integrity of this North American archaeologist.

In his recent comprehensive book on biblical archaeology Dever has done it again (Dever 2017), and this is the real and only reason that I take up the issue of William G. Dever one more time. In this new monograph, Dever promotes the idea that without archaeological evidence you can do very little as far as historical investigations are concerned. While this is indeed true, it is not his idea but instead has its roots in the very arguments put forward by Thompson and this writer over many years. Our main argument has for a generation been that so-called historical information in the Bible does not verify itself. In order to establish a biblical text as a historical source we need external evidence of the events narrated in the Bible, either written documents or physical remains. Maybe we should congratulate Dever on his late 'discovery', if this would not also sound hollow. As a matter of fact, reading his new book shows that little has changed.

Dever devotes his chapters on the earliest Israelite history to a model of the Israelite settlement that was prepared by this writer in *Early Israel* (Lemche 1985). He attacks Israel Finkelstein because of his low chronology (among the relatively new discussion of the low chronology, see Finkelstein 2005), which would effectively remove Jerusalem from the tenth-century BCE scene, as if Finkelstein is the only person to support it, though it is indeed a dating that is supported by a series of Israeli archaeologists from the University of Tel Aviv, including David Ussishkin and Ze'ev Herzog, not forgetting the late Orna Zimhoni. This he does in his usual fashion, with the addition of derogatory comments and without much discussion (or maybe he will consider his bias against Finkelstein to be arguments?).[7] In his new book, though, he mostly attacks Finkelstein on the basis of anthropology, accusing Finkelstein of interpreting the archaeological evidence in the wrong way. He is here referring to Finkelstein's study on the Israelite settlement (1988). He claims Finkelstein's position to be outdated in the light of modern anthropological knowledge on the relation between the desert and the sown, but he has totally misunderstood the basis of Finkelstein's position, namely, the idea of the cultural *continuum* that Finkelstein takes from my aforementioned study. Accordingly he claims a position close to George E. Mendenhall (1962, 1973) and Norman K. Gottwald (1979), arguing for an inner Canaanite (he still uses this obsolete term) development. He puts forward a scenario of peasants and city-dwellers on the one hand vis-à-vis a nomadic tribal population on the other, and thus perpetuates the old misconceptions that we are speaking about two cultures in a dimorphic society as described in a series of articles by Michael B. Rowton (1973, 1974, 1976, 1977) that appeared more than forty years ago.[8] Rowton's model was partly wrong. The nomads are not living in a dimorphic society, but represent an encapsulated life form as described by Fredrik Barth (e.g. Barth 1973). Nomads do not automatically represent a different ethnos from the one found among the villagers and city-dwellers in the region, where all life forms co-exist at the same time. So in conclusion Dever's model is in no way 'new'. It is close to my explanation of societal development in the highland of central Palestine published in *Early Israel* but at the same time forgetting the criticism here of especially Gottwald's reconstructions. It is almost the same model, but any reference to *Early Israel* is absent.

It is obvious that biblical studies is in many ways handicapped by having to fulfil the expectations of the religious groups that form its basis. If you are brought up within a religious group, which would often have strong ideas about the historical foundation of its religion, and the same group is also providing economic support for your scholarly activities, it

---

7. E.g. Dever 2017: 261: 'Finkelstein's idiosyncratic low chronology'.

8. Dever duly mentions Michael B. Rowton but does not seem to know of the criticism of Rowton's position, which from an anthropological point of view is hardly tenable.

is clear that you should not or could not break with your own background. It would be expected that your scholarly activity should enhance rather than destroy the beliefs of your back-up group.

When a scholar like Dever has for decades attacked his minimalist opponents and accused them of destroying Western civilization, of being counter-cultural, and especially of simply being not honest scholars, these accusations are themselves particularly dishonest, because it was never intended that his diatribes should be read by other critical scholars, for whom such words are intolerable. The allegations are put forward for the pleasure of his religious back-up group, and have one important aim; namely, to discourage the members of this group from becoming acquainted with the arguments of the minimalists, a move that is typical of conservative or fundamentalist congregations.[9]

When we were young, we – the scholars belonging to the critical group that encompassed Thomas Thompson as well as me – did not know, or were not concerned about the effect that our scholarship would have had on the lay person. Of course the respective backgrounds of Thompson and me are very different. Thompson grew up a Catholic of Irish extraction in Detroit, while my home was in the most wealthy part of Denmark, solidly Lutheran-evangelical. When I was at a very early stage in my studies, and presented with the conflict between fundamentalists and critical positions as found in protestant environments, I naturally found the fundamentalist position ridiculous and of no scholarly value at all. It never occurred to me that the fundamentalists had something to contribute to critical scholarship. This was a mistake, although their contribution was mostly very negative in nature. My position was practically identical to the one James Barr presented in his work on fundamentalism. Barr's view on fundamentalism very much covered what a critical scholar of my generation would have thought about the phenomenon (Barr 1977).

For Thomas Thompson, the realization that he had challenged a dominant Protestant religious set-up became abundantly clear when, for several years after the publication of his *Historicity*, he was cut off from the academic world, and only in a fairly advanced age allowed to return to it, albeit not in his own country but in faraway Thule, in icy Scandinavia. The absolutely free and unbiased academic environment that the University of Copenhagen provided made it possible for Thompson, as it had for me for many years, to unfold an enormous range of provocative new ideas and theories. One could say that Thomas Thompson went into exile, but not one from which he would some day return.

---

9. On this 'technique', cf. Barr 1977: 120–59.

Reviewing the field of Old Testament studies today, it is very clear that many scholars of the present have changed their positions considerably, at least as far as the history of ancient Israel is concerned. The traditional positions have been undermined by developments in biblical studies and Palestinian archaeology among their more progressive exponents. Nothing is really as it used to be. Among the scholars who have been spearheading the progress in scholarship over the last twenty-five years, practically none of them accept today the positions that dominated Old Testament scholarship fifty years ago. It is not necessary to mention them all, and details are immaterial. However, it could well be argued that it is the general environment that has changed. To illustrate the changes one example is enough: while a generation ago almost every critical scholar placed the composition of the various parts of the Old Testament between c. 1000 and 400 BCE, today the discussion centres on the period from c. 500 to 100 BCE (if not later). The relations between the biblical tradition and the culturally superior Greek-Hellenistic world are today one of the real hot spots in biblical studies.

Cultural Memory:
The Reliance on Tales instead of Historical 'Facts'

Still, the basic conditions have not changed (very much). Whatever advances scholars make, we are still met on the street with reactions that seemingly deny that any changes have occurred at all. Although we are in this case talking about religious people who are afraid of losing their tradition, i.e., their faith, the problem should not be seen as exclusively a religious one. On the contrary, it reflects a general attitude among people from all backgrounds. In several articles over the last years, I have stressed that when we discuss history writing in ancient times, we must never make the mistake of taking it to be anything like modern history writing (Lemche 2012a, 2012b, 2012c, 2013a, 2013b). It was not, and it never tried to be. It was cultural memory, a term that refers not to the memory of individuals, but to a memory nourished by a special population about its past. How it came about may be a point of discussion, but cultural memory is not made up of recollections by individuals living in the periphery; it depends on the elite in the society being able to write and read and accordingly controlling the exchange of ideas inclusive of the recollections of their own society. Collective memory is not history in the modern meaning of the word, and as memory it is not bound by the rules of history that it should present the past as it really was. It was something taught to people. History is a weapon of mass instruction, to use an expression coined by John Gatto (2008).

We may think of history writing today as reporting in writing something that really happened in the past. It is certainly not. History writing is related to cultural memory by being a kind of national propaganda aiming at creating a common basis for the new national states of the last two hundred years. It was always highly selective and partial. But it was expected that the historians who were entrusted with the historiography did not invent events that are not reflected by surviving evidence, especially written sources. That is the big difference between former chronicles and methodically controlled history writing from, say, 1800. As the general public at the same time in most Western countries learned history in the elementary schools that sprang up everywhere, it was at the same time the 'victim' of the historical constructions presented to them from childhood onwards. History became a means of national self-identification, reflecting the prevailing ideology of the many national states that appeared around the same time as critical historiography arose.

We have many examples even in recent times of what may happen when an accepted and official history is challenged, especially in the media. A recent television program, in several parts, retelling the history of Denmark from ancient times to the present, created a stir because many people were unable to identify with the producer's perhaps somewhat left-leaning reconstructions. It turned out that there were several interpretations of Danish history in existence at the same time. Only very few commentators – mostly in the media – presented a detailed criticism based on historical research. In general, most commentators fell back on their own ideas about Danish history and did not understand the point, namely that all historical reconstruction is construction; historical reconstructions represent the way certain people understand history. You might say that the 'official' Danish history, the one that meets you, for example, at the National Museum in Copenhagen, has become the cultural memory of most Danes, and they don't want to be challenged by new ideas and reconstructions. This is of course only one among many examples, but nonetheless a telling one: When people have accepted a certain tale as theirs, they are not at all inclined to exchange this tale that has become their collective cultural memory with another story. Not particularly interested in how and why a new historical construction came about, they often react angrily to ideas that are seen as revisionist and foreign – in my own country as those ideas that are 'un-Danish'.

It seems that this is the situation whenever the general public has accepted a certain version of a story created by the specialists as its 'history'. This public is not likely to accept changes out of hand and it will instinctively try to fight such changes, not by scholarly arguments, which would be beyond its capabilities, but with rejection and ridicule. However, national histories – especially in Europe with so many conflicting national narratives – are of course highly indicative when it comes to gauging ordinary people's reactions to change. My argument is that this type of reaction is not limited to critical issues like religion or national history; it is a general attitude to change found among those parts of a population that have not been trained to critically assess what they have been told.

Bibliography

Arnold, B. T. and R. S. Hess, eds. (2014), *Ancient Israel's History: An Introduction to Issues and Sources*, Grand Rapids, MI: Baker Academic.
Avalos, H. (2007), *The End of Biblical Studies*, Amherst, NY: Prometheus Books.
Barr, J. (1977), *Fundamentalism*, London: SCM Press.
Barth, F. (1973), 'A General Perspective of Nomads-Sedentary Relations in the Middle East', in C. Nelson (ed.), *The Desert and the Sown: Nomads in the Wider Society*, 11–21, Berkeley: Institute of International Studies, University of California.
Dever, W. G. (1977), 'The Patriarchal Traditions', in J. H. Hayes and J. Maxwell Miller (eds), *Israelite and Judaean History*, 102–19, London: SCM Press.
Dever, W. G. (1990), *Recent Archaeological Discoveries and Biblical Research*, Seattle: University of Washington Press.
Dever, W. G. (2001), *What Did the Biblical Writers Know and When Did They Know it? What Archaeology Can Tell Us about the Reality of Ancient Israel*, Grand Rapids, MI: Eerdmans.
Dever, W. G. (2003), 'Contra Davies', *Bible and Interpretation* (January), http://www.bibleinterp.com/articles/Contra_Davies.shtml.
Dever, W. G. (2017), *Beyond the Texts: An Archaeological Portrait of Ancient Israel and Judah*, Atlanta: SBL Press.
Finkelstein, I. (1988), *The Archaeology of the Israelite Settlement*, Jerusalem: Israel Exploration Society.
Finkelstein, I. (2005), 'A Low Chronology Update: Archaeology, History and Bible', in T. E. Levy and T. Higham (eds), *The Bible and Radiocarbon Dating*, 31–42, London: Equinox.
Gatto, J. T. (2008), *Weapons of Mass Instruction: A Schoolteacher's Journey Through the Dark World of Compulsory Schooling*, Gabriola, BC: New Society Publishers.
Gottwald, N. K. (1979), *The Tribes of Yahweh: A Sociology of Liberated Israel, 1250–1050 BCE*, Maryknoll, NY: Orbis Books.
Kitchen, K. A. (1966), *The Ancient Orient and Old Testament*, London: The Tyndale Press.
Kitchen, K. A. (2003), *On the Reliability of the Old Testament*, Grand Rapids, MI: Eerdmans.
Kofoed, J. B. (2005), *Text and History: Historiography and the Study of the Biblical Text*, Winona Lake, IN: Eisenbrauns.
Lemche, N. P. (1985), *Early Israel: Anthropological and Historical Studies on the Israelite Society before the Monarchy*, VTSup 37, Leiden: E. J. Brill.
Lemche, N. P. (2003a), 'Review of Long, V. H., Baker, D. W., Wenham, G. J. (2002), *Windows into Old Testament History*', *JAOS*, 123: 386–8.
Lemche, N. P. (2003b), 'Review of Provan, I., Long, V. P., Longman III., T. (2003), *A Biblical History of Israel*', *JAOS*, 123: 925.

Lemche, N. P. (2005), 'Conservative Scholarship on the Move,' *SJOT*, 19: 203–52 (= 'Conservative Scholarship-Critical Scholarship: Or How Did We Get Caught by This Bogus Discussion: On Behalf of the Dever-Davies Exchange', *Bible and Interpretation* (Sept. 2003), http:// www.bibleinterp.com/articles/Conservative_Scholarship.shtml.

Lemche, N. P. (2011), 'Evading the Facts: Notes on Jens Bruun Kofoed: *Text and History: Historiography and the Study of the Biblical Text* (2005)', in L. L. Grabbe (ed.), *Enquire of the Former Age: Ancient Historiography and Writing the History of Israel*, 139–63, LHBOTS 554, London: T&T Clark.

Lemche, N. P. (2012a), 'How to Do History? Methodological Reflections', in A. Hunt (ed.), *Second Temple Studies IV: Historiography and History*, 6–16, LHBOTS 550, New York: T&T Clark.

Lemche, N. P. (2012b), 'The Copenhagen School and Cultural Memory', in P. Carstens, T. Bjørnung Hasselbalch, and N. P. Lemche (eds), *Cultural Memory in Biblical Exegesis*, 81–94, Piscataway, NJ: Gorgias Press.

Lemche, N. P. (2012c), 'Cultural Amnesia', in P. Carstens, T. Bjørnung Hasselbalch and N. P. Lemche (eds), *Cultural Memory in Biblical Studies*, 159–72, Piscataway, NJ: Gorgias Press.

Lemche, N. P. (2013a), 'Historie og Kulturel erindring i Det Gamle Testamente', *DTT*, 76: 18–30.

Lemche, N. P. (2013b), 'History as an Argument for Land Possession', in E. Pfoh and K. W. Whitelam (eds), *The Politics of Israel's Past: The Bible, Archaeology and Nation-Building*, 102–19, Sheffield: Sheffield Phoenix Press.

Lemche, N. P. (2017), 'A Sectarian Group Called Israel: Historiography and Cultural Memory', in J. West and J. Crossley (eds), *History, Politics and the Bible from the Iron Age to the Media Age: Essays in Honour of Keith W. Whitelam*, 72–96, LHBOTS 651, London: Bloomsbury T&T Clark.

Lindhardt, P. G. (1970), 'To breve fra Frants Buhl til Peder Madsen', *DTT*, 33: 55–61.

Long, B. O. (1997), *Planting and Reaping Albright: Politics, Ideology, and Interpreting the Bible*, University Park, PA: The Pennsylvania State University Press.

Long, V. H., D. W. Baker and G. J. Wenham, eds (2002), *Windows into Old Testament History: Evidence, Argument, and the Crisis of 'Biblical Israel'*, Grand Rapids, MI: Eerdmans.

Mendenhall, G. E. (1962), 'The Hebrew Conquest of Palestine', *BA*, 25: 65–87.

Mendenhall, G. E. (1973), *The Tenth Generation: The Origins of the Biblical Tradition*, Baltimore: Johns Hopkins University Press.

Müller, M. (2013), *Det Teologiske Fakultet i det 20. Århundrede: En Skitse*, Copenhagen: Det Teologiske Fakultet.

Provan, I., V. P. Long and T. Longman III (2003), *A Biblical History of Israel*, Louisville, KY: Westminster John Knox Press.

Rowton, M. B. (1973), 'Urban Autonomy in a Nomadic Environment', *JNES*, 32: 201–15.

Rowton, M. B. (1974), 'Enclosed Nomadism', *JESHO*, 17: 1–30.

Rowton, M. B. (1976), 'Dimorphic Structure and Topology', *OA*, 15: 17–31.

Rowton, M. B. (1977), 'Dimorphic Structure and the Parasocial Element', *JNES*, 36: 181–98.

Thompson, T. L. (1974), *The Historicity of the Patriarchal Narratives: The Quest for the Historical Abraham*, BZAW 133, Berlin: de Gruyter.

The Need for a Comprehensive Sociology of Knowledge of Biblical and Archaeological Studies of the Southern Levant*

Emanuel Pfoh

A Prelude

'In the social sciences, the progress of knowledge presupposes progress in our knowledge of the conditions of knowledge' (Bourdieu 1992: 1). Thus opened the renowned French sociologist Pierre Bourdieu's study on the logic of social practice. Bourdieu has also contributed – especially relevant for the present discussion – with a sociology of the academic realms, namely its production and reproduction in France during the 1980s, coining the term *Homo academicus* to refer to the agent/s responsible for the logic of producing and reproducing knowledge in the scholarly field (Bourdieu 1984). Such a sociological study has never, at least in a systematic and comprehensive manner, been attempted in biblical studies – including here *biblical archaeology*, which in many ways, and in spite of its many methodological improvements in the last decades, can still be considered in terms of epistemology a central part of biblical scholarship (cf., for instance, Hoffmeier and Millard 2004; Levy 2010) rather than a part of the international discourse of archaeology. Nonetheless, and in sight of future endeavours, we may already hypothesise about the

* It is with great pleasure that I dedicate this essay to Thomas in honour of his 80th birthday and in recognition of his scholarship. His 1999 book *The Bible in History* (Thompson 1999) was decisive in my career choices while I was an undergraduate. Ever since we first met in Copenhagen in February 2009 – and I should say much before then, if we consider e-mail exchanges – he has always been a source of support and encouragement. I am happy to count myself among his intellectual children.

existence of a *Homo biblicus occidentalis*, with distinct regional variations: the *Homo biblicus europaeus* and the *Homo biblicus americanus*.[1] This species has some two hundred years of existence, and in more recent times has produced a third variation, the *Homo biblicus israelensis*, of some seventy years of existence now. These academic creatures, their living and reproductive conditions, the changes in their intellectual habits, together with the discourses they create and produce, need indeed to be sociologically explored.

Calling for a Sociology of Knowledge

I would like in this article to make a call for a serious and comprehensive study of the conditions by which institutional knowledge about the biblical texts and the history of ancient Israel/Palestine is manufactured as an international discourse through universities, academic societies (ASOR, IAA, SBL, AAR, IES, etc.)[2] and meetings, research projects, journals, media and popular culture, etc., touching upon issues of national memories, cultural heritage and religious identities, as well as past and current politics in the Middle East. Furthering such an approach may in effect contribute, firstly, to grasping a clearer understanding of the concept of ancient Near Eastern and biblical intellectual heritage in the modern Western world, and secondly, to providing current biblical scholarship with more critical epistemologies, with a scholarly self-awareness precisely of how knowledge is produced and reproduced, where this knowledge is located and contextualized, for what purposes, and which are the potential political implications – in the face of the current political situation in Israel/Palestine and the Middle East – of such a research.

This proposal, being ambitious in research scope and resources, should definitely be carried out by a collective effort of scholars over a considerable amount of time. The task should also be divided into national traditions and within them into universities and institutes' traditions. Research on the conditions affecting the production of knowledge, as it has developed in other fields of the humanities and the social sciences, and no less in the archaeology of the ancient Near East, is most necessary to transcend an empirical level of documentation – and here we might attend for

---

1. My memory indicates that it was Philip R. Davies who was one of the first to use the term *Homo biblicus americanus* in a forum on the internet in the mid-2000s, although this might be disputed, of course.

2. On the SBL, see preliminarily the critical notes in Avalos 2007: 307–24. Further, Avalos's insights on the 'infrastructure of biblical studies', beyond his particular conclusions, are relevant to the present discussion; cf. Avalos 2007: 289–342.

instance to recent important contributions with epistemological concerns by Reinhard Bernbeck and Susan Pollock (2004), regarding the political economy of ancient Near Eastern archaeology, or by Zainab Bahrani (1998, 2003, 2006), regarding Mesopotamia's imaginative geographies, Iraq's cultural heritage, questions of race and ethnicity in Mesopotamia, to name but a few interests and problem-oriented topics. These insights provide paramount guidance for the task in biblical scholarship.

In the field of Middle East studies, two recent comprehensive studies worth being attended to for their orientation are Zachary Lockman's book *Field Notes: The Making of Middle East Studies in the United States* (2016), documenting the creation of areas studies between the 1920s and the 1980s and relating political needs in the US and geopolitical conditions in the Middle East to the process of knowledge production by specialists in this area, and Lara Deeb and Jessica Winegar's *Anthropology's Politics: Disciplining the Middle East* (2016), exploring the (usually concealed) politics and the institutionalization of American anthropology of Middle Eastern societies. Apart from some exceptions – which I shall be referring to later – in general, as noted before, we have so far nothing of the like in biblical studies or in the archaeology of the Southern Levant.[3]

Besides national traditions of research, and apart from distinctive locations in which research is carried out, the question of funding research projects should be addressed as well in a critical fashion. American and European excavations in Israel/Palestine have at least for the last hundred years received financial support from universities but also from private investors and associations, usually of some religious orientation and interest. Let us then imagine a private organization, or a private individual, openly religious and willing to contribute to find material evidence of some biblical event or situation: can we think that such private, religious funding does not produce a certain expectation or bias in the archaeologists working regarding what to find?[4] A very clear, and concrete example of this is ELAD, an American real estate development company which is funding archaeological digs in East Jerusalem in order

---

3. We do have 'histories of scholarship', for instance, of biblical archaeology (i.e., Moorey 1991) or of American archeology in the Middle East (i.e., King 1983), but we do not have thorough sociologies of such disciplines yet.

4. Cf. notably Zevit 2004: 7 n. 9, who observes: 'As recently as summer 2001, archaeologists from denominational institutions indicated to me that they would procure neither private nor denominational institutional financial support unless they could make significant connections between their site and the Bible. Electing to excavate Iron Age levels of an identified biblical city was the safest route to financial support.'

to reveal the historicity of the biblical City of King David and with that reclaiming the materiality of Jewish heritage in that place: in this situation the sociology of the production of knowledge by scholars associated with this organization is not so hard to guess.[5] This is just one example related to Israel/Palestine but, similarly, the situation can also be found in different locations of the Middle East, be it Egypt, Turkey, Syria or Iraq.

That politics, religion and other personal beliefs affect in some way and to some degree the scholars interpreting evidence in the world is a fact that has been very well known in the sociology of knowledge since the pivotal publication of Peter Berger and Thomas Luckmann's *The Social Construction of Reality* in 1966 (Berger and Luckmann 1991 [1966]). Of course, this condition can be traced back to previous developments by modern thinkers and scholars like Max Weber, Karl Marx, Immanuel Kant, David Hume and Rene Descartes; but Berger and Luckmann were pioneers in detailing the workings of – as they called it – institutionalization, legitimization and internalization processes of knowledge in society. In this landmark work, we have in effect a clear theoretical basis to analyse the functioning of both academic and popular knowledge about ancient Israel and the archaeology of Palestine in modern times.

All these preliminaries are of course but a search for orientation and a commentary on the need to study the scholars who study the ancient Near East (including here, of course, biblical scholars and historians and archaeologists of ancient Israel/Palestine/Southern Levant), where they do it, in what socio-economic conditions, where the funding comes from, what is their implicit and explicit relation to politics, religion and other institutions, how the produced knowledge is processed and transmitted institutionally and academically by universities and academic associations, etc. (see already Pfoh 2013: 2–4; 2018: 93–5; Ben Zvi 2018: 34–40).

Some Precedents in Old Testament Studies

In what follows, I would like to present now some examples of how a sociologically informed enquiry about ancient Near Eastern and biblical knowledge production operates, presenting only criticism about results – the manner in which such knowledge is produced is only assumed in this instance, mostly because no proper research has been conducted yet.

---

5. Cf. Greenberg 2018: 82–5. Reference must be made here to a thorough study by Raz Kletter on the recent archaeology of the Western Wall Plaza in Jerusalem, uncovering the politics of scientific research in that location (Kletter 2019). See also on these issues, from a broader historiographical perspective, Pfoh (in press).

Perhaps Jack M. Sasson was one of the first ancient Near Eastern and biblical scholars who noted in a seminal article from 1981 that the idea of ancient Israelite statehood as treated by late nineteenth- and early twentieth-century American and German biblical scholars was crafted upon the idea of either national independence, in the first case, or the national unification realised by Bismarck, in the second, and that the idea of Israelite peoplehood was very much dependent on the model of the Western European nation-state (Sasson 1981). Later on, during the 1990s, in a context of harsh debate between the so-called biblical maximalists and minimalists in Old Testament studies, several critical voices appeared. Although not fully addressing the question of the sociology of knowledge in biblical studies, already Thomas Thompson, along with the rest of the 'minimalist' scholars, made clear the need for having clear epistemologies, in particular regarding our construction of knowledge about 'ancient Israel' and the history of the Southern Levant.[6] In particular, Philip Davies and Robert Carroll provided in a couple of papers presented in the context of the European Seminar in Historical Methodology (1996–2012), chaired by Lester L. Grabbe,[7] some guiding questions, problematizations and answers orientated towards some sociological criticism of biblical studies (Davies 1997; Carroll 1997), and so also did Niels Peter Lemche when discussing the politics and ideologies in Old Testament historical scholarship (Lemche 2000, 2005). Equally, already in 1997, Burke O. Long published a socio-historical study, based on a wealth of private archival data, on William F. Albright and his 'Baltimore school', detailing the matrix of biblical archaeology in the US in the twentieth century and advancing a perspective fitting to what is called for in this paper (Long 1997). Also most relevant in this connection is Nadia Abu El-Haj's anthropology of early Israeli archaeology (Abu El-Haj 2001) and Raz Kletter's study on the inception of Israeli archaeology in the 1950s and 1960s, working with archival documents (Kletter 2006).

---

6. See especially the following early examples of 'minimalist' epistemology and methodology aiming at a change of historical paradigm in Old Testament studies – building their criticism here (except for Davies) in the then recently discovered Tel Dan stele – in Davies 1992; Lemche and Thompson 1994; Lemche 1995; Thompson 1995; Whitelam 1995; Cryer 1996; more recent evaluations are found in Lemche 2008; Thompson 2013, 2018; Pfoh forthcoming.

7. Regarding the European Seminar on Historical Methodology, it is useful in this regard to check the anthology and evaluation in Grabbe 2019.

However, it was in effect Keith W. Whitelam who published, right in the middle of the debates of the 1990s in Old Testament historical studies, what is probably the most radical and controversial critique of the ways the history of ancient Israel has been reconstructed by Western scholars: *The Invention of Ancient Israel: The Silencing of Palestinian History* (Whitelam 1996). Beyond the criticism – mostly ideological, rather than properly 'scientific' or historiographical – that this book received,[8] it is clear that Sasson's critical insights were developed by Whitelam into full scale. In perspective, Whitelam's book marked a watershed in Old Testament studies regarding the potentialities of a sociological perspective in the construction of knowledge about the ancient past of Israel/Palestine. It is relevant, for instance, to quote at length Whitelam's opinion of the matrix of one of the classical origins' models for explaining the emergence of ancient Israel in Canaan/Palestine:

> Albrecht Alt's seminal essay 'Die Landnahme der Israeliten in Palästina', published in 1925 [...], led to the development of what has come to be called the Infiltration or Immigration model of Israelite origins, frequently characterized as the peaceful infiltration/immigration of Israelites into Palestine. This hypothesis, associated with German scholarship, notably Alt, Noth, and M. Weippert, has been very influential in the discourse of biblical studies, nearly three-quarters of a century after its classic formulation by Alt, not only in current reformulations of the hypothesis, but through a series of ideas which have been taken for granted in the discourse of biblical studies and therefore rarely articulated. It still retains considerable support, most notably in the recent important work of the Israeli archaeologist Israel Finkelstein (1988). However, *it is a construction of the past, an invention of Israel, which mirrors perceptions of contemporary Palestine of the 1920s at a time of increasing Zionist immigration.* (Whitelam 1996: 74, my emphasis)

Also:

> Alt's work is set in one of the most crucial periods of modern Palestinian history: a period of increasing Zionist immigration into the area in the early decades of the century, along with aspirations of a national homeland, which completely changed the social, political, and demographic characteristics

---

8. And for sure it received criticism when it appeared: see, for instance, Levine 1996; Provan 1997; Dever 1998: 44–6; 1999. It also received more balanced and even praiseful criticism, as found in Lemche 1996 and Holloway 2000. Whitelam addressed in general the critique of 'minimalism' in Whitelam 2002. Further on the historiographical possibilities that his initial outlook opened, see Whitelam 2013.

of the region [...] *The central feature of Alt's construction, significant immigration of groups in search of a national homeland, needs to be considered in the context of these dramatic developments in Palestine at the time he was conducting his research – developments of which he could hardly have been ignorant.* (Whitelam 1996: 76, my emphasis)

This kind of critique proper of the sociology of knowledge, focuses not on the question of data interpretation but rather on the crafting of models for interpreting data and on the influence of the historical, social, national, religious and political contexts of the scholar at work and his/her productions. As such, Whitelam's critique produced a clear precedent to rethink the epistemologies current in Western biblical scholarship.

A more recent example of how well-researched archaeological data can lead to the proposition of social institutions and practices that result in not only historical anachronisms but that also politically legitimate modern historical situations, also related to national and identity issues, is provided by the work of Avraham Faust, a prominent archaeologist from Bar Ilan University in Israel. Faust, in two major studies (2006, 2012) and in many scholarly papers, has advocated for an understanding of early Israelite society (c. 13th–11th centuries BCE) as essentially egalitarian and democratic, first in its social structure, and then, when class differences appeared with statehood, with a surviving egalitarian ethos. Faust indicates in his *Israel's Ethnogenesis*:

> The almost complete lack of decoration on pottery manufactured during the Iron Age II in the kingdoms of Israel and Judah, and earlier in the territories presumably inhabited by Israelites or Proto-Israelites, must therefore be very meaningful. Its mere absence is a powerful statement, which might be directed to within the group or in relation with the outside world. Deciphering it is a complex endeavor. What were the messages transmitted by a lack of decoration? Internally, the lack of decoration could indicate an ideology of simplicity and egalitarianism [...]. (Faust 2006: 45)

Further:

> Four-room houses, by the very uniformity of their plans, the egalitarian ethos reflected by them, and their dominant position within the society discussed, were used to reinforce the community's values and ideology, and to strengthen the sense of togetherness of the population; by building a house according to the traditional code of the society, the inhabitants transit of a message of 'we are part of the community', and therefore enhance the coherence of that community. At the same time, however, the differences in size and quality of the houses sent indexical messages of superiority and wealth. (Faust 2006: 81)

And finally:

> It is clear in light of the above that the Israelite society had a strong egalitarian/democratic ethos, resulting from its location among similarly disposed Near Eastern societies, the specific circumstances through which it evolved, and the fact that it emerged through interaction (and hostility) with other groups seen by the Israelites as hierarchical. The egalitarian ethos became for the Israelites an important part of their distinct identity vis-a-vis other groups [...]. It is even likely that in Israel, more than in many other similar societies, the ethos had some impact on social reality (which still remained, nevertheless, hierarchical). It is also clear that this ethos had an impact on many facets of material culture that were discussed earlier, both during the Iron Age I, when the discrepancy between the ethos and social reality was small, and Iron Age II, when the disparity was great. (Faust 2006: 106–7; cf. also Faust 2012: 9, 28–38, 220–3)

Of course, as Faust himself acknowledges, he is not the first scholar to refer to 'democratic' situations in the ancient Near East: more than seventy years ago, Thorkild Jacobsen famously proposed in a paper to understand prehistoric Mesopotamia in terms of a 'primitive democracy', a situation later replaced by the appearance of 'autocracy' with the development of Mesopotamian statehood (Jacobsen 1943). Closely following Jacobsen in its model, Faust proposed an ideal egalitarian and democratic social situation during the Iron Age I, subsumed later by the appearance of the state but – as noted – with a surviving force as a social ethos.

Kletter has recently criticized Faust's understanding of early Israelite society, correctly in my opinion, by noting the transference of modern diacritics (like egalitarianism and democracy) into a pre-modern, Near Eastern context:

> Faust raises an imaginary vision of ancient Israel as a democratic, egalitarian, pure and simple society. This ideal picture may bear relation to the life of those of us who, like Faust, saw childhood in modern Israel of the 1950–60s: a young, relatively socialist state. Houses did not have high fences and differences of wealth were fewer (and less pronounced) than today. However, this nostalgic picture must also be set against the present capitalist state, where gaps between rich and poor are vast and where democracy is limited to only one side of the fence. (Kletter 2016a: 124; see further Lemche 2010; Kletter 2016b)

Like Whitelam's criticism of Alt's articulation of his explanation for early Israel's appearance as mirroring Zionist colonisation in Palestine in the early twentieth century, Kletter's insight on Faust's reconstruction of social structure and ancient Israelite ethos hits precisely at the core of a scholar's analytical choices: we most probably cannot escape our cultural and socio-economic upbringing, but we always can be epistemologically conscious about it in order to ponder how much our reconstructions of historical realities depend on critical method and sound data or on distortions of a personal past into a historical landscape.

Concluding Remarks

The insights and examples considered in this brief contribution show but a glimpse of a matter that, once again, needs undoubtedly further systematic and comprehensive study and development in the field of biblical studies. Discussions among scholars and different historiographical models are not a novelty at all, of course, but the implicit reasons why scholars adopt theoretical positions and are led to make particular conclusions are often ignored or left aside because they are usually unknown – in the sense of not being scientifically explored. Sometimes these issues are understood simply as political bias in scholarship, be it from the right, or of nationalist-religious or liberal or leftist orientations, all of which without a doubt exists, as all scholarship is political in one way or the other. However, just noting the politics – and condemning or blissfully discarding them accordingly – and interpreting them seriously and scientifically, engaging them epistemologically, are two quite different approaches and attitudes to the question. My point therefore is that the context for the production of knowledge should at least be considered by everybody as a necessary moment of any research, a moment of reflexivity in which we think about our own categories and models and our own social locations to understand and explain our production of knowledge. To gain consciousness of such an epistemological situation would unquestionably make our research processes not only more explicit and scientific but also more honest.

Bibliography

Abu el-Haj, N. (2001), *Facts on the Ground: Archaeological Practice and Territorial Self-Fashioning in Israeli Society*, Chicago: The University of Chicago Press.

Alt, A. (1953), 'Die Landnahme der Israeliten in Palästina' [1925], in A. Alt, *Kleine Schriften zur Geschichte des Volkes Israel. Band I*, 89–125, ed. M. Noth, Munich: Beck.

Avalos, H. (2007), *The End of Biblical Studies*, Amherst, NY: Prometheus Books.

Bahrani, Z. (1998), 'Conjuring Mesopotamia: Imaginative Geography and a World Past', in L. Meskell (ed.), *Archaeology Under Fire: Nationalism, Politics and Heritage in the Eastern Mediterranean and the Middle East*, 159–74, London: Routledge.

Bahrani, Z. (2003), 'Iraq's Cultural Heritage: Monuments, History, and Loss', *Art Journal*, 62: 10–17.

Bahrani, Z. (2006), 'Race and Ethnicity in Mesopotamian Antiquity', *World Archaeology*, 38: 48–59.

Ben Zvi, E. (2018), 'Clio Today and Ancient Israelite History: Some Thoughts and Observations at the Closing Session of the European Seminar for [*sic*] Historical Methodology', in L. L. Grabbe (ed.), *'Even God Cannot Change the Past': Reflections on Seventeen Years of the European Seminar in Historical Methodology*, LHBOTS 663 / ESHM 11, 20–49, London: T&T Clark.

Berger, P. and T. Luckmann (1991 [1966]), *The Social Construction of Reality: A Treatise in the Sociology of Knowledge*, London: Penguin Books.

Bernbeck, R. and S. Pollock (2004), 'The Political Economy of Archaeological Practice and the Production of Heritage in the Middle East', in L. Meskell and R. W. Preucel (eds), *A Companion to Social Archaeology*, 335–52, Oxford: Blackwell.

Bourdieu, P. (1984), *Homo academicus*, Paris: Les Éditions de Minuit.

Bourdieu, P. (1992), *The Logic of Practice*, Stanford: Stanford University Press.

Carroll, R. P. (1997), 'Madonna of Silences: Clio and the Bible', in L. L. Grabbe (ed.), *Can a 'History of Israel' Be Written?*, 84–103, JSOTSup 245 / ESHM 1, Sheffield: Sheffield Academic Press.

Cryer, F. H. (1996), 'Of Epistemology, North-West Semitic Epigraphy and Irony: The "*bytdwd*/House of David" Inscription Revisited', *JSOT*, 69: 3–17.

Davies, P. R. (1992), *In Search of 'Ancient Israel'*, JSOTSup 148, Sheffield: Sheffield Academic Press.

Davies, P. R. (1997), 'Whose History? Whose Israel? Whose Bible? Biblical Histories, Ancient and Modern', in L. L. Grabbe (ed.), *Can a 'History of Israel' Be Written?*, 104–22, JSOTSup 245 / ESHM 1, Sheffield: Sheffield Academic Press.

Deeb, L. and J. Winegar (2016), *Anthropology's Politics: Disciplining the Middle East*, Stanford: Stanford University Press.

Dever, W. G. (1998), 'Archaeology, Ideology, and the Quest for an "Ancient" or "Biblical" Israel', *NEA*, 61: 39–52.

Dever, W. G. (1999), 'Histories and Nonhistories of Ancient Israel', *BASOR*, 316: 89–105.

Faust, A. (2006), *Israel Ethnogenesis: Settlement, Interaction, Expansion and Resistance*, London: Equinox.

Faust, A. (2012), *The Archaeology of Israelite Society in Iron Age II*, Winona Lake, IN: Eisenbrauns.

Finkelstein, I. (1988), *The Archaeology of the Israelite Settlement*, Jerusalem: Israel Exploration Society.

Grabbe, L. L., ed. (2019), *The Hebrew Bible and History: Critical Readings*, T&T Clark Critical Readings in Biblical Studies, London: Bloomsbury T&T Clark.

Greenberg, R. (2018), '50 ans de fouilles israéliennes dans la ville historique de Jérusalem', *Les Cahiers de l'Orient*, 130: 71–86.

Hoffmeier, J. K. and A. Millard, eds (2004), *The Future of Biblical Archaeology: Reassessing Methodologies and Assumptions*, Grand Rapids, MI: Eerdmans.

Holloway, S. W. (2000), 'Review of Keith W. Whitelam, *The Invention of Ancient Israel: The Silencing of Palestinian History*', *RBL*, 31 July.

Jacobsen, T. (1943), 'Primitive Democracy in Ancient Mesopotamia', *JNES*, 2: 159–72.

King, P. J. (1983), *American Archaeology in the Mideast: A History of the American Schools of Oriental Research*, Philadelphia: ASOR.

Kletter, R. (2006), *Just Past? The Making of Israeli Archaeology*, London: Equinox.

Kletter, R. (2016a), 'Land Tenure, Ideology, and the Emergence of Ancient Israel: A Conversation with Philippe Guillaume', in L. L. Grabbe (ed.), *The Land of Canaan in the Late Bronze Age*, 112–24, LHBOTS 636 / ESHM 10, London: Bloomsbury.

Kletter, R. (2016b), 'Water from a Rock: Archaeology, Ideology, and the Bible', *SJOT*, 30: 161–84.

Kletter, R. (2019), *Archaeology, Heritage and Ethics in the Western Wall Plaza, Jerusalem: Darkness at the End of the Tunnel*, CIS, London: Routledge.

Lemche, N. P. (1995), 'Bemerkungen über eines Paradigmenwechsels auf Anlaß einer neuenddeckte Inschrift', in M. Weippert and S. Timm (eds), *Meilenstein. Festgabe für Herbert Donner zum 16. Februar 1995*, 99–108, ÄAT 30, Wiesbaden: Harrassowitz.

Lemche, N. P. (1996), 'Clio Is also among the Muses! Keith W. Whitelam and the History of Palestine: A Review and a Commentary', *SJOT*, 10: 88–114.

Lemche, N. P. (2000), 'Ideology and the History of Ancient Israel', *SJOT*, 14: 165–94.

Lemche, N. P. (2005), 'Conservative Scholarship on the Move', *SJOT*, 19: 203–52.

Lemche, N. P. (2008), *The Old Testament between Theology and History: A Critical Survey*, LAI, Louisville, KY: Westminster John Knox Press.

Lemche, N. P. (2010), 'Avraham Faust, Israel's Ethnogenesis, and Social Anthropology', in E. Pfoh (ed.), *Anthropology and the Bible: Critical Perspectives*, 93–104, BI 3. Piscataway, NJ: Gorgias Press.

Lemche, N. P. and T. L. Thompson (1994), 'Did Biran Kill David? The Bible in the Light of Archaeology', *JSOT*, 19: 3–21.

Levine, B. (1996), 'Review of Keith W. Whitelam, *The Invention of Ancient Israel: The Silencing of Palestinian History*', *IEJ*, 46: 284–8.

Levy, T. E., ed. (2010), *Historical Biblical Archaeology and the Future: The New Pragmatism*, London: Equinox.

Lockman, Z. (2016), *Field Notes: The Making of Middle East Studies in the United States*, Stanford: Stanford University Press.

Long, B. O. (1997), *Planting and Reaping Albright: Politics, Ideology, and Interpreting the Bible*, University Park, PA: The Pennsylvania State University Press.

Moorey, P. R. S. (1991), *A Century of Biblical Archaeology*, Cambridge: The Lutterworth Press.

Pfoh, E. (2013), 'Some Reflections on the Politics of Ancient History, Archaeological Practice, and Nation-Building in Israel/Palestine', in E. Pfoh and K. W. Whitelam (eds), *The Politics of Israel's Past: The Bible, Archaeology and Nation-Building*, 1–17, SWBA 2nd Series 8, Sheffield: Sheffield Phoenix Press.

Pfoh, E. (2018), 'Rethinking the Historiographical Impulse: The History of Ancient Israel as a Problem', *SJOT*, 32: 92–105.

Pfoh, E. (in press). 'Western Scholarship, Ethnogeographies and Cultural Heritage in Israel/Palestine', in W. Sommerfeld (ed.), *Proceedings of the 63rd Rencontre Assyriologique Internationale 'Dealing with Antiquity – Past, Present & Future' Marburg 24–28 July 2017*, AOAT 460, Münster: Ugarit-Verlag.

Pfoh, E. (forthcoming), 'Considering "Minimalism", History and Historiography'.

Provan, I. W. (1997), 'The End of (Israel's) History? K. W. Whitelam's *The Invention of Ancient Israel*: A Review Article', *JSS*, 42: 283–300.

Sasson, J. M. (1981), 'On Choosing Models for Recreating Israelite Pre-Monarchic History', *JSOT*, 21: 3–24.

Thompson, T. L. (1995), 'A Neo-Albrightean School in History and Biblical Scholarship?', *JBL*, 114: 683–98.

Thompson, T. L. (1999), *The Bible in History: How Writers Create a Past*, London: Jonathan Cape.

Thompson, T. L. (2013), 'Changing Perspectives on the History of Palestine', in T. L. Thompson, *Biblical Narrative and Palestine's History: Changing Perspectives 2*, 305–41, CIS, Sheffield: Equinox.

Thompson, T. L. (2018), 'The Problem of Israel in the History of the South Levant', in L. L. Grabbe (ed.), *'Even God Cannot Change the Past': Reflections on Seventeen Years of the European Seminar in Historical Methodology*, 70–87, LHBOTS 663 / ESHM 11, London: T&T Clark.

Whitelam, K. W. (1995), 'Sociology or History: Towards a (Human) History of Ancient Palestine?', in J. Davies, G. Harvey and W. G. E. Watson (eds), *Words Remembered, Texts Renewed: Essays in Honour of John F. A. Sawyer*, 149–66, JSOTSup 195, Sheffield: Sheffield Academic Press.

Whitelam, K. W. (1996), *The Invention of Ancient Israel: The Silencing of Palestinian History*, London: Routledge.

Whitelam, K. W. (2002), 'Representing Minimalism: The Rhetoric and Reality of Revisionism', in A. G. Hunter and P. R. Davies (eds), *Sense and Sensitivity: Essays on Reading the Bible in Memory of Robert Carroll*, 194–223, JSOTSup 348, Sheffield: Sheffield Academic Press.

Whitelam, K. W. (2013), 'Shaping the History of Ancient Palestine: Nationalism and Exclusivity', in E. Pfoh and K. W. Whitelam (eds), *The Politics of Israel's Past: The Bible, Archaeology and Nation-Building*, 183–211, SWBA, 2nd Series 8, Sheffield: Sheffield Phoenix Press.

Zevit, Z. (2004), 'The Biblical Archaeology versus Syro-Palestinian Archaeology Debate in Its American Institutional and Intellectual Contexts', in J. K. Hoffmeier and A. Millard (eds), *The Future of Biblical Archaeology: Reassessing Methods and Assumptions*, 3–19, Grand Rapids, MI: Eerdmans.

Part 2

HISTORY, HISTORIOGRAPHY AND ARCHAEOLOGY

The Abraham and Esau-Jacob Stories in the Context of the Maccabean Period*

Łukasz Niesiołowski-Spanò

One of the most important achievements of Thomas L. Thompson was the falsification of the hypothesis of the historical validity of the context of the patriarchal narratives in Genesis. His seminal book (Thompson 1974), next to the work of John Van Seters (1975), changed the scholarly paradigm for good. After publication of these two studies, it was practically impossible to claim – in line with the scholarly consensus – that narratives about the Patriarchs in Genesis contain any traces of the historical memory originating in the Bronze Age.

One might say that Thompson's ground-breaking study is dominated by *pars destruens*, it being argumentation against the former scholarly paradigm. Thomas Thompson in his later works (as well as other scholars) expressed his view on the possible historical context of the so-called patriarchal narratives preserved in Genesis; however, less systematically (cf. Thompson 2011; 1992: 356, 365–6). Thompson claims that it was the Hellenistic era which fits best the historical context of the stories written in Genesis. This claim may not look like the result of systematic studies of the Hellenistic history of the Jews and development of Jewish writings in this period. It seems rather to be the natural effect of the shifted paradigm, accepted by Thompson, expressed in its best-known form by Niels Peter Lemche, in his – already classic – article (1993). This contribution is intended as an *addendum* to the claims about the possible creation / rewriting of the key elements in the Abraham and Jacob-Esau stories during the second century BCE.

---

* This paper originated in studies made possible thanks to research grant number 2016/23/B/HS3/01880 funded by the National Science Centre, Poland.

This is not the right place to discuss in depth the possible origins of the traditions about Abraham and Jacob-and-Esau. I am also not going to discuss the historical period of the earliest attestation of these biblical figures, which incidentally still remains a very complicated issue. The aim of this study is to look at these two stories from Genesis and investigate their possible role in the late second century BCE (cf. my earlier work, dealing with a similar topic, but from a different point of departure: Niesiołowski-Spanò 2006). Therefore, I am not going to discuss how old the stories are or the figures of the patriarchs and where they came from. I may, however, try to shed light on the possible historical context that might have influenced and inspired the current version of these stories and their place within the framework of Genesis.

* * *

The main focus of this article will be on the account of Abraham as the father of multiple nations, and on the story of Jacob and Esau's conflict and their reconciliation, in the light of the process leading to the creation of the identities of the groups living in Palestine. In both these cases we will deal with the classical aetiological myths of ethnogenesis but of a contradictory nature. The story about Abraham, as the father of Ishmael and Isaac, clearly includes others in the community. Both the groups that claim to be descendants of Isaac and Jacob-Israel, as well as the group supposed to descend from Ishmael (regardless of whether they really knew they were Ishmaelites, or whether they were described as such) are depicted as kin. On the other hand, the story about the competition between Jacob and Esau, described in Genesis, with an important variant in *Jubilees*, looks rather like the aetiology of the relationship between two real, existing groups, for which the biblical authors try to fix family bonds. The issue which deserves further attention concerns whether those relationships illustrate friendly or hostile attitudes, or rather, represent biblical authors' positions on including or excluding other groups.

Abraham has been depicted as the figure disconnected from any historical realities, by being alien and of a nomadic way of life. The stories connected with Abraham are set within the mythical *illo tempore*, in the same way as Greek heroes are described in un-historical realities of the tragedies or Homeric epic for which a coherent historical background does not exist. The realities of myth are usually different from the real world or what may be realised by the creation of an unreal world, e.g. of the Amazons, the Lotophagi, or the unreal past-time, regardless of nuclei of realistic realities used in the description. In this light one shall consider mythical the realities of Exodus, of the conquest of Palestine by Joshua, of the so-call period of Judges, David, Solomon, and the subsequent kings of Israel and Judah, as well as the court of Nebuchadnezzar in the book of Daniel. If one accepts such a definition of myth, it therefore constructs the realities far from those considered unreal and as such false and deceptive. The reality of myth is not a lie, but a truth; truth *par excellence* – the object of undisputed faith (on the theme of the use of myth in the Hebrew Bible see recently Wajdenbaum 2010; cf. Niesiołowski-Spanò 2011: 1–5). As a matter of fact, the quest for the historical realities of most of the biblical stories is baseless. As mythical, i.e. being the object of religious beliefs, they may have been filled with real historical information, but they are still un-historical in the scholarly sense of the word. The realities of the biblical stories shall not determine their historical trustfulness or lack thereof, because they were composed for different reasons: as stories for believers (cf. Niesiołowski-Spanò 2018).

I consider two issues in the biblical story of Abraham the most important: (1) the covenant between God and Abraham, and through him with the promised multitudes of Abraham's descendants, who become the chosen people of God, i.e. the community of faithful ones, and (2) the sacrifice of Isaac (*Akedah*). The *Akedah* (Gen. 22:1-13) has notably a gnomic nature, and evokes the philosophical and etic reflections similar to those intended by the book of Job and Ecclesiastes. Are there limits to trust in God? Shall the believer expect reward for his/her pious life, and if so, would it be an earthly or eternal reward? This is not the proper place to discuss this issue in depth, so let us conclude with the general remark that the *Akedah* looks like one of the biblical voices focused on philosophical questions, along with other biblical wisdom texts. I would not consider this tradition as having originated in popular thought, so thus not based on folkloristic stories (for example the *Akedah* does not reflect the original aetiology for sacrifice), but rather it is a reflection of the Jewish elites of the late Hellenistic period (second–first century BCE), an expression of their intellectual, highly sophisticated interest.

The key element in the Abraham story is therefore the covenant between God and Abraham, and his (expected, and promised) offspring. Abraham – in contrast e.g. to Jacob – is deprived of any distinctive aspects linking him with any particular group. Abraham is a figure pure in nature, and as such more of a model figure than one that is concrete. As a matter of fact, the intended aspect of Abraham may be interpreted in the light of the well-defined aspects of his sons: Ishmael, standing for Ishmaelites, Isaac, personifying Jews, and sons born by Keturah (Gen. 25:1-4) openly linked with the inhabitants of Arabia. As the offspring of Abraham clearly indicates certain peoples, of clear and distinctive nature and dwellings, Abraham undoubtedly deserves the name of the ecumenical patriarch (de Pury 2000) as well as the pan-ethnic patriarch.

In the Abraham story, or precisely in the Isaac-Ishmael part, the narrative is far from clear and the plot is not straightforward. If one expected here a typical mythical narrative about the origins of the group, written down by those claiming to be descendants of Isaac, then some distinctive aspects of Isaac should be expected. In some cases the narrative fulfils the need to describe the 'our' hero in the typical way: the child is born in unusual conditions, as the result of God's will, which is a well-known literary device to mark the unparalleled hero (cf. Moses, Exod. 2:1-10; Samson, Judg. 13:2-24; Jesus, Matt. 2:1-16). The miraculous origin of Isaac is also strengthened by the *Akedah* story, i.e. the miracle of Isaac's life being saved by the direct intervention of God. These aspects of Isaac clearly show his particular role in the narratives, allowing the audience to identify with Isaac as their mythic forefather.

On the other hand, Isaac is Abraham's younger son. In the entire narrative it is the older son – Ishmael – who is treated by Abraham as legal and a full-fledged son. Despite the fact that Hagar is called Sarah's slave, which may indicate the lower status of her son, the biblical texts (e.g. Heger 2014: 113–24), as well as numerous attestations from extra-biblical sources (Ze'evi 2000), indicate that a son born by the wife's slave get the status equal to legal sons. It is even openly stated that Abraham did not want to treat Ishmael as the lesser son (Gen. 21:9-11). Moreover, the Egyptian identity of Hagar may indicate an ambivalent meaning: in the light of the xenophobic view every stranger is bad, but on the other hand, in confronting the historical realities, regardless of the period, Egyptian origins may have pointed to the elevated economic and political position of Ishmael. Casting out Hagar and Ishmael comes about because of the will of jealous Sarah, and is initially conducted in spite of Abraham's objections (Gen. 21:8-21). The text openly states that 'God was with the boy [Ishmael], and he grew up' (Gen. 21:20) and Abraham wanted the best for his first-born son: 'And Abraham said to God, "O that Ishmael might live in your sight!"' (Gen. 17:18). The legal status of Ishmael, not lower than Isaac's, can be seen at the scene of Abraham's burial, where both brothers act hand in hand (Gen. 25:9).

Therefore, what was the purpose of complicating the plot and instead of making Isaac the apparently chosen hero, making Ishmael the first-born son of Abraham?

It looks like the ecumenical Abraham, and the semi-equal positions of Isaac and Ishmael, serve to declare the open attitude of the Jewish community (Isaac) toward these people who may be understood as the descendants of Ishmael, Hagar and Keturah. If such was the case, this sophisticated, and in a way twisted narrative device, might have served a few different purposes. Firstly, it might have served as inter-propaganda directed to members of the Jewish community, with the statement about Arabs, who shall not be treated as aliens. This may have served certain political needs. Secondly, the Abraham-Isaac-Ishmael tradition might have been addressed to the Arab population with the same friendly information. In this case, we would be dealing with the declaration of friendship, which in the reality of politics might have been understood as an invitation toward the Arab population to join the political unity of the Jews.

One may ask the question about the circumstances in which both scenarios might have been possible. Up for consideration – I assume – are only cases when the Jews might have favoured an improvement in relations with the Arabs. Did this condition occur in the period of the Judahite monarchy (e.g. 7th–6th century BCE), when the Arab population inhabited southern regions of Judah, and territories South and South-East of it? I see no clear reasons why the state of Judah, with its functionaries, state and royal ideology, its formal ways of extending political and fiscal control over inhabitants, and its system of military service, had to call for any improvements in the relations between Judahites and Arabs. The state had enough means by which keep the inhabitants loyal (in this regard see e.g.: Niesiołowski-Spanò 2016). In the past, during the stateless period in the history of the Jews – a time when the consolidating means of the state obviously did not exist – there perhaps was a motivation to convince populations of different origins and cultures, including the neighbouring Arabs, to reassess and improve relations, or even to include them within the community. One may assume that as the community was not guaranteed by the state, it was possible to use other tools for extending this 'imagined community'.[1]

Whatever the most plausible period when the Abraham-Isaac-Ishmael story might have been used for propagandistic purposes, aiming to better the relationships between the Jews and the Arabs, one should ask the question whether the patriarchal figures were invented out of nothing or adopted out of the older 'proto-historical' tradition? In offering such stark contrast between the invented heroes and traditional figures, I am inclined

---

1. This is an intended allusion to Benedict Anderson's book (1983).

to opt for the second. The most efficient propaganda is usually constructed on the basis of plausible elements which do not appear coarse or brazen. Furthermore, having traditional, popular and well-known figures involved in the new propagandistic content would strengthen the significance of the message. It would even authenticate the story.

On the other hand, one cannot overlook the fact that Abraham and his sons are almost absent from the Hebrew Bible outside Genesis. This fact does not, naturally, allow us to rule out the possibility of the early existence of the tradition of Abraham, but it may suggest the sudden, and even momentous 'career' of this figure. It is certainly not accidental that Abraham became very popular in New Testament literature as the patriarch who made a covenant with God (in contrast to Moses, the law-giver). I suppose it is mostly because Abraham represents the person included in God's community. Although he was born outside of it, he was included in the group of the chosen ones. Moses and Jacob-Israel were born as members of the community, bound by the covenant with God. This may explain why the New Testament authors made extensive usage of this figure in their writings.

* * *

The second story to be dealt with here is typically etiological in nature. Two figures, whose names directly link them to certain populations, Jacob/Israel-the Jews and Esau/Edom-the Idumaeans (and earlier the Edomites), set their bilateral relationships (Gen. 25:23): 'And the Lord said to her, "Two nations are in your womb, and two peoples born of you shall be divided; the one shall be stronger than the other, the elder shall serve the younger"'. This brotherhood clearly evokes the relation between another pair: Isaac-Ishmael. In both cases, the 'other' brother – Ishmael and Esau – is a first-born son, with the apparent favour of their fathers (Gen. 21:10-11; 25:28).

The relationship between Esau and Jacob, the selling of Esau's birthright, in a way a kind of cheating, and reconciliation between the two brothers, seems to construct the centre of the narrative about Isaac's sons. Here also the reader may be surprised as to why 'our' hero – Jacob – is not the better of the two from the very beginning of the story. Such a literary device was used a few chapters later to underline the position of Jacob's chosen sons. In the story about Jacob's sons, the reader knows from the beginning what the attitude of the father is toward his sons, and what the hierarchy and mutual relations are between them. In the case of the story of Jacob-Israel his non-dominant position at the beginning of the story cannot be accidental. Jacob identifies, therefore, as the eponymic hero *par excellence*, evoking imagined community. Hence, Israel is to be equated with Jacob and does not refer to the kingdom of Samaria, but to the virtual and literary entity constructed on the mythical basis of common origins. Therefore, why is Jacob not simply the only child, and as one of two brothers, why is he not the more important one from the very beginning?

There are – in my opinion – two ways to explain this issue. According to one explanation, we have to do here with a literary device of diminishing the importance of the protagonist, allowing his subsequent exaltation. Such a narrative tool was used in the Joseph story, whose poor faith contradicts with his sudden success at the Pharaoh's court (Gen. 37 and Gen. 41:37-57). Similarly, Gideon presents himself as the youngest son of his father, originating from within the weakest clan of his tribe (Judg. 6:15), but this does not preclude his possessing servants (Judg. 6:27), and having a royal-like nature (Judg. 8:22-26). The same device was used to signal the humble origins of David (1 Sam. 16:4-13), which – by contrast – underscores the later David's career. Yet if this device has been used in the Jacob story, a clear and more straightforward message should be expected. Being the younger twin-brother makes much less of an impact than being the youngest out of many. Still, the entire story does not represent the clear Rocky Balboa-like scenario. Jacob depicted in Genesis is not the hero who falls, and loses, to rise to a triumphal victory. He is rather described as the lucky dodger. The stories about Jacob struggling with an angel, staying at Laban's house and especially competing with his brother do not represent the typical plot of the falling-and-rising hero. The Jacob story – in the light of the narrative devices used in similar cases – does not represent a simple and straightforward account.

The second way to explain the narrative structure would be based on emphasising the appreciation of the second brother – Esau. Readers obviously sympathise with Jacob, yet it might have been Esau who was intended to be the central figure of this part of the story. Therefore, the story allows the interplay of the protagonists' successes and failures. In this way, the narrative's attractiveness and the intellectual value of the story are proportionally higher since the story is less straightforward. The demanding reader needed more sophisticated accounts.

Special attention must be paid not only to the account about the brothers' relationship in Genesis, but also in the version preserved in *Jubilees*. Interestingly, the account in *Jubilees* in general follows the Jacob-Esau story from Genesis, with one important exception: the Jacob-Esau story ends in Genesis, rather surprisingly, with the brothers' reconciliation (pointing to the generosity of Esau versus Jacob being a lucky imposter), while in *Jubilees* the tension culminates with the violent struggle between Esau and his clan and Jacob and his sons, fighting in the name of the whole of Israel. The version in *Jubilees* seems to be better-constructed in regard to the narrative's dynamics: Jacob's fears, leading him to protect the most beloved ones by placing them at the end of the caravan (Gen. 33:1-3), does not find a logical culmination in Genesis. The canonical version, in which two brothers hug one another (Gen. 33:4), is dramaturgically less natural than the version in *Jubilees*, where the tension ends with war as the narrative climax:

> And afterward Judah spoke to Jacob, his father, and he said to him, 'O father, stretch your bow and shoot your arrows and strike down the enemy and kill the adversary. And may you have might because we will not kill your brother (inasmuch as) he is near to you and with us he is like you with respect to honor'. And then when Jacob drew his bow and shot an arrow and stuck Esau, his brother, on his right breast, he killed him. (*Jub*. 38:1-3)

Furthermore, this conflict is openly depicted in *Jubilees* as the conflict between two populations:

> And Jacob's sons besieged the children of Esau on the mountain of Seir. And they bowed down their necks to become servants of the children of Jacob. (...) And Jacob sent notice to his sons to make peace. And they made peace with them and placed a yoke of servitude upon them so they might pay tribute to Jacob and his sons always. And they continued paying tribute to Jacob until the day that he went down to Egypt. And the children of Edom have not ceased from the yoke of servitude, which the twelve sons of Jacob ordered upon them until today. (*Jub*. 38:10. 12-14) (trans. O. S. Wintermute)

General scholarly consensus points to the late second century BCE as the date of *Jubilees*, which is interpreted as depending on the canonical Genesis. In this light the key difference between the two texts of the Jacob-Esau story may suggest two phenomena. Firstly, in Maccabean Judah there was a group which did not accept the peaceful message presented in Genesis, interpreted as the postulate of friendly relationships between the Jews and the Idumaeans. Their view, presented in *Jubilees*, postulated instead a violent conquest of Idumaea, leading to 'a yoke of servitude upon them so they might pay tribute to Jacob and his sons always'. According to *Jubilees* the sons of Esau are strangers to Israel, and deserve to be conquered and subdued (Mendels 1987: 57–8). Secondly, despite very close narrative similarities between the two texts, the differences in the conclusions of the Jacob-Esau story are striking. Hence, one may argue that this deviation in narratives was possible not only because of a difference of worldviews, but also because the canonical version was not as stable as might be assumed. While a large majority of *Jubilees*' narrative faithfully agrees with Genesis, divergences in narrative plot do occur, albeit rarely. The version in Genesis might have been challenged by a different frame of reference, which may suggest that the Genesis version did not have the status of unchangeable truth-text. The unstable status of the narrative may suggest a recent date. The Genesis version of the Jacob-Esau story was not an old, covered with patina, holy, unquestionable text, but rather a recently elaborated version which might have been rejected and transformed by *Jubilees*. The author of the Genesis version of the Jacob-Esau story inserted there his worldview and his agenda, while the author of *Jubilees* disregarded them and replaced them with his own propagandistic demands – in place of brotherly love, he placed the decisive military struggle, followed by the political domination of the Jews over the Idumaeans.

The Jacob-Esau case, in an even more obvious way than in the case of Abraham and his sons, points to the fact that we deal here with archaic, legendary figures. It is impossible to establish when these legendary figures were invented, or even when they were mentioned for the first time (cf. i.e.: Deut. 32:9; 33:10; Pss. 14:7; 78; Isa. 9:7; Hos. 12:13). Suffice it to say that – with a high degree of plausibility – they originated in the pre-Hellenistic period. Thus Jacob and Esau may serve as good examples of figures originated in the old mythical tradition, which were used in a later time for propagandistic purposes.

Is it possible to establish the period when certain Jewish communities might have advocated the improvement of relationships with the Idumaeans? Through the centuries the relations between the neighbours were typically dominated by either violence or peaceful tension, as well as ongoing competition. Border disputes and double-sided attacks on a local scale were supplemented by wars, some of which are referred to in the Hebrew Bible (cf. Isa. 34:9-13; 1 Sam. 14:47; 1 Kgs 11:15-16; Mal. 1:4). This must have been typical of neighbourly relationships in the monarchic period. It is, however, not impossible that in the monarchical period there were people in Judah who might have postulated good relationships with the Edomites. Such a postulation – for political reasons – must not have been accepted by the state politicians, who plausibly preferred the solid military-based relationship. If the idea of Jacob and Esau being kin originated in the monarchical period, it most likely remained on the fringe of official state discourse.

The most obvious event that points to hostile relationships is remembered in the guilt of Edom, that is, participation in the destruction of Jerusalem, along with the Chaldeans (Lam. 4:21-22; Obadiah). Despite the fact that Obadiah equates Esau with Edom and makes use of the notion of an Esau-Jacob brotherhood, hardly anyone would have postulated good relationships with Edomites in these times (cf. Ben Zvi 1996: 230–46).

The period after the fall of Jerusalem may provide the ideal circumstances for the possibility of improving relations with the Edomites. The remnants of the Judahites, living under Chaldean rule, might have considered the Edomites – the allies of the Babylonians – as appropriate allies. Such a situation makes sense, but one could question whether the Judahites, living on the poor remnants of the destroyed kingdom of Judah, would still identify themselves with Jacob. In particular, would they be inclined to identify with such a Jacob as is depicted in Genesis? One may doubt that this would be the case.

During the Persian period one may expect the postulates about neighbourly peaceful relations between the Idumaeans and Judahites. These may have come down from the ruling Persian authority, aiming to calm local tensions. The Persians wanted the local communities to obey the local authorities, and any local conflict, especially close to the Egyptian border, might weaken the strategic situation of Achaemenid Persia in the region. In this light it could be concluded that any possibility of improvement of the relationship between the Jews and the Idumaeans expressed during the fifth or fourth century BCE first of all might serve the strategic needs of the Persians (cf. Ben Zvi 2006; 2014: 26–7). Nonetheless, one may posit the idea that the only well-dated attestation about Jewish-Idumaeans relationships points to strong antagonism: the effort to establish an administrative centre in Jerusalem, referred to in the book of Nehemiah, which causes a hostile reaction from the neighbours, including Geshem the Arab. Here also it would be difficult to accept the Genesis-like version of Jacob as the ideal eponymic figure for the inhabitants of the province of Yehud.

On the other hand, while Ammonites and Moabites were not supposed to be admitted to the assembly (Deut. 23:3-6), the Edomites and Egyptians may have been permitted: 'You shall not abhor any of the Edomites, for they are your kin' (Deut. 23:7). This statement may well fit with the political realities of the fifth century BCE, when the Persians extended their rule over Egypt, and Southern Judah and the region of the Northern Negev became strategic zones for military reasons. This was the period when the inhabitants of Yehud might have disregarded the people in Transjordan, but were obliged to keep good relationships with the people of the South. This may have been the possible period when the idea of the Jacob-Esau brotherhood was promoted (or invented) for political reasons to ensure a safe border.

The historical data about the relationships between the Jews and the Idumeans from the third century BCE are practically absent. The lack of decisive data does not allow for unequivocal hypotheses; however, one cannot rule out the possibility that proposals for peaceful relations with the Idumaenas might have been expressed among the Jews. This hypothesis, without any firm sources supporting it, has to remain, however, purely speculative.

Jewish-Idumaean relations are better known only from the late Maccabean period, when the Jews under the Hasmonaeans expanded their state southward. Josephus reports the conquest of Idumaea, pointing to the regions of Adora and Marisa (*Ant.* 13.257-258), followed by the note about the religious conversion of the Idumaeans to Judaism. This account sheds new light on relations between the neighbours. The possibility of the normalization and improvement of relations between the Jews and the Idumaeans might have been expressed as well in the imperialistic propaganda before the conquest of John Hyrcanus, or after it.

All of the chronological scenarios mentioned above may find support and respective followers. It is, however, difficult to deny that the political expansions of John Hyrcanus provide a kind of 'game-changer' in relations between the Jews and the Idumaeans. It is not difficult to imagine the importance and relevance of the probability of friendly relations between these two peoples, especially in the context of these military events during their preparation and planning before as well as after the conquest. The propagandistic and political value of the biblical story would thus be very apparent.

I am inclined to say that the military expansion under John Hyrcanus provides the most plausible historical context for the possibility of improvement in the relations between the Jews and the Idumaeans, turned into literary form in the story of Jacob and Esau's reconciliation (Niesiołowski-Spanò 2016: 198–200). According to this reconstruction, the late Hasmonaean period would offer the political background for the literary intervention of the older Jacob-Esau tradition (possibly originating in the Persian period). This literary invention was based on the insertion of the friendly peace-making motif, replacing the version of a military clash between the brothers, which nonetheless was preserved in *Jubilees*.

The same period, c. 130–80 BCE, seems to be the suitable political background for the creation of the international and ecumenical figure of Abraham also. This was the period when Judaism was reshaped considerably. The changes in ritual and the new position claimed by the Scriptures provide an adequate context for that deep theological reflection. In both cases, the changes in the Jacob-Esau story, from military conflict to friendly peaceful reconciliation, as well as the new figure of Abraham, father of all nations, fit well into the political situation of this period. The turn of the second century and the beginning of the first century BCE was the time when politics mixed heavily with theology, of which the latter considerably influenced the rewriting of the Hebrew Bible.

Bibliography

Anderson, B. (1983), *Imagined Communities: Reflections on the Origin and Spread of Nationalism*, London – New York: Verso.

Ben Zvi, E. (1996), *A Historical-Critical Study of the Book of Obadiah*, BZAW 242, Berlin: de Gruyter.

Ben Zvi, E. (2006), 'Ideological Constructions of Non-Yehudite/Peripheral Israel in Achaemenid Yehud: The Case of the Book of Chronicles', in E. Ben Zvi (ed.), *History, Literature and Theology in the Book of Chronicles*, 195–209, London: Equinox.

Ben Zvi, E. (2014), 'Othering, Selfing, "Boundarying" and "Cross-Boundarying" as Interwoven with Socially Shared Memories: Some Observations', in D. Edelman and E. Ben Zvi (eds), *Imagining the Other and Constructing Israelite Identity in the Early Second Temple Period*, 20–40, LHBOTS 456, London: Bloomsbury T&T Clark.

Heger, P. (2014), *Women in the Bible, Qumran and Early Rabbinic Literature: Their Status and Roles*, Leiden – Boston: E. J. Brill.

Lemche, N. P. (1993), 'The Old Testament – A Hellenistic Book?', *SJOT*, 7: 163–93.

Mendels, D. (1987), *The Land of Israel as a Political Concept in Hasmonean Literature: Recourse to History in Second Century B.C. Claims to the Holy Land*, TSAJ 15, Tübingen: Mohr Siebeck.

Niesiołowski-Spanò, Ł. (2006), 'Two Aetiological Narratives in Genesis and Their Dates', *Studia Judaica*, 9: 367–81.

Niesiołowski-Spanò, Ł. (2011), *Origin Myths and Holy Places in the Old Testament: A Study of Aetiological Narratives*, London: Routledge.

Niesiołowski-Spanò, Ł. (2016), 'Functional Ethnicity: Or How to Describe the Societies of Ancient Palestine', *UF*, 47: 191–203.

Niesiołowski-Spanò, Ł. (2018), 'Athens and Jerusalem, Again: The New Paradigm of the Jewish and Greek Intercultural Relationships?', in R. Koliński, J. Prostko-Prostyński and W. Tyborowski (eds), *Awīlum ša ana la mašê – man who can not be forgotten: Studies in in Honor of Prof. Stefan Zawadzki Presented on the Occasion of his 70th Birthday*, 161–9, AOAT 463, Münster: Ugarit-Verlag.

de Pury, A. (2000), 'Abraham: The Priestly Writer's "Ecumenical" Ancestor', in S. L. McKenzie, T. Römer and H. H. Schmid (eds), *Rethinking the Foundations: Historiography in the Ancient World and in the Bible: Essays in Honour of John Van Seters*, 163–81, BZAW 294, Berlin: de Gruyter.

Thompson, T. L. (1974), *The Historicity of the Patriarch Narratives: The Quest for the Historical Abraham*, BZAW 133, Berlin: de Gruyter.

Thompson, T. L. (1992), *Early History of the Israelite People from the Written & Archaeological Sources*, SHANE 4, Leiden: E. J. Brill.

Thompson, T. L. (2011), 'Memories of Esau and Narrative Reiteration: Themes of Conflict and Reconciliation', *SJOT*, 25: 174–200.
Van Seters, J. (1975), *Abraham in History and Tradition*, New Haven: Yale University Press.
Wajdenbaum, P. (2010), 'Is the Bible a Platonic Book?', *SJOT*, 24: 129–42.
Wintermute, O.S. (1985), 'Jubilees', in J. H. Charlesworth (ed.), *The Old Testament Pseudepigrapha*, vol. 2, 35-142, New York: Doubleday.
Ze'evi, D. (2000), 'My Slave, My Son, My Lord: Slavery, Family and State in the Islamic Middle East', in M. Toru and J. E. Philips (eds), *Slave Elites in the Middle East and Africa: A Comparative Study*, 71–9, London: Kegan Paul International.

Tell Balata (Shechem): An Archaeological and Historical Reassessment

Hamdan Taha and Gerrit van der Kooij

Introduction

The establishment of the Tell Balata Archaeological Park was a major project of the Palestinian Ministry of Tourism and Antiquities (MoTA), especially its Department of Antiquities and Cultural Heritage (DACH). This Park-project was designed and realized jointly with Leiden University and the UNESCO-Ramallah office. Its goal was the management of this significant heritage site of Tell Balata, identified with historical Shechem, which was realized between 2010 and 2014. In terms of the management aspect, a reassessment of the results of previous research was an essential part of this in order to deal with the variety of 'values' attributed to the site. The assessment concerned study of the excavations and their results, not only those that had been published and documented in archives, but also those currently visible on site. In terms of the latter, two field seasons of clearance and excavation were included in 2010 and 2011. After assessment the attributed values were used to guide the physical management of the site, among these being preventive conservation, accessibility and being 'visitor friendly', as well as 'educating' the public through the dissemination of information in a variety of different ways.

Considering the context of the *Festschrift*, this contribution has its focus on the values attributed to the site and the excavated remains of past societies, in particular as a function of biblical and historical studies and of archaeological research. For that reason a good starting point would be the history of research and interpretations of Tell Balata, in order to better understand what informs the management of the site.

History of Research: Goals and Results

Discovery of the Site

Archaeological interest in the site of Tell Balata, two kilometers ESE of the old centre of Nablus, began when remains of a large ancient stone wall were found there and identified as part of the historical city of 'Shechem'. On a fieldtrip in 1903, Thiersch and Hölscher observed the low tell-mound with this wall at the western edge ('ein Stück guter kyklopischer Umfassungsmauer'). The site had already been indicated as 'ruins' on the British map of *The Survey of Western Palestine* in 1882, lying close to Joseph's Tomb and Jacob's Well. Already in 1697 Maundrell had noted 'pieces of very thick wall' there, but took it to be the eastern extension of ancient Shechem, because for him, following Hieronymus, Nablus was the site of the biblical city. This was common knowledge in the nineteenth century, as discussed by Robinson (1856: 292). Thiersch, however, used Eusebius's view (and the Madaba map) to site the city east of (Roman) Nablus. This apparent connection between a historical city and an archaeological site gave biblical scholars-archaeologists a reason to raise money and explore the archaeological site through excavations.

Austrian-German-Dutch Excavations

The German Old Testament scholar and archaeologist, Ernst Sellin, professor in Vienna, began excavations in 1913 and 1914. He hoped to verify the identification of the site, and was also motivated not least by the discovery in 1908 of a hoard of MB-Age metal tools and weapons. He began by exposing more of the visible city wall and the NW city gate, and by making test trenches. When based in Berlin, Sellin continued to oversee large-scale excavations in 1926, 1927 (both with the Dutch Old Testament scholar and Assyriologist Franz Böhl), and 1928 (directed by the archaeologist Gabriel Welter). German fieldwork ended in 1934.

The excavation method consisted of two principles: vertical trenching to detect strata and building remains, and a horizontal method that was used to expose buildings completely and give 'contemporary' contexts to objects found in soil-layers, thus supposedly giving a synchronic picture of ancient inhabitants' lives (a method preferred by Welter and Böhl). The digging was roughly done, with little attention paid to non-stone details of architecture and stratigraphy, a result of the limited goals and questions asked at that time. Consequently the results were chronologically and functionally highly vulnerable for all sorts of interpretation and manipulation.

Funding came from German public and religious sources, from American Methodists (Bishop Du Bose for 1926) with religious motives (the ruined buildings being regarded as a setting for biblical stories), and from the Dutch *Sichem-comité* which was organized by Böhl and had biblical-historical goals – one of the main goals being 'how the Israel-tribes obtained a firm footing in Canaan for the first time', considering the Abimelech story and the 'entrance of the "Lea-tribes" from the East'. Like Sellin, Böhl optimistically expected 'the answer from the ruins of the old city of Shechem' (Böhl 1926: 7). Böhl was also interested in the fourteenth-century BCE rebellious person Labaya, who features in the Amarna Letters as king of Shikmu.

Sellin wrote his preliminary excavation reports in a descriptive way and with archaeological interpretations. The few historical or biblical references included were for dating purposes, e.g. the identification of the large temple of Tell Balata with the biblical temple of Shechem (the house of *El-berith*) that was destroyed by Abimelech (Sellin 1926: 311, 316).

At this time, archaeological outcomes served historical research, as can be seen in this quote from Böhl (1927: 6): in biblical studies 'we are looking for the facts, the historical background... How did the people live in this remote past, and what did they experience? Archaeological excavations provide building materials towards this synthesis.' However, some archaeologists, for example Peter Thomsen in Tübingen, preferred a separation of archaeological sources from written ones, and an 'Archaeology of Palestine' that does not favour a specific period or ethnic label that is suggested through the written sources (Thomsen 1913: 1).

American Excavations
In 1956 George Ernest Wright and Bernard Anderson, theologians at McCormick Theological Seminary and Drew University respectively, began field campaigns to continue Sellin's work at the site. Wright's specialism in pottery chronology and his interest in stratigraphy, together with the fact that he was assisted by three foremen trained at Kenyon's Tell es-Sultan excavations, led to the expectation that the additional excavations he would carry out would be more precise about dating the exposed ruins. The purpose of the dating was to connect the history of the site with biblical and secular histories (and vice-versa). Additional excavation at the East Gate 'gave' precisely that dating result. The subsequent series of excavations, involving many staff, continued until 1968, with a smaller staff team remaining until 1973 to resolve some outstanding issues and to prepare the site for conservation and visitors, in particular by William Dever and the local foreman Nasr Diab Mansour.

The excavations used a much more stratigraphic analysis and recording, especially evident in the work of some supervisors trained by Kenyon, such as Larry Toombs and Joseph Callaway, but also Siegfried Horn and a younger generation (e.g. Paul Lapp). This made it possible to reconstruct a detailed relative chronology of the strata, supplemented by Wright's stylistic pottery analysis (apart from other artifacts), which it was hoped would supply more absolute chronological points in the relative time-line, and was expected to be less dependent on historical projections on the site's chronology.

It was not only the archaeological interpretations but also the historical and biblical ones that were the subject of continuous staff discussions (Campbell 2002: 5), and staff members published these ongoing debates in a series of articles, following Wright's 1965 influential volume *Shechem*. Wright wanted to teach a lesson to those in 'theological circles' who claimed not to be interested in archaeology, and show them that they should be 'deeply concerned with history for religious reasons', because 'the recovery of the biblical world and the vast scholarly attempt to place the Bible in its proper context in ancient history have revolutionized the understanding and teaching of it...' (Wright 1965: xvii).

In his book the archaeological conclusions are strongly combined with historical and biblical events; for example, the phasing of the city's fortifications is connected with Egyptian destructions and biblical narrative (phase 6: 'The East Gate of Lab'ayu and Abimelech, ca. 1550–1100 B.C.' [Wright 1965: 75–6]). In Chapter 8 Wright connects 'the sacred area of Shechem' with an 'early Biblical tradition'. The broad-room 'temple 2' (LB) is connected with Abimelech, with the *migdal* (fortress) and the name 'house of *El-berith*' being identified as temples 1 and 2 respectively.

Wright also identified a *temenos* and temple tradition just east of the 'fortress temple'. This he dated to the eighteenth–seventeenth century BCE, and named the 'courtyard temples' (Wright 1965: 110–22). Thus, the biblical cultic tradition (the *maqom*) of Shechem, appearing in the narratives about Abraham/Jacob, Joshua and Abimelech, including a 'terebinth' tree and a 'great stone' ('pillar'), has been rediscovered in this part of Tell Balata.

In the Iron Age remains of 'Israelite Shechem' Wright sees proof of a state-system attributed to the reign of David and Solomon, with provinces and districts. A role for Shechem is indicated by the 'granary' (rebuilt 'temple 2'). According to biblical narrative Shechem was essential to the successors of Solomon, 'as the old religious centre of the north...the place for solemn meeting and covenant with the new monarch' (1965: 22).

However some younger staff members became very critical of Wright's claim that his results were scientific and not connected to his religious choices. Paul Lapp, for example, wanted methodological rigor and transparency, as described in this passage from Sherrard (2001: 163): 'Rather than determine what a given dig had to do with the Bible, develop an interpretation of what that meant for faith, and push that thesis – Wright's methodology – Lapp explored various points of view to impress upon his non-specialist audience the inability of archaeologists to provide incontrovertible proof of anything, only to advance hypotheses they felt best fit the data and to welcome the development of better hypotheses' (cf. Lapp 1975: 56). Wright believed that the Old Testament had 'an eternal validity'; Israelite religion was unchanging, rather than the result of historical development (Sherrard 2011: 134). This mono-vocal view on biblical narrative, which had already been voiced in his contribution to *The Westminster Historical Atlas to the Bible* concerning the value of the conquest of Canaan, was completely opposed to Lapp's view on society, especially when it is used to justify Zionist colonization (cf. e.g. Sherrard 2011: 147),

> We have thus seen that when Israel under Joshua entered Palestine during the thirteenth century B.C., Canaanite civilization was weak and decaying. It was small loss to the world when in parts of the Palestinian hill country it was virtually annihilated. The purity and righteous holiness of the God of Israel were now to be demonstrated against this background of pagan and immoral religion. The intransigence and hostility of the religious leaders of Israel toward the people and religion of Canaan is thus to be seen in its true perspective. There could be no compromise between Jehova and Baal. (Wright and Filson 1945: 36)

Interestingly the American team had also discussed the site's 'historical' connections with local workers (cf. Ammons 1978: 121–23), for example foreman Abu Isa (Nasr Diab), who also worked on the Park project in 2010 and clearly remembered the historical associations attributed to the site by the American Expedition. Furthermore at least one copy of Wright's *Shechem* was still around and being read in the village in 2010. However, as was usual at that time, the local community was not aware of the archaeological nature of the expedition.

'Maximalism and Minimalism'
Outside of the archaeological team, Karl Jaroš maximally combined Tell Balata's archaeological remains with biblical narrative, within the framework of the classical source distinction J, E, P, D, etc. He did this in a

critical and dialectic way: first, he tried to establish the biblical picture of 'the political and religious value of Shechem' which would then be 'useful to connect with archaeological results, confront with the texts and finalize the picture' (1976: 67 n. 1). He accepted Thompson's 1974 critical view on the historicity of Abraham, but gave the 'co-existence' of Jacob/Israel and Josef with Shechem 'geschichtliche Glaubwürdigkeit'.

The theoretical background to Wright and Jaroš is the scholarly tradition of considering the biblical narratives as basically of historical value, to be confirmed by results from archaeology as an 'independent witness'. This is an example of value-testing through 'the balance of probability' (in John Bright's words). Claiming to use independent research tracks, as Jaroš had, does not necessarily equate to independence from scholarly bias.

Edward Campbell, assistant director among the excavation staff, was placed in charge of the American Joint Project and its publications after Wright's death in 1974. Dealing with the general excavation results (stratigraphy and architecture), he took some of the historical discussions into consideration for the interpretation of the discovered remains, but he could not accept Wright's 'courtyard temples' of the MB IIB period as temples, except to say that perhaps one building may have been a 'sanctuary room of some sort', and so he saw no relevance here for the Abraham narratives (1993: 1349). However, in his more detailed final excavation report (2002, with G. R. H. Wright) Campbell was more cautious: *'Text and archaeology may converse'* for interpretation (e.g. 2002: 232). But again later (2014) he concluded that a 'paradigm shift' had taken place since the Joint Expedition at Tell Balata, in terms of interpretations and data collecting, with 'a deepened mistrust of written sources...' Abraham no longer played a role and that of David–Solomon became uncertain. On the other hand, Campbell referred to Lawrence Stager, who adapted the archaeological dating of use of the *migdal*-temple (built in MB IIC, 'temple 1') to fit the biblical story of the temple of *El/ Ba'al-berith* and Abimelech being declared king at the 'Oak-of-the-Pillar in Shechem' (Stager 2003: 28), 'so well into Iron Age', not accepting the archaeological reconstruction by Bull of 'temple 2'.

A New Paradigm in Archaeology and Historiography
In archaeology the old claim of arriving at independent historical results had been challenged since the 1960s by 'New Archaeology' and other theoretical movements (e.g. Lewis Binford and David Clarke), which included social sciences and philosophy of science. This challenge has sharpened archaeological data collecting and interpreting.

Historiographers noticed this change in the archaeological discipline and so the difficulty of using archaeology. They also realized that biblical studies needed additional input from sociological studies and the philosophy of science, becoming aware of biases of biblical scholars that were not only religious but also political. The reconstructions of historical realities were taken as 'constructions' that had to be deconstructed as part of the methodology.

After Thompson's early impetus, most comprehensive studies with this approach, published in the 1990s, were skeptical about distilling a historical reality from the biblical narratives (the so-called 'minimalistic' approach). According to Niels Peter Lemche (1998) we have to regard the Old Testament as a compilation of searching for self-identities, rather than taking it as a text where real history is to be found. As is the case for many populations, a largely created history is only useful for the group that is serves (Lemche 1998: 148–56). This is referred to as the 'crisis in Old Testament studies' (see e.g. Zwelling 2000; Long 2002; and Kofoed 2002).

Archaeology and Historiography as Factors for Heritage Management

The *Tell Balata Archaeological Park* project was funded by the Dutch Ministry of Foreign Affairs, in line with UNESCO and ICOMOS policies. The Palestinian Ministry and Department (established in 1995 following the Oslo agreement) had published, together with UNESCO, the *Inventory of Cultural and Natural Heritage Sites of Potential Outstanding Universal Value in Palestine* (Taha 2005). This inventory included Tell Balata as part of the *Old Town of Nablus and its Environs*, because of the value of the site (see below) and due to it being endangered by long-term neglect and current population pressure (see site photo, Fig. 6.1). For the UN (UNESCO), all archaeological and historical objects and materials are public property in the hands of a Department of Antiquities that not only has to take care of them, but also to develop public interest and responsibility for them. For the first time in history Palestinian society became responsible for its past, to study it and to teach it.

Thus the project was not only set within the domain of Archaeology, a discipline meant to develop a view of the past scientifically, but also in the domain of Heritage Management – a term designed by UNESCO and ICOMOS – in order to provide sustainable care for items of archaeological and cultural heritage. The basic question of 'who owns heritage?' involves decolonization and focusing on the sustainable 'economic and social development' of local population groups. This has a parallel with recent developments in archaeology, which deal with the social factors around current research and its biases in reconstructing the past ('who owns the past?').

Heritage management has to take all possible stakeholders into account, including their interests. This implies *multi-vocality* concerning heritage. Multi-vocality is in opposition to *mono-vocality*, which means that one stakeholder-group uses heritage (and an interpretation of it) for its own benefit at the expense of other, underrepresented groups. Multi-vocality gives importance to alternative interpretations of remains from the past. This social aspect was further developed in the ICOMOS Ename-Charter 2008 and the ICOMOS Paris-Declaration 2011 (cf. Van den Dries and Van der Linde 2014: 128–9, etc.).

Applying these international standards and procedures to the Archaeological Park came under the direct responsibility of MoTA-DACH, at that time represented by the first author. MoTA-DACH's heritage policy was indeed neutral/scientific, without preference towards specific periods, historic population groups and religions, but instead accepting the value of all historical periods represented at the site. The intrinsic archaeological value of the site may be supplemented by written sources if the identification of the site is successful. Some periods of Tell Balata are hypothetically identified with historic Shechem/Shikmu and applied as long as no alternative identification is preferred. The intrinsic archaeological value and view of the last phase of the MB- and LB-periods may be supplemented by information from a 'direct' literary source, the Amarna archive.

Figure 6.1 Tell Balata in its recent urban setting, after clearance in 2010, view to south (courtesy Tell Balata Archaeological Park).

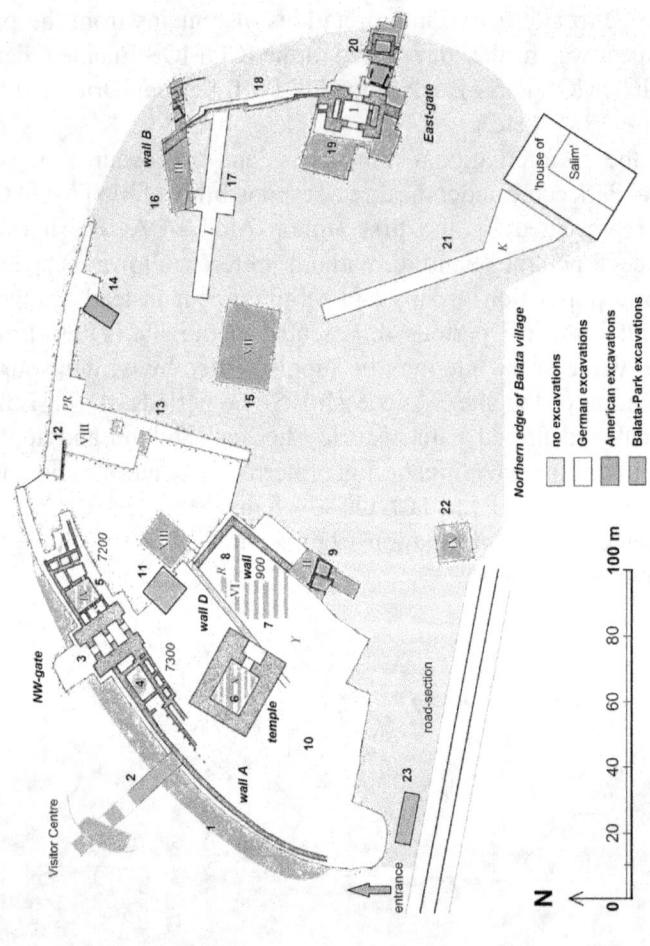

Figure 6.2 Tell Balata plan showing the excavated parts with numbered areas of special attention. It also shows the location of the new entrance and the 'Interpretation Center' for visitors (courtesy Tell Balata Archaeological Park, drawing based on G. R. H. Wright 2002: Ill. 2).

Effect on Archaeological Results
Tell Balata and its exposed remains have been studied by Western scholars within a research framework of biblical studies (and connected religions) and during a period within which biblical studies moved from optimism towards skepticism with regard to finding a historical reality behind the texts' narratives. At the same time archaeology became a discipline that tries to produce a defensible (and non-refutable) view of a historical reality, independent from textual information, especially if the texts are difficult to read as historical sources. For the Park project this meant a 'deconstruction' of many published constructions of the historical reality of Tell Balata. This assessment was done partly by studying the archives of Tell Balata fieldwork (in the Semitic Museum of Harvard University, the Palestine Archaeological Museum in Jerusalem, the Museum of Antiquities and the Netherlands Institute for the Near East, both in Leiden), and by excavation in four areas (see site map, Fig. 6.2). The archival documents and the excavations led to some alternative conclusions of which three may be mentioned here (see Taha and van der Kooij 2014c for details):

- (Area 1) The German-excavated 'marl' over the ruins of the acropolis is not the 'covering' thrown over the Hellenistic city after destruction by Hyrcanus (Wright 2002: 184), but the disintegrated remains of MB walls;
- (Areas 1 and 2) The Park excavations made clear, combined with archived documents, that the lime-grit ramp was made during the construction of 'wall A' (the probably MB IIC 'cyclopean' wall) and kept as a ramp;
- (Area 14) New excavations made clear that the current chronological view about the LB and Iron I period has to change to one of a direct transition from a fierce fire destruction of the town at the end of LB to a new settlement at the beginning of Iron Age I (e.g. dating of strata by two consecutive types of collared rim pithos).

Challenge of the Site's Values
In modern site management all stakeholders of a specific heritage item should be involved with its management, because each one would give it a *value* (a key-word in this domain) that may be neglected by others, sometimes intentionally. For the Tell Balata Archaeological Park project this meant that all stakeholders should be identified and that the value they attribute to the site should be described, understood and taken into account. This would give them a connection with the site and a sense of

responsibility for it – all ingredients of sustainable management. With some stakeholders this may generate economic benefits, for example pilgrimage and general tourism.

In the framework of this article we may focus on three stakeholders:

- Archaeologists (researchers/the academic world): for them the site and uncovered remains from the past have the value of research objects aiming at knowledge about past societies. Depending on their framework their results are more or less biased, but they should be arrived at only after determining the intrinsic historic value of the remains, and by using the best tested theory and method of excavation and interpretation, which indicate the quality of retrieval of materials and their contexts and interpretations. DACH, directed by the first author, adopted this value (see Taha and Van der Kooij 2014c).
- The local community may include several stakeholders, but common values come from those living near to the site. Its use as a stone quarry (during the 1914–18 war) or as a rubbish dump are not in line with sustainable management, but other values are (to some extent): as a park-oasis and children's playground (kites) and stage (plays) in a cramped urban setting; as a source of historical knowledge and self-identity (including knowledge about interpretations by the American Expedition, referred to above, such as the role of Ibrahim); as a resource for local jobs and income through tourism, etc. (see Taha and Van der Kooij 2011 for local value-opinions, 2014a for heritage items, 2014b for education, and 2014d for site management; see also Van den Dries and Van der Linde 2014). After the project, additional study of the local community in relation to the site was made by MoTA and Leiden University, directed by Jehad Yasin and Monique van den Dries, funded by the EU (NEARCH-project).
- External visitors, tourists: Visitors vary greatly in their appreciation of the site, be it for archaeological interest or for religious/pilgrimage purposes, including religious experiences (see Van den Dries and Van der Linde 2014: 158–9). Their views on history in relation to Tell Balata vary between those of maximalists and of minimalists. The religious tourists that come as groups often have a maximalist's view and tend to limit their visit to the large temple and its forecourt as partly constructed for that purpose by the American Joint Expedition.

Applying the focus of the Palestinian Department of Antiquities and Cultural Heritage, the University of Leiden and UNESCO on education, the Park project established an 'Interpretation Centre' to bring information, discussions, and a variety of values to the attention of the local visitor as well as those from further afield. This is supported by a meeting room, museum room, small library, an introductory documentary movie with 3D animations of the MB IIC city, a timeline and illustrative wall pictures, as well as a corner for interactive searching. Project books and leaflets are available for distribution and viewing.

These values also determine the way the site and its excavated remains from the past are treated. To this end, the project has implemented the following:

- Damage prevention, such as consolidations (also by the American Joint Expedition), and partial restoration (to prevent collapse, etc.); refilling of excavation pits and trenches if not needed for any other 'value'; control of tree-roots and rain-water, etc.
- Measures to make the site accessible and 'visitor friendly' were: a visitors trail with signs (together with the Guidebook) and fencing, as well as information panels and leaflets; measures to make the trail partially accessible for wheelchairs, etc.

The application of values may result in dilemmas: which stakeholder's value takes preference in these decisions? The answer is to be found in the local community that has been disconnected from archaeological work on the site, and in the missing stakeholder, namely, the ancient societies represented in the site. They left behind this heritage, and it is the archaeologist who has the task of retrieving and interpreting the remains in such a way that he or she comes closest to what that society was and did, and defend that, in the same way that a solicitor would.

Bibliography

Ammons, Linda L. (1978), 'West Bank Arab Villagers: The Influence of National and International Politics on Village Peasant Life', unpublished PhD thesis, Harvard University.

Böhl, Franz M. T. (1926), *De geschiedenis der stad Sichem en de opgravingen aldaar*, Mededelingen der Koninklijke Akademie van Wetenschappen, afdeling Letterkunde Deel 62, Serie B, No. 1, Amsterdam: Koninklijke Akademie van Wetenschappen.

Böhl, Franz M. T. (1927), *De Opgraving van Sichem. Bericht over de voorjaarscampagne en de zomercampagne in 1926*, Zeist: Ruys.

Campbell, Edward F. (1993), 'Shechem; Tell Balata', in E. Stern (ed.), *The New Encyclopedia of Archaeological Excavations in the Holy Land*, 1345–54, Jerusalem: Carta.

Campbell, Edward F. (2002), *Shechem III. The Stratigraphy and Architecture of Shechem/ Tell Balatah, Vol. 1: Text*, ASORAR 6, Boston: ASOR.

Campbell, Edward F. (2014), 'Archaeological Campaigns at Shechem (1913–1973)', in B. Wagemakers (ed.), *Archaeology in the Land of 'Tells and Ruins': A History of Excavations in the Holy Land Inspired by the Photographs and Accounts of Leo Boer*, 91–100, Oxford/Philadelphia: Oxbow.

Jaroš, Karl (1976), *Sichem: Eine archäologische und religionsgeschichtliche Studie mit besondere Berücksichigung von Jos 24*, OBO 11, Göttingen: Vandenhoeck & Ruprecht.

Kofoed, Jens Bruun (2002), 'Epistemology, Historiographical Method, and the 'Copenhagen School', in V. P. Long, D. W. Baker and G. J. Wenham (eds), *Windows into Old Testament History: Evidence, Argument, and the Crisis of 'Biblical Israel'*, 23–43, Grand Rapids, MI: Eerdmans.

Lapp, Nancy L., ed. (1975), *The Tale of a Tell: Archaeological Studies by Paul W. Lapp*, Pittsburgh: Pickwick Press.

Lemche, Niels Peter (1998), *The Israelites in History and Tradition*, LAI, Louisville, KY: Westminster John Knox Press.

Long, V. Phillips (2002), 'Introduction', in V. P. Long, D. W. Baker and G. J. Wenham (eds), *Windows into Old Testament History: Evidence, Argument, and the Crisis of 'Biblical Israel'*, 1–22, Grand Rapids, MI: Eerdmans.

Robinson, Edward (1856), *Biblical Researches in Palestine and the Adjacent Regions, Vol. II*, Boston: Crocker & Brewster.

Sellin, Ernst (1926), 'Die Ausgrabung von Sichem: Kurze vorläufige Mitteilung über die Arbeit im Sommer 1926', *ZDPV*, 49: 304–20.

Sherrard, Brooke (2011), 'American Biblical Archaeologists and Zionism: The Politics of Historical Ethnography', PhD thesis, The Florida State University.

Stager, Lawrence E. (2003), 'The Shechem Temple, Where Abimelech Massacred a Thousand', *BAR* 29 (4): 26–35, 66, 68–9.

Taha, Hamdan, ed. (2009 [2005]), *Inventory of Cultural and Natural Heritage Sites of Potential Outstanding Universal Value in Palestine*, Ramallah: MoTA-DACH.

Taha, Hamdan and Gerrit van der Kooij, eds (2011), *Stories about Tell Balata*. Nablus: MoTA-DACH (bilingual Arabic-English).

Taha, Hamdan and Gerrit van der Kooij, eds (2014a), *Tell Balata Archaeological Park Guidebook*, Ramallah: MoTA-DACH (English and Arabic editions).

Taha, Hamdan and Gerrit van der Kooij, eds (2014b), *Teachers Handbook for Archaeological Heritage in Palestine, Tell Balata*, Ramallah: MoTA-DACH (English and Arabic editions).

Taha, Hamdan and Gerrit van der Kooij, eds (2014c), *Tell Balata: Changing Landscape*, Ramallah: MoTA-DACH (English, Arabic summary).

Taha, Hamdan and Gerrit van der Kooij, eds (2014d), *Tell Balata Archaeological Park: Management Plan*, Ramallah: MoTA-DACH (internal publication, English).

Thomsen, Peter (1913), *Kompendium der palästinischen Altertumskunde*, Tübingen: Mohr.

Thompson, Thomas L. (1974), *The Historicity of the Patriarchal Narratives: The Quest for the Historical Abraham*, BZAW 133, Berlin: de Gruyter.

Thompson, Thomas L. (1999), *The Bible as History: How Writers Create a Past*, London: Jonathan Cape.

Van den Dries, Monique H. and Sjoerd J. van der Linde (2014), 'Part D: Heritage Management and Public Archaeology 1', in H. Taha and G. van der Kooij (eds), *Tell Balata: Changing Landscape*, 127–59, Ramallah: MoTA-DACH.

Wright, George Ernest (1965), *Shechem: The Biography of a Biblical City*, London: Duckworth.

Wright, George Ernest and Floyd Vivian Filson (1945), *The Westminster Historical Atlas to the Bible*, London: SCM Press.

Wright, G. R. H. (Mick) (2002), *Shechem III: The Stratigraphy and Architecture of Shechem/Tell Balatah, Vol. 2: The Illustrations*, ASORAR 6, Boston: ASOR.

Zwelling, Jeremy (2000), 'The Fictions of Biblical History (Review of Thomas L. Thompson, *The Mythic Past: Biblical Archaeology and the Myth of Israel*. New York 1999)', *History and Theory*, 39: 117–41.

'SOLOMON' (SHALMANESER III) AND THE EMERGENCE OF JUDAH AS AN INDEPENDENT KINGDOM

Russell Gmirkin

In the past, under the scholarly approach now known as Maximalism, the history of the monarchies of Judah and Israel relied heavily on an uncritical use of the biblical text, especially Samuel–Kings, as a collection of ancient texts purportedly containing reliable, near-contemporary data about ancient times in the biblical lands. Thompson L. Thompson observed that the biblical historiographical texts contained considerable story elements and may have been written as late as the Persian or Hellenistic eras, which rendered their usefulness as historical sources questionable. The criticisms of the high regard for the historical value of biblical texts under Maximalism by Thompson and other Minimalist voices of the Copenhagen School necessitated a new approach to history-writing about the monarchic period. One of Thompson's most important contributions to the study of ancient history and literature was to construct a history of the southern Levant, including the Iron II kingdoms of Israel and Judah, independent of the later literary and religious stories of the biblical text. Thompson sought to write histories of the region relying solely on archaeological, climatological, sociological and other non-literary data (Thompson 1992, 1999).

In the current article I seek to assemble and analyze evidence relevant to the emergence of the ancient kingdom of Judah and the construction of Jerusalem's temple using methods allied to those of Thompson, although my efforts rely more heavily on documentary sources. First I survey and discuss ancient contemporary Iron II inscriptional sources that touch on political and religious developments in Judah, Israel and the nearby areas. Next, in somewhat of a departure from traditional Minimalism – I would label myself a post-Maximalist – I discuss Iron II source documents cited in the Hellenistic-era book of Kings, namely the Royal Annals of Israel and Judah and the Acts of Solomon.

This article's major conclusions may be summarized as follows:

- That the area later known as the kingdom of Judah was under direct rule from Samaria from c. 875 to c. 735 BCE.
- That Yahweh worship was also centered at Samaria during this early period and only appeared at Jerusalem as a result of Samarian regional influences.
- That Judah only emerged as an independent political entity in the time of Tiglath-pileser III under Jehoahaz of Judah in c. 735 BCE.
- That the Acts of Solomon originated in the Neo-Assyrian province of Samaria to celebrate Shalmaneser III as legendary conqueror and founder of an empire south of the Euphrates.
- That old local monumental architecture that the Acts of Solomon attributed to Shalmaneser III, including Jerusalem's temple, is best understood as reflecting Omride building activities c. 875–850 BCE.

1. *A Survey of Sources*

In this investigation of the historical origins of the kingdom of Judah and of Jerusalem's temple, primary weight must be assigned to contemporary and near-contemporary[1] references to Judah, its kings, and Yahweh worship in inscriptional sources. I will open this article with a survey of kings of Judah and Israel (Bit Humri, Samaria) in Assyrian, Babylonian and (in one instance) Moabite inscriptions, noting in passing (but not relying upon) their mention in biblical sources.[2]

Event	Ruler	Date	Reference	Biblical parallel
Ahab at Qarqar	Shalmaneser III	853 BCE	*LAR*, I, §611	omitted
Jehu at Ba'li-ra'si	Shalmaneser III	841 BCE	*LAR*, I, §590, 672	omitted

1. By near-contemporary, I mean retrospective reference to earlier events in a king's reign published during that king's lifetime. It goes without saying that all royal monumental inscriptions served propagandistic purposes and in this light must be read critically.

2. For a survey of inscriptions mentioning rulers of Judah and Israel, see Millard 1990: 271–3; Galil 1996: 153–4; Kelle 2002.

Omri + son of Omri	Mesha	c. 825 BCE	Mesha Stele 4-11,18-19	2 Kgs 3:1-27
Jehoash tributary	Adad-nirari III	803 BCE	*LAR*, I, §739	omitted
Menahem tributary	Tiglath-pileser III	738 BCE	*LAR*, I, §772	2 Kgs 15:19-20
Jehoahaz tributary	Tiglath-pileser III	c. 735 BCE	*LAR*, I, §801	2 Kgs 16:7-10
Pekah + Hoshea	Tiglath-pileser III	732 BCE	*LAR*, I, §815-816	2 Kgs 15:29-30
Siege of Samaria	Shalmaneser V	722 BCE	*Chronicle* no.1, i.28	2 Kgs 17:3–18:10
Fall of Samaria	Sargon II	720 BCE	*LAR*, I, §§55, 99	omitted
Judah tributary	Sargon II	720 BCE	*LAR*, II, §§137, 194	omitted
Hezekiah tributary	Sennacherib	701 BCE	*LAR*, II, §§240, 312	2 Kgs 18:13; 19:19
Manasseh tributary	Esarhaddon	674 BCE	*ANET*[3] 291	omitted
Manasseh tributary	Assurbanipal	668 BCE	*LAR*, II, §876	omitted
Jehoiachin captive	Nebuchadnezzar II	597 BCE	*ANET*[3] 308	2 Kgs 25:27
Fall of Jerusalem	Nebuchadnezzar II	586 BCE	*Chronicle* no. 5, r. 11-13	2 Kgs 24:10-16

The most striking fact that emerges from this survey of inscriptional sources is that while several ancient inscriptions refer to kings of Israel starting with Omri and Ahab, there is no mention of Judah, as either a kingdom or as a geographical region, prior to the annals and inscriptions of Tiglath-pileser III (c. 735 BCE), Sargon II (720 BCE) and Sennacherib (701 BCE). This leads to the hypothesis that the kingdom of Judah first emerged under Jehoahaz ('Ahaz') in c. 735 BCE and was directly ruled in earlier times from Samaria, likely beginning no later than the time of Omri or Ahab.

A second striking fact also emerges from this survey of ancient sources, namely that the names and biblical regnal data of the kings of Israel starting with Omri and Ahab, and of Judah starting with Jehoahaz and Hezekiah correspond closely in sequence and absolute chronology to the kings of Israel and Judah as determined from contemporary ancient Near

Eastern inscriptional sources. Although the books of Samuel–Kings were composed in the early Hellenistic era,[3] it seems clear that the regnal data found in the Royal Annals of Judah and Israel in Kings traced back in large part to authentic Iron II royal traditions, broadly corroborated from the time of Omri in Israel and Jehoahaz in Judah to the fall of the northern and southern kingdoms.[4] Excerpts directly quoted from these two Iron II sources (as opposed to other late and highly dubious content in Kings, such as the novelistic Tales of the Prophets) may in some cases provide useful information that supplements earlier inscriptions.

2. Inscriptional Sources

The key inscriptions for the period prior to Tiglath-pileser III and the first mention of Judah as an independent kingdom are as follows.

The Kurkh Monolith Stele. The battle of Qarqar took place in 853 BCE between the armies of Shalmaneser III of Assyria and those of the assembled members of the South Syrian league that had formed to prevent Assyria from extending its territory south of the Euphrates. The third member of the list of allies was Ahab of Israel who contributed 2,000 chariots and 10,000 soldiers.

The Black Obelisk. In the year 841 BCE, the Assyrian king Shalmaneser III mounted another western offensive in the Hauran, details of which were recorded on the Black Obelisk. This text mentions (and pictures) Shalmaneser III receiving tribute from five kings of the southern Levant, including Jehu the son of Omri.

The Mesha Stele. As a memorial inscription (Drinkard 1989), the Mesha Stele was likely erected near the end of Mesha's reign, sometime c. 840–800 BCE. The Mesha Stele mentions Israel as a prominent regional power ruled by 'Omri, king of Israel' and his sons, who had conquered and ruled parts of northern Moab east of the Dead Sea.

---

3. The Hellenistic-era date of Kings is demonstrated by the use of the Pentateuch (c. 270 BCE) and Berossus (c. 280 BCE), notably at 2 Kgs 19:35-37, which draws directly on a fragment of the *Babyloniaca* at Josephus, *Ant.* 10.20-21.

4. Tyrian royal annals quoted in Josephus (*Apion* 1.106-27) go back to c. 1000 BCE. It is likely that this palace literary genre was adopted in Omride Samaria, along with the Phoenician script, as a result of close political and economic ties with Phoenician (cf. 1 Kgs 16:31). These in turn were transmitted to Jerusalem as a result of Omride rule in Jerusalem.

The Inscriptions at Kuntillet 'Ajrud. The archaeological remains at Kuntillet 'Ajrud on an isolated hilltop in the eastern central Sinai consist of a single layer of occupation (in two phases) dated to c. 820–750 BCE. The inscriptions at Kuntillet 'Ajrud famously mentioned 'Yahweh of Teman and his Asherah' and 'Yahweh of Samaria and his Asherah' (Meshel 2012: 3.1, 3.6, 3.9, 4.1.1), but omitted Jerusalem and its temple.

Al-Rimah Stele and Nimrud Slab. In a campaign of 805 or 803 BCE, Adad-Nirari brought into subjection 'Hatti, Amurru in its totality, Tyre, Sidon, the land of [Bit]-Humri, Edom, Philistia, as far as the great sea of the setting sun' (Kelle 2002: 652). Jehoash of Bit-Humri was mentioned as a tributary.

Neither Judah, Jerusalem or its temple was mentioned in any of these sources. Their omission in the inscriptions at Kuntillet 'Ajrud and in the Nimrud Slab seem particularly telling.

Inscriptions mentioning Judah or Israel do not appear in the period c. 800–740 BCE. The land of Judah is first mentioned in connection with campaigns of Tiglath-pileser III in the 730s BCE, when both Menahem of Bit-Humri and Jehoahaz of Judah made tribute payments. Samaria's weakened military power after Tiglath-pileser conquered significant territory in Galilee likely allowed Judah to emerge as an independent kingdom c. 735 BCE (cf. Kelle 2002: 657). Earlier figures appeared in the Royal Annals of Judah, but one may question their status as kings.[5]

3. *Omri and the Inscriptions*

An analysis of the inscriptional evidence from c. 850–800 BCE supports the hypothesis that Judah was under direct rule from Samaria during this period. The prominence of Israel under Omri and Ahab as a regional power of the southern Levant has been extensively discussed elsewhere (e.g. Finkelstein 2013: 83–117). In economic and political alliance with the Phoenicians, Ahab's Israel controlled the coastal route through the ('Solomonic') chariot cities of Gezer and Megiddo, the northern inland trade route through Hazor, portions of the King's Highway from Gilead through northern Moab (Dearman 1989: 159, 169), and the southern trade to the Red Sea (Meshel 2012: 69). The zenith of Omride military power

---

5. It was not uncommon for the founder of a new dynasty to give themselves a royal or divine ancestry to legitimize their reigns (Bienkowski and Millard 2000: 97 s.v. 'Dynasty'). Compare Jehu, who was described as a usurper who ended the Omride dynasty in the biblical text, but was called 'Jehu the son of Omri' in Assyrian texts (*LAR* I, §§590, 672; 2 Kgs 9:2; Na'aman 1998).

and territorial expansion was during the reign of Ahab (874–853 BCE),[6] whose activities as a builder is attested by monumental architectural remains at Samaria, Jezreel, Megiddo, Gezer, Hazor and elsewhere.

Omride interest in controlling trade routes in both the Transjordan and the Negev in this period calls into question the existence of a kingdom centered at Jerusalem in this period. The geographical territory of Judah was adjacent to the hills of Ephraim and immediately opposite Ammon and Moab. It is difficult to imagine a strong military power such as Israel under Omri and Ahab having overlooked Judah, a relatively easy target whose possession would consolidate Omride control of Ammon and northern Moab as well as giving Samaria full control of the fertile Jericho plain (cf. 1 Kgs 16:34). Omride rule of Jerusalem and Judah would also have given Israel control of the trade route that ran south from Samaria through Judah and the Negev to the Red Sea. Indeed, the royal establishment of the site of Kuntillet 'Ajrud as a Samarian outpost indicated to excavator Meshel that Israel must have ruled Judah during the period Kuntillet 'Ajrud was occupied (Meshel 2012: 69).

The above discussion points to the strong likelihood that Samaria ruled Judah and Jerusalem during the period c. 875–800 BCE. Construction of the Temple Mount's palace and temple in the ninth century BCE, modeled on the royal compounds on the artificially leveled acropolises at Samaria and Jezreel (Wightman 1993: 29–31; Ussishkin 2003: 535; 2011: 18–21; Finkelstein and Silberman 2006: 105), is best attributed to the Omrides in line with their building activities (Omri at 1 Kgs 16:24, Ahab at 1 Kgs 22:39) well-documented in other cities such as Megiddo, Gezer and Hazor (Finkelstein and Silberman 2006: 163–7, 275–81). Several of these cities had a palace for the governor of the city. Jerusalem in the ninth century BCE is best understood as another such Omride city with governor's palace and temple (like the temples at nearby ninth-century BCE Tel Motza and eighth-century BCE Arad; cf. Garfinkel and Mumcuoglu 2016: 166–72).

Likewise, archaeological evidence for a ninth-century BCE temple at Jerusalem admits an interpretation as a religious outpost of Samaria rather than a local 'Jewish' (Judahite) construction. Inscriptional evidence indicates that the territorial expansion of the Omrides was accompanied by an exportation of Yahweh worship to regions conquered and controlled by Samaria. Vessels of Yahweh seized by Mesha at Nebo (Mesha Stele vv. 17-18) point to the establishment of Yahweh cult sites in territories

---

6. Ahab's regnal dates are usually fixed by his death at the battle of Qarqar in 853 BCE.

under Omride rule. Indeed, an identification of Yahweh as the primary national god of Omri's Israel is suggested by the opposition of Yahweh and Kemosh, the national god of Moab, in the Mesha Stele. The exportation of Yahweh worship to regions under Samarian control is reinforced by the discoveries at Kuntillet 'Ajrud, which its excavator interpreted as a Yahwistic cultic center occupied by priests and founded on royal authority from Israel (Meshel 2012: 66–9).

Important finds at Kuntillet 'Ajrud included pictorial representations of the gods on *pithoi* and other scenes and decorative materials on plastered walls along with priestly writings of a religious character that mention Yahweh, Baal and El. The blessing inscriptions from Kuntillet 'Ajrud constitute the oldest Hebrew dedicatory inscriptions discovered to date. The only place names mentioned were Teman and Samaria, which appear within the phrases 'Yahweh of Teman and his Asherah' and 'Yahweh of Samaria and his Asherah' (Meshel 2012: 3.1, 3.6, 3.9, 4.1.1). It is striking that there is no mention of a 'Yahweh of Jerusalem'. However, the inscribed letters קר (thought to be an abbreviation for *qorban* or sacrifice) on a *pithos* made of Motza marl clay from the vicinity of Jerusalem indicates that offerings collected at Motza or Jerusalem were sent to supply the priests resident at Kuntillet 'Ajrud (Meshel 2012: 67–8, 291–83). This suggests cultic activities that took place at Motza and Jerusalem's temples were under Samarian control. A temple to Yahweh likely existed at Jerusalem in the ninth century BCE as a religious satellite of 'Yahweh of Samaria' but was evidently neither significant nor well known in its own right.

Based on comparisons with Kuntillet 'Ajrud, one may hypothesize that Jerusalem's temple functioned primarily for the worship of Yahweh and his Asherah, but also accommodated the worship of other 'Canaanite' deities such as El and Baal (cf. Meshel 2012: 110, 131), and was likely operated by priests from Samaria (cf. Meshel 2012: 67–8) who incidentally brought with them the basics of temple scribal culture to Jerusalem (cf. Meshel 2012: 68, 102–3). The absence of cultic apparatus at Kuntillet 'Ajrud, perhaps removed when the site was abandoned (Meshel 2012: 68–9), allows little inference about religious activities at Jerusalem, except to suggest the existence of a *bamah* and *massebot* (cf. Meshel 2012: 66). But a more complete picture may be provided by the Royal Annals of Judah in 2 Kings 21–25, especially the description of Jerusalem's temple under Manasseh, which was likely taken from our Iron II source. This described the house of Yahweh at Jerusalem as a high place with *asherah* and altars where incense was burned to Baal and other gods. The comparison of the religious practices at Jerusalem's temple with those of 'Ahab king of Israel' (2 Kgs 21:3) seems particularly telling if this derived from the Royal Annals of Judah, suggesting the existence of an Iron II tradition that Jerusalem's temple was founded by Ahab, and perhaps operated by cultic personnel from Samaria like Kuntillet 'Ajrud. One may take the description of Jerusalem's temple under Manasseh as typifying the cultic practices of the Iron II temple at Jerusalem throughout its existence from the time of Ahab to the destruction of Jerusalem's temple in 586 BCE. The evidence for Jerusalem's temple as a cultural outpost of Samaria as found in the Royal Annals of Judah scandalized the Hellenistic-era Jewish authors of Kings, who viewed the polytheistic and idolatrous practices in Jerusalem's temple as having provoked the wrath of Yahweh and caused the fall of Jerusalem. One may discount the accounts of Hezekiah and Josiah as Yahwistic reformers as late, Hellenistic-era literary fictions in which idealized Davidic kings briefly overthrew the apostate religious practices imported there from Samaria.[7]

4. *The Acts of Shalmaneser*

Another Iron II source document cited in Kings was the Acts of Solomon. Under the usual Maximalist interpretation, the description of Solomon's empire from the Euphrates to the River of Egypt is discounted as legendary, while a limited rule at Jerusalem as Jewish king and builder of Jerusalem's temple c. 970–930 BCE is credited as historically possible. This article takes a contrary position: that Solomon's reign in Jerusalem is the stuff of legend, and that his rule over vast territories in trans-Euphrates is historical.

One can detect three literary strata of different dates in the account in 1 Kings 3–11 that 1 Kgs 11:41 attributed to the Acts of Solomon.[8]

---

7. The earliest portrayal of the kings of Judah from Manasseh to Zedekiah (the 'era of Manasseh') was uniformly negative in the books of Kings, Zephaniah, Jeremiah and Ezekiel. The original negative portrayal of Josiah in 2 Kings 22–23 was later revised and supplemented with a positive depiction of Josiah as reformer, as I argued in Gmirkin 2011. I assigned 2 Kgs 21:1–22:1; 22:3-10, 12-17; 23:26–25:26 to the earlier DtrM or Manasseh redaction, and restricted the later DtrJ or Josiah redaction to 2 Kgs 22:2, 11, 18-20; 23:1-25. As so assigned, DtrJ materials display consistent literary dependence on DtrM, while DtrM shows none on DtrJ, demonstrating the chronological priority of DtrM. It is also apparent that 2 Kgs 22:2 originally contained a negative formula that described Josiah as wicked like his forefathers, a formula also found at 2 Kgs 21:20; 23:32, 37; 24:9, 19.

8. A detailed literary and historical analysis of 1 Kings 3–11 will eventually appear in *Berossus and Kings* (forthcoming).

The oldest literary stratum of the Acts of Solomon (1 Kgs 4:26-28; 5:13-18; 10:28-29; cf. 2 Sam. 8; 10), which described campaigns and empire-building in the vicinity of the Euphrates river, conforms closely to the well-known genre of monumental inscription, recounting the impressive deeds of a single king, published during his lifetime. The Acts of Solomon contains many political references anachronistic prior to c. 840 BCE, and arguably was based on the inscriptions of Shalmaneser III (likely the one set up at Ba'li-Ra-sa near Mount Carmel in 841 BCE, the oldest royal monumental inscription of any king in the region; cf. Drinkard 1989: 140–54).[9] The description of Solomon in this literary stratum closely resembles the aggrandized picture of Shalmaneser III in Assyrian inscriptions: his vast empire, his chariot forces, his harems, and his acquisition of chariots and horses from Egypt, Que, Aram and the Neo-Hittite states at the battle of Qarqar in 853 BCE.[10] Shalmaneser appeared as שלמו in the biblical text (Hos. 10:14), very close to the spelling of Solomon as שלמה (LXX Σολομών) in 1 Kings 3–11. The appearance of Shalmaneser III in the biblical text as a mighty king who ruled the territories south of the Euphrates is easily accounted for as a local tradition among the Assyrian ruling class in the later province of Samerina.

5. *The Neo-Assyrian Edition of the Acts of Shalmaneser*

The second literary stratum of the Acts of Solomon (1 Kgs 4:20-28; 6:1-10, 14-38; 7:1-51; 9:15-24, 26-28; 10:1-27; 11:14-25), in which Shalmaneser III (Solomon) was portrayed as a great builder of monumental works of architecture in the southern Levant, has several chronological indicators pointing to the time of Assyrian rule over Samerina, perhaps as late as the time of Sennacherib. These include the correspondence of Solomon's territorial holdings with Assyrian provinces in the southern Levant (1 Kgs 4:7-19, in which Assyrian provincial centers such as Megiddo, Gezer and Gilead figure prominently, but no sites from Judah appear); the prominence of trade with Arabia;[11] and the affinities of the

---

9. The identity of Solomon and Shalmaneser III was first suggested by Greg Doudna in private conversation c. 2000.

10. The Kurkh Monolith lists the first five members of the South Syrian league as Adad-'idri of Aram, Irhuleni of Hamath (named as a Hittite city at *LAR*, II, §§55, 92), Ahab of Israel, and the rulers of Guea (Que) and Musri (Egypt; cf. Tadmor 1961; Ash 1999: 119 n. 64). The mention of these same countries in connection with Solomon's horses and chariots at 1 Kgs 10:29-29 is striking.

11. References to the Arabs in Assyrian records begin in the eighth century BCE (*LAR*, I, §§772, 778, 817; *LAR*, II, §§18, 55).

Solomon building account with Sennacherib's Palace Without Rival (discussed below). The monumental architecture attributed to Solomon in this later literary strata appears to reflect actual constructions under King Ahab of Bit Omri, building projects which included the monumental gates and fortifications at the chariot cities of Megiddo, Gezer and Hazor (Finkelstein and Silberman 2006: 163–7, 275–81; cf. 1 Kgs 9:15-19), and the temple of Yahweh and other impressive buildings at Jerusalem, which was arguably ruled from Samaria in earlier times. The Acts of Solomon is best understood as a Neo-Assyrian composition that incorporated translations of the cuneiform inscription at Ba'li-Ra'si into Aramaic and contained amplifications that included legendary accounts of international relations and his regional achievements as builder. This Neo-Assyrian text, authored and locally preserved by the educated ruling class of Neo-Assyrian Samerina, celebrated Shalmaneser III as the first great Assyrian king whose rule extended to this region.

6. Jerusalem's Temple as Solomonic Foundation

It is widely accepted that the accounts of Solomon's royal residence and temple in Jerusalem at 1 Kings 5–8 broadly conform to ancient Near Eastern building accounts (Hurowitz 1992: 106–310). The architectural details generally correspond to building features at various tenth- to eighth-century BCE sites in Syria and Israel, pointing to an authentic source underlying the biblical description of the temple in the Iron II period.[12] Most recently, the discovery of two small clay models of temples at Khirbet Qaiyafa, datable to the tenth century BCE, and sharing some features of the description of Solomon's residence and temple, has been touted as a triumph of Maximalism, showing that the biblical account derives from an authentic ancient Jewish source on Solomon's building activities (Garfinkel and Mumcuoglu 2016: 37–69).

The building account of the temple follows Assyrian rather than Neo-Babylonian patterns, showing that this account predated the fall of Nineveh in 614 BCE (Hurowitz 1992: 313–16). The prominent Assyrian influences on the biblical description of the temple point specifically to 1 Kgs 5:13–7:51 as originally a seventh-century BCE composition of Assyrian authorship. Many details in the description of Solomon's temple directly parallel Sennacherib's description of his Palace Without Rival in inscriptions dating to 694 BCE. Parallels in the two building accounts include: the emphasized use of forced labor for quarry work

---

12. Archaeological parallels are conveniently assembled at Dever 2001: 144–57.

(1 Kgs 5:15; cf. *LAR*, II, §§364, 383, 407); description of quarrying and hewing of stone (1 Kgs 5:17-18; 6:7; *LAR*, II, §§390, 408, 411, 421, 426), felling of cedar trees from Syria (1 Kgs 5:6, 14, 18; cf. *LAR*, II, §§366, 388, 392, 410–11, 426, 430), the difficult transport of building materials, partially by raft (1 Kgs 5:9; cf. *LAR*, II, §§366, 384, 408); the description of building dimensions and other architectural features (1 Kgs 6:2-9, 15-38; 7:1-12; cf. *LAR*, II, §§365, 372, 384, 388, 392, 410, 413, 426, 430, 432); dedication ceremonies accompanied by sacrifices (1 Kgs 8:63-65; cf. *LAR*, II, §§370, 416); the decorative motif of lions, bulls and cows (1 Kgs 7:25, 27, 36, 43; cf. *LAR*, II, §§390–92, 411–13), the twelve lion sculptures leading to Solomon's throne, six on a side (1 Kgs 10:18-20), and the twelve lion colossi similarly arranged in pairs at the entrances to Sennacherib's palace (*LAR*, II, §391); 'a portico, patterned after a Hittite (Syrian) palace, which they call in the Amorite tongue a *bît-hilâni*' (*LAR*, II, §§366, 425) like that of Solomon's temple (1 Kgs 6:3; 7:6-8, 12, 21; cf. Ussishkin 1966: 174–9); and innovative bronze-working as an expression of royal wisdom and cunning (*LAR*, II, §§407, 412; cf. 1 Kgs 7:13-14). The close correspondence between Sennacherib's building account of Solomon's temple and palace suggests that the biblical authors were not only broadly familiar with the literary conventions of Mesopotamian building accounts but had actually read the cuneiform inscriptions at Sennacherib's Palace Without Rival. One may posit Assyrian authorship of the building account in Kings by educated Assyrian or Babylonian scribes from Samerina who travelled back to Nineveh for the international celebrations associated with the Palace Without Rival (*LAR*, II, §§367, 394, 413, 424; cf. Russell 1991: 260–2).

Although the Acts of Solomon credited Shalmaneser III with a building program of ancient monumental architecture that included chariot cities at Gezer, Megiddo and Hazor, and Jerusalem's temple and palace, these fortresses and impressive buildings of an earlier era are best understood as historically having been constructed by Ahab of Israel. Archaeological evidence pointing to correlations between the temple building account and temple architecture of the tenth to eighth centuries BCE in the southern Levant fully supports the construction of Jerusalem's temple by Ahab rather than a construction by a local king of Judah (much less Solomon). The attribution of Jerusalem's temple and other ancient monumental constructions in the southern Levant to the legendary ruler Shalmaneser III (Solomon) was an expression of local patriotic pride among the Mesopotamian (Assyrian and Babylonian) ruling class of Neo-Assyrian Samerina.

7. The Survival of Neo-Assyrian Samarian Literary Traditions

With the fall of Samaria and the deportation of local Israelite elites, Assyrian officials and Babylonian colonists became the new educated ruling class elites of Neo-Assyrian Samerina. According to prevailing modern scholarly theories, these Mesopotamian educated elites were gradually assimilated by intermarriage and cultural intermixing into the dominant Yahweh-worshipping local Samaritan culture and had effectively disappeared by Persian and Hellenistic times (Levin 2013). This seems to be based on little more than assumption and is contradicted by network theory, which supports a strong persistence of educated and ruling class elites guarding their privileged positions and intellectual traditions down through time (cf. Popović 2014). Although Mesopotamians in Samaria eventually adopted the local worship of Yahweh (cf. 2 Kgs 17:24-34), they still remained a strong intellectual and cultural force. Several lines of evidence point to Babylonian and Assyrian traditions having been preserved intact by educated ruling class elites in Samaria across the Neo-Babylonian and Persian eras into the early Hellenistic era, where these same elites exerted a strong literary influence on the biblical texts of Genesis–Kings. Indications of local Mesopotamian traditions infiltrating the Pentateuch include the following:

- A significant body of Babylonian traditions set in primordial times (Gen. 1–11).
- Strong traditions about their ancestors originally having lived in Mesopotamia and later having emigrated to the southern Levant. Both Jews and Israelites were autochthonous people of the southern Levant, but the Babylonians resettled in Neo-Assyrian Samerina did in fact come from Chaldea, as Genesis narrates.
- Mesopotamian calendrical and legal traditions, including provisions taken from the Law of Hammurabi and other Old Babylonian and Middle Assyrian law collections (Gmirkin 2017: 144, 175 n. 366).

There is thus no need to invoke Jewish exiles returning from Babylonia to account for pervasive Mesopotamian influences on the Pentateuch, when such influences are more economically and persuasively explained as cultural artifacts preserved by the Babylonian and Assyrian educated elites who still exerted a persistent influence in Hellenistic-era Samaria. These educated Mesopotamian ruling class elites preserved and transmitted the Acts of Solomon down to the Hellenistic era, much as local native Jewish and Samaritan elites of royal descent transmitted the Royal Annals of Judah and Israel. The authors and editors of the Jewish, Jerusalem-centric books of Samuel and Kings found all three of these source documents problematic. Although approving of the kings of Judah down to Hezekiah, they rejected the entire line of northern kings as uniformly wicked, as well as the line of later kings of Judah starting with Manasseh, in light of the scandalous description of Jerusalem's temple in the Royal Annals of Judah. Lacking any tradition about a local Jewish construction of Jerusalem's ancient temple and palace, but finding a ready-made building account in the Acts of Solomon preserved among the Samaritans, the Hellenistic-era authors of Kings appropriated this Iron II source document and adapted it to their own purposes, claiming that Solomon was the son of David, the fictional heroic founder of Jerusalem. The final Hellenistic-era literary stratus of the Acts of Solomon (1 Kgs 3; 4:1-6; 5:1-12; 6:11-13; 8; 9:1-14, 25; 11:1-13, 26-43; 12:1-31) incorporates artificial literary connections between David and Solomon, and between Solomon and the later kings of Judah and Israel. Additional connections were inserted into the earlier novelistic David stories in 2 Samuel, where Shalmaneser III's conquests in trans-Euphrates were credited to David (2 Sam. 8 and 10; cf. Na'aman 2002: 207–10) and where David was only prevented by God's prophet Nathan from constructing Jerusalem's temple and palace as he desired (2 Sam. 7), leaving that task to Solomon. In this new literary tradition, Solomon was transformed from a famous Assyrian ruler and Samaritan hero to a Jewish king at Jerusalem, the son of David and ancestor of the royal house of Judah. The artificial grafting of Solomon into the Jewish tradition between David and Rehoboam had the effect of transferring Neo-Assyrian traditions about Shalmaneser III from c. 850 BCE to c. 970–930 BCE, when Maximalists still seek archaeological evidence for the mythical Jewish kingdom of Solomon.

A serious consideration of the Acts of Solomon as an Iron II source thus leads to the complete deconstruction of the notion of a United Monarchy under Jerusalem's rule, but ironically confirms the existence of Solomon's kingdom. Solomonic building activities in Jerusalem, however, evaporate under close inspection. It is likely that Jerusalem's temple and the governor's house that later served as palace were indeed ninth-century BCE constructions, as broadly confirmed by archaeological evidence, but are best attributed to Ahab, Jerusalem's ruler at that time.

Bibliography

Ash, P. S. (1999), *David, Solomon and Egypt: A Reassessment*, JSOTSup 297, Sheffield: Sheffield Academic Press.

Bienkowski, P. and A. Millard, eds (2000), *Dictionary of the Ancient Near East*, Philadelphia: University of Pennsylvania Press.

Dearman, A. (1989), 'Historical Reconstruction and the Mesha Inscription', in A. Dearman (ed.), *Studies in the Mesha Inscription and Moab*, 155–210, ABS 2, Atlanta: Scholars Press.

Dever, W. G. (2001), *What Did the Biblical Writers Know and When Did They Know It? What Archaeology Can Tell Us about the Reality of Ancient Israel*, Grand Rapids, MI: Eerdmans.

Drinkard, J. (1989), 'The Literary Genre of the Mesha Inscription', in A Dearman (ed.), *Studies in the Mesha Inscription and Moab*, 131–54, ABS 2, Atlanta: Scholars Press.

Finkelstein, I. (2013), *The Forgotten Kingdom: The Archaeology and History of Northern Israel*, Atlanta: Society of Biblical Literature.

Finkelstein, I. and N. A. Silberman (2006), *David and Solomon: In Search of the Bible's Sacred Kings and the Roots of the Western Tradition*, New York: Simon & Schuster.

Galil, G. (1996), *The Chronology of the Kings of Israel and Judah*, SHCANE 9, Leiden: E. J. Brill.

Garfinkel, Y. and M. Mumcuoglu (2016), *Solomon's Temple and Palace: New Archaeological Discoveries*, Jerusalem: Bible Lands Museum.

Gmirkin, R. (2011), 'The Deuteronomistic History: A Hellenistic Era Composition in Two Redactions', unpublished paper presented at SBL.

Gmirkin, R. (2017), *Plato and the Creation of the Hebrew Bible*, CIS, London: Routledge.

Hurowitz, V. (1992), *I Have Built You an Exalted House: Temple Building in the Bible in Light of Mesopotamian and Northwest Semitic Writings*, JSOTSup 115, Sheffield: Sheffield Academic Press.

Kelle, B. (2002), 'What's in a Name? Neo-Assyrian Designations for the Northern Kingdom and Their Implications for Israelite History and Biblical Interpretation', *JBL*, 121: 639–66.

Levin, Y. (2013), 'Bi-Directional Forced Deportations in the Neo-Assyrian Empire and the Origins of the Samaritans: Colonialism and Hybridity', *ACR*, 28: 217–40.

Luckenbill, D. D. (1926), *Ancient Records of Assyrian and Babylonia*, 2 vols, Chicago: University of Chicago Press.

Meshel, Z. (2012), *Kuntillet Ajrud (Horvat Teman): An Iron Age II Religious Site on the Judah-Sinai Border*, Jerusalem: Israel Exploration Society.

Millard, A.R. (1990), 'Israelite and Aramean History in the Light of Inscriptions', *Tyndale Bulletin*, 41: 261–75.

Na'aman, N. (1998), 'Jehu Son of Omri: Legitimizing a Loyal Vassal by his Overlord', *IEJ*, 48: 236–8.

Na'aman, N. (2002), 'In Search of Reality Behind the Account of David's Wars with Israel's Neighbours', *IEJ*, 52: 200–224.

Popović, M. (2014), 'Networks of Scholars: The Transmission of Astronomical and Astrological Learning between Babylonians, Greeks and Jews', in J. Ben-Dov and S. L. Sanders (eds), *Ancient Jewish Sciences and the History of Knowledge in Second Temple Literature*, 153–93, New York: New York University Press.

Russell, J. (1991), *Sennacherib's Palace Without Rival at Nineveh*, Chicago: University of Chicago Press.
Tadmor, H. (1961), 'Que and Musri', *IEJ*, 11: 143–50.
Thompson, T. L. (1992), *Early History of the Israelite People: From the Written and Archeological Sources*, SHANE 4, Leiden: E. J. Brill.
Thompson, T. L. (1999), *The Bible in History: How Writers Create a Past*, London: Pimlico.
Ussishkin, D. (1996), 'King Solomon's Palace and Building in Megiddo', *IEJ*, 16: 174–9.
Ussishkin, D. (2003), 'Jerusalem as a Royal and Cultic Center in the 10th–8th Centuries BCE', in W. G. Dever and S. Gitin (eds), *Symbiosis, Symbolism, and the Power of the Past: Canaan, Ancient Israel and their Neighbors from the Late Bronze Age through Roman Palestina*, 529–38, Winona Lake, IN: Eisenbrauns.
Ussishkin, D. (2011), *On Biblical Jerusalem, Megiddo, Jezreel and Lachish*, Chuen King Lecture Series 8, Hong King: Chinese University of Hong Kong.
Wightman, G. J. (1993), *The Walls of Jerusalem from the Canaanites to the Mamluks*, Mediterranean Archaeology Supplement 4, Sydney: University of Sydney.

On the Pre-Exilic Gap between Israel and Judah

Étienne Nodet

The starting point of this paper is a question about the pre-exilic period: After the fall of the Northern Kingdom, why did the new settlers ask for an Israelite priest from the exiles, rather than a sage from Jerusalem? A related question is: Why was that kingdom called Israel, since the true Israel, under the legitimate Davidic dynasty, should have been in Judah (and Benjamin)?

The tentative answer will be a retrospective effect of the emergence of Judaism in the Persian period and later, that is, the Babylonian reform brought in by Ezra and Nehemiah, which rejected the local Israelites. Several steps are involved: a reassessment of the religion of the settlers; an examination of the tenets of the reformers Ezra and Nehemiah; some higher criticism of 1–2 Kings. The main sources are well known, but Josephus Flavius is to offer a significant contribution.

Assyria Resettles Samaria

The story has major version variants in the Bible, as well as in Josephus's paraphrase. After the deportation of Samaria, new settlers were sent (2 Kgs 17:24-28): 'And the king of Assyria brought people from Babylon, Kuthah, Avva, Hamath, and Sepharvaim, and placed them in the cities of Samaria instead of the sons of Israel'. But they did not know the god of the land, and Yhwh sent lions, which killed them. Then one of the exiled priests was sent by the king to Bethel (and not to the city of Samaria) and this priest taught them how to worship Yhwh, which incidentally indicates that there was a form of Yahwism in the Northern Kingdom. As a result, the five nations practiced a kind of syncretism, for they put their own gods in the shrines, and they feared Yhwh as well (vv. 29-33).

We observe in the next section (vv. 34-41) an interesting difference between the LXX and MT, in two separate places.

v. 34   עד היום הזה הם עשים   ἕως τῆς ἡμέρας ταύτης αὐτοὶ ἐποίουν
         כמשפטים הראשנים   κατὰ τὸ κρίμα αὐτῶν (= כמשפטם)
         אינם יראים את־יהוה ואינם עשים   αὐτοὶ (= הינם) φοβοῦνται καὶ αὐτοὶ
                                                 ποιοῦσιν
         אשר צוה יהוה את־בני ... כחקתם   κατὰ τὰ δικαιώματα αὐτῶν...
         יעקב אשר־שם שמו ישראל   ἐνετείλατο κύριος τοῖς υἱοῖς Ιακωβ...

MT: To this day they do according to the *earlier* customs: they *do not* fear Yhwh, *nor do* they follow their statutes…which Yhwh commanded the sons of Jacob, whom he named Israel.

LXX: To this day they do according to their customs: they fear Yhwh, they follow their statutes…which Yhwh commanded the sons of Jacob, whom He named Israel.

The next five verses (35-39) are common to both versions: '…and with whom Yhwh made a covenant and commanded them, saying: "You shall not fear other gods, nor bow down yourselves to them nor serve them nor sacrifice to them". But Yhwh, who brought you up from the land of Egypt with great power and with an outstretched arm, him you shall fear', etc. Then the next verse is different:

v. 40   ולא שמעו כי אם   καὶ οὐκ ἀκούσεσθε (= ולא תשמעו)
         כמשפטם הראשון הם עשים   ἐπὶ τῷ κρίματι αὐτῶν, ὃ αὐτοὶ ποιοῦσιν

MT: And *they did not* listen, but according to their *earlier* custom they did.

LXX: And *you shall not* listen to their custom, which they do.

These variants convey very different meanings. According to the MT, the settlers, after a period of mixed worship, have abandoned Yhwh. For the LXX, by contrast, 'they' are faithful, as if they were a kind of remnant from the time before the deportation, since they are ordered not to follow the settlers and their mixed cult. Their identity is not clear, however, all the more since the final verse (v. 41 MT and LXX) returns to syncretism and blurs the picture: 'So while these nations feared Yhwh, they also served their idols…so they do to this day'.

The inescapable conclusion is that Samaritanism is at best a degraded Yahwism or even a second-class Judaism, although the LXX introduces some unexplained doubts. This is the common interpretation, but it can hardly be reconciled with other sources, and particularly later rabbinic views. The Rabbis of old cannot be suspected of having been fond of Samaritanism, but they had interesting sayings: according to *b. Sanh.* 21b, Israel first received the Torah in Hebrew script (כתב עברי), then by

Ezra's time it was given again in Aramaic script (כתב אשורי), while the ancient one was left to the people of Flavia Neapolis (Nablus), that is, the city built by Vespasian after 70 on the ruins of Shechem. Of course, this entails an anachronism, since both scripts were in use together until the Hasmonean period, as can be seen on the coins, but the statement is clear: the Samaritans had the Torah before Ezra's reform, namely, the beginning of Judaism proper. In another context, there was a controversy about unleavened bread, and the ethnarch Simon b. Gamliel stated (*t. Pes.* 1:15): 'For every commandment that the Samaritans observe, they are more meticulous than Israel', that is, 'than the Jews'. In other words, he appreciated their biblical accuracy, while rabbinic Judaism includes 'oral Torah' of Mosaic authority, poorly connected to Scripture. This is obvious in the classical *Midreshei Halakhah*.

Now Josephus, who loathed the Samaritans, involuntarily gives us a solution. For his biblical paraphrase in the *Antiquities*, he did not use a previous Greek translation, as it is usually thought, but only Hebrew scrolls, though unfortunately in a loose way.[1] Here, he first paraphrases the biblical account of the fall of Samaria, the deportation of the population and the settling of foreigners (*Ant.* 9.277-789). These people were then destroyed by 'pestilence' (instead of biblical 'lions'), so that the king of Assyria sent 'priests' (instead of biblical 'priest'). Then, Josephus's account diverges:

Ant. 9	2 Kgs 17 LXX
(290) And they, after being instructed in the ordinance and religion of this God, worshipped him with great zeal, and were at once freed from the pestilence.	[28] (The priest) taught them how they should fear Yhwh.
	[29-33] But every nation still made gods of its own and put them in the high places, which the Samaritans had made [...] They feared Yhwh and served their own gods according to the custom of the nations.
These same rites have continued in use even to this day,	[34] To this day they do according to their customs: they fear, and they do according to the statutes [...],
among those who are called Kuthim in Hebrew, Samaritans in Greek.	

---

1. For a study of all his paraphrase, see Nodet 2018, with bibliography; Josephus's source came from the Jerusalem temple archives.

(291) When they see the Jews prospering, they call them their kinsmen as descending from Joseph,	[35-39] which Yhwh commanded the sons of Jacob, whom he named Israel, and with whom Yhwh made a covenant and commanded them, saying: 'You shall not fear other gods [...] [40] And you shall not listen to their custom, which they do'.
but, when they see the Jews in trouble, they declare to be aliens of another race.	

Elsewhere, Josephus scorns the opportunism of the Samaritans, who claim to be either related to the Jews as sons of Joseph, or aliens of another race, depending on the circumstances (e.g. *Ant.* 11.302; 12.257, see Pummer 2009: 122–6[2]). However, he recognizes here that they have replaced the ancient Israelite tribes, and he never suggests that they had any kind of non-Yahwistic worship, in contrast to 2 Kgs 17:29-33. We may surmise that he would have been glad to accuse them of syncretism, but elsewhere he only says that they practice a downgraded Judaism (*Ant.* 11.302-311). He obviously did not know this passage. In fact, until the Maccabean crisis (167–164 BCE), the Israelite nation had its two temples, Gerizim[3] and Jerusalem (see 2 Macc. 5:22). Some Delos shrine inscriptions of that period show that the Samaritans considered themselves to be true Israelites.[4]

In terms of literary criticism, we may conclude: first, that 2 Kgs 17:29-33 and 41 are later Jewish insertions introduced to disparage the Samaritans, and second that the LXX variants at vv. 34 and 40 reflect the text as it was before the Jewish additions. In other words, Josephus did read the original version of the whole story: the Samaritans were (and still are) true Yahwists, whatever their origins. As for the 'downgraded Judaism' he stigmatizes, we have to consider the reforms of Ezra and Nehemiah.

---

2. The prejudice against the Samaritans (because of the MT story) is so strong that some say that Josephus could not have written *Ant.* 9.290, e.g. Egger 1986: 48–50.

3. The excavations at Mount Gerizim have shown that the shrine was built earlier than the fourth century, with an important transformation around 200 BCE; see Magen 2007. Dušek 2012 shows that the numerous Hebrew inscriptions are not earlier than this transformation.

4. See Bruneau 1982; White 1987.

The Reformers: Ezra and Nehemiah

The books of Ezra and Nehemiah are notoriously difficult and entail inextricable chronological problems. Here, we will consider only some aspects. As for Ezra himself, we see him in two capacities that hardly fit together. First, he is a teacher, well trained in the law of Moses, who opens the holy book and reads it aloud before the returnees from exile, who do not know it (Neh. 8:1-8; 1 Esd. 9:37-55). Second, on his arrival in Jerusalem, his only major deed as a leader is to expel the foreign wives and their children, which has nothing to do with the laws of Moses, for he does not take circumcision into account. An interesting list of the culprits is given, for it includes sons of the high priest Jeshua and his brothers, priests, Levites and lay people (Ezra 10:18-44). Jeshua, together with Zerubbabel, was the restorer of the Temple, but Ezra's genealogy puts him above him. According to Ezra 7:1, Ezra was the son of the high priest Seraiah, of Aaronide descent, but in Aaron's genealogy (1 Chron. 6:3-15), Seraiah's son was Jozadak, who was sent into exile by Nebuchadnezzar. From this we learn first that Jeshua was a legitimate high priest, and second that Ezra was a would-be high priest, as an uncle of Jeshua, which means that his authority is deemed to be higher. All this simply cannot be accurate (Zadok 2012: 151–81). Now, in Artaxerxes' very favorable Aramaic letter to Ezra (Ezra 7:11-26), the king allows any one of the sons of Israel to go with him to Jerusalem, offers considerable gifts for the temple worship, and urges him to make sure that everyone in the province Beyond the River knows the laws of his God – or incurs major penalties. Such a benevolence is not explained, but the king enforces Ezra's authority over all of his kingdoms.[5]

Before concluding about Ezra, it is useful to consider some of Nehemiah's works, extracted from the tortuous stories of the book. Upon his arrival at Jerusalem, he secretly inspects the walls, but only over a small portion of the city, the Ophel hill, which broadly corresponds to the ancient City of David (Neh. 2:11-19). The rebuilding of the walls is then launched by the high priest Elyashib, but on a much larger scale. The work is divided into sections that are entrusted to many inhabitants from the surrounding towns, but Nehemiah himself does not appear in the picture (3:1-32). Later, we learn that the wall is finished in 52 days, despite the fact that Nehemiah has plenty of enemies within the city and outside who

---

5. There is a similarity between this letter and Antiochus III's decrees concerning the Jews (*Ant.* 12.138-146), after he conquered Coele-Syria around 200 BCE. His political motivation is apparent. But this topic is beyond the scope of this study.

try to frighten him. He then sets the doors of the wall in place, and appoints gate-keepers, Levites and singers, thus creating a holy space for observing the Sabbath day, but he complains that there are almost no dwellers within the area (6:15–7:4; cf. 13:15-22). The position looks strange, but in his paraphrase, Josephus provides a clue, for he says that the work on the wall was completed in 2 years and 4 months (*Ant.* 11.179, see Nodet 2018: 247). This variant allows us to disentangle two very different projects: a big one, led by Elyashib, and a much smaller one, by Nehemiah, who was obviously a Babylonian reformer. Later the latter finds that a grandson of the high priest Elyashib has married a Samaritan woman and expels both. Such a policy is akin to Ezra's, and we find a very similar story in *Ant.* 11.306-312: some Jerusalem elders chase away to Samaria the numerous priests, Levites and lay people who have married Samaritan women. In fact, the two main tenets enforced by those elders are genealogical purity and a strict observance of the Sabbath.

As for Nehemiah's view about Scripture, we have a meaningful story (Neh. 13:1-3):

> On that day they read aloud from the book of Moses in the hearing of the people; and there was found written in it that no Ammonite or Moabite should ever enter the assembly of God, because they did not meet the sons of Israel with bread and water [...]. So, when they heard the law, they separated all 'mixture' from Israel.

The passage quoted is Deut. 23:3-5, which was never intended to imply this kind of ethnic cleansing. This means that the Babylonian rule is put under the authority of Scripture, though it is obviously unrelated. Quoting Deut. 7:3-4 (prohibition of intermarrying with the Canaan nations) would have hardly been better.

We have elsewhere a glimpse of Nehemiah's library, which was inherited by Judas Maccabee. According to 2 Macc. 2:13, Nehemiah 'gathered together the books of the kings and prophets, and those of David, as well as the letters of the kings concerning the offerings'. The 'letters' may have included King Darius's decree about the rebuilding of the Jerusalem temple, which includes significant aid for the cult (Ezra 6:1-12), or the letter of Artaxerxes to Ezra (7:11-26). The other items may cover a part of the biblical books, but Moses is conspicuously absent, which is in some ways consistent with Nehemiah's action.

It would also be pertinent at this point to mentions something about Sabbath warring. At the beginning of the Maccabean crisis, some faithful Jews were killed in the wilderness by the Syrians on a Sabbath, and the rebels decided to allow armed defense on the Sabbath day, but without invoking any precedent (1 Macc. 2:29-41). This peculiar decision was kept in the Hasmonean state. This is close to Nehemiah's Babylonian views, since, for him, although city walls offer some protection on the Sabbath day, it is impossible to protect the entire state in this way.

Ezra and Nehemiah shared the same special Babylonian culture, and, like the Jerusalem elders of Josephus, thought that they represented the true Israel, against the local Israelites of Judea and Samaria. Thus, we can conclude the following about Ezra: first, his skill in the laws of Moses is a literary device;[6] second, the foreign women he chases are not pagan Canaanites, but local Israelites; third, Ezra may have been a fictitious character, whose task was to combine the laws of Moses with the Babylonian reform. In fact, in Ben Sirach's series of biblical portraits, we read at the end that Zerubbabel and Jeshua built the Temple, then Nehemiah raised the walls, but Ezra is ignored (Sir. 49:11-13).

On the Books of Kings

These books certainly depend on ancient archives, local or otherwise, but this does not preclude some reworking. We may observe, for instance, that the position of King Solomon is somewhat shaky. According to 1 Kgs 5:15 LXX, after David's death, 'Hiram, king of Tyre, sent his servants to anoint Solomon instead of David his father, for Hiram had always loved David', but the MT conceals the dependence. This friendship refers to 1 Sam. 5:11-12, after David's conquest of Jebus-Jerusalem: King Hiram sent cedar trees and workers to build a house for David, so that 'David knew that Yhwh had established him as king over Israel'. Phoenician influence (or rule) appears, too, when Solomon builds the temple: the same Hiram helps with workers and materials, and the chronology is given in the Phoenician calendar (1 Kgs 6:1, 37). Moreover, after Solomon's death, all Israel come to Shechem to make his son Rehoboam king (1 Kgs 12:1). This indicates at least that Jerusalem was not very important for 'all Israel'. Then, after the secession, it is stated that 'Israel has been in rebellion against the house of David to this day' (12:19; see 2 Kgs 17:21). So, Israel's identity was detached from Judah.

After this, the Northern Kingdom was ruled by Jeroboam, who organized a dissident worship, with high places and golden calves. After him, several dynasties reigned until the fall in 722 BCE and the deportation of

---

6. In spite of a common view since Wellhausen, that they were finalized at Babylon, but this is not the place for an in-depth discussion on this point.

the population.[7] However, the very name 'Israel' remained attached to that kingdom, while the domain of David's heirs was simply 'Judah' (sometimes including Benjamin).

Another story of the deportation is given in 2 Kgs 18:11-12, after Samaria was taken:[8] 'And the king of Assyria carried away Israel to Assyria […], because they did not obey the voice of Yhwh their God, but transgressed his covenant, even all that Moses the servant of Yhwh commanded'. We may wonder why such a punishment happens after so many years of idolatry, all the more that the foreign settlers are not mentioned. But if we compare this with the first account, we have some understanding of why the newcomers asked for a priest from among the exiled Israelites and not from Jerusalem. If we bring together that event and the Jewish reformers Ezra and Nehemiah, we see that the priest was supposed to convey a true Mosaic Yahwism, while Judah was the home of Babylonian Judaism.

This may seem fanciful, but the subsequent Hasmonean dynasty, which surfaced in Judea after the Maccabean crisis (167–164), provides us with an actual illustration. Judas Maccabee himself was Nehemiah's heir, and the problem of armed defense on the Sabbath day belongs to his doctrines. A letter preserved in 2 Macc. 1:1-9 shows that some forty years after the crisis, the Jews of Egypt still would not accept Hasmonean rule and notably its founding feast (*Hanukkah*). As for the Samaritans of Mount Gerizim, Josephus reports that around 150 BCE they tried to obtain from King Ptolemy VI of Egypt the destruction of the Jerusalem Temple (*Ant.* 13.74-79). Later, when he saw that his power was firmly established, the high priest John Hyrcanus (135–104) was careful to destroy the Gerizim temple (around 111 BCE; see Pummer 2009: 250–5); he Judaized the Idumeans (*Ant.* 13.255-258), but the Hasmonean rulers never attempted to enforce Judaism upon the Samaritans. In other words, both the Egyptian Jews, somehow connected with the Onias temple,[9] and the Samaritans were more faithful to the laws of Moses.

---

7. Finkelstein 2013 gives an excellent, updated archeological survey, but his historical conclusions are skewed by a Judean prejudice.

8. For the relationship between the two parallel accounts, see Macchi 1994: 47–72.

9. See Taylor 1998, but her 'Zadokite temple' should be replaced with 'Oniad temple', for there never was any Zadokite dynasty of Jerusalem high priests. See also Kooij 2012: 51–69.

Final Remarks

This short paper is just an outline of what should be a more detailed study. That the books of Kings have been reworked in various ways has long been well known, since the MT and LXX are quite different. Concerning the origins of the Samaritans, we have identified two stages. The final one, detected by a comparison with Josephus's paraphrase, is a large modification of 2 Kings 17, to the effect that Samaritanism is to be recognized as a very poor Yahwism. Before this, something was introduced to give substance to the good Yahwist teaching of the deported priest who was sent to Bethel in order to teach the foreign settlers. The two different accounts of the deportation of the Northern Kingdom, put together, indicate that this teaching was the law of Moses, in connection with 'the sons of Jacob, whom he named Israel'. This may be related to the 'chosen place', since the original reading of Deut. 12:4 (and after) is 'the place that I have chosen, to make my name dwell there' (cf. Neh. 1:9; see Schenker 2008). In the context, Mounts Ebal and Gerizim are mentioned, which is suggestive. However, the issue is not simple, for the 'place' is not clearly named, and we know that until the Maccabean crisis there were two legitimate temples, Jerusalem and Gerizim.

Broadly speaking, the overall narrative of 1–2 Kings is independent of the law of Moses, though a 'law of Yhwh' frequently occurs. When the 'Book of the Law' or 'Book of the Covenant' was found in the Temple and brought to King Josiah, it is stated that it was ignored since the time of the judges, and during 'all the days of the kings of Israel and the kings of Judah' (2 Kgs 23:22; see too Neh. 8:17). Following the previous line of reasoning, we could suggest that the story of the discovery is a subtle hint at the arrival in Judah of the law of Moses.[10] As for the main ideas of the author who introduced the two accounts of the deportation in their original form (Josephus), we can say that he accepted being a Judean Jew with both biblical and Babylonian traditions, but wished to remain faithful to the Davidic dynasty.

All the considerations proposed so far involve various historical problems, which cannot be dealt with here. The identity of the ancient Israelites and the settlers is not clear. Both kingdoms had some kind of Yahwism by the time of their deportations, but it is difficult to assess.[11] In the same way, we do not know the origins of the Babylonian reformers'

---

10. The usual view that it was the discovery of Deuteronomy cannot be maintained, because of the Samaritan Yahwism of old.

11. E.g. an inscription of the eighth century bears a blessing of 'Yhwh of Samaria and his Ashera'; see Puech 2014.

sectarian views and the roots of their authority, since Nehemiah's new 'city' was quite small. We could tentatively bring to the discussion the case of the Qumran document 4QMMT, ascribed to the Sadducees, who were faithful to Scripture (Nodet 2012): they humbly urge King Alexander Janneus of Judea (103–76), after his rejection of Pharisean traditions, to organize the temple worship according to Moses, the Prophets and the Writings, but they do not invoke any precedent. This leads to a question about the dating of priest Ezra's synthesis of Scripture and Babylonian traditions.

Bibliography

Bruneau, Ph. (1982), 'Les "Israélites de Délos" et la juiverie délienne', *BCH*, 106: 465–504.

Dušek, J. (2012), *Aramaic and Hebrew Inscriptions from Mt. Gerizim and Samaria between Antiochus III and Antiochus IV Epiphanes*, Leiden: E. J. Brill.

Egger, R. (1986), *Josephus Flavius und die Samaritaner. Eine terminologische Untersuchung zur Identitätsklärung der Samaritaner*, Freiburg (CH): Universitätsverlag.

Finkelstein, I. (2013), *The Forgotten Kingdom: The Archaeology and History of Northern Israel*, Atlanta: Society of Biblical Literature.

Kooij, A. van der and J. Cook (2012), *Law, Prophets, and Wisdom: On the Provenance of Translators and Their Books in the Septuagint Version*, Leuven: Peeters.

Macchi, J.-D. (1994), *Les Samaritains. Histoire d'une légende*, Geneva: Labor et Fides.

Magen, Y. (2007), 'The Dating of the First Phase of the Samaritan Temple on Mount Gerizim in Light of the Archaeological Evidence', in O. Lipschits, G. N. Knoppers and R. Albertz (eds), *Judah and the Judeans in the Fourth Century B. C. E.*, 157–212, Winona Lake, IN: Eisenbrauns.

Nodet, E. (2012), 'Sadducéens, sadocides, esséniens', *RB*, 119: 186–212.

Nodet, E. (2018), *The Hebrew Bible of Josephus: Main Features*, Leuven: Peeters.

Puech, E. (2014), 'Les inscriptions hébraïques de Kuntillet 'Ajrud (Sinaï)', *RB*, 121: 161–94.

Pummer, R. (2009), *The Samaritans in Flavius Josephus*, TSAJ 129, Tübingen: Mohr-Siebeck.

Schenker, A. (2008), 'Le Seigneur choisira-t-il le lieu de son nom ou l'a-t-il choisi ? L'apport de la Bible grecque ancienne à l'histoire du texte samaritain et massorétique', in A. Voitila and J. M. Jokiranta (eds), *Scripture in Transition*, 339–51, Leiden: E. J. Brill.

Taylor, J. E. (1998), 'A Second Temple in Egypt: The Evidence for the Zadokite Temple of Egypt', *JSJ*, 29: 297–321.

White, M. (1987), 'The Delos Synagogue Revisited: Recent Fieldwork in the Graeco-Roman Diaspora', *HTR*, 80: 133–60.

Zadok, R. (2012), 'Some issues in Ezra-Nehemiah', in I. Kalimi (ed.), *New Perspectives on Ezra-Nehemiah: History and Historiography, Text, Literature, and Interpretation*, 160–71, Winona Lake, IN: Eisenbrauns.

Perceptions of Israel's Past in Qumran Writings: Between Myth and Historiography

Jesper Høgenhaven

Thomas L. Thompson, to whom this essay is dedicated in friendship and gratitude, proposed in an article from 1998 what he termed a 'Copenhagen Lego hypothesis' with regard to the manuscript 4QTestimonia (4Q175) from Qumran, a text that appears to combine selected scriptural passages in an otherwise unknown order (Thompson 1998). Thompson's suggestion is that literary traditions may have circulated as smaller more or less finalized 'Lego blocks' which could be used and reused in a wide variety of contexts.

In recent decades scholars have appreciated the variety and diversity of the literary genres and compositions represented in the more than 900 fragmented Qumran scrolls. Passages dealing with past events and figures are no rarity among these texts. Much attention has been given to passages pertaining to the past of the so-called Qumran community itself. Many scholars have attempted to reconstruct a history of the community on the basis of various bits and pieces of information allegedly revealing how Qumran authors envisaged their own past. The feasibility of such a project, however, has also received strong criticism. The late Philip R. Davies made the following pointed remark on scholars striving to collect the elements necessary for writing a 'sectarian history' based on Qumran scriptural commentaries (*pesharim*):

> The first direction in exegesis of the *pesharim* must always be towards their midrashic function, for until we understand how these commentaries work – and that means as midrashim – we have no warrant to plunder them for historical data, especially given that (a) no continuous tradition can be established as lying behind them and (b) where they do contain – as we know

that they do (I think in particular of 4QpNah) – some historical information, any kind of plausible analogy we could invoke would warn us that it will be mixed up with invention, will be distorted, garbled and anachronistic. (Davies 1989: 27–8)

The endeavor to establish a history of how the Qumran community must have originated and developed, on the basis of possible hints scattered among the retrieved documents, is not likely to produce reliable results, regardless of whether or not the ancient Greek and Latin sources on the Essenes are taken into account. In the following pages, however, we shall look at the broader perspective of how the past of Israel is represented and interpreted in Qumran scrolls, employing literary motifs from earlier traditions.

Israel's Past in the Damascus Document

An often-cited example of how the origins of the Qumran community are written into a perception of scriptural traditions is found in the opening admonition section of the Cairo Damascus Document (CD 1–8). Here, past events that appear to be somehow linked to community origins and/or background are merged into a scripturally based (or literature-based) representation of Israel's past, and, indeed, the past of humankind. The admonitions set out, not at the outset of a chronologically organized sequence but *in medias res*, with God in his wrath delivering Israel and his sanctuary into the hands of Nebuchadnezzar, king of Babylon (CD 1.1-6). However, after 390 years, God recalls his covenant with the 'first ones' (ברית ראשנים) and, having left a 'remnant' (שארית) for Israel, lets a 'root of planting' (שורש מטעה) grow forth from Israel and Aaron to inherit the land (CD 1.7-8). He then after an initial twenty-year period of blindness endows the remnant with a 'Teacher of Righteousness' (מורה צדק) as their guide. Regardless of how these lines may reflect or construct memories of community origins, it is evident that, in the understanding of the author, the remnant of Israel is the product of a coherent history of divine actions and human responses. These opening lines set the scene for the following recalling of Israel's past, the overall theme being the inevitable wrath of God caused by the continued acts of disobedience perpetrated by humans, as stated in CD 1.2: 'He has a dispute with all flesh and will make judgment against all who scoff at him' (כי ריב לו עם כל בשר ומשפט יעשה בכל מנאציו). The destruction of the temple seems here to be perceived as the central and most tangible symbol in the literary tradition for God's dispute with all flesh.

As the admonition goes on to elaborate on the dualistic notion of how God has chosen and raised up his elect ('those called by name', קריאי שם, CD 2.11), while causing those that he hated to stray, a series of examples from the literary traditions of past events and figures is cited. Representatives of those who walked 'after the wantonness of their heart' (בשרירות לבם, CD 2.17-18) are the Watchers, the sons of Noah, and the sons of Jacob in several generations (CD mentions explicitly the Exodus and desert generation, and their descendants who lived in the land). As a positive counter-example, Abraham is introduced, followed by Isaac and Jacob: Abraham 'did not walk in it [the wantonness of heart]' (אברהם לא הלך בה), CD 3.2). To the contrary, he observed God's commandments, and transmitted this way to Isaac and Jacob. Abraham, Isaac and Jacob are accepted as 'friends' or, from a more active perspective, 'lovers' (אוהבים), CD 3.3-4) of God.

The next positive example of how God upholds his everlasting covenant, building 'a sure house in Israel' (ויבן להם בית נאמן בישראל, CD 3.19), is presented in the words of Ezekiel, as 'the priests and the Levites and the sons of Zadok who kept the watch of my sanctuary when the children of Israel strayed from me' (CD 3.21–4.1, cf. Ezek. 44:15). Here the priests and the prophets are introduced as a positive continuation of the patriarchs' line of conduct:

CD MS A 3

18 ואל ברזי פלאו כפר בעד עונם וישא לפשעם ...
19 ויבן להם בית נאמן בישראל אשר לא עמד כמהו למלפנים ועד
20 הנה המחזיקים בו לחיי נזח וכל כבוד אדם להם הוא כאשר
21 הקים אל להם ביד יחזקאל הנביא לאמר הכהנים והלוים ובני

CD MS A 4

1 צדוק אשר שמרו את משמרת מקדשי בתעות בני ישראל
2 מעליהם יגישו לי חלב ודם הכהנים הם שבי ישראל
3 היוצאים מארץ יהודה והנלוים עמהם ובני צדוק הם בחירי
4 ישראל קריאי השם העמדים באחרית הימים ...

CD MS A 3
18 But God in his wonderful mysteries atoned for their iniquity and forgave their sin
19 and built them a sure house in Israel, such as never stood from their earliest times until
20 now. Those who hold fast to it are to have eternal life, and all human glory is theirs. As
21 God swore to them, through the hand of Ezekiel the prophet, saying, 'The priests and the Levites and the sons of

CD MS A 4
1   Zadok, who kept the watch of my sanctuary, when the children of Israel strayed
2   from me, they shall present to me fat and blood'. The priests are the penitents of Israel
3   who depart(ed) from the land of Judah, (the Levites are whose who) accompany them, and the sons of Zadok are the chosen ones of
4   Israel, those called by name, who stand in the end of days…[1]

There is a *verbatim* correspondence between priests, Levites and sons of Zadok, and Abraham and his descendants, who are said to have 'kept' (וישמרו) God's commandments, or to have 'kept' (שמרו) the watch (משמרת) of his sanctuary. In this way, the text achieves an unbroken chain between Abraham via Isaac and Jacob, and the priests, Levites and Zadokites who embody God's covenant. The passage goes on to identify the latter groups using 'exegetical' terms known from the *pesharim*: The priests are the 'penitents of Israel' (שבי ישראל) or 'those of Israel who return (שבי ישראל) who depart(ed) from the land of Judah', with the Levites accompanying them (a wordplay on the meaning of the root לוה is intended). The Sons of Zadok are 'the chosen ones of Israel, those called by name' (קריאי השם), who stand 'in the end of days' (באחרית הימים). Here again, the text seems to intend some degree of identification between the elect and the group associated with the author. The elect are represented as the true descendants of Abraham and as the true priests and Levites.[2]

Israel's past, in other words, is construed in terms of a coherent meaningful narrative determined by God's election of the righteous and his rejection of the wicked. The patriarchs play an important part as prime examples of righteousness and obedience, while, on the other hand, the destruction of the temple and the exile is perceived as the central act of divine punishment, which, however, also forms the background for God's renewed act of grace and his establishment of a 'sure house' in Israel.

Israel's Past in the Reworked Pentateuch Texts

When we move outside this framework, we encounter in Qumran scrolls a number of representations of the past without explicit 'sectarian' formulations. Some Qumran compositions represent various forms of what has been termed 'scriptural rewriting'. The usefulness and definition of

---

1. Text and translation follow Baumgarten and Schwartz 1995.
2. I have dealt more extensively with this passage and the reference to the Abraham tradition in Høgenhaven 2018b.

'rewritten bible' or 'rewritten scripture' has been a much-debated issue. Thompson has made the observation that in the ancient world writing literature was always a rewriting of existing texts and traditions, and suggested that we speak of 'reiterative rhetoric' rather than 'rewritten bible/scripture' (Thompson 2018). The so-called *Reworked Pentateuch* texts comprise five manuscripts from Cave Four, 4Q158 and 4Q364-367.[3] This group of Qumran manuscripts could be seen as a borderline case between biblical transmission and biblical rewriting. However, attempting to draw a precise line between composition and transmission would seem to be a less fruitful endeavor. The Qumran scrolls document a great extent of variety in the ongoing transmission and reshaping of literary material, some of which eventually ended up forming the canonical biblical collections, and the *Reworked Pentateuch* manuscripts are interesting, above all, because they demonstrate some of the concerns and mechanisms that were driving forces behind this process (see Holst 2012). The manuscript 4Q158 seems to contain more expansions and additions to the textual tradition than any of the other manuscripts in the group.[4]

4Q158 consists of 15 fragments of various sizes, which can be paleographically dated to the early first century BCE. Most of the preserved text runs parallel to the book of Exodus. A number of passages have text known from Genesis and Deuteronomy, but they seem to have been worked into a common narrative framework based on the storyline from Exodus. Some of the additions from Deuteronomy seem to be part of an expansionist or harmonizing textual tradition similar to the Samaritan Pentateuch.[5]

---

3. 4Q158 was published by John M. Allegro in 1968 under the title 'Biblical Paraphrase: Genesis, Exodus' (Allegro 1968: 1–6). 4Q364-367 were published by Emanuel Tov and Sidnie White Crawford in 1993 as '4QReworked Pentateuch' (Tov and White Crawford 1993: 187–351). Tov and White Crawford regard 4Q158 and 4Q364-367 as witnesses to the same literary composition (cf. Tov 1992). Michael Segal has suggested that 4Q158 differs from 4Q364-367, which should be regarded as 'biblical' manuscripts (Segal 1998, 2000). George J. Brooke has challenged Tov's and White Crawford's understanding of 4Q158 and 4Q364-367, and pointed out that in cases where the preserved texts of these manuscripts actually overlap, they do in fact exhibit textual differences. According to Brooke (2001), then, the five manuscripts represent different literary compositions belonging to the same genre.

4. Moshe Bernstein characterizes 4Q158 as 'more exegetical' than 4Q364-367 (Bernstein 1998: 134 n. 7).

5. A new text edition of 4Q158 by Molly Zahn is under preparation (see Zahn 2011).

One of the longer passages in which 4Q158 goes beyond what is known to us from other textual representations of the Pentateuch is found in fragment 4, in a context that seems to be a paraphrase of Exod. 24:4-6, where Moses celebrates the conclusion of God's covenant with Israel:

4Q158, frag. 4

1 [צוה לכה]
2 העם ממצרים תעבד[ון]
3 למספר שנים עשר שבטי[ישראל]
4 ויעל את העול[ה] על המזב[ח] ויזבח זבחים שלמים ליהוה פרים בני בקר ויקח מושה חצי הדם וישם
5 באגונות וחצ[י ה]דם זרק על ה[מזבח ויקח ספר הברית
6 אשר היראתי אל אברהם ואל ///[יצחק ואל יעקוב והקמותי את בריתי]
7 אתם לה[י]ו[ת] להמה ול[זרע]ם לאלוהים

4Q158, frag. 4
1 ...he commanded you...
2 the people from Egypt: You shall serve...
3 according to the number of the twelve tribes of [Israel]
4 And he offered the burnt offer[ing] on the alt[ar, and he sacrificed peace offerings of oxen, the sons of cattle, to the Lord. And Moses took half of the blood and put it]
5 in basins, and hal[f of the] blood he threw against the [altar. And he took the book of the covenant ...]
6 which I showed to Abraham and to [Isaac and to Jacob...and I raised up my covenant]
7 with them to b[e] God for them and for their [offspring]

The preceding lines state that Moses built an altar at the foot of the mountain, and erected twelve stones (cf. Exod. 24:4). After bringing the sacrifices he divides the blood into two portions, casting one portion on the altar. In all likelihood, the text once related how Moses read the 'book of the covenant' to the people, and sprinkled the remaining portion of blood on the people as part of the covenant-making (cf. Exod. 24:8). In the 4Q158 version of the narrative Moses is the sole subject of the sacrificial act, which is in the Masoretic performed by the young men of Israel. 4Q158 may be reflecting a general tendency to enhance the importance and position of Moses, and, possibly, the author also wished to avoid having lay people performing sacrificial rites. At any rate, the first lines of fragment 4 (lines 1-2) do not reflect the Masoretic narrative of Exodus 24. Rather, we have what looks like a reference to Exod. 3:12, where God commands Moses to worship 'on this mountain' when he has led the people out of Egypt. The events related in Exodus 24 may be seen as the fulfilment of the divine command in this earlier part of the Moses story. In 4Q158 the correspondence is made explicit and unambiguous (cf. Zahn 2011: 20–1).

The last lines (lines 6-7) also do not resemble any known version of the Exodus narrative. The reference to Abraham seems to echo Exod. 6:3 (וארא אל אברהם אל יצחק ואל יעקב באל שדי, 'I appeared to Abraham, to Isaac, and to Jacob, as El Shaddai'). In the biblical text, however, God states that he appeared (וארא, *niphal* of ראה) to the patriarchs. 4Q158 has the verb in the active *hiphil* (היראתי), implying that God showed or revealed something to Abraham, and in all probability also to Isaac and Jacob.[6] The surviving text does not state what it was that God revealed to the fathers. The subsequent reference to God as 'God for them and for their offspring' could also be related to Exod. 6:3, and furthermore we may have a hint at God's covenant with Abraham, as described in Gen. 17:7-8 (cf. especially Gen. 17:7: והקמתי את בריתי ביני ובינך ובין זרעך אחריך לדרתם לברית עולם להיות לך לאלהים ולזרעך אחריך, 'And I will establish my covenant between me and you and your offspring after you throughout their generations for an everlasting covenant, to be God to you and to your offspring after you'). Indeed, the covenant could be the idea connecting the Exodus context (Exod. 24) and Gen. 17:7-8: the author of 4Q158 may have intended to remind his readers that the covenant God concludes with the Israelites at Sinai is a realization of what was already inherent in his covenant with Abraham (Zahn 2011: 51–2). Read in this light, that which God revealed to Abraham could have been the covenant itself or possibly the possession of the land. In fact, the Promised Land is the only thing God is explicitly said to have 'shown' to Abraham in Genesis (Holst 2012: 133). The reference to the 'book of the covenant', which Moses reads to the people (Exod. 24:8) could have prompted the author of 4Q158 to remind his readers of the earlier covenant with Abraham. Another possibility, though, is that the focus of the passage is on the sacrificial act, and that the object revealed to Abraham could have something to do with sacrificial rules or practices, which were later communicated to Moses (cf. Holst 2005: 184).

---

6. 4Q158 probably made mention here of all three patriarchs. After 'Abraham' and the preposition ל before the lacuna we find the remains of a word which was erased. The original word here seems to be 'Jacob'. The scribe, then, appears to have jumped by mistake to Jacob, and then to have erased the name in order to write 'Isaac'.

At any rate, the author of 4Q158 has achieved a creative combination of tradition pieces documented in the Masoretic tradition in Gen. 17:7-8 and Exod. 6:3-7. A coherent narrative framework is construed, within which the divine acts of grace are viewed as an unbroken chain of events unfolding the promise to the patriarchs (I have treated this passage, and the strategies and tendencies of 4Q158 at more length in Høgenhaven 2012a; see also Holst 2012).

Israel's Past in Commentary on Genesis A (4Q252)

The so-called 'commentaries on Genesis' (4Q252-254a) would seem to represent a highly interesting middle position between rewriting and commenting.[7] The best preserved manuscript, *Commentary on Genesis A* (4Q252), combines extensive passages from Genesis, which are interspersed with expansions that are not exegetical or as explicitly interpretative as those found in Qumran *pesharim*, but rather explanatory notes containing, e.g., calendrical information which could be regarded as 'missing' in the Genesis text. These passages of 4Q252 resemble reworking or rewriting more than the passage-by-passage interpretation normally associated with the commentary genre. In several cases, 4Q252 supplements the source text by additional narrative passages, providing extra details. At certain points, however, the composition inserts interpretations of the *pesher* type, once using the term פשרו אשר (4Q252 5 iv 5), identifying particular elements from the text with specific meanings, which are generally associated with eschatology and the life of the community in much the manner familiar to us from Qumran *pesharim*.[8]

4QCommentary on Genesis A (4Q252) consists of six fragments, preserving text from six columns. The script is datable to the second half of the first century BCE (Brooke et al. 1996: 190).[9] The manuscript quotes Genesis 6; 7–8; 9; 11; 15; 17; 18; 22; 28; 36; 49. Columns I-III reproduce parts of the flood story and the Abraham narrative. Column IV depicts the fate of Amalek, with Gen. 36:12 as its point of departure, and

---

7. Genesis Commentary A (4Q252) was edited by George J. Brooke (Brooke et al. 1996: 185–207; cf. Trafton 2002).

8. Brooke argues that while the 'implicit exegesis' in 4Q252 represents 'more widely accepted and acceptable interpretations of tradition', the explicit (*pesher* type) exegesis is influenced by 'the community's eschatological perspective' and represents a 'sectarian' stance (Brooke 1996: 399–400).

9. Earlier scholars termed the scroll 'Patriarchal Blessings', and a fragment of the text was published in 1956 by John M. Allegro under this title (Allegro 1956).

with reference to Deut. 25:19; 1 Sam. 14:48; 15:1-9. Column IV contains Jacob's blessing of Reuben (Gen. 49:3-9). Column V quotes and interprets Jacob's blessing of Judah (Gen. 49:10), and col. VI, of which only small fragments have survived, seems to quote Jacob's blessing of Gad.

Scholars have expressed different opinions with regard to the genre of 4Q252, and the presence or absence of an inner thematic coherence. Moshe Bernstein regards 4Q252 as an example of exegetical interest properly speaking, focusing on biblical passages that are difficult to understand, but with no specific common theme (Bernstein 1994, 1994/1995). George J. Brooke has argued that the selection of quotations and interpretative passages reflects a specific interest in divine blessings and curses that have not yet been fulfilled (Brooke 1994/1995). Shani Tzoref has suggested that 4Q252 should be regarded as a 'compilation', affiliated, as far as genre is concerned, with texts like *Testimonia* (4Q175), *Tanhumim* (4Q176) and *Eschatological Midrash* (4Q174, 4Q177), and as far as contents are concerned, with *Pesher on the Periods* (4Q180) and the Damascus Document (Tzoref 2012). Recently, Émile Puech has presented an interpretation of 4Q252 as a coherent composition with the theme 'God's blessing for the sons of Jacob and their election' (Puech 2013/2014). The theme, in Puech's view, is developed in a great narrative, which takes its point of departure from God's intervention in the age of Noah, and extends as far as the eschatological fulfilment of the divine promise. The determining motifs are the election of the righteous and the rejection of the wicked, and the author exhibits a particular interest in the pure line of descent. The outlook of 4Q252, then, reflects the situation and worldview of the Qumran community, which regarded itself as the truly righteous as opposed to the corrupt priesthood of Jerusalem.[10] There is no need to assume that the text was compiled from various sources, and there is, in fact, no essential difference between the two parts of the manuscript, one reflecting biblical rewriting, and the other biblical commentary (Puech 2013/2014: 247–9).

In 4Q252 as in the Damascus Document, no distinguishing line is drawn between the mythological events of the Primeval History and the patriarchal narratives. The text joins the Abraham story rather elegantly to the flood story: As the conclusion to the part that concerns the flood, we have a paraphrase of Gen. 9:1 and Gen. 9:27, referring to God's

---

10. The text, according to Puech, seems to know 4QMMT, and should be regarded as an Essene composition from around 100 BCE.

blessing of Noah's sons, and to his dwelling 'in the tents of Shem'. To this reference, then, the mention of the land given to Abraham is added more or less as an explanatory note:

4Q252, frags. 1 and 3, col. ii

7 ... כי ברך אל את בני נוח ובאהלי שם ישכן
8 ... ארץ נתן לאברהם אהבו

4Q252, frags. 1 and 3, col. ii
7 ...because God blessed the sons of Noah and in the tents of Shem he will dwell,
8 a land he gave to Abraham his friend.

The following passage then relates Terah's departure from Ur, and Abram's departure from Haran. Apparently, the text goes on to paraphrase the account of the covenant-making, as it is described in Gen. 15:10-17. The text is fragmentary, but clearly mentions the animals heifer, ram, and goat, as well as the fire passing in between the pieces. The next passage (col. III, lines 1-6) deals with the story of Sodom and Gomorrah.

More text is preserved from the following passage, which refers to the binding of Isaac. The narrative is reproduced in 4Q252 in a condensed and abbreviated version, beginning with Abraham stretching out his hand (Gen. 22:10), and being halted by the intervention of an angel from the heavens (Gen. 22:11-12). There are two lines missing, then the text refers to the blessing of El Shaddai, and to the 'blessing of your father Abraham':

4Q252, frags. 1, 3-5, col. 3

12 אל שדי יב]רך
13 [א]ת ברכת אביכה [אברהם

4Q252, frags. 1, 3-5, col. iii
12 El Shaddai will bl[ess ...
13 the blessing of your father [Abraham

The wording echoes Gen. 28:3-4, and the 'you-addressee' and recipient of the divine blessing seems here as in Gen. 28:3-4 to be Isaac. His relation to Abraham is made quite explicit as the latter is referred to as 'your father' (אביכה). The combination of the Aqedah narrative and the motif blessing directed towards Isaac is interesting, also because a similar phenomenon may be registered in *4QPseudo-Jubileess* (4Q225):

4Q225 frag. 2, col. ii

ויברך אל יהוה את יִשׂ[ח]ק כל ימי חיו ויוליד את 10
יעקוב ויעקוב הוליד את לוי דֹוֹ]ר שלישי ויהיו כול 11
ימי אברהם וישחק ויעקוב ולֹוֹ]יׄ 12

4Q225, frag. 2, col. ii
10 God the Lord blessed Is[aac all the days of his life. He became the father of]
11 Jacob, and Jacob became the father of Levi, [a third generation... all
12 the days of Abraham Isaac, Jacob, and Lev[i ...[11]

Here as in 4Q252, God bestows his blessing not on Abraham but on Isaac, and the text explicitly enhances Isaac's role as the forefather of Levi through Jacob. The focus thus seems to be on the direct and unbroken connection between the patriarchs and the priestly line. In a similar fashion, as we have seen above, Abraham is represented in the Damascus Document as the forefather of the true priests, Levites and Zadokites.

4Q252 should probably not be understood as either a commentary or an example of 'biblical rewriting' but rather as a learned composition dealing with the themes of divine blessings and curses, the election of the righteous and the rejection of the wicked.[12]

Israel's Past in Words of the Luminaries (4Q504, 4Q506)

The prayers prescribed for the days of the week in the liturgical composition *Words of the Luminaries*, and uttered by the voice of a collective first person plural, are arranged in a sequence that appears to be chronological in the sense that it follows, or accords largely with, the narrative

---

11. *Pseudo-Jubilees* is the title given by the modern editors to three Qumran manuscripts (4Q225, 4Q226, and 4Q227) which 'employ language that is familiar from and to some extent characteristic of *Jubilees*' (Attridge et al. 1994: 142) without actually being copies of *Jubilees*. The relationship between 4Q225 and *Jubilees* remains unclear, however. Perhaps *Jubilees* is one among several sources used by the author of 4Q225 (the text was edited in Attridge et al. 1994).

12. Cf. the acute remarks by Tzoref (2012: 357): 'To mix the metaphors of our common trade – the ancient scholar had both itches to scratch and axes to grind, and for his work in these interrelated endeavours, he could rummage in a toolbox full of traditions and intertexts, techniques and strategies. I see the compiler of 4Q252 and those who produced his sources, as having engaged in a dynamic and fluid process, using language and ideas from scripture and other corpora in active reading and composition.' On the coherence and tendencies in 4Q252 see also: Høgenhaven 2018a.

order known from scriptural tradition. Indeed, the prayer for each day has a particular theme which is taken from this narrative, and elaborated on as a motivation for the days' address to the Deity. The prayer for the first day focuses on the creation of man, whom God fashioned in the image of his glory (יצרתה בדמות כבוד[כה], 4Q504 frag. 8 4) and then goes on to dwell on God's special relationship with Israel, which he has elevated to a unique position over against all nations. The divine favour granted to Israel is manifest through God's revelation in the form of the column of fire and the cloud (4Q504 frag. 6 10) and his appearance to Moses (4Q504 frag. 6 12). Against the background of this summarizing recapitulation of creation and election, the text pleads with God not to hold the iniquities of the forefathers against his people, Israel (4Q504 frag. 4 5-8).

The prayer for the fourth day explicitly recalls the narrative of God's revelation and covenant-making at Horeb: He is said to have appeared before the Israelites, spoken to them and established his covenant through Moses (4Q504 frag. 3 ii 7-17). The prayer for the fifth day mentions the rebellious behavior of the Exodus and desert generation, and God's declared intention to destroy them, and how Moses atoned for their sin (כיא כפר מושה בעד חטאתם, 4Q504 frag. 1-2 ii 9-10) and makes an appeal to God to turn his anger away from his people (4Q504 frags. 1-2 ii 11).

The subsequent preserved passages from the prayers for the fifth and sixth day present Israel's past viewed from the double perspective of divine anger and punishment and divine blessing and favour. The text explicitly states that the events referred to had already been foretold in writing by Moses and the prophets sent by God (4Q504 frags. 1-2 iii 12-13). No detailed account is given of either the Israelites' transgressions or the divine acts of blessing, but a series of examples are given: The mention made of 'our kings' who 'acted perversely' (וישחיתו, 4Q504 frags. 1-2 iii 15-16) would seem to constitute a general reference to the iniquities committed by kings of Israel and Judah, according to the literary tradition. Expressions of divine grace are God's election of Jerusalem as a 'resting place' (מנוחה, 4Q504 1-2 iv 2), his election of the tribe of Judah and his everlasting covenant with David (4Q504 1-2 iv 5-8). The people, as a result of the peace and tranquillity granted to them, 'ate, were replete and became fat' (ויוא[כ]לו וישבעו וידשנו, 4Q504 frags. 1-2 iv 14), and worshipped foreign gods. As a consequence, God poured out his anger and their land became a wasteland (4Q504 1-2 v 3-6). Despite his destructive wrath, God still remembered his covenant, redeemed his people, showed them favour among the countries where he had scattered them and made them turn back and listen to his voice (4Q504 frags. 1-2 v 6-14).

Within the narrative framework of Words of the Luminaries, the reference to the exile seems to constitute the decisive turning-point. The text continues, stating that the 'we'-group has indeed experienced God's purifying action, and is now capable of atoning for their iniquities including those of their fathers and of recounting the mighty works of God 'to eternal generations':

4Q504, frags. 1-2, col. vi.

2 [ ]°[ו]תשליךְ מֵ[ע]לֵינוּ כול פשעיֵ[נ]וּ[ו]תֵ[ט]הֲרֵנוּ
3 מחטתנו למענכה לכה אתה אֲדוני הצדק
4 אתה עשיתֵה את כול אלה ועתה כיום הזה
5 אשר נכנע לבנו רצינו את עוונו ואת עוון
6 אבותינו במעלנו ואשר הלכֵיו בקרי ולוא מאסנו
7 בנסויֵיכה ובנגיעיכה לוא געלה נפשנו להפר
8 את בריתכה בכול צרת נישנו אשר השלחתה בנו את אויבינו כיא אתה
9 זקתה את לבבנו ולמען נספר גבורתכה לדורוֵת
10 עולם

4Q504, frags. 1-2, col. vi
2 [... You have thrown awa]y f[r]om us all ou[r] failings and have [pu]rified us
3 from our sin for yourself. To you, to you, Lord, belongs the justice, for
4 you are the one who has done all this. And now, on this very day
5 on which our heart has been humbled, we atone for our iniquity and the iniquity
6 of our fathers, for our disloyalty and our {their} rebellious behavior. We have not rejected
7 your trials, and our soul has not despised your punishments to the point of breaking
8 your covenant, in spite of all the anguish of our soul. For you, who sent our enemies against us
9 have strengthened our heart so that we can recount your mighty works to
10 everlasting generations[13]

The presentation of Israel's past in *Words of the Luminaries* is seamlessly connected to the universal events of the primeval history, as is the case with the overview in the Damascus Document. In *Words of the Luminaries* it is the creation story known from Genesis 2–3 rather than the narrative of the Watchers that forms the background for the recapitulation of God's

---

13. 4Q504 was published in Baillet 1982: 137–68 + planches XLIX-LIII. The translation here follows García Martínez and Tigchelaar 1998: 1016–17.

election of, and covenant with Israel. The liturgical text likewise presents the past of Israel within a dualistic framework, but here no explicit reference to a 'remnant' is made. The 'we'-group present in the text identifies itself with 'Israel', and the identity is expressed in the words addressed to God: 'Remember, please, that all of us are your people' (זכור נא כיא[ז] עמכה כולנו, 4Q504 frag. 6, l. 6).

Israel's Past in Apocryphal Lamentations A and B

The liturgical composition *Apocryphal Lamentations A* (4Q179) depicts the misery and desolation of a devastated Jerusalem and its inhabitants. Intertextual points of contact with the book of Lamentations and the prophetic books are numerous. The first, partly preserved column describes the desolate city, focusing on the sanctuary, the streets and buildings, the missing inhabitants and the land, which has become like a desert:

4Q179, frag. 1, col. I

1   [°]
2   [°°°ר̇ כל עוונותינו ואין לאל ידנו כי לוא שמע]נו
3   [יהו̇דה לקרותנו כל אלה ברוע]
4   והפרנ[ו̇] את בריתו *vacat* אוי לנו]
5   [היה לשרפת אש והפכה]
6   [ר̇ תפארתנו וניחוח אין בו במז̇]בח
7   [חצרות קדשנו היו
8   [°כנ̇] [° י̇תום ירושלים עיר
9   מרב[ץ לחיה ואין מ̇]חריד [ורחובותיה
10 [ה̇] הוי כל ארמונותיה שממו
11 [° ובאי מועד אין בם כל ערי
12 [נחלתנו היתה כמדבר ארץ לוא
13 [לשמ[ח]ה לוא נשמשעה בה ודורש
14 [ל] [אנוש למכאוב̇י]נו [כול חובינו
15 פ[ש̇עינו י̇נ̇] [ח̇טאותינו

4Q179, frag. 1, col. I

2 ... all our sins, and it is not in the power of our hand, for we did not obe[y
3 ... Judah, so that all these things have happened to us because of the evil
4 ... [we broke] his covenant. *vacat* Woe to us ...
5 ... has been burnt by fire, and an overthrow
6 ... our beauty. And there is no pleasing odour in it on the al[tar ...
7 ... the courtyards of our sanctuary have become
8 ... an orphan ... Jerusalem, the city of
9 ... a lair] for wild beasts, and there is no one [to frighten them away,] and her streets
10 ... Alas! All her palaces are desolated
11 ... and those who come to the festival are not among them. All the cities

12 ... our inheritance has become like a desert, a land not
13 ... j[o]y is not heard in her, and he who seeks
14 ... our wound is incurable ... all our guilt
15 ... our [t]ransgressions ... our sins[14]

In 4Q179 literary images of a desolate and ruined city and a broken and exiled people would seem here to have been transformed into a metaphor for people experiencing marginalization and oppression.[15] Scholars have debated whether or not the description should be linked to any specific historical events, the destruction of Jerusalem in 587 BCE or possibly some later occasion.[16] However, in view of the importance ascribed to the memory of the Babylonian exile as it was recalled and constructed in literary traditions, it seems likely that the imagery of exile of destruction is here extended to cover the entire notion of divine anger and punishment against a guilty people. This metaphorization is further developed in *Apocryphal Lamentations B* (4Q501), where images of destruction and abandonment are explicitly applied to the lamenting group itself:

4Q501

1 [   ]י אל תתן לזרים נחלתנו ויגענו נכר זכור כיא
2 [אנחנו עצור]י עמכה ועזובי נחלתכה זכור בני בריתכה
   השוממים
3 [ ]ה המנודבים תועים ואין משיב שבורים ואין חובש

4Q501
1 ...Do not give our inheritance to foreigners, nor our produce to the sons of foreigners. Remember that
2 [we are the removed one]s of your people and the forsaken ones of your inheritance. Remember the sons of your covenant, the desolate,
3 ...the spurred ones, the wanderers, who no one brings back, the sorely wounded, who no one bandages[17]

14. The text was published in Allegro 1968: 75–7. For the transcription and translation see also Høgenhaven 2002.

15. Cf. Berlin's expression (2003: 17) that 4Q179 and 4Q501 are 'not poems of mourning, they are poems of alienation'.

16. Maurya Horgan points to the siege and destruction of Jerusalem by Antiochus IV Epiphanes in 169–167 BCE as a possible historical background for 4Q179 (Horgan 1973: 222–3). However, it is hardly fruitful to speculate about historical events as the background for the composition (cf. Høgenhaven 2012b).

17. The text was published in Baillet 1982: 79–80 + planche XXVIII. The English translation follows García Martínez and Tigchelaar 1998: 993–5.

Apocryphal Lamentations A does not contain any specific 'sectarian' terminology, but it has been suggested that the text might be interpreted in light of polemics against the prevailing regime in Jerusalem known from several Qumran texts (Berlin 2003: 16–17). Be that as it may, these poetical lamentations corroborate the overall expression that Israel's past was construed in a variety of genres represented in the Qumran texts, as a coherent narrative with God's acts of blessing and of punishment as the focal point, and with the destruction of Jerusalem, as perceived in the literary tradition, as the central manifestation of divine anger.

Concluding Observations

We may sum up the tendencies characteristic of representations of the past in the texts we have briefly surveyed here: In general, Israel's past is presented in Qumran texts as a coherent narrative, connecting seamlessly with the Primeval History. No distinction is made between the 'mythological' events of the distant past (including the creation of mankind and the fall of the Watchers) and the more recent 'historical' events. There is a tendency to smooth out inconsistencies and apparent contradictions occurring in earlier literary traditions.

At the same time, certain aspects of the narratives are emphasized and enhanced. This is the case with the role of the patriarchs and the priestly elements of the tradition. In particular, Abraham's role as forefather of Levi is underlined, so as to achieve an unbroken narrative chain between the patriarchs and the priests and Levites. These figures represent the elect of God in different phases of the narrative, both groups standing out, by virtue of their righteous behavior, in contrast to the evildoers whom God rejects and punishes. In these representations of the past, the division line between the elect and the doomed is made more explicitly visible. Thus, the representation of Israel's past is characterized by a general tendency to include all parts of the narrative in a comprehensive pointed 'salvation history' (or 'perdition history') with a dualistic perspective. There are different nuances as regards the identification of the elect with a renewed and repentant 'Israel' or the faithful and obedient remnant of Israel. Nevertheless, the fundamental features of how the past is perceived seem to be common to compositions documented in the Qumran scrolls, regardless of whether they belong to the 'sectarian' literature or not.

Bibliography

Allegro, J. M. (1956), 'Further Messianic References in the Qumran Literature', *JBL*, 75: 174–87.
Allegro, J. M. (1968), *Qumran Cave 4. I (4Q158-4Q186)*, DJD 5, Oxford: Clarendon Press.
Attridge, H. et al. (1994), *Qumran Cave 4. VIII. Parabiblical Texts. Part 1*, DJD 13, Oxford: Clarendon Press.
Baillet, M. (1982), *Qumrân Grotte 4. III (4Q482-4Q520)*, DJD 7, Oxford: Clarendon Press.
Baumgarten, J. M. and D. R. Schwartz (1995), 'Damascus Document (CD)', in J. H. Charlesworth (ed.), *The Dead Sea Scrolls: Hebrew, Aramaic, and Greek Texts with English Translations, Vol. 2: Damascus Document, War Scroll, and Related Documents*, 4–57, Tübingen: Mohr Siebeck; Louisville: Westminster John Knox Press.
Berlin, A. (2003), 'Qumran Laments and the Study of Lament Literature', in E. G. Chazon (ed.), *Liturgical Perspectives: Prayer and Poetry in Light of the Dead Sea Scrolls: Proceedings of the Fifth International Symposium of the Orion Center for the Study of the Dead Sea Scrolls and Associated Literature, 19–23 January, 2000*, 1–17, STDJ 48, Leiden: E. J. Brill.
Bernstein, M. J. (1994), '4Q252: From Rewritten Bible to Biblical Commentary', *JJS*, 45: 1–17.
Bernstein, M. J. (1994/1995), 'Method and Context, Genre and Sources', *JQR*, 85: 61–79.
Bernstein, M. J. (1998), 'Pentateuchal Interpretation at Qumran', in P. W. Flint and J. C. VanderKam (eds), *The Dead Sea Scrolls After Fifty Years: A Comprehensive Assessment. I*, 128–59, Leiden: E. J. Brill.
Brooke, G. J. (1994/1995), 'The Thematic Content of 4Q252', *JQR*, 85: 33–59.
Brooke, G. J. (1996), '4Q252 as Early Jewish Commentary', *RevQ*, 17: 385–401.
Brooke, G. J. (2001), '4Q158: Reworked Pentateuch[a] or Reworked Pentateuch A?', *DSD*, 8: 219–41.
Brooke, G. J. et al. (1996), *Qumran Cave 4. XVII: Parabiblical Texts, Part 3*, DJD 22, Oxford: Clarendon Press.
Davies, P. R. (1989), *Behind the Essenes: History and Ideology in the Dead Sea Scrolls*, BJS 94, Atlanta: Scholars Press.
García Martínez, F. and E. J. C. Tigchelaar (1998), *The Dead Sea Scrolls Study Edition. 2: 4Q274–11Q31*, Leiden: E. J. Brill.
Holst, S. (2005), 'Abraham at Qumran', in M. Müller and T. L. Thompson (eds), *Historie og konstruktion. Festskrift til Niels Peter Lemche i anledning af 60 års fødselsdagen den 6. september 2005*, 180–91, FBE 14, Copenhagen: Museum Tusculanums Forlag.
Holst, S. (2012), 'Hvornår er en tekst bibelsk? Bearbejdede Mosebøger blandt Dødehavsrullerne', in J. Høgenhaven and M. Müller (eds), *Bibelske genskrivninger*, 111–38, FBE 17, Copenhagen: Museum Tusculanums Forlag.
Høgenhaven, J. (2002), 'Biblical Quotations and Allusions in 4QApocryphal Lamentations (4Q179)', in E. D. Herbert and E. Tov (eds), *The Bible as Book: The Hebrew Bible and the Judaean Desert Discoveries*, 113–20, London: The British Library; New Castle: Oak Knoll Press.
Høgenhaven, J. (2012a), 'Den uforudsigelige Jahve i 4QRewritten Pentateuch A: På grænsen imellem genskrivning og afskrift af Bibelen i Qumran', in J. Høgenhaven and M. Müller (eds), *Bibelske genskrivninger*, 139–63, FBE 17, Copenhagen: Museum Tusculanums Forlag.

Høgenhaven, J. (2012b), 'Communal Laments from Qumran and Their Biblical Background', in T. Davidovich (ed.), *Plogbillar & svärd. En festskift till Stig Norin*, 78–88, Farsta: Molin & Sorgenfrei.

Høgenhaven, J. (2018a), 'Fortschreibung und Kanonisierung in der Bibliothek von Qumran: Bemerkungen mit besonderem Hinblick auf Genesis-Kommentar A (4Q252)', in J. Høgenhaven, J. T. Nielsen and H. Omerzu (eds), *Rewriting and Reception in and of the Bible*, 11–31, WUNT 396, Tübingen: Mohr Siebeck.

Høgenhaven, J. (2018b), 'Abraham and his Family in Qumran Biblical Exegesis', in L. Bormann (ed.), *Abraham's Family: A Network of Meaning in Judaism, Christianity, and Islam*, 145–65, WUNT 415, Tübingen: Mohr Siebeck.

Horgan, M. (1973), 'A Lament over Jerusalem ("4Q179")', *JSS*, 18: 222–34.

Puech, É. (2013/2014), '4Q252: Commentaire de la Genèse ou "Bénédictions patriarcales"?', *RevQ*, 26: 227–51.

Segal, M. (1998), 'Biblical Exegesis in 4Q158: Techniques and Genre', *Textus*, 19: 45–62.

Segal, M. (2000), '4QReworked Pentateuch or 4QPentateuch?', in L. H. Schiffman, E. Tov and J. C. VanderKam (eds), *The Dead Sea Scrolls Fifty Years After Their Discovery: Proceedings of the Jerusalem Congress, July 20–25, 1997*, 391–9, Jerusalem: Israel Exploration Society/The Shrine of the Book, Israel Museum.

Thompson, T. L. (1998), '4QTestimonia and Bible Composition: A Copenhagen Lego Hypothesis', in F. H. Cryer and T. L. Thompson (eds), *Qumran between the Old and New Testaments*, 261–76, JSOTSup 290 / CIS 6, Sheffield: Sheffield Academic Press.

Thompson, T. L. (2018), 'Rewritten Bible or Reiterative Rhetoric: Examples from Yahweh's Garden', in J. Høgenhaven, J. T. Nielsen and H. Omerzu (eds), *Rewriting and Reception in and of the Bible*, 49–63, WUNT 396, Tübingen: Mohr Siebeck.

Tov, E. (1992), 'The Textual Status of 4Q364-367 (4QPP)', in J. Trebolle Barrera and L. Vegas Montaner (eds), *The Madrid Qumran Congress: Proceedings of the International Congress on the Dead Sea Scrolls, Madrid 18–21 March, 1991, Vol. 1*, 43–82, STDJ 95, Leiden: E. J. Brill.

Tov, E. and S. White Crawford (1993), *Qumran Cave 4. VIII: Parabiblical Texts, Part 1*, DJD 13, Oxford: Clarendon Press.

Trafton, J. L. (2002), 'Commentary on Genesis A (4Q252 = 4QCommGen A = 4QPBless)', in J. H. Charlesworth (ed.), *The Dead Sea Scrolls: Hebrew, Aramaic, and Greek Texts with English Translations: Vol. 6B, Pesharim, Other Commentaries, and Related Documents*, 203–19, Tübingen: Mohr Siebeck; Louisville: Westminster John Knox Press.

Tzoref, Sh. (2012), '4Q252: Listenwissenschaft and Covenantal Patriarchal Blessings', in A. M. Maier, J. Magness and L. H. Schiffman (eds), *'Go Out and Study the Land' (Judges 18:2): Archaeological, Historical and Textual Studies in Honor of Hanan Eshel*, JSJSup 148, 335–57, Leiden: E. J. Brill.

Zahn, M. (2011), 'Building Textual Bridges: Towards an Understanding of 4Q158 (4QReworked Pentateuch A)', in G. J. Brooke and J. Høgenhaven (eds), *The Mermaid and the Partridge: Essays from the Copenhagen Conference on Revising Texts from Cave Four*, 12–32, STDJ 96, Leiden – Boston: Brill.

Is Josephus's John the Baptist Passage a Chronologically Dislocated Story of the Death of Hyrcanus II?*

Gregory L. Doudna

On the one hand John the Baptist plays a central role in the Gospels. On the other hand, neither rabbinic tradition nor, with one exception, ancient historians seem to know anything of a first-century CE John the Baptist. The exception is Josephus's *Antiquities of the Jews*, produced in Rome in the early 90s CE. John the Baptist appears in a passage at *Ant.* 18.117-119, situated by Josephus in a context dated 35 CE, a few years after many scholars understand Jesus to have been crucified.

This article proposes that Josephus's 'John the Baptist' passage in *Antiquities* is a chronologically displaced story of the death of Hyrcanus II, the aged former high priest, by Herod the Great in either c. 34 or 30 BCE.

As a matter of method the Gospels are set completely to one side and the focus is solely on analysis of the Josephus passage.

---

* Dedicated to Thomas L. Thompson, mentor, friend, teacher with conscience and courage. I remember his first written comment on a paper of mine. I had written: 'It could be argued that…' Thompson in the margin: 'Please do'. Another Thompson aphorism: 'When everyone is agreed on something, it is probably wrong'. In other words, as Thompson has also put it, 'in our fields, if all are in agreement, it signifies that no one is trying to falsify the theory: an essential step in any scientific argument'. I thought of what I have come to call Thompson's Rule when I encountered this scientific study showing that, as counterintuitive as it sounds, unanimous agreement actually does reduce confidence of correctness in conclusions in a wide variety of disciplines (Gunn et al. 2016).

The passage in *Antiquities* is in Josephus's language and style, yet at the same time the passage reads as an insertion into pre-existing text, like an ancient excursus or footnote set into a text that would read perfectly smoothly without it (Schwartz 2013: 106–9). This description does not mean the passage is an interpolation by a later Christian scribe. For a number of reasons the passage is unlikely to have come from a later Christian forger, not the least of which is that Josephus's John the Baptist is not in any way portrayed as Christian.[1] Rather, the insertion of a story into preexisting narrative is a well-known phenomenon in the composition process of Josephus.[2] But this composition process results in precisely the kind of passage that can be subject to Josephus making a chronological mistake, in this case attaching an undated story from a source to the wrong Herod. Here is the Josephus John the Baptist passage:[3]

> But to some of the Jews it seemed that the army of Herod was destroyed by God – indeed, God quite justly punishing [Herod] to avenge what he had done to John, who was surnamed the Baptist.
>
> For Herod killed him, although he was a good man and [simply] bade the Jews to join in baptism, provided that they were cultivating virtue and practicing justice toward one another and piety toward God. For [only] thus, in John's opinion, would the baptism [he administered] indeed be acceptable [to God], namely, if they used it to obtain not pardon for some sins but rather

---

1. On the forgery issue see the discussion of Kirby (2015). A recent argument for forgery (Nir 2012) identifies the ideology of Josephus's John the Baptist passage as that of 1QS and considers Qumran texts not part of mainstream Judaism, in contrast to the Essenes considered to have been part of mainstream Judaism and unrelated to the Qumran texts. Nir argues that Josephus could not have favorably portrayed a view that purification would be effective only if moral sin was eliminated first, which Nir argues was held only by fringe groups on the edges of Judaism such as represented in the Qumran texts; therefore, Nir argues, the John the Baptist passage is a forgery and interpolation. However each of these assumptions – that the Qumran texts were fringe, that 1QS and the Essenes are unrelated and that Josephus could not have represented the purification teaching of 1QS favorably – is doubtful.

2. As just one example, compare Noam (2018: 59–69), on an interpolation by Josephus at *Ant.* 13.282-283 of a story from a Jewish source concerning a heavenly voice in the temple heard by John Hyrcanus I, into a narrative otherwise following *War*. Noam discusses the way in which the story was 'interpolated into an existing narrative in *Antiquities*…a further illustration of Josephus's addition of sources with parallels in rabbinic sources to his later work [*Antiquities*]' (p. 69).

3. Translation of John Meier, with Meier's explanatory comments in brackets (Meier 1992: 233). Other translations from Josephus in this article are from Loeb Classical Library editions (LCL).

the cleansing of their bodies, inasmuch as [it was taken for granted that] their souls had already been purified by justice.

And when the others [namely, ordinary Jews] gathered together [around John] – for their excitement reached fever pitch as they listened to [his] words – Herod began to fear that John's powerful ability to persuade people might lead to some sort of revolt, for they seemed likely to do whatever he counseled. So [Herod] decided to do away with John by a preemptive strike, before he sparked a revolt. Herod considered this a much better [course of action] than to wait until the situation changed and [then] to regret [his delay] when he was engulfed in a crisis.

And so, because of Herod's suspicion, John was sent in chains to Machaerus, the mountain fortress previously mentioned; there he was killed. But the Jews were of the opinion that the army was destroyed to avenge John, God wishing to inflict harm on Herod. (*Ant.* 18.116-119)

In this passage John is said to have been a righteous man. To those who were practicing virtue and piety (which it is implied John teaches), John instructed them βαπτισμῷ συνιέναι, to be 'joined' in immersing. But when 'others' (τῶν ἄλλων) – presumably not under religious discipline – also heard John, 'their excitement reached fever pitch as they listened to [his] words'. When Herod, the ruler, saw that the people 'seemed likely to do whatever [John] counseled', Herod 'began to fear that John's powerful ability to persuade people might lead to some sort of revolt'. Herod therefore arrested John in 'a preemptive strike' and sent John as a prisoner to Machaerus (a fortress across from Qumran on the other side of the Dead Sea). There, at Machaerus, Herod had John executed. The method of execution is not stated. Following that Herod's army was destroyed, which many Jews believed was divine punishment for what Herod had done to John. As part of the insertion Josephus added the cross-reference to the mention of Machaerus.

This, then, is Josephus's story of John. In this story there is no mention of Galilee, asceticism or wilderness associated with John. There is no criticism by John of Herod's marital behavior. There is no mention of strange dress or diet. Herod is presumed ruler over the area in which John is active, and Herod controls Machaerus. John is portrayed favorably, unlike Josephus's negative portrayals of wilderness wonder-workers of the first century CE. Josephus uses a word widely in use meaning immersion, βαπτισμός, not the word used in the Gospels and the rest of the New Testament as a *terminus technicus* for Christian baptism, βάπτισμα.

On the baptism of John in the Josephus passage, key points of interpretation and/or assumptions (without going into detail to argue each of these points) are: (1) The immersions are repeated, not one-time, and are best understood in terms of a study of Étienne Nodet (2009), of initiation to social levels of formal status and purity requirements as reflected in Josephus's description of Essene practices of *War* 2.129, 137-139, 150, and the *haburim* of rabbinic tradition.[4] There is an initiatory, legal-witnessing component to first-time purification upon entry but there is also continuing purification following entry to that social circle. (2) The immersions accomplish purification in Jewish terms, not removal of sin. (3) The procedure is uncertain but may have been immersions done by oneself with or without witnesses assisting, indistinguishable from Jewish purification in the stepped-pool *mikvehs* found archaeologically in large numbers. (4) John's ideology of purification, in which purification is to be done only by those already in a prerequisite state of moral sinlessness accomplished through right behavior for the purification to be acceptable to God, is exactly that of 1QS 3.6-12 and 1QS 5.13-14 of the Qumran *yachad* texts. It is not Pharisaic/rabbinic (purification is for all without precondition and unrelated to sin) or Christian (one time initiatory, removes sin). (5) John's instruction that observant Jews 'be united (with one another)' in practicing purification suggests social organization; compare access to communal food and drink of the Qumran *Serekh* texts for which purification by immersion is a prerequisite for participation. (6) Josephus or his source may be criticizing Christian baptism, but it is also possible that Josephus, writing to gentiles, or his source is simply clarifying a common misunderstanding held by gentiles concerning Jewish purification. (7) The surname, 'the Baptist', 'the Immerser' (Ἰωάννου τοῦ ἐτικαλουμένου βαπτιστοῦ), carries no necessary connotation that John was immersing other persons; the surname could come about because he was known for being an immerser or bather, or a teacher of such or leader of a disciplinary order practicing such. (8) It is not John's purification-immersion teaching which prompts Herod's murderous response, but rather John's popularity among the public who are swayed by his words or public sermons – the implication is John is an alternative locus of popular authority raising the specter of insurrection – which is the issue to Herod.

The point of interest here is that every word of Josephus's story of John would read perfectly well in the time of Herod the Great (37–4 BCE). The figure 'Herod' of the story, if the story were read in isolation, would read perfectly well and naturally as Herod the Great.

4. Cf. *War* 2.150 speaking of the Essenes: 'They are divided, according to the duration of their discipline, into four grades; and so far are the junior members inferior to the seniors, that a senior if but touched by a junior, must take a bath, as after contact with an alien' (also: Klawans 2006: 145–74; Sanders 1990: 37–8; and Haber and Reinhartz 2008: 93–124).

Meanwhile, Hyrcanus II, the aged ex-high priest executed by Herod the Great, has long been presumed and understood to have been named 'John' on the basis of papponymy – the common Jewish practice of naming a firstborn son after the paternal grandfather (on the prevalence of papponymy, Hachlili 2005: 195). The paternal grandfather of Hyrcanus II was John Hyrcanus I (high priest 135–104 BCE).

The name 'John' for Hyrcanus II has not, however, gone unchallenged. In a 1987 article Tal Ilan noted that there is no ancient attestation of a Hebrew name for Hyrcanus II, questioned whether Hyrcanus II had a Hebrew name, and if he did, challenged the assumption that it must have been 'John' (Ilan 1987). Yet while it is true there is no confirmed attestation of a Hebrew name for Hyrcanus II, it seems unwarranted to suppose he did not have one. If it were not for coins, it would not be known that the final Hasmonean king, Antigonus, had a Hebrew name, Mattathias. Hyrcanus II minted no coins according to the most current information.[5] This means that Hyrcanus II's Hebrew name cannot be discovered by means of coins, yet just as Antigonus had a Hebrew name (known only from coins), so it can be presumed Hyrcanus II (who had no coins) did as well, given that other Hasmonean rulers certainly did and there is no evidence or reason to suppose any did not.

As for the identity of Hyrcanus II's Hebrew name, Ilan cites the example of Jonathan Aristobulus III (*War* 1.438; *Ant.* 15.51) whose Hebrew name was that of his great-grandfather Alexander Jannaeus (Jonathan), which suggests that papponymy while common may not have been absolute. Nevertheless, although not attested or certain, Yohanan or John is the leading candidate for Hyrcanus II's Hebrew name based on papponymy, the same name as Josephus's John the Baptist. In the end Ilan's argument is more of a demonstration of incompleteness of evidence in favor of, than a falsification of, the prevalence of papponymy as it bears on Hyrcanus II's Hebrew name.

Hyrcanus II had a long history as high priest of the Jewish people, 76–67 and 63–40 BCE, ending in 40 BCE when he was overthrown, cast out of his native land and taken prisoner to the Parthian Empire.

---

5. It has been conclusively ruled out that any of the 'John high priest' Hasmonean coins can be attributed to Hyrcanus II (Hendin 1991: 6). It has also separately nearly been ruled out that any of the 'Jonathan high priest' Hasmonean coins can be attributed to Hyrcanus II (Hendin and Shachar 2008). Nor are any other coins attributed to Hyrcanus II. A reasonable explanation for why Hyrcanus II minted no coins is that, except for c. 67 BCE when he was king for only a few months according to Josephus – too brief to mint coins – Hyrcanus II held no civil authority other than as ethnarch and therefore was in no position to mint coins (see Sharon 2017).

According to Josephus the Jewish diaspora east of the Euphrates, at least after the new Parthian ruler Phraates IV set Hyrcanus II free and honored him, considered Hyrcanus II their legitimate high priest and king, even though he was in exile.[6]

Hyrcanus II as Ethnarch (or, John the Authority on Purification)

According to a study of Nadav Sharon, Hyrcanus II was recognized as *ethnarch* of Jews throughout the Roman empire by Julius Caesar in 47 BCE; the term 'ethnarch' meant ruler of a people in a territory, not ruler of the territory; and, as ethnarch Hyrcanus II had formal authority under Roman law over affairs of the Jewish people of the diaspora as well as in Judea (Sharon 2017: 126–9, 260–80, 357–9).[7]

Julius Caesar honored Hyrcanus II in this way after commending Hyrcanus II for providing military support to Julius Caesar in Egypt and for bravery. Julius Caesar promised Hyrcanus II and his descendants the ethnarchy of Jews empire-wide and the high priesthood in Jerusalem in perpetuity, as part of a restoration of ancestral law and *de facto* self-rule to the Jews following Roman conquest, in keeping with Julius Caesar's practice with other peoples who had been conquered by the Romans.[8]

---

6. *Ant.* 15.14-15: 'When Hyrcanus was brought there, the Parthian king Phraates treated him very leniently because he had learned of his distinguished and noble lineage. For this reason he released him from his bonds and permitted him to settle in Babylon, where there was a great number of Jews. These men honored Hyrcanus as their high priest and king, as did all of the Jewish nation occupying the region as far as the Euphrates.'

7. In Sharon's analysis Hyrcanus II's ethnarchy starting in 47 BCE related to the Jews as a people throughout the Roman Empire, and there is no evidence Hyrcanus II held civil authority over all people in any geographical area in the period of Roman rule. If Sharon is correct it would not be expected that Hyrcanus II would have minted coins, thus removing the mystery of the missing Hyrcanus II coins.

8. That the restoration of rights to practice ancestral customs and a return of *de facto* self-rule to the Jews under the ethnarchy of Hyrcanus II in 47 BCE was in keeping with the practice of Julius Caesar with other conquered peoples is discussed in Pucci Ben Zeev (1995). Julius Caesar's designation of Hyrcanus II as authoritative in matters of *halakhic* law is illustrated at *Ant.* 14.192-195, described as a letter from Julius Caesar to the magistrates of Sidon: 'Whereas the Jew Hyrcanus, son of Alexander, both now and in the past, in time of peace as well as in war, has shown loyalty and zeal toward our state, as many commanders have testified on his behalf, and in the recent Alexandrian war came to our aid with fifteen hundred soldiers, and being sent by me to Mithridates, surpassed in bravery all those in the ranks, for these reasons it is my wish that Hyrcanus, son of Alexander, and his children, shall

In other words, Hyrcanus II, 'high priest of the Most High God' (*Ant.* 14.163), was legally recognized as lawgiver or law-decider for the Jewish people throughout the Roman empire.

Although Hyrcanus II would have been ethnarch of the Jews formally only within the territory of the Roman empire, he may also have been regarded informally as authoritative by diaspora Jews outside the Roman empire in light of his status within the Roman empire. In this light Hyrcanus II's high standing in the diaspora after his exile in 40 BCE may have continued the status or authority he held before that time, rather than representing something new. Sharon (2017: 279 n. 87) notes that Hyrcanus II's authority over Jews living outside Judea seemed to be 'mainly in issues that have to do with religion – "manner of life" (*Ant.* 14.195)'.

Following the downfall of the Antigonus Mattathias regime in Jerusalem (40–37 BCE), Hyrcanus II returned to Judea about 36 BCE, after which he may have divided his time between Jerusalem and Jericho. Despite the likelihood that Hyrcanus II remained until his death the single most respected and esteemed religious authority to Jews throughout the ancient world, never again would Hyrcanus II officiate as high priest in the temple in Jerusalem.

Hyrcanus II's Death and a Destruction of an Army of Herod

According to Josephus (*Ant.* 15.165-179), Herod – seeing the legitimacy with which the returned Hyrcanus II was popularly regarded as a threat in contrast to Herod's own much more questionable legitimacy to rule – treacherously executed Hyrcanus II on a legal pretext in 30 BCE in the context of an unsuccessful attempted flight of Hyrcanus II to take refuge with the Nabatean king Malichus I (reigned 59–30 BCE). Josephus situates Herod's execution of Hyrcanus II as occurring later than a destruction of an army of Herod in 32 BCE – the only destruction of an army of a Herod found in Josephus other than the one of Antipas of 36 CE (*Ant.* 18.114-115). According to Josephus, Herod invaded Nabatean territory but Herod's army was nearly annihilated at Canatha deep in Coele-Syria, in 32 BCE.

---

be ethnarchs of the Jews and shall hold the office of high priesthood of the Jews for all time in accordance with their national customs… And if, during this period, any question shall arise concerning the Jews' manner of life, it is my pleasure that the decision shall rest with them.'

[Herod's forces] suffered great losses...the Arabs...returned and killed them after their rout. The Jews therefore suffered death in various forms, and only a few of those who escaped found shelter in their camp. Then King Herod in despair of the outcome of the battle rode off to get aid but in spite of his haste he was not quick enough in bringing help, and the Jews' camp was taken...so unexpected a victory...in destroying a large part of [Herod's] force. (*Ant.* 15.112-120)

However, the failed escape attempt and execution of Hyrcanus II is arguably better situated c. 34 BCE, preceding rather than following the First Nabatean War of 32–31 BCE which Herod ultimately won, reflecting a larger issue of systematic three-year offset errors in Josephus's datings of some events in the reign of Herod which have long been noticed. As discussed by Thomas Corbishley (1935: 22–4) and others since:

Every one who has gone into the subject at all is aware that there are obvious blunders in the chronology of Josephus [for the time of Herod]... all the existing discrepancies [in the time of Herod] can be found on the supposition that Josephus, in compiling his history, has failed to notice that, whilst in general his sources used the 'official' method of dating [from the start of Herod's reign in 37 BCE], some document or documents used a different scheme – regarding the year 40/39 B.C. as the first year of the reign... Thus, having described the events of 40–34 B.C. with considerable fullness, Josephus passes (*Ant.* 15.108) to the events of the seventh year, sc. 31/30 B.C., without apparently noticing that he has jumped three years...

Corbishley (1935: 24–5) noted similar unusual gaps of three years in Josephus's history-telling in two other places: from 20 BCE to 17/16 BCE, and 12/11 BCE to 9/8 BCE. *Antiquities* 15.380 has the rebuilding of the Temple begun in the eighteenth year of Herod whereas *War* 1.401 has the Temple rebuilding begun in the fifteenth year of Herod; Corbishley reconstructed both as referring to 23/22 BCE reflecting the two methods of dating. At *Ant.* 16.136 the building of Caesarea takes ten years, whereas *Ant.* 15.341 has twelve years; Corbishley suggested the ten may have been the accurate number and the twelve mistakenly calculated by Josephus based on the two methods of reckoning.

A further example (not brought out by Corbishley): at Antioch in 37/36 BCE and at Alexandria in 34 BCE, in public ceremonies, Mark Antony, ruler of the eastern Roman Empire, gave title to territories comprising nearly the whole of the Eastern Roman Empire to a restored Egyptian Ptolemaic dynasty of kings and queens. According to historian Hendrikus van Wijlick (2013: 135–48), the Donations of Antioch of 37/36 BCE to Cleopatra VII, consort of Mark Antony, included Coele-Syria, parts of

Nabatea and the 'balsam-producing parts of Judaea' (Plutarch), which Josephus identifies as within 'the region about Jericho' (*Ant.* 15.96). These territories were given to Cleopatra 'towards the end of 37 or at some point in 36' (van Wijlick 2013: 142). Cleopatra allowed Herod to lease back her Judean territory starting in 36 BCE according to both Dio Cassius and Plutarch. However Josephus in both *War* and *Antiquities* places the leaseback from Cleopatra in 34 BCE, with Josephus's date being erroneous in van Wijlick's opinion. Similarly, Plutarch and Dio have Lysanias, ruler of Iturea, executed by Mark Antony at Cleopatra's instigation in 36 BCE, but Josephus (*Ant.* 15.92) has Lysanias's execution in 34 BCE.

With this in mind, in the present case Herod's army was destroyed by the Nabateans with help from the forces of a general of Cleopatra in 32 BCE. A year later Herod (with a new army) was victorious over the Nabateans in 31 BCE. After that is when Josephus situates in *Antiquities* Hyrcanus II's attempt to flee to the Nabateans which failed and ended in Hyrcanus's execution. Josephus has Hyrcanus II (concerning whom Josephus has been completely silent in his history for four years prior to this point) trying to flee to the Nabateans for sanctuary – with the Nabatean ruler's active assistance including promises to send a force ($\delta\upsilon\nu\alpha\mu\iota\nu$, military power) to bring Hyrcanus's party safely to Nabatea – *after* the Nabateans, according to Josephus, had been defeated and had acclaimed Herod 'ruler (or, protector) of their nation' (*Ant.* 15.160, 172).

Hyrcanus's intended flight to the Nabateans and execution by Herod arguably makes better sense dated c. 34 BCE in the context surrounding Herod's trip to Mark Antony in Laodicea – *before* rather than *after* Herod's defeat by and then victory over Malichus I in the First Nabatean War of 32–31 BCE.

In 35 BCE Herod murdered the new, popular, eighteen-year old high priest Jonathan Aristobulus III, grandson of Hyrcanus II. (At least the family members believed Herod had had the young man murdered, according to Josephus; Herod claimed it was an unfortunate accident in a swimming pool.) A year earlier Herod had written to Mark Antony that Jonathan was so well-liked that the whole land could very easily be filled with disorder and war 'because the Jews had formed hopes of an overturn of the government and the rule of another king' (*Ant.* 15.30). According to Josephus, Herod feared that Hyrcanus II's daughter Alexandra, Jonathan's mother, 'would try to overthrow his government if she found an opportunity' (*Ant.* 15.42).

> [Herod] called a council of his friends and bitterly accused Alexandra of having secretly plotted against his throne, saying that through Cleopatra she was working to get Antony to deprive him of his power and have the

youth [Jonathan Aristobulus III] take over the government in his place. (*Ant.* 15.31-32)

After a complaint from the aggrieved mother, Alexandra, to Cleopatra, following the death of her son, Herod was summoned by Mark Antony to Laodicea in 34 BCE to answer for the death of Jonathan Aristobulus III. The complaint from Alexandra seems to have been part of more far-reaching moves and hopes for Herod's removal by Mark Antony and a restoration of the Hasmoneans to power at that time, whether by means of Hyrcanus II himself or by having a Hasmonean woman as queen.

According to Josephus these moves included the governor of Idumea and trusted general of Herod, Costabarus, conspiring with Cleopatra to align with her and no longer be subject to Herod (*Ant.* 15.255-257; cf. 15.79); Alexandra scheming to have Mark Antony become sexually enamored with her beautiful daughter Mariamne (even though Mariamne was currently inconveniently married to Herod) and by this means 'they might recover the throne' (*Ant.* 15.73; cf. 15.23-28); and an escape attempt by Alexandra and Mariamne from Herod's house arrest to a Roman military unit (*Ant.* 15.72), all in what Josephus portrays as a climate of popular hostility to Herod and support for a Hasmonean restoration. The alleged conspiracy of Hyrcanus II with Nabatean king Malichus I would be well understood as one more element in this context. According to *War* 7.300 Herod's building restorations at Masada c. 34 BCE were part of this context as well:

> Herod finished this fortress as a refuge for himself, suspecting a twofold danger: peril on the one hand from the Jewish people lest they should depose him and restore their former dynasty to power; the greater and more serious from Cleopatra, queen of Egypt. For she never concealed her intention, but was constantly importuning Antony, urging him to slay Herod, and praying him to confer on her the throne of Judea.

But alas for these hopes, the meeting with Mark Antony in 34 BCE went well for Herod. Herod came out of the meeting having 'strengthened Antony's goodwill toward [Herod's] throne and his government' (*Ant.* 15.75). Either shortly before or shortly after Herod's journey to Mark Antony in 34 BCE makes the best sense for the attempted flight of Hyrcanus II to the Nabateans and then failure of that attempt and Hyrcanus II's execution.

This date actually agrees with the picture given by Josephus in the earlier *War*. At *War* 1.433-434 Josephus tells of Herod's execution of Hyrcanus II without dating it. But then Josephus mentions that Mariamne, on the eve of Herod's trip to Mark Antony of 34 BCE, 'openly upbraided him [Herod] with the fate of her grandfather Hyrcanus and her brother Jonathan' (*War* 1.437, 439-444), thus situating Herod's execution of Hyrcanus II as having already occurred by that point, in agreement with the reconstruction argued here. In *Antiquities*, which has redated Hyrcanus II's execution later, note that until Josephus's story of Hyrcanus II's execution at the time of Herod's trip to Octavian in Rhodes of 30 BCE, Josephus mentions only daughter Alexandra and granddaughter Mariamne, never Hyrcanus, following 34 BCE. At *Ant.* 15.72-73, 80, it is only Alexandra and 'the women' attempting to flee to the safety of Roman forces in 34 BCE, with no mention of Hyrcanus II. Arguably, Josephus when writing *Antiquities* did not know exactly when Hyrcanus II was executed and mistakenly dated Hyrcanus II's execution three or four years late.

Themes of Hyrcanus II and John the Baptist in Josephus Compared

The themes in Josephus's John the Baptist story of Herod fearing revolt, and preemptively executing, agree extremely well with the portrayal of Herod the Great of Josephus. Herod the Great's executions of rivals and threats to his rule, his paranoia and suspicions, are a major theme in Josephus in a way that is not paralleled at all in Josephus for Herod Antipas, with the sole exception of the John the Baptist passage at issue of *Ant.* 18.116-119. That passage (*Ant.* 18.116-119) reads as if it were other language for Josephus's descriptions surrounding Hyrcanus II in the time of Herod the Great.

> Fearing that everyone would incline to Aristobulus [grandson of Hyrcanus II], [Herod] put him to death at Jericho... (*Ant.* 20.248)
>
>> *Herod began to fear that John's powerful ability to persuade people might lead to some sort of revolt...decided to do away with John... Machaerus...there he was killed. (Ant. 18.118-119)*
>
> [Herod] believed...it would be safest not to have a man who was far worthier than himself of obtaining the kingship wait to seize his opportunity...[he] ordered the man [Hyrcanus II] to be strangled. (*Ant.* 15.164, 176)
>
>> *[Herod] decided to do away with John by a preemptive strike, before he sparked a revolt. Herod considered this a much better course of action than to wait until the situation changed and then to regret his delay. (Ant. 18:118)*

> Herod married Aristobulus' sister Mariamme, hoping to capture the goodwill of the people for himself, thanks to their recollection of Hyrcanus [II]... (*Ant.* 20.248)

>> *[John] was a good man... And when the others (ordinary Jews) gathered together around John... they seemed likely to do whatever he counseled...* (*Ant.* 18.117-118)

Josephus's John the Baptist story emphasizes condemnation by the Jews at large for Herod's unjust execution of John. Here is Josephus stating a similar belief held by Jews concerning Herod's perfidy and Hyrcanus II's innocence in the matter of Herod's execution of Hyrcanus II.

> And as proof that it was without committing any crime that [Hyrcanus II] came to such an end they specify his mildness of character and the fact that not even in his youth did he give any sign of boldness or recklessness... [the] charges were a pretext invented by Herod... what was most painful of all, as we have said before, was that in his old age [Hyrcanus II] came to an unworthy end... That Antipater and Herod advanced so far was due to his mildness, and what he experienced at their hands in the end was neither just nor an act of piety. (*Ant.* 15.165-182)

>> *For Herod killed him, although he was a good man and simply bade the Jews to join in purification, provided that they were...practicing justice toward one another and piety toward God.* (*Ant.* 18.117)

Josephus's story of the execution of John the Baptist corresponds with his story of Herod's execution of Mariamne, Hyrcanus II's granddaughter, both featuring a popular belief that divine punishment fell on Herod as a result.

> [T]here arose a pestilential disease which destroyed the greater part of the people and also the most honored of [Herod's] friends, and this caused all to suspect that their misfortune had been brought upon them by God in His anger at what had lawlessly been done to Mariamme. (*Ant.* 15.243)

>> *But the Jews were of the opinion that the army [of Herod] was destroyed to avenge John, God wishing to inflict harm on Herod.* (*Ant.* 18.119)

But is it plausible that Josephus would make a chronological mistake of the magnitude suggested in the case of the John the Immerser passage – of attaching an undated story from a source to the wrong Herod, over a half century removed in time?

The answer is yes it is plausible; the phenomenon has a number of parallels.

Of Doublets and Chronological Dislocations

At *Ant.* 14.145-148 Josephus mistakenly wrote a Roman Senate decree from 139 BCE as applying to Hyrcanus II in 47 BCE. At *Ant.* 14.150-155 Josephus mistakenly wrote a decree of Athens from 105 BCE as applying to Hyrcanus II of 47 BCE (Eilers 2008). Following these two examples Josephus then sets forth a further dossier of Caesarian documents (*Ant.* 14.190-264), which Josephus presents as all applicable to Hyrcanus II. However some of those documents apply to John Hyrcanus I of the preceding century, not Hyrcanus II. As Claude Eilers (2003: 194) commenting on these errors of Josephus put it succinctly: 'Unfortunately, he had the wrong Hyrcanus'. Wrong Hyrcanus, wrong Herod, same principle.

Daniel Schwartz has done work on doublets in Josephus from sources in which, just as in biblical texts, variant versions of the same figure or event are narrated in the text as if they are two persons or two events. For example Josephus separately presents two accounts of a visit of the Roman governor of Syria, Vitellius, to Jerusalem at the time of a Jewish festival, which have usually been assumed in scholarly discourse, based on Josephus's portrayal, to be distinct historical visits (*Ant.* 18.89-122). Schwartz argues convincingly that the two visits of Josephus are two versions of a single visit of Vitellius and Herod Antipas to Jerusalem at Passover 37 CE (Schwartz 2013: 100–104; cf. also Nodet 2014: 274–6).

Similar analysis has been done by David Goodblatt on what Josephus presents as two unrelated sets of events in Parthian Babylonia following successively in chronological sequence, commonly dated c. 20–35 CE and 41 CE (*Ant.* 18.310-379). Goodblatt (1987) showed that these are stories of the same context told different ways, with the correct datings being 36–52 CE (rule of Asinaios and Anilaios in Nehardea) and 40/41 CE (pogrom in Seleucia) respectively.

The study of Corbishley (1935) referred to above showed a doublet concerning Herod's second trip to Rome of 12 BCE at *Ant.* 13.66-270. As Josephus has it a series of events of 14–12 BCE is essentially repeated in 12–10 BCE. Josephus misunderstood two versions of the same events of 14–12 BCE as being different and consecutive in sequence and mistakenly situated the second version of the same events in the following two years of 12–10 BCE.[9]

A Judas son of Sepphoraeus, 'unrivaled interpreter of the ancestral laws...educated the youth...', inspired an anti-Roman insurrection in Jerusalem c. 4 BCE at a time of a removal of Joazar from the high priesthood (*Ant.* 17.149, 207-208, 339). A Judas of Gamala, characterized by Josephus as the founder of the Fourth Philosophy dedicated to liberty from Rome, is said to have inspired another anti-Roman insurrection at a time of removal of the same Joazar from the high priesthood again in 6 CE (*Ant.* 18.3-4, 23-26). Some scholars have held that this is too much coincidence and reflects a doublet; if so, one of the variants is chronologically dislocated in Josephus by about nine years (Lagrange 1911; Rhoads 2011).

In the same way, Josephus's John the Baptist story reads as a doublet or different version of Hyrcanus II chronologically dislocated to the time of the wrong Herod. In this case Josephus did not place the two versions of the death of Hyrcanus II close together in the same time setting as in some of the other cases of doublets. If Josephus had done that, the doublet in this case would have been recognized before now. Instead, Josephus mistakenly attached one of the traditions of the death of Hyrcanus II to the wrong Herod, just as he separately mistakenly attached documents to the wrong Hyrcanus.

Summary of Comparisons between Josephus's
John the Baptist and Hyrcanus II

1. *Same name*: Hyrc. II: Though unverified, 'John' is suggested from papponymy.
2. *Judea sphere of activity*: likely.
3. *Popular support*: Hyrc. II: *Ant.* 15.15; 20.248.
4. *Herod fears threat to power*: Hyrc. II: *Ant.* 15.178, 183.
5. *Righteous man considered innocent*: Hyrc. II: *Ant.* 15.174-178.

---

9. Corbishley (1935: 30): 'The narrative of the quarrels in Herod's family as given in 13.66-135, taken by itself, is coherent, although incomplete... On the other hand, the story of what Josephus calls the δευτέρα ἔρις in Herod's family, as given in 13.189-270, is merely another version, from a different angle, of the former quarrel, and its dislocation must be due to the fact that it was attributed in the sources to the "twenty-seventh" and "twenty-eighth" years of the reign; and since Josephus knew that Herod had gone to Rome in the "twenty-sixth" year (on his own dating) he naturally presumed that this was a fresh quarrel, not another story of the earlier quarrel dated on a different system.'

6. *Executed by Herod*: Hyrc. II: *Ant.* 15.174-178.
7. *Site of imprisonment/execution*: Josephus's John the Baptist: Machaerus on the Judean/Nabatean border across from the Dead Sea. Hyrc. II: unstated, but occurs when seeking refuge with the Nabatean king who planned to send horsemen to escort Hyrcanus II's party from the Dead Sea and 'bring them in safety' to Nabatea (*Ant.* 15.167-173).
8. *Herod condemned by Jews for the execution*: Hyrc. II: *Ant.* 15.174, 182.
9. *Execution is followed by a destruction of Herod's army*: Hyrc. II: *Ant.* 15.118-119 (with death of Hyrc. II in Josephus's *Antiquities* redated c. four years earlier, per argument).
10. *Purification by immersion*: Hyrc. II: purification by immersion central to his practice as first-century BCE high priest and ex-high priest. As ethnarch of Jews of the diaspora would have been the principal figure known in the diaspora associated with purification by immersion.
11. *Purification ideology and communal organization like that of 1QS*: Hyrc. II: both when he was high priest, and later as high priest emeritus spending much of his time at the Royal Estate of Jericho, it would be highly unusual if Hyrcanus II did *not* have a familiar relationship with the site of Qumran and its purification installations in physical proximity to Jericho.

Every element of the Josephus John the Baptist passage agrees with, or can agree with, Hyrcanus II in relation to Herod the Great. On the one hand there are these positive circumstantial indicators, cumulative in impact. On the other hand there is no detail in Josephus's John the Baptist passage in contradiction to Hyrcanus II, apart from the single factor of the chronological setting in which the story is found in Josephus. But that chronological setting is neither internal to the story nor necessary to the story. It was an ancient judgment of the historian, Josephus, known for fallibility elsewhere on chronological matters.

Therefore the thesis should be considered.

Emic and Etic

Little is known of Hyrcanus II's activity after his return to Judea c. 36 BCE. Josephus represents Hyrcanus II as esteemed by 'all of the Jewish nation' east of the Euphrates as their legitimate high priest and king (*Ant.* 15.14-15). If after his return to Judea in c. 36 BCE Hyrcanus II lived in the residences of previous Hasmoneans and now of Herod, at whose invitation he had returned, he would have spent much of his time at the royal estate in Jericho, at a time of peak activity of the scrolls later found to have been placed in caves at the nearby site of Qumran.

In agreement with the point of view of some of the Qumran texts with respect to the power center in Jerusalem, Hyrcanus II had been estranged from a regime in control of Jerusalem which had driven him from Judea. An adversary had seized the high priesthood by force. The usurper regime had held power in Jerusalem before succumbing to a Roman invasion. The usurper had died violently at the hands of the Romans, in his death evoking the imagery of the fate of a 'Wicked Priest' in 1Q Pesher Habakkuk. When Hyrcanus II, instead of being restored to power and honor after his return to Judea in accord with Herod's promises, was killed by Herod and every male of Hyrcanus II's lineage killed too (*Ant.* 15.266), did that have anything to do with the end of all compositions of Qumran texts which occurred at that time, for reasons no one knows?[10]

Hyrcanus II and Baptizing

Josephus says nothing of Hyrcanus II baptizing. Josephus also does not mention that Hyrcanus II engaged in mystical rites of ascension to heaven, issued *halakhic* rulings, was involved in calendric decisions, officiated in temple administration, wrote or had issued in his name hymns and liturgies, or corresponded with Jewish officials abroad and at home. Yet it is likely that Hyrcanus II engaged in all of these things, because he was high priest for thirty-two years and those are the kinds of things a high priest is believed to have done. To this list can be added purification by immersion. The immersions of Josephus's John the Baptist are nothing other than purification immersions, in running water or in the full-body-immersion *mikvehs*, which have been abundantly attested archaeologically in Judea and Galilee starting from about the beginning of the first century BCE.[11] If an identity of Josephus's John the Baptist with Hyrcanus II is

---

10. Atkinson and Magness 2010: 340: '[T]he Essenes apparently stopped composing new religious texts after the middle of the first century B.C.E., as there are no historical references in the scrolls [of Qumran] to events after 31 B.C.E.'; Wise 2003: 84: '[J]udging by the latest references [in an inventory of thirty-one historical allusions in Qumran texts], all of the sectarian writings on the list were probably composed between 60 and 30 B.C.E.'.

11. Arguing for a slightly later date than the c. 100 BCE date most commonly judged for the start of *mikvehs* used for ritual immersions, Berlin 2005: 452, 469 n. 148: '*mikva'ot* first appear in contexts of the early–mid first century B.C.E.; there is no evidence for such installations in Jewish settlements before then…there is no

contested on the grounds that there is no ancient testimony that Hyrcanus II baptized (immersed for purification), that reflects an underlying presupposition that Josephus's John's immersions differed from the purification practices of most Jews in first-century BCE Judea. Such assumptions can arise from anachronistically reading into Josephus Christian conceptions of what Josephus's John the Baptist's immersings must have been.

Josephus does not discuss Jewish purification practices much anywhere in his works, perhaps because his attention was on political history. Josephus obtained most of his information for Hyrcanus II from Herod's court historian Nicolaus of Damascus and other sources concerned with political history. That Josephus did not make a point of stating that Hyrcanus II, who as high priest was the leading Jewish figure in the world involved with purification for over three decades, immersed himself for purification, is not a significant omission.

But the question nevertheless remains in a different form: if purification by immersion was not noteworthy for Hyrcanus II, why was it noteworthy in the case of John the Baptist? A curious finding has been that the *mikvehs* used by Jews for ritual immersions, so pervasive in Judea and areas under the control of the Hasmonean state in the first century BCE, seem not to have been found at all in the diaspora.[12] Would Hyrcanus II in Babylon, given the means and opportunity to do so, have resumed purification by immersion as had been his practice in Judea?

According to Josephus the Parthian ruler, Phraates IV, when he came to power in 38/37 BCE, 'released [Hyrcanus II] from his bonds and permitted him to settle in Babylon, where there was a large number of Jews' (*Ant.* 15.14). Did Hyrcanus II, perhaps now in a house of his own, have *mikvehs* installed? In first-century BCE Judea purification by immersion would not be noteworthy. But in the diaspora, in Babylon, a Jewish practice of purification by immersion in *mikvehs*, especially by Hyrcanus II, a public figure, would have been unusual and noteworthy. Although hypothetical,

---

positive evidence for so early a date [late second century BCE] from any of these locales [Jericho, Upper City of Jerusalem, Qumran, Gezer, Gamla]... Michael Wise has recently proposed that the Teacher of Righteousness...should be dated to the mid-first rather than the mid-second century B.C.E. If correct, then it is interesting to note that this is the same period in which the more widespread but less rigorous practices of "household Judaism" appear'.

12. E.g. Haber and Reinhartz 2008: 164 n. 13, 174: 'As of yet, there have been no *mikvaot* found in the Diaspora (...) The archaeological evidence suggests that ritual ablutions were associated with synagogues in the Diaspora and that these purification procedures did not involve immersion in a *mikveh*.'

this is one way Hyrcanus II could have become known as 'the Immerser', with the name following him in certain circles back to Judea.

Conclusion and Implications

This article has proposed that Josephus's John the Baptist is an independent tradition of Hyrcanus II of the time of Herod the Great, which has been chronologically displaced in *Antiquities*. Josephus's John the Baptist story is to be understood as in the class of additional material from Jewish stories inserted by Josephus into the preexisting narrative of *War* in the composition process of *Antiquities*. These are the same kinds of stories that are found in later rabbinic traditions, although this particular story is not attested in later rabbinic compilations.

If this analysis is correct – that Josephus misplaced this story to the wrong Herod in *Antiquities* – then there is no attestation external to the New Testament of the Gospels' figure of John the Baptist of the 30s CE. The implication would seem to be this: either the Gospels' John the Baptist has been generated in the story world of the Gospels, or he derives from a different figure than Josephus's John the Baptist, secondarily conflated with Josephus's John the Baptist. These issues are beyond the scope of this paper.

Bibliography

Atkinson, K. and J. Magness (2010), 'Josephus's Essenes and the Qumran Community', *JBL*, 129: 317–42.

Berlin, A. (2005), 'Jewish Life Before the Revolt: The Archaeological Evidence', *JSJ*, 36: 417–70.

Corbishley, T. (1935), 'The Chronology of the Reign of Herod the Great', *JTS*, 36: 22–32.

Eilers, C. (2003), 'Josephus's Caesarian *Acta:* History of a Dossier', in *Society of Biblical Literature Seminar Paper Series 42*, 189–213, Atlanta: SBL Press.

Eilers, C. (2008), 'Forgery, Dishonesty, and Incompetence in Josephus' "Acta": The Decree of Athens ("AJ" 14. 149-155)', *ZPE*, 166: 211–17.

Goodblatt, D. (1987), 'Josephus on Parthian Babylonia (*Antiquities* XVIII, 310-379)', *JAOS*, 107: 605–22.

Gunn, L. et al. (2016), 'Too Good to be True: When Overwhelming Evidence Fails to Convince', in *Proceedings of the Royal Society A: Mathematical, Physical and Engineering Sciences*, 472: 20150748, http://dx.doi.org/10.1098/rspa.2015.0748.

Haber, S. and A. Reinhartz, eds (2008), *'They Shall Purify Themselves': Essays on Purity in Early Judaism*, Atlanta: Society of Biblical Literature.

Hachlili, R. (2005), *Jewish Funerary Customs, Practices and Rites in the Second Temple Period*, Leiden: E. J. Brill.

Hendin, D. (1991), 'New Data Sheds Light on Hasmonean Coin Theories', *Celator* 5 (6): 6–8.

Hendin, D. and I. Shachar (2008), 'The Identity of YNTN on Hasmonean Overstruck Coins and the Chronology of the Alexander Jannaeus Types', *INR*, 3: 87–94.

Ilan, T. (1987), 'The Greek Names of the Hasmoneans', *JQR*, 78: 1–20.

Kirby, P. (2015), 'The Authenticity of John the Baptist in Josephus' (21 May), http://peterkirby.com/john-the-baptist-authentic.html.

Klawans, J. (2006), *Purity, Sacrifice, and the Temple: Symbolism and Supersessionism in the Study of Ancient Judaism*, Oxford: Oxford University Press.

Lagrange, M.-J. (1911), 'Où en est la question du recensement de Quirinius?', *RB*, 8: 60–94.

Meier, J. (1992), 'John the Baptist in Josephus: Philology and Exegesis', *JBL*, 111: 225–37.

Nir, R. (2012), 'Josephus' Account of John the Baptist: A Christian Interpolation?', *JSJH*, 10: 32–62.

Noam, V. (2018), *Shifting Images of the Hasmoneans: Second Temple Legends and Their Reception in Josephus and Rabbinic Literature*, Oxford: Oxford University Press.

Nodet, É. (2009), 'Le baptême des prosélytes, rite d'origine essénienne', *RB*, 116: 82–110.

Nodet, É. (2014), 'Machéronte et Jean-Baptiste', *RB*, 121: 267–82.

Pucci Ben Zeev, M. (1995), 'Caesar and Jewish Law', *RB*, 102: 28–37.

Rhoads, J. (2011), 'Josephus Misdated the Census of Quirinius', *JETS*, 54: 65–87.

Sanders, E. P. (1990), *Jewish Law from Jesus to the Mishnah: Five Studies*, London: SCM Press.

Schwartz, D. R. (2013), *Reading the First Century*, Tubingen: Mohr Siebeck.

Sharon, N. (2017), *Judea under Roman Domination: The First Generation of Statelessness and its Legacy*, Atlanta: SBL Press.

van Wijlick, H. (2013), 'Rome and Near Eastern Kingdoms and Principalities, 44–31 BC: A Study of Political Relations during Civil War', PhD thesis, Durham University, http://etheses.dur.ac.uk/9387/.

Wise, M. (2003), 'Dating the Teacher of Righteousness and the *Floruit* of his Movement', *JBL*, 122: 53–87.

Thompson's Jesus:
Staring Down the Wishing Well*

Jim West

Historical Jesus scholars have each 'looked down the long well of history and [seen their] own face reflected at the bottom'[1]

This essay re-evaluates the book by Thomas Thompson titled *The Messiah Myth: The Near Eastern Roots of Jesus and David* and discusses the appropriateness of his methodology, the correctness of his interpretation, and the continuing importance of his contribution on the topic of the historical Jesus. In the present essayists view, this is Thompson's most important work and is critical to a correct understanding of his academic agenda. It is, accordingly, quite surprising that it has not received either adequate or even marginal attention. Nor, in the very few reviews it has received, has it been correctly understood.

So, for instance, when Thomas Thompson's volume appeared in the United States in 2005 it was not charitably reviewed by all its readers. *Kirkus Reviews* opined:

> ...the book is too technical to appeal to most general readers, since Thompson presupposes a comfortable familiarity with Hebrew Scripture and the New Testament that most nonspecialists lack. Even the sections where he explicitly engages the academic landscape can be puzzling: in his historiographic overview, he curiously fails to discuss the work of N.T. Wright, arguably today's most influential historian of the New Testament and a scholar whose careful historical readings of the New Testament seem

---

* It is with heartfelt gratitude to Tom Thompson that I offer this small token of my appreciation for both his scholarship and his friendship over the decades. I hope that he finds it a joy to read.

1. Tyrell 1909: 44.

an obvious point of engagement for Thompson. Finally, the production team gets demerits for the impossibly tiny print. At turns tendentious and stuffy. *The Messiah Myth* reads like nothing more and nothing less than a promising doctoral dissertation.[2]

Publisher's Weekly is equally nonplussed, writing:

> For Thompson, Jesus and David emerge merely as characters in stories that reveal the value of the good king. Although Thompson provides a valuable service by situating the Jesus and David tales in the context of other ancient Near Eastern literature, his argument that the biblical writers used such literature to write their fictions of David and Jesus is neither new nor startling. In addition, the lack of a coherent structure and a definitive conclusion lessens the effectiveness of Thompson's book.[3]

Alongside respectable reviews were an army of 'Jesus Mythicists' who latched onto Thompson's work as support for their view that Jesus actually never existed and who were bolstered by Thompson's book. Doing so, they misunderstood both Thompson and his work. Others ignored Thompson's work. Indeed, the *Review of Biblical Literature*, the book reviewing 'arm' of the Society of Biblical Literature, never even reviewed the book, as though it never existed.

In what follows the volume will be assessed more charitably and carefully than has yet been done and its purpose and intent will be described more fairly. In the quotation at the heading of this essay the famous notion that scholars of the Historical Jesus are merely gazing at themselves was cited. And in many instances that is true. Liberation theologians see Jesus as a liberation theologian. Feminist theologians see him as a feminist. LGBTQ scholars see Jesus as a homosexual male. Protestant Theologians from nineteenth-century Germany saw Jesus as a crusty Protestant. And on it goes.

But Thompson's Jesus is not a liberal Catholic. Thompson's Jesus is a theological construct comprised of bits and pieces of Old Testament theological historiography. Thompson's Jesus is a real man who really existed but he is a man about whom we know nothing at all aside from the understanding foisted upon him by the theologians of the early Church who wrote his story: the Gospels.

---

2. https://www.kirkusreviews.com/book-reviews/thomas-l-thompson/the-messiah-myth/, accessed 15 July 2018.
3. https://www.publishersweekly.com/978-0-465-08577-4, accessed 16 July 2018.

Thompson, in other words, does not see his own reflection at the bottom of the well. He sees the reflection provided by the Old Testament. And that reflection is very much worth considering. He, like Rudolf Bultmann before him, rightly perceives the historian's task. As Bultmann (1934: 9–10) put it:

> However good the reasons for being interested in the personalities of significant historical figures, Plato or Jesus, Dante or Luther, Napoleon or Goethe, it still remains true that this interest does not touch that which such men had at heart; for *their* interest was not in their personality but in their *work*. And their work was to them not the expression of their personality, nor something through which their personality achieved its 'form', but the cause to which they surrendered their lives. Moreover, their work does not mean the sum of the historical effects of their acts; for to this their view could not be directed. Rather, the 'work' from *their* standpoint is the end they really sought, and it is in connection with their purpose that they are the proper objects of historical investigation. This is certainly true if the examination of history is no neutral orientation about objectively determined past events, but is motivated by the question how we ourselves, standing in the current of history, can succeed in comprehending our own existence, can gain clear insight into the contingencies and necessities of our own life purpose.

There is no doubt in my mind that Thompson would agree fully with this assessment.

The book, for those who have not yet read it, begins in Part One, 'The Kingdom of God', with a series of chapters which invite the reader to consider the ancient Near Eastern background (or better, underpinning) of the messianic concept. How are we to understand, historically, the person of Jesus? What is a Prophet? Who are the children of the Kingdom of God? How do ancient texts lay the groundwork for the fully developed question of the messianic figure?

In Part Two, 'The Royal Ideology', Thompson questions the various myths (used in the classical sense of the word and not the modern sense of 'falsehood') connected to the messianic figure: the Good King, the Conquering Holy Warrior and the Dying and Rising God.

The final section of the book draws all of what precedes it together in what Thompson calls 'The Never Ending Story'. In three successive chapters he discusses Holy War, the Good King and the Bad King and the figure of David in story and song. The volume concludes with a series of appendices, notes, a bibliography, an index of biblical citations and a subject index.

Thompson's book, long overlooked and very much worth a fresh consideration is not an attempt to join him to the 'Jesus Mythicist' camp. Nor is it a denial of the existence of Jesus of Nazareth. Thompson is far too intelligent to fall into that category. Rather, the volume, in my view Thompson's most important, painstakingly and carefully shows readers the various streams which make up the great river of Jewish messianism. In his own words:

> This book attempts to answer the question I first raised some five years ago: What is the Bible if it is not history? (Thompson 2005: ix)

Furthermore:

> Part I deals with the perspective of the gospels, which builds its narrative figures on the basis of the myth drawn primarily from earlier Jewish tradition. Part II considers three of the most central figures of ancient Near Eastern royal ideology – the good king, the conquering holy warrior and the dying and rising god – and discusses their reuse in biblical tradition and especially in the Hebrew Bible. Part III describes the biblical revision of holy war ideology and the way this tradition has affected the composition of the narratives about the kings of Judah and Israel and finally the development of the messiah figure in narrative and song. (Thompson 2005: x–xi)

How did ancient Judaism understand messianic figures and how did they formulate their views based on precedent? That is the issue of the present work. The importance of that question cannot be exaggerated.

The chief question at hand, though, is whether or not Thompson accomplishes his goal. Does he lay bare the roots of messianic understanding in Early Judaism?

He certainly shows that Early Judaism's understanding of a messianic figure has roots in other ancient Near Eastern materials. As he shows:

> The same or similar saying can be given to different figures in different narratives without disturbing the conviction that it belongs to each. Nevertheless, a particular saying out of its author's context can hardly be identified as belonging to Job, a Psalter's David or Isaiah's suffering servant. (Thompson 2005: 26)

The biblical authors, then, had a library of ideas to draw from when it came to describing its heroes, and they used those materials with great skill to weave together their stories of great men. This does not imply that those great figures did not exist nor does it imply that they did not accomplish great deeds. It simply recognizes the fact that the historical bones of great persons have been covered with muscle and flesh and decorations drawn from the stories of other great heroes from other times and places. Heroes are amalgams.

This also applies to the descriptions of Jesus in the Gospels. As Thompson opines:

> No author of the first century CE invented these roles [i.e., the roles exemplified in the story of Jesus; JW]. Nor did he invent the figures that bear them in his stories. One who wishes to separate and distinguish such roles historically needs to begin much earlier than the gospels. The fabric of the gospels was long in preparation. No author of merit – and Luke is an extraordinarily gifted storyteller – has written apart from a literary community and a common tradition. (Thompson 2005: 65)

Is this true? It seems undeniably so. Has Thompson proven his thesis? To this point, he has. But he also has more evidence to muster. Next, then, he turns to one of the most important hero story tropes: 'The reversal of this world's power and wealth'.

> It can be found in every major ancient Near Eastern wisdom tradition and in nearly every ancient text tradition that gives voice to the ideology of kings and kingship. As it has been transmitted and reinterpreted within biblical tradition, this trope has played a decisive role in the development of the Jesus story. It goes far in defining his character, personality and mission. (Thompson 2005: 105)

Jesus was a hero figure and the stories told of him in the Gospels utilize hero story tropes to give fullness and form to his life story. But not only that, these tropes connect Jesus to an audience that can better understand him because these tropes are utilized.

Thompson continues to develop his carefully constructed argument by observing that

> The process of biographical story creation is complex. It is especially difficult to determine whether we are in fact dealing with the story of a particular man's life and a biography illustrating values we hold because of him. We may be dealing with a narrative figure whose function is to illustrate universal or eternal values. The difference between the two rests on our ability to separate the bearing figure of a narrative from its message. (Thompson 2005: 134–5)

This, it seems, is the very heart of the issue. What material in the Gospels stems from the unique behaviors and deeds of Jesus of Nazareth and what stems from hero tropes adopted by the Gospel writers? The answer to this critical question is that we simply do not have any way of disentangling the threads and the Gospel authors would not wish us to do so.

What we can be sure of, however, is that the tropes adopted by the Gospel writers have a long and firmly established history. When, for instance, Jesus is likened to a king, it is because this trope was in place long before even David came on the scene. And so was the kind of king. As Thompson shows, 'The virtues of humility, social justice and integrity are all marks of a piety oriented toward an ideal kingdom' (2005: 169).

The tropes that were applied to the life and kingdom of David are also applied to the life and ministry of Jesus. The Near Eastern roots of Jesus and David are in fact not simply Israelite or Judean tropes, but nearly 'universal'. Ancient Israel and the Early Church both made use of materials found in their respective intellectual environments in order to 'flesh out' their heroic tales.

Does this imply that the tales told of David, and of Jesus, are 'untrue'? Quite the contrary. A trope can be true and it can be applied to a wide range of persons and still be true. Such is the case of the borrowed tropes applied to both David and Jesus. And what is the aim of the utilization of such tropes to describe David and Jesus? Thompson observes:

> The interactive roles of the messiah as prophet, king, judge and priest are well-known aspects of the messiah's profile. These roles of illustration struggle constantly to maintain a doorway between transcendent and ephemeral worlds. (Thompson 2005: 297)

The various tropes, in other words, are illustrations. In the same way that preachers illustrate their sermons with stories that are sometimes a mixture of historical fact and metahistorical fiction, so too the biblical authors.

Does, then, Thompson have it right? Does the present book contribute anything meaningful to our understanding of the great heroes of Judaism and Christianity, David and Jesus? If we understand the biblical text as 'history' then the answer is no. If we take the Old Testament, and the New, as simple recitations of historical fact then Thompson's solution to the problem of historicity will be extraordinarily unhelpful and even frustrating and annoying.

Fortunately, though, the Old Testament and the New are not mere historical tales telling the bare facts of historical events. The Old Testament and the New are theological works, which happily and unselfconsciously mix historical remembrance with illustrative materials without any concern that postmodern readers take them as something other than sermons.

If we take the text of the Bible seriously and on its own terms than we will find Thompson's disentangling of the disparate threads which make it up both engaging and enthralling. Rather than standing at the edge of the well and staring down to see a reflection which is his own, Thompson has stared down the well and seen the reflection of the biblical authors. And we should be grateful for it.

This key work of Thomas Thompson deserves a fresh hearing and a fair hearing from those in the guild of biblical scholarship. On this, the occasion of his 80th birthday, my humble hope is that this contribution to his *Festschrift* encourages such a fresh hearing.

Bibliography

Bultmann, R. (1934), *Jesus and the Word*, trans. L. P. Smith and E. H. Lantero, New York: Scribners.

Thompson, T. L. (2005), *The Messiah Myth: The Near Eastern Roots of Jesus and David*, New York: Basic Books.

Tyrell, G. (1909), *Christianity at the Crossroads*, London: Longman, Green & Co.

THE QUR'AN AS BIBLICAL REWRITING

Mogens Müller

1. *Introduction*

Biblical studies has changed significantly from its earlier focus on history. Not least, the Enlightenment set a new standard in claiming the Bible not to be in itself revelation, but rather human testimonies about revelation, including its interpretation. This way of resolving the claim of divine infallibility opened the eyes of critical scholarship to a history behind the texts and to the human efforts that created and collected the books, which became the Pentateuch of Samaritanism, the TANAK of Judaism and the Bible of Christianity.

From its beginning, the goal of Enlightenment scholarship was to reconstruct the history behind the biblical story. The effort was to reach the historical bedrock supporting all later interpretation and myth-making. Such historical-critical scholarship, however, reduced the biblical message by insistently asking the question of referentiality. Only what could be proven or, at least, made likely, to render what really had happened, could be labelled 'truth' and thereby be reckoned trustworthy.

It was in the 1970s that biblical studies effectively first shifted its focus from creating a history behind the texts to interpreting the biblical story itself. It was no longer primarily looked upon as a trustworthy source for factual history. It was rather assessed as a narrative, the message of which in principle was independent of its referentiality. Its truth value was more to be ascertained from its ability to create faith and affect the behavior of its readers and listeners. Thus, the biblical texts were fundamentally viewed as sources for understanding the beliefs, convictions and intentions of their creators.

2. The Introduction of the Concept 'Biblical/Scriptural Rewriting'

This change of focus away from the question of eventual referentiality to that of biblical authors and their intentions in producing their writings, brought attention to the particular phenomenon of rewriting in the Bible and a vast Apocryphal and Pseudepigraphic literature. Hitherto, variations had mainly raised the question of which version could claim to be the original or, at least, the most original among many variants. Now, such variations acquired independent interests for reissuing a message in new situations and changed circumstances.

It was the Jewish biblical scholar, Geza Vermes (1924–2013), who back in 1961 coined the term 'Rewritten Bible'.[1] Much discussion has concentrated on the appropriateness of the very term, but this should not hide its heuristic value in drawing attention to the extensive literature consisting in rewriting existing books and stories. Obviously, these rewritings did not owe their formation to new knowledge about a text's referential history, but rather to an interest in making existing stories suitable to new contexts. In the Jewish Bible itself, Chronicles clearly consists of a later rewriting of the stories told in the books of Samuel and Kings. Among the Pseudepigrapha, the book of *Jubilees*, from the second century BCE, stands out as a new version of Genesis and introduction to Exodus, while Pseudo-Philo's *Liber Antiquitatum Biblicarum*, from around the middle of the first century CE, rewrites the biblical stories from Adam to King David.

In regard to the New Testament, viewing the gospels as rewritten Bible, or, what in this context is the more correct term, as biblical rewritings, offers a fruitful approach. The Gospel of Matthew, from the 80s, for example, stands out as a rewriting of the earliest gospel, of Mark, from c. 70 CE, to be followed, c. 100, first by the Gospel of John and, still later, some decades into the second century, by the Gospel of Luke. Although it is an anachronism to speak about a Bible as a fixed collection of writings so early, I would venture to label the New Testament gospels as biblical rewritings, in the sense that their authors intend them to be seen as authoritative stories to be used in Christian service alongside readings from the Jewish Holy Scriptures.

---

1. See Vermes 1973. Vermes later developed the genre concept in numerous articles and books. Of course, the phenomenon of interpreting by creative retelling was noted long before and given various labels, among them Midrash. However, it was only with Geza Vermes's elaboration of the genre or interpretation strategy that it became a heuristic tool in understanding the rewriting as creative reception.

In comparing the development of the Jesus story through the variations of the four gospels, with their expansions, shortenings, and often radical restructuring, a reader detects a surprising freedom on the part of the author not only to supplement existing stories with new characteristics, but also to invent events and speeches. A biblical scholar has to work with the concept of creative 'fiction'. As critical scholarship increasingly changed its perspectives towards the writing of the narratives, it ceased to be as interested in eventual historical facts, which had been assumed to be embedded in the texts. Eyes were opened towards viewing these stories as vehicles for unfolding and maintaining beliefs and convictions rather than history writing in our sense of the word. With reception history, fiction became a legitimate category for understanding what occurs in rewriting. At the same time, it exposes what those who rewrote thought of their original.

It is of some interest in this context to introduce Aristotle's definitions in his *Poetics*, where (ch. 9) the philosopher distinguishes between poetry as being more philosophical and serious than history writing. Where history writing pertains to the particular, poetry relates to the common. Thus, the poet depicts what is understood as real, what Aristotle calls *mimesis*. In doing so, he created an awareness that literary texts could be fictional, thereby contributing to the understanding of mimetic activity as implying more than the alternatives of true and untrue. As expressions of a legitimate and necessary human activity, *mimesis* first of all addresses the reality of reception, opening such reality in a new way by letting what is told become the receiver's own experience. In this, Aristotle operates with what we could call *mimetic competence*. Mimetic competence describes, for instance, what the tragedian is doing when he presents the Homeric myth that had almost lost its original meaning, in a manner that recreates its impact for the audience.

This is exactly what the authors of the gospels did in their writing and rewriting of the Jesus story (Müller 2014). This understanding of the gospels in particular and the biblical story in general as at least partly fictional, revisits pre-critical Bible reading.[2] Its value is no longer measured by its degree of referentiality. The truth of the story is free from its dependence on the factuality of its content. However, this is not a

---

2. See the still important book by Frei, *The Eclipse of Biblical Narrative* (1974), showing how the shift to a historical-critical understanding of the Bible involved a serious reduction in the assumed biblical 'truth'. The 'narrative turn' in the 1970s first opened a way out of this confusion of historical truth and religious truth, not by giving up a critical scholarship but by refining it.

return to an uncritical attitude, which today would mean fundamentalism. Instead, the reading of a narrative occurs in respect to a truth that is only accessible through what we today would understand as fiction; namely, through myth, symbol and metaphor.

In reading biblical texts, we should not attend so exclusively to the story's tale as if it were a window into a world of the distant past. Far more, we should attend to what the authors wanted to achieve in terms of their readers or listeners – which beliefs, convictions and behavior they aimed at creating in the lives of the congregations to which they owe their existence and want to support. They did not primarily intend to inform us about historical facts, but rather to convey a revelation, which does not allow itself to be reduced to merely what can be neutrally acknowledged. Their message is addressed rather to *faith*. For example, the author of the Gospel of John closes with a declaration that what has been written in his book was 'recorded in order that you may hold the faith that Jesus is the Christ, the Son of God, and that through this faith you may possess life in his name' (Jn 20:31).

3. *'Rewritten Bible' as a New Approach to Understanding the Qur'an*

Reading the Qur'an as a biblical scholar in an age that is no longer necessarily determined by polemics allows us to conceive much of what is contained in its *sura*s as a biblical rewriting of the Samaritan, Jewish and Christian Bibles. By 'biblical' I mean a story or text that is conceived as a religious, authority-bearing revelation. To a scholar of Samaritanism, Judaism or Christianity, it is obvious that Muhammad, in creating the *sura*s of the written Qur'an, among other things, reformed a series of biblical figures and their stories. The earlier, polemical interests of such scholarship had primarily led to fault-finding through a comparison of the Qur'an with the canonical scriptures and their versions. Today, however, a reading formed by the concept of reception history would rather concentrate on the modifying intention behind such revision. Historical failures, such as, for example, the mistaking of Moses' sister Miriam for the mother of Jesus (*sura* 3.35-37, 19.28, and 66.12), were noticed by Christian writers as early as the beginning of the eighth century.[3] Such

---

3. As early as in the beginning of the eighth century John of Damascus (born c. 650/675 and diad before 754), in the part concerning heresies in his great work *The Fountain of Wisdom*, also has a chapter on the heresy of the Ishmaelites, as he names the Muslims. Although John of Damascus is ridiculing and polemical against what he conceived as an expression of Arianism, nevertheless he is well informed,

'mistakes', however, find parallels in the Bible itself. Who, for instance, was it that killed the giant Goliath? Was it David as told in 1 Samuel 17, or was it one of David's men, Elhanan, as in 2 Sam. 21:19 (the 'reconciling' of the two traditions in 1 Chron. 20:5 by letting it be a brother of Goliath that was killed by Elhanan may seem nothing but a miraculous save)?

It is a remarkable fact that the Qur'an apparently does not reflect the period between Jesus and Muhammad himself. Besides genuinely biblical traditions, however, the Qur'an obviously also elaborates on interpretations and traditions known from Old Testament Pseudepigrapha and New Testament Apocrypha and later traditions. Such dependence on pseudepigraphic material is also evident in the New Testament itself, where, for instance, a wandering rock, to be identified as Christ in 1 Cor. 10:4, does not stem from any canonical text, but rather from contemporary Jewish interpretation – it is known from Pseudo-Philo, *LAB* 10:7, but is probably older. Correspondingly, the picture of Abraham as a fanatic monotheist, fighting the idolatry of his father and people, depicted in many *sura*s in the Qur'an, especially in *sura* 21.51-70, is not in accordance with what is told in biblical Genesis, but in turn very similar to what the book of *Jubilees* relates.

One also may ask from where the narrative additions and alterations in the *sura* 12, Joseph, come, if not from retellings circulating in milieus visited by Muhammad. And the only 'deed' of Jesus referred to in the Qur'an, namely his creating a bird out of clay and making it come alive, does not resemble anything in the canonical gospels, but, in turn, reminds of a story from the apocryphal *Gospel of Thomas*, not to be mistaken with the *Gospel of Thomas* from the Nag Hammadi find. Thus, the *sura*s of the Qur'an indirectly reflect various receptions of biblical stories from the centuries from around the beginning of the Common Era and until the time of Muhammad, just as an interaction with Jewish and Christian biblical interpretation found its place in the following centuries, not least thanks to the many converts from these religions to Islam. However, this openness obviously came to an end in the eleventh century, when the reading of Jewish and Christian Scripture by Muslims came to be regarded with suspicion, if not simply forbidden (see Griffith 2012: 140–1).

---

knowing the Qur'an and the early Muslim traditions. See Sahas (1972), who also states (p. 129): 'What distinguishes John of Damascus as a Christian interlocutor in the Muslim-Christian dialogue is that he was motivated to refute Islam as, primarily, a theological heresy and as a "false" religious tradition, whereas the later Byzantine writers were involved in anti-Muslim polemics which, more often than not, had political dimensions and support'.

There has been a long scholarly discussion of how Muhammad became acquainted with biblical and para-biblical traditions. More than a hundred years ago, the Danish Semitist, Frants Buhl (1850–1932), who was also an eminent expert on Islamic studies, wrote about the inclusion of biblical figures in the Qur'an in a dictionary article from 1904:[4]

> It can be viewed as fully certain, that he [Muhammad] has not collected this material by reading books, because at that time, there did not exist any Arabic literature with such content and he was able to read neither the Old nor the New Testament in their original language. What he received, he owed, as also the Qur'an itself and the historical reports suggest, exclusively to conversations with Christians and Jews.

Frants Buhl goes on to claim that Muhammad arbitrarily changed the traditions or distorted them because of either misunderstanding or failing memory. Moreover, the material itself was often dubious, his informants drawing from unclean sources such as Old and New Testament Apocrypha, Talmudic literature and simple novels such as the *The Alexander Novel*.

This may come near to the historical truth. Nevertheless, I think that Frants Buhl, at the same time, narrows our perspective by leaving out the question about the possible theological creativity on behalf of Muhammad. What was his aim in including the biblical stories and figures in his 'prophecies'? Instead of studying eventual discrepancies between supposedly original versions of the traditions and his renderings, one could ask what his intentions in rewriting were, if not to bring – according to his conviction – the true message of the stories. It is possible to consider the changes as Muhammad adapting the traditions to align with the message the he wished to convey. In his own self-perception, he was not a 'rewriter' of existing written traditions, but the recipient of the final revelation, 'God's envoy and the seal of the prophets' (*sura* 33.40). As such, he had access to parts of the heavenly Qur'an only partly revealed to the earlier prophets of which Jesus was the last and greatest before Muhammad himself. This construction, of course, serves the goal of securing the primacy of the Qur'an against the Jewish Holy Scriptures and the Christian Bible. Modern scholarship speaks rather of creative reception and interpretation.[5]

---

4. Buhl 1904: 840 (my translation from Danish).
5. This is also remarked by Neuwirth (2012: 738): 'It is no strong exaggeration… to classify the Qur'ān – in addition to its being prophecy – as "exegesis"'.

4. Jesus in the Qur'anic Rewriting

Readers of the Christian Bible know most of the figures in the Qur'an. However, because of the Qur'anic rewriting, they are all more or less transformed, to serve the special interest of Muhammad's preaching and teaching.[6] The Qur'an, however, does not normally seek to achieve this by expanding the biblical traditions through adding new narrative elements. Where it happens as, for instance, in the introduction of a fourth son of Noah (*sura* 11) and in the *sura* Joseph (*sura* 12), where for once the narrative is given free rein, the non-biblical narrative material often stems from para-biblical writings or traditions either Jewish or Christian.

A very clear example of rewriting in the Qur'an is, of course, the transformation of the Jesus figure.[7] While it retains some of the central gospel features such as the virgin birth, the bringing of the gospel – though without much indication of its content – wonder-working and resurrection, it all the same emphasizes that in all his uniqueness, even as the greatest of the prophets before Muhammad, Jesus is not Son of God. It should be noted, though, that the Qur'anic story about Jesus never gives the impression of employing written sources other than the heavenly book.

A series of places mentioning Jesus simply offer a short characteristic of him as prophet, son of Mary, and receiver of the Spirit of God (for instance 2.87, 136, 253). His being one of the prophets is repeated several times (2.136; 3.84; 4.163; 6.85; 33.7; 42.13; 57.27), and twice it is mentioned that he is one of those with whom God has made a covenant. At several places, we find summaries of Jesus' activities. The first time, 3.48-49, occurs in words uttered by Jesus himself:[8]

> [49] I have come to you with a sign from your Lord: I will make the shape of a bird for you out of clay, then breathe into it and, with God's permission, it will become a real bird; I will heal the blind and the leper, and bring the dead back to life with God's permission; I will tell you what you may eat and what you may store up in your houses. Another possible translation is 'to tell you what you eat and what you store…' There truly is a sign for you in this, if you are believers. [50] I have come to confirm the truth of the Torah which preceded me, and to make some things lawful to you which used to

---

6. See, for a nearly complete overview of the Qur'anic reception of the biblical gallery of characters, Müller 2012, an article which, regrettably, only exists in Danish.

7. The following reproduces the paragraph about Jesus in the article mentioned in the note above (Müller 2012: 408–11). Of the relevant literature I only mention Parrinder 1965; Räisänen 1971; and Robinson 2003.

8. The translation here and in the following is according to Abdel Haleem 2010.

be forbidden. I have come to you with a sign from your Lord. Be mindful of God, obey me: ⁵¹God is my Lord and your Lord, so serve Him – that is a straight path.

In the following (3.52-53) it is told that Jesus feels people's disbelief and asks who helps him. Suddenly, the disciples turn up declaring: 'We will be God's helpers; we believe in God – witness our devotion to Him. ⁵³Lord, we believe in what You have revealed and we follow the messenger: record us among those who bear witness [to the Truth].'

Sura 5 also contains two other statements about Jesus spoken by God himself. Thus in 5.46-47:

> ⁴⁶We sent Jesus, son of Mary, in their footsteps, to confirm the Torah that had been sent before him: We gave him the Gospel with guidance, light, and confirmation of the Torah already revealed – a guide and lesson for those who take heed of God. ⁴⁷So let the followers of the Gospel judge according to what God has sent down in it. Those who do not judge according to what God has revealed are lawbreakers.

The description in 5.110-111 is more elaborate and repeats motifs to be found in other places:

> ¹¹⁰Then God will say, 'Jesus, son of Mary! Remember My favour to you and to your mother: how I strengthened you with the holy spirit, so that you spoke to people in your infancy and as a grown man; how I taught you the Scripture and wisdom, the Torah and the Gospel; how, by My leave, you fashioned the shape of a bird out of clay, breathed into it, and it became, by My leave, a bird; how, by My leave, you healed the blind person and the leper; how, by My leave, you brought the dead back to life; how I restrained the Children of Israel from [harming] you when you brought them clear signs, and those of them who disbelieved said, "This is clearly nothing but sorcery"; ¹¹¹and how I inspired the disciples to believe in Me and My messengers – they said, "We believe and bear witness that we devote ourselves [to God]".'

The motif that Jesus has received the Gospel also turns up in 57.27, and the idea that he has got clear evidence and has been strengthened by the Holy Spirit is repeated in 2.87, 253 and 43.63, where also Wisdom is mentioned. The story of Jesus creating a bird of clay and giving it life has – as mentioned above – an 'original' in the *Gospel of Thomas* 2, where, however, it pertains to the child Jesus and to twelve sparrows which he even causes to fly.

Sura 5 has its name, 'The Table', because of what is told in 112-115:

[112]When the disciples said, 'Jesus, son of Mary, can your Lord send down a feast to us from heaven?' he said, 'Beware of God if you are true believers'. [113]They said, 'We wish to eat from it; to have our hearts reassured; to know that you have told us the truth; and to be witnesses of it'. [114]Jesus, son of Mary, said, 'Lord, send down to us a feast from heaven so that we can have a festival – the first and last of us – and a sign from You. Provide for us: You are the best provider.' [115]God said, 'I will send it down to you, but anyone who disbelieves after this will be punished with a punishment that I will not inflict on anyone else in the world'.

This story seems to reflect the institution of the Last Supper, mixed with elements from the 'Eucharist speech' in John 6.

It is remarkable that the Qur'an, with the few exceptions mentioned above, does not include Jesus sayings.[9] The Gospel is something that Jesus received; it is not, as in the New Testament, the message about him. We hear nearly nothing about the content of his teaching and preaching, nor what his distinct contribution as a prophet was, other than being the last of the great prophets before Muhammad. The nearest we come to the 'content' of the Gospel is perhaps in *sura* 57.27, where the statement about God giving Jesus the Gospel is followed by the declaration: 'We gave him the Gospel and put compassion and mercy into the hearts of his followers'. However, it is followed by the statement: 'But monasticism was something they invented – We did not ordain it for them – only to seek (Alternatively, "only that they should seek") God's pleasure, and even so, they did not observe it properly'.

It is also part of the Qur'anic picture of Jesus that he is not killed by the Jews.[10] In 4.157-159 we read that the Jews said,

[157] 'We have killed the Messiah, Jesus, son of Mary, the Messenger of God'. (They did not kill him, nor did they crucify him, though it was made to appear like that to them; those that disagreed about him are full of doubt, with no knowledge to follow, only supposition: they certainly did not kill him – [158]God raised him up to Himself. God is almighty and wise. [159]There is not one of the People of the Book who will not believe in [Jesus] before his death, and on the Day of Resurrection he will be a witness against them.)

---

9. This is in contrast to the relatively extensive Jesus-tradition that arose later in Islam. See for instance the collection edited and translated in Khalidi 2003.

10. The medieval Muslim rewriting of especially the Gospel of Matthew under the title *Gospel of Barnabas* solves this problem by the introduction of four angels helping Jesus away, while the traitor, Judas, is changed by God to look like Jesus and so himself suffering the death he had planned for Jesus.

That God took Jesus directly up to himself in this way reflects a docetic Christology and resembles what we find in gnostic texts. On the other hand we see in 5.75 an anti-docetic feature in a remark about Jesus and Mary as both taking food.

At the same time as Jesus occupies an exceptional place in the Qur'an, it is also emphasized that he is not divine, but a servant, made of earth just as Adam (see *sura* 3.59). In *sura* 4.171-172, it is said:

> [171]People of the Book, do not go to excess in your religion, and do not say anything about God except the truth: the Messiah, Jesus, son of Mary, was nothing more than a messenger of God, His word, directed to Mary, a spirit from Him. So believe in God and His messengers and do not speak of a 'Trinity' – stop [this], that is better for you – God is only one God, He is far above having a son, everything in the heavens and earth belongs to Him and He is the best one to trust. [172]The Messiah would never disdain to be a servant of God, nor would the angels who are close to Him.

Further, one could also further refer to *sura* 5.72-5, 9.30-31 and 43.57-59 in this regard. Finally, in the Qur'an, we find Jesus himself openly confessing this (*sura* 5.116-118):

> [116]When God says, 'Jesus, son of Mary, did you say to people, "Take me and my mother as two gods alongside God"?' he will say, 'May You be exalted! I would never say what I had no right to say – if I had said such a thing You would have known it: You know all that is within me, though I do not know what is within You, You alone have full knowledge of things unseen – [117]I told them only what You commanded me to: 'Worship God, my Lord and your Lord'. I was a witness over them during my time among them. Ever since You took my soul, You alone have been the watcher over them: You are witness to all things [118]and if You punish them, they are Your servants; if You forgive them, You are the Almighty, the Wise.'

When Jesus finally speaks in the Qur'an, just as in the Gospel of John, it is essentially about himself.

5. Conclusion

The extensive reception of stories and characters in the Qur'an, from the Samaritan and Jewish Holy Scriptures and the Christian Bible, shows that the forming of religious consciousness and beliefs took place primarily in the manner of a transforming reinterpretation of existing tradition. In this connection the employment of the genre or interpretation strategy known as 'rewritten Bible', especially in the version of 'biblical rewriting', intending to produce new authoritative religious texts, is helpful, not only in perceiving what is going on in the New Testament, but also in the Qur'an. In both cases, existing religious or theological universes are transformed in several respects, the most important being that a new character of fundamental significance is introduced with the effect of changing the existing hierarchy. From the perspective of the understanding formed in the tradition of historical criticism and its repeated question about the referentiality of what is narrated, this transforming change in our perspective is a challenge, not to say a problem. However, when scholarship takes into consideration that religious truth never converges with historical truth but always arises out of an interpretation of certain events, and that this interpretation can take place in the shape of story-telling, many things become more understandable. It is extremely important not to mistake story for history. The religious message is not necessarily subverted by the eventual fictionality of its narrative. It is the intended message that determines what is to be told and how. The *tertium comparationis* between history and story is not the historical facts that can be proved to lie within the narrative, but the belief and behavior the message intends to create in its audience. That becomes far clearer in the Qur'an than in the Samaritan and Jewish Scriptures or the Christian Bible, as the Qur'an does not, itself, consist of a continuing narrative or a coherent salvation history. Rather, such is presupposed in a way that often demands more knowledge than what is contributed by the *suras* of the Qur'an.

Because of the relationship between history and creative interpretation, it is in my mind the intended effect on belief and behavior that should rouse our interest when comparing the traditions of the Pentateuch, the TANAK, the New Testament and the Qur'an. Such an approach will further make it clear that no generation is excluded from reinterpreting its traditions in a responsible way, and that nobody can reinterpret traditions without relating them to their own horizons of understanding. When such 'rewriting' no longer produces new authoritative religious writings, the role will be given over to preaching and teaching, which is fully aware of its character as an interpretive discourse. The Samaritan and Jewish Holy Scriptures, the Christian Bible and the Qur'an all live through their interpreters – and no religion is neither better nor worse than their interpreters.

Bibliography

Abdel Haleem, M. A. S., trans. (2010), *The Qur'an*, Oxford: Oxford University Press.
Buhl, P. (1904), In *Kirke-Leksikon for Norden, vol. II*, 839–41, Aarhus: Albert Bayer.
Frei, H. W. (1974), *The Eclipse of Biblical Narrative: A Study in Eighteenth and Nineteenth Century Hermeneutics*, New Haven and London: Yale University Press.

Griffith, S. H. (2012), 'The Bible in Arabic', in R. Marsden and E. A. Matter (eds), *The New Cambridge History of the Bible: Vol. 2, From 600 to 1450*, 123–42, Cambridge: Cambridge University Press.

Khalidi, T. (2003), *The Muslim Jesus: Sayings and Stories in Islamic Literature*, Cambridge, MA: Harvard University Press.

Müller, M. (2012), 'Koranen som "bibelsk genskrivning"', in J. Høgenhaven and M. Müller (eds), *Bibelske genskrivninger*, FBE 17, 377–412, Copenhagen: Museum Tusculanum Forlag.

Müller, M. (2014), 'The New Testament Gospels as Biblical Rewritings: On the Question of Referentiality', *StTh*, 68: 21–40.

Neuwirth, A. (2012), 'The Qur'ān and the Bible', in R. Marsden and E. A. Matter (eds), *The New Cambridge History of the Bible, Vol. 2: From 600 to 1450*, 735–52, Cambridge: Cambridge University Press.

Parrinder, G. (1965), *Jesus in the Qur'an*, London: Sheldon Press.

Räisänen, H. (1971), *Das Koranische Jesusbild*, Helsinki: Schriften des Finnischen Gesellschaft für Missiologie und Ökumenik.

Robinson, N. (2003), 'Jesus', in Jane McAuliffe (ed.), *Encyclopaedia of the Qur'an, Vol. III*, 7–20, Leiden: E. J. Brill.

Sahas, D. J. (1972), *John of Damascus on Islam: The 'Heresy of the Ishmaelites'*, Leiden: E. J. Brill.

Vermes, G. (1973 [1961]), *Scripture and Tradition in Judaism*, SPB 4, Leiden: E. J. Brill.

Part 3

BIBLICAL NARRATIVES

The Food of Life and the Food of Death in Texts from the Old Testament and the Ancient Near East*

Ingrid Hjelm

Johann Wolfgang von Goethe, who lived from 1749 to 1832, pronounced that 'Anyone who cannot give an account to oneself of the past three thousand years remains in darkness, without experience, living from day to day'.[1] One must remember that Goethe's dictum was uttered before the archaeological discoveries of the northern and eastern Orient from the mid-nineteenth century, but after the Egyptian and Hellenistic booty from Napoleon's wars gave inspiration to the ever more intensified search for historical warrant in biblical tradition. This search concerns not only the historical validity of the Bible's narratives *per se*, but also its reception as basis for theology and dogmatism. Who meant and said or wrote what and when? Goethe's 3,000 years take him back to biblical Israel's golden age, the settlement of the tribes in the Promised Land and the fulfilment of Yahweh's promise to the Patriarchs. It is biblical Israel, and not Greece, the Near East or Palestine as such, which is the cradle of European history. This has been convincingly argued by Keith Whitelam in his

---

* It is my outmost pleasure to contribute to the celebration of Thomas's more than 50 years of pursuit of knowledge and wisdom, which he has graciously distributed in innumerable lectures and publications worldwide. As founder and editor of the Copenhagen Seminar Series (1996–2016), he has furthered the works of many scholars. This article is a translation with minor revisions of Hjelm 2015, which is reproduced here with permission of the University of Copenhagen's Faculty of Theology.

1. 'Wer nicht von dreitausend Jahren sich weiss Rechenschaft zu geben bleib im Dunkeln unerfahren. Mag von Tag zu Tage leben' (Goethe 1819). The translation into English is mine.

much criticized book, *The Invention of Ancient Israel* from 1996. The book's most important matter, however, is represented by its subtitle: *The Silencing of Palestinian History*. This silencing results from the development of a Western self-understanding that based itself in an ecclesiastical authorization of biblical narrative and in biblical scholars' reconstruction of an ancient Israel that might serve Western identity and ideology. None of these narratives represent the real and complex history of the region or take seriously the fact that the purpose of biblical narratives was to develop and prescribe contemporary theology rather than being history writing in a modern sense of the term. The adoption and development of the 'Bible' in Western culture have impacted interpretation of some of the most valued biblical texts and the Old Testament as a whole.

The title 'the Old Testament' in itself designates that it has been replaced or fulfilled with something new, 'the New Testament', an expression of a Christian covenant that artificially combines Jer. 31:31's new covenant for Israel and Judah with Isaiah's vision for all nations wandering to Zion (Isa. 2; 60 and 66). Anne Gudme and Jesper Høgenhaven's very fine presentation of Old Testament exegesis in *Fønix* 2009 gives examples of such interpretations, with their reading of Genesis 2–3's Garden story, which draws on the New Testament, dogmatics and practical theology. The narrative is clearly mythological and, as stated by the authors, less oriented towards the Fall paradigm, which its reception traditionally claims. Nevertheless, their interpretation remains within the 'Christian' 'sin and redemption' pattern in a demythologized socio-anthropological reading, which seeks to explain humanity's hardship in an unwelcoming world. This reception's authoritative status is most obvious in dogmatic theology's thematic understanding of Genesis 1–3 as 'creation and fall'. One may ask if this traditional interpretation discloses the Garden story's theological potential. We may perhaps gain a better grip on the text by looking behind the myth and drawing on its antecedents and function in the intellectual world of the ancient Near East.

I here offer an interpretation that reads Genesis 1–3 together with the Mesopotamian myth of Adapa, the book of Proverb's discourse on Wisdom and Folly and 1 Samuel 25's story about Nabal and Abigail, focusing on how these texts play with motifs of wisdom, divinity and immortality.[2]

---

2. My former students, now Cand. theol. Jonatan Dyre and Cand. theol. Lotte Broberg, made me aware of the possibilities of an intertextual reading of these biblical texts.

The Myth of Adapa

Libraries already existed in Sumer in the fourth millennium BCE. These were unknown to Goethe. As mentioned above, it was ancient Egypt's literary, pictorial and cultural world that first became part of Western culture, leading to a strong interest in the Moses tradition's connection to Egypt and Egyptian parallels to the biblical creation stories. With intense archaeological activity in Mesopotamia, Syria and Palestine since the middle of the nineteenth century, and a better understanding of the Egyptian material, biblical scholars received a lot of new material to work with. From the libraries in Mesopotamia we now have the well-known creation myths, *Enuma Elish*, *Atrahasis* and *Gilgamesh*, which all have strong parallels to Old Testament myths and ideas that we find in Genesis 1–11. A lesser known myth is the Mesopotamian *Adapa* myth, which is known from the Egyptian El-Amarna archive (fr. B; fourteenth century BCE), and the Assyrian King Ashurbanipal's library in Nineveh (frr. A and C-D; seventh century BCE).[3] Up to now, the tale has been found in six Akkadian fragments, of which the Amarna fragment is the longest. It lacks the introduction (fr. A), and possibly also the ending found in fragment D. Recently, a Sumerian version from the old Babylonian period has appeared. By and large, it parallels the later versions mentioned above (Cavigneaux and Al-Ravi 1993). Apart from these fragments, we also find several references to the myth in Mesopotamian literature (Picchioni 1981: 82–101; Wilcke 1991: 263–9; cf. Mettinger 2007: 100).

In fragment A, l. 1-21 (*ANET*: 101), the story begins with a description of Adapa as the wisest (*atra-ḫasīsu*) of the seven semi-divine sages (*apkallu*) from before the flood. His creator, [the water god] Ea [father of Marduk] perfected him with wide understanding to disclose the design of the land. He has given him wisdom, but not eternal life (l. 4). Ea has created him as a model of men, whose command no one can corrupt. He is blameless, pure of hands and responsible for the daily offering and rites on behalf of Ea in Eridu [near the Persian Gulf]. One day, when Adapa is in his sailboat catching fish for the offering, the wind rises and he drifts into open sea. Here fr. A breaks off, but fortunately

---

3. The fragments A-D can be found in E. A. Speiser's translation in *ANET* (Pritchard 1969: 101–3). A recent English translation of all the Akkadian fragments can be found in Izre'el 2001. Summaries can be found in Foster 1997: 449. References to other editions can be found in Liverani 2004: 4–5 and Mettinger 2007: 100.

fr. B continues the narrative to its apparent conclusion.[4] The south wind (*Shutu*) casts him overboard and Adapa curses the wind and breaks its wing. The stilling of the wind for seven days causes drought, hunger and disease. Anu [god of the cosmos] summons him to explain his act to the heavenly council of gods. Ea advises Adapa to appear in mourning garb and with unkempt hair before Tammuz and Gizzida [gods of vegetation], who have left Eridu and may be persuaded to speak 'a good word' to Anu when they see him in mourning. Furthermore, when Anu offers him bread and water, he should refuse, because, says Ea, it is the food of death (*a-ka-la ša mu-ti*) and the water of death (*me-e mu-u-ti*), but he shall accept a garment and oil for his body. It goes as predicted by Ea. Adapa explains how he was cast into the sea and spent the rest of the day in the world of the fish. Tammuz and Gizzida plead 'mercy', and Anu takes pity on him. He considers what to do to a man, an uncouth mortal, to whom Ea has disclosed what pertains to heaven and earth. He decides to bring him the food and water of life, as well as clothing and oil. Adapa accepts the clothing and oil, but refuses to eat and drink, because Ea had forbidden it. Anu laughs at Adapa's ignorance and sends him back to earth:

> His [Anu's] heart grew calm, he became quiet.
> 'Why did Ea disclose what pertains to heaven and
> Earth to an uncouth mortal,
> And give him a violent temper?
> Since he has so treated him,
> (75) What, for our part, shall we do for him?
> Bring him food of life, let him eat.'
>
> They brought him food of life (*a-ka-al ba-la-ṭi*), he did not eat.
> They brought him waters of life (*me-e ba-la-ṭi*), he did not drink.
> They brought him a garment, he put it on.
> (80) They brought him oil, he anointed himself.
>
> Anu stared and burst out laughing at him,
> 'Come now, Adapa, why did you not eat or drink?
> Won't you live? Are not people to be im[mor]tal?'

---

4. Although fr. B is the earlier, both Izre'el (2001: 111–19) and Mettinger (2007: 101) consider that fr. A must belong to the original narrative, because of its focus on wisdom and eternal life.

Ea my lord told me,
'You must not eat, you must not drink'.

(85) 'Let them take him and [ret]urn him to his
earth'.[5]

Fragment D from Ashurbanipal's library contains an incomplete continuation, which may suggest that the myth has been used as an incantation against sickness, because the curse of Eridu caused by the absence of the vegetation gods, Tammuz and Gizzida, is lifted (Liverani 2004: 4). The fragment also contains a critique of Ea for exceeding Anu's command:

Anu laughed aloud at the doing of Ea [saying]:
'Of the gods of heaven and earth, as many as there be,
Who [ever] gave such a command,
So as to make his own command exceed the command of Anu?'[6]

This continuation, which is missing in the other fragments, adds an element to the myth that presents Ea as revolting against Anu. This detail is significant when reading the myth in the light of Genesis 2–3. Attempts at interpreting Ea as consciously misleading Adapa in order to keep his humanity and prevent him from gaining divinity so that he may remain in the service of the temple at Eridu, presents Ea as a trickster figure. Such is also Ea's role in tradition and legends (esp. *Atrahasis* and *Gilgamesh*): 'the cleverest of gods, the one who can plan and organize and think of ways out when no one can', 'who persuades, tricks and evades to gain his ends' (Jacobson 1976: 116). It was Ea who came up with the idea of creating humans when the gods got tired of working. Against the will of the gods, he also saved humankind when their increasing noise forced the gods to annihilate the entire creation with a flood, from which Ea saved a single wise man, Atrahasis/Utnapishtim. Instead, he suggested ways of limiting human life (Mettinger 2007: 105). This cunning, which is a general characteristic of Ea, fits badly the suggestion by some scholars that Ea had misread the situation and expected that Anu would give Adapa a death penalty.[7] Fragment D in *ANET*'s version can be read as a confirmation of Ea's cunning, which ensured that Adapa remained in his office of priesthood forever (l. 10-11). However, the text is uncertain

---

5. Foster's section of fr. B in Hallo (1997: 445). Reproduced with permission – see bibliography for full details.
6. Fr. D in *ANET*, 102–3.
7. References to the bibliography in Liverani (2004: 5).

and full of ambiguities. Based on Izre'el's translation, 'Anu se[t] Adapa at his service [...] he established his freedom from Ea' (l. 9-10; Izre'el 2001: 39), we rather find a structural similarity with Genesis 3's curse and dethronement of the snake, suggesting that Ea did not get away with challenging the supreme god.

Ea's role reflects the ambiguity in portraits of the snake in Egyptian and Mesopotamian iconography and literature: as threat and salvation, fertility and chaos, life and death, rebirth, protection and sexuality. We also find such ambiguity in Num. 21:8-9, when Moses orders the Israelites to make a copper snake and put it on a stake so that they will survive a snake bite. The snake is endowed with supernatural powers, and it is telling that the Hebrew word נחש also means to divinize and make sorcery. Snakes were symbols of eternity, because they could renew their skin, but snakes can be deadly, so they were also symbols of death, disaster and evil. The Old Testament does not view snakes as representing wisdom and this is not the role of the snake in Genesis 3. Its role is as the shrewdest of creatures, the seducer and the trickster, which is not recognised until it is too late. It is hardly incidental that it is a snake that snatches the plant of life, by Gilgamesh called 'man becomes young in old age', when he is momentarily unaware. As a mockery, it leaves its skin behind (Gilgamesh XI; *ANET*, 96; Westenholz and Westenholz 1997: 134).

Limits of Divinity

Both the myth of Adapa and Genesis 2–3 seek to answer questions about man's divinity. Liverani is hardly right when he argues that Adapa is not a human archetype (Liverani 2004: 17). Adapa is presented as a model for man in fr. A, l. 6, and Anu calls him an 'uncouth mortal' (l. 72 in Foster 1997) and a 'worthless human' (*ANET* fragment B, l. 57). It is true that Adapa is a priest and Gilgamesh a royal figure, as pointed out by Liverani in his argument against seeing these narratives as concerning man's immortality. Gilgamesh, however, goes to the ends of the world to get the plant of life needed to revive his non-royal friend Enkidu, not himself.

In the myth of Adapa, we find a priest, who is exceedingly wise and associates with the gods. He provides his gods' food, but does that mean that he is allowed to eat of the food himself? According to Liverani's analysis of hospitality rules in the ancient Near East, Adapa would have moved from the outer to the inner realm if he had eaten with the gods. He would have become untouchable, 'because the gods – like men – could not permit someone to whom they had given bread and water to die' (Liverani 2004: 17). Adapa had performed a divine act when he broke the wing of the south wind, and he might be considered a god. It is therefore also possible to view his act as a challenge to Ea's authority: Who controls the world? The test with the food and water provides the answer. Does Adapa's wisdom equal the wisdom of the gods and can he see through their plans? The result is that he could not: Ea, the trickster has misled him. In light of fr. D, however, we might think that this later version rather sees Ea as having fallen victim to his own hubris.

In Genesis' Garden story, the holiest of the temple is replaced by the divinity's private garden, where humankind associates with the god. Does that make humans divine, and where is the border between god and man? With Adam's rejection of animals as fitting company and the creation of a woman as his equal, it is established that 'man' is essentially different from 'animal'. Now it is time to establish the status of 'man' in relation to the divine. The distinction is already clear: it is the difference between the divine creator and the created human as gardener of the creation. However, as said by McKinlay (1999: 74): '…in dependency there is already a power differential'. The garden is for all and everyone, but eating of its produce is differentiated. A small distinction, one may say, when man can eat from 'every' tree, except one: the Tree of Knowledge of Good and Evil (Gen. 2:16-17). The sequence 'good *and* evil' (טוב ורע) is not incidental! Far too many interpreters see the idiom as an expression of totality: alpha and omega, absolute knowledge, etc., but from Thompson's interpretation we have learned that the woman already knows 'the good' before she eats (Thompson 2009: 143–4). The author not only plays with his/her characters, but also his/her readers. When the snake says that 'When you eat of it your eyes will be opened and you will be like god, knowing good and evil' (כאלוהים ידעי טוב ורע; alternatively: 'as gods who know good and evil'; Gen. 3:5),[8] Eve immediately sees and judges the tree's qualities as delightful (נחמד) and good (טוב) (Gen. 3:6). From this follows that in addition to the 'good' that man already knows, the tree will provide knowledge of the 'evil' man doesn't know.

There are, however, two trees in the garden, which are not intended for man, but the man and his woman are tricked by Yahweh Elohim to focus on the tree of wisdom from which they must not eat, lest they die (Gen. 2:16-17). The snake plays Ea's role, questions the god's ordinance and turns focus away from the issue of death to the issue of divine wisdom. The elusive Tree of Life, mentioned first and last (Gen. 2:9 and 3:22) in the narrative, is the drama's framework and essential theme.

8. Generally, I use my own translations from *Biblia Hebraica Stuttgartensia* (Elliger and Rudolf 1990).

We know the result: Eve, who already knew the 'good', comes to know 'evil' as well. The Tree of Knowledge became the tree of death and we are confronted with the motif of two sorts of food from the Adapa myth: for life or for death: tree of life or tree of death. Could Adapa see through the play of the gods? Could man and woman, in their seeming divinity, formed by the god and with the god's spirit in them, see through their lord, god's and the snake's ploy? They could not and, like Adapa, they are cast back to the earth.

The Book of Proverbs

The problem of seeing through and judging the agenda of gods is also central in the book of Proverb's discourse on Wisdom (חכמה) and Folly (אשת כסילות) in chs. 1–9. Research has generally characterized the two figures as positive and negative characters respectively (Camp 2000: 75). Since the term 'a foolish woman' (אשת כסילות) only appears in Prov. 9:13 it is usually interpreted in light of the book's numerous utterances about the foreign woman (אשה זרה / אשה נכריה), whom man shall be aware not to visit (Prov. 2:16; 6:24; 7:5).[9] Proverbs' use of matrimonial metaphors associates female wisdom with the wise and faithful wife (Prov. 5:15-19), while the foreign and foolish woman is associated with prostitution, harlotry (זונה; Prov. 6:26) and adultery (נאף; Prov. 6:32). This dualism presents Wisdom as creation, love, truth, social order, wisdom and life, while Folly represents falsehood, folly, silliness, social disorder and death. Reflecting Ps. 1:1's 'blessed man' (אשרי האיש), Prov. 3:13 considers the man happy who has found wisdom (אשרי אדם מצא הכמה). In addition to Wisdom's extraordinary qualifications as provider of a long and pleasant life, riches, honor and happiness, worth more than silver, gold and pearls (vv. 14-17), she, echoing Genesis 2–3, is 'the tree of life' (עץ חיים היא) to those who take hold of her (v. 18).

But how do the two women use their power to catch the men, and where does their power come from? Is it only Folly who plays the role of trickster and lures the men into her realm?

Proverbs 8:1-4 pictures a scene in which Wisdom addresses her victim. From the highest points along the way, from the crossroads, from beside the gates, and from the entrance of the portals she cries to the men (אישים) and to the humans (בני אדם) about the wisdom she offers: 'Oh simple ones (פתאים) learn prudence; oh foolish ones (כסילים) get understanding' (v. 5; cf. also Prov. 1:22). In contrasting terms, she characterizes her talk

---

9. Discourses on the foreign woman are found in Prov. 5:1-23; 6:20-35 and 7:1-17.

and words as right, righteous, straight, true and wise for those who seek knowledge, versus wicked, twisted, shrewd and perverted, which is the speech that her lips hate (vv. 6-13). Wisdom cries out aloud everywhere, in the streets, in the market places, on the top of the walls and in the city gates (Prov. 1:20-21). She seems as restless as the foreign and seductive woman, who cannot rest at home but lies in wait in the street, in the market and at every corner to seduce men (Prov. 7:11-12). The author of Proverbs 1–9 has consciously created linguistic ambiguity about the positive and negative figures by using identical terms for both (Aletti 1977: 132–4; cf. Camp 2000: 76). Proverbs 4:8 assures the young man that Wisdom will honor him if he embraces her (חבק), while in Prov. 5:20 the speaker asks why on earth he should embrace (חבק) a foreign woman's bosom. In Prov. 3:18 and 4:13, the young man is advised to hold on (חזק) to Wisdom, while in 7:13 the foreign woman seizes (חזק) him and entices him with sex. Both women want to infatuate him with love and passion (Prov. 5:19; 7:18). Both women encourage him to accept and increase (לקח) wisdom and understanding, but the words of the foreign woman are seductive (Prov. 7:21), her lips drip honey and her speech is smoother than oil (Prov. 5:3). Both women will urge the man to choose the right way, but Wisdom's path leads to life (Prov. 4:10; 8:35; 9:11) while Folly's leads to death (Prov. 2:18; 5:5; 7:27; cf. also the two ways in Deut. 30:15-20).

We are now ready to look at the great scene of comparison in Proverbs 9 where Wisdom and Folly issue invitations to a feast in their respective houses. Wisdom has built her house; she has set up the seven pillars (Prov. 9:1), which alternatively can be translated 'the seven have set up its foundations' (Greenfield 1985), alluding to the Mesopotamian *apkallu* tradition's seven sages, bringers of civilization and culture. Wisdom's self-designation as אמון ('confidante') in 8:30 may also be a variant of the Akkadian *ummānu*, which means adviser, workman, artist or sage. In the *Poem of Erra* we find a combination of these terms (Kvanvig 2011: 450). The number of seven symbolizes totality and grandeur (Clifford 1999: 106). Loretz (1990: 38 n. 29) has suggested that it is a late addition with a hidden reference to Proverb's seven headlines. Wisdom has slaughtered her beasts, mixed the wine, set the table and sent out young girls (נערות) to shout from the highest places in the town: 'Whoever is simple let him turn in here' (מי פתי יסר הנה). Wisdom herself says to he who is without sense (חסר לב; can also mean 'lacks courage'): 'Come eat of my bread and drink of the wine I have mixed. Leave simpleness (פתאים)[10] and live, and walk in the way of insight' (vv. 4-6). Here the narrative breaks off to give

---

10. Literally, the word means 'the simple ones'/'the inexperienced'. The apparatus suggests other forms of the word based on earlier witnesses.

proverbial admonition and warning (vv. 7-12), which separates the section on Wisdom from the section on Folly (vv. 13-18). In contrast to the considerate preparation and order in Wisdom's house, Folly (אשת כסילות) is characterized as a restless, seductive or noisy (המיה)[11] and imprudent woman (פתיות)[12] who understands nothing (בל ידעה מה). She has no girls to send, but sits at the entrance to her house, on a chair at the heights of the village, and shouts to those who pass by, those walking straight on their way: 'Whoever is simple let him turn in here' (מי פתי יסר הנה). And to him without sense (חסר לב), she says: 'Stolen water (מים גנובים) is sweet and hidden / secret bread (לחם סתרים) is pleasant'. As an antithetic echo of v. 6, the narrator comments in v. 18: 'but he does not know that the dead (רפאים) are there and that her guests are in the valley of death/Sheol' (בעמקי שאול; cf. also 5:5). With this commentary, the author has pointed to the fact, which unfortunately many commentators miss, that the passersby cannot see the difference between the women. As the woman in Genesis 3 couldn't see the wood for trees, also Proverbs' play with destinies offers the possibility that what seems positive is in fact the opposite. Fox's rationalistic interpretation is wishful thinking when arguing that the eating in Proverbs is 'second course eating' because man can make use of the wisdom from Eden (Fox 1997: 622). The text does not imply such an understanding. The unmasking comes from the eating, but then it is too late. Maybe that is the reason that Folly, in all texts save this one, is called the 'foreign woman', because such may be recognizable. The essence of the text may not be a distinction between wisdom and folly, but rather a warning against the dangerous other, as in Prov. 5:15: 'Drink water from your own cistern, flowing water from your own well'. In *Gilgamesh*, the role of the dangerous other is played by Shamkhat, the prostitute, who civilizes Enkidu during six days and seven nights of lovemaking (tabl. I, l. 183-89; Westenholz and Westenholz 1997: 66). After this the animals do not recognize him and will not share their food with him, but he does not yet know the food of man. Then the prostitute opens her mouth and speaks to Enkidu: 'Eat the bread, Enkidu, for it is the symbol of life; drink the beer as it is the custom of the country'.[13] Although the bread is the symbol of life, it does not give eternal life. When Enkidu dies later in the story, Gilgamesh does not succeed in getting the plant of life and reviving

---

11. The verb can mean both, because its basic meaning is 'hum'/'buzz' → be noisy. It is used to describe sounds of bees, bears and pigeons.

12. Notice that it is the same root as in v. 6.

13. This scene is found only in the old Babylonian OB Penn tablet II, l. 55-67; cf. Westenholz and Westenholz 1997: 145–50; *ANET*, 77.

his friend. The book of Proverbs has set a contrast between the food for life and the food for death, which related to Wisdom and Folly might have had the power to abolish Genesis' deathly wisdom. The book's realism, however, remains intact: embracing Wisdom leads to a long life (3:16).

There is, however, more at play in Proverbs and Genesis' Garden story, for who has planted the trees, created the snake, set the table, and who are, in fact, the women? In order to answer these questions, I will follow McKinlay (1999) and Broberg (2014) and include the story about Nabal and Abigail in 1 Samuel 25 in my examination.

1 Samuel 25

The narrative about Nabal, Abigail and David is interpolated between two narratives about David's clashes with Saul in chapters 24 and 26. Together these narratives form a triad, which has the purpose of settling David's royal dignity through three temptations.

1. In ch. 24, David abstains from killing Saul and only stealthily cuts off the skirt of his robe, saying to his men that Yahweh forbid that he [and they] should lay his hand on Yahweh's anointed (1 Sam. 24:7).
2. In ch. 25, David abstains from killing Nabal and his household and he blesses Abigail for having kept him from bloodguilt (דמים: 1 Sam. 25:33) and self-revenge.
3. In ch. 26, David once again abstains from killing Saul and only takes his spear and jar of water, saying that Yahweh forbid that he should lay his hand on Yahweh's anointed (1 Sam. 26:11, 23).

With the passing of these trials, David's royal assignment is secured. It began with the covenant he made with Saul's son Jonathan (1 Sam. 18:3-4; 20:12-17; 23:16-18), which was secured in Saul's inauguration of David as his successor (1 Sam. 24:21) and in his blessing of him (1 Sam. 26:25). The narratives can be read as a process of development during which David matures for his assignment. Along the way, he is tempted by Folly (Nabal)[14] who is hard and evil (קשה ורע; 1 Sam. 25:3), and advised by Wisdom (Abigail) who is wise and beautiful (טובת שכל ויפת תאר; 1 Sam. 25:3), to choose whether to accept or reject the food he is offered.

---

14. The root נבל has many meanings, but foolish, worthless and godless are the most common in the OT. The word can, however, also mean 'noble'. Hebrew usually use feminine endings ה-, ות- or ית- for concepts, which one can observe also in Abigail's interpretation of Nabal's name (1 Sam. 24:25).

The story goes like this: Nabal is a wealthy farmer who also has far away possessions. During wintertime, David and his men 'guarded'[15] Nabal's shepherds and flocks. At springtime's shearing festival, David sends ten of his men to Nabal to claim payment for their service. Nabal refuses to pay and pretends not to know David, whom he indirectly calls a runaway slave (vv. 10-11). Hearing about the incident, David arms 400 men (v. 13) and swears to kill every male (literally: 'everyone who pisses against the wall'; משתין בקיר[16]) in Nabal's house (v. 22). With his rough expression David's utterance alludes to v. 3's designation of Nabal as doggish (כלבי). In the meantime a servant of Nabal has told Abigail about the meeting between David's men and her husband. He appeals to her to take action, because the evil will make an end (כלתה הרעה) of Nabal's house because he is so ill-natured and stupid (הוא בן בליעל) that no one can speak to him (v. 17). Without her husband's knowledge, Abigail takes a huge amount of bread, wine, sheep, grain, raisins and fig cakes and loads them on asses, which she sends on ahead (cf. also Jacob's reconciliation with Esau and his 400 men in Gen. 32–33).[17] Meeting David, she completely submits herself, takes the blame upon herself and makes excuses for her evil husband (איש בליעל), whose name reflects his character: 'Fool is his name and folly is with him' (נבל שמו ונבלה עמו; v. 25).

Abigail's further speech to David contains three 'now' (ועתה) sentences in vv. 26-27, appealing to him to avoid bloodguilt, wishing that his enemies be like Nabal and urging him to accept the gift for his men. In vv. 28-31, she adds four 'prophetic' utterances, which, with Yahweh as subject, pronounces David's future royal position (vv. 28 and 30) and justifies his wars as Yahweh's wars (v. 28), who will protect his life against pursuers (v. 29) and his soul against grief or pangs of conscience for having shed blood without cause (v. 31a). Her speech ends in a petition to David not to forget her ('your handmaid') when Yahweh has done well to him (v. 31b).

David's answer to her speech is an acceptance of her gift and a praise of her (ברוכה את) and her judgement (טעמך; v. 33) incorporated in a praise of Yahweh, God of Israel, who has sent her (vv. 32-35).

---

15. The text, in fact, indicates that David has appeared as a mafioso and the 'protection' has mostly been a protection against David and his gang (e.g. 1 Sam. 25:7).

16. Participle *hiphil* of שתן, which occurs only here in 1 Samuel and also in 1 Kings 14 and 2 Kings 9. All occurrences are in contexts of power confrontation.

17. McKinlay 1999: 80: 'Like Wisdom she sends her messengers on ahead. This woman clearly knows what she is about'.

When Abigail comes home, Nabal is holding a feast 'like the king's feast', too drunk to be told what has happened, so Abigail waits until the following day. When Nabal is told about the incident, he has a stroke and dies ten days later (vv. 36-38). In David's view, it is justifiable that Yahweh has avenged him and returned Nabal's evil on his own head (v. 39). He marries Abigail, who lays aside her maiden role (אמה) and takes on the role of housewife (שפחה)[18] for David's men (vv. 40-42).

As in Proverbs, the Nabal–Abigail story has two contrasting characters, two feasts, and a young man who has the choice of going to the feast of life with Abigail or the feast of death with Nabal. The food is the same, but the service different. David chooses the feast of life and praises Abigail, as one would praise a god (McKinlay 1999: 81). In this scene of praise it is hinted that Abigail, like Wisdom and the woman in Genesis' Garden story, do not act on their own, but are 'agents of God' (McKinlay 1999: 76).

In a tripartite development of similar scenes, we find that '[t]he gift of discernment that came from Eve [is] tested by Wisdom, and then taken and tried out in the "real" world of power and conflicts' (McKinlay 1999: 82–3). The god has planted the tree, created the snake and the woman, set the conditions and delivered the food. In other words, the narratives operate within a mode of ambiguity, which led McKinlay to ask whether ambiguity is part of the deity's essence: 'It makes persuasive reading to understand God's role as that of a trickster, who both prescribes the fruit but who all along intends humankind to have the knowledge that it gives' (McKinlay 1999: 76, with reference to Magonet 1992: 42; Fewell and Gunn 1993: 34).

But as Broberg (2014: 49) correctly asks, what is the character of women, when McKinlay also states that 'Eve, the mother of all living, together with the snake, has provided the gift from the tree that will grant humans a divine gift of discernment' (McKinlay 1999: 76)?

In a comparative analysis of the goddesses Athirat, Qudshu, Tannit, Anat and Astarte in texts from the ancient Near East, inscriptions mentioning Asherah (and Yahweh) from Khirbet el-Qom and Kuntillet Ajrud and Old Testament texts, Broberg finds so much similarity in the symbol of Ashera's linking of trees, snakes, fertility and woman that it is plausible that McKinlay's 'agents of God' hide an Ashera goddess (Broberg 2014: 50–64).[19] The use of the plural forms in Gen. 1:26's and

---

18. אמה: vv. 24 (×2), 25, 28, vv. 31 and 41; שפחה: vv. 27 and 41.

19. Regarding Asherah, see Carstens (1998), and for additional information, Wyatt (1995).

3:22's 'let us' and 'like us' functions as an *inclusio* around this hidden goddess (Broberg 2014: 64), who is present at the creation as god's wife, but in the course of the narrative is transformed to become Adam's wife as the 'mother of all living' (Gen. 3:20; Broberg 2014: 59; cf. also Wallace 1985: 158). A similar transformation takes place when Abigail as David's wife 'is moved into the ranks of the many wives' (McKinlay 2014: 82).

If, as argued by Broberg (2014: 61), Genesis 2–4's woman/Eve narratives contain a conscious dethronement of Asherah similar to the anti-Asherah bashing the in the books of Kings (e.g. 1 Kgs 18:19; 2 Kgs 21:7; 23:4-7), it is likely that Proverbs 1–9 and 1 Samuel 25 are written as contrasting narratives, aiming at transferring Asherah's positive traits as mother of all living onto the female figure. As heir of the life-sustaining qualifications of the fertility goddess, the wise woman secures the good life and holds death in check. Ambiguities in Proverbs' portrait of Wisdom allows for seeing her as 'a separate female divine figure', such as found also in *1 Enoch* 42 and the Wisdom of Solomon (Crawford 1998: 365). Her transformation into a mere conceptual figure stresses her equation with the Torah in Ben Sira, Baruch and 4Q525 = 4QBeatitudes: 'Thus Wisdom has lost the special status we observed in Proverbs 1–9, Job 28, *1 Enoch* 42 and the Wisdom of Solomon, and become subsumed under the Torah as in Sir. 15:1, 24:23 and Bar. 4:1' (Crawford 1998: 365).

Conclusion

The myths of the ancient Near East and the Old Testament deal with questions about human's status in the cosmos and its character and role in relation to the god(s). The myths also deal with the qualities of humanity's and gods' worlds. In the world of the gods, the food hangs on trees, it is easy to get, but not all food is permitted. In man's world, it is a daily struggle to get enough food, and life ends in death and a return to the soil.

The myths also concern humanity's rebellion, its desire to transgress borders and its lust for evil such as the Bible's Flood story begins and ends with. The origin of this motif is not made clear in the Old Testament, but in the Mesopotamian creation myth, *Enuma Elish*, humans are created from clay and the blood of a rebellious god, Ups. Now we know where the rebellious mind came from. The myths' characterization of humans as rebellious earthly creatures has not only influenced the development of ancient Near Eastern societies' laws, social order and cult (Schmid 1997), but has also been defining for the New Testament's and Christianity's theology of sin. Not least has the development of portraits of Folly from a human figure (Prov. 1–9) to a semi-divine being (*1 En.* 42) to a chthonic demon (4Q184) put an unfortunate emphasis on women's sexuality as sinful (Crawford 1998: 366) and distorted interpretations of Genesis' Garden narrative.

The study of ancient myths may also add to our understanding of the Lord's Supper as a radical transformation of drinking from the *ṣarṣaru* cup of Isthar in Near Eastern covenant ideologies' confirmation and remembrance of the covenant. The additional interpretation of this act in Matthew (26:28) regards forgiveness of sins, but originally it was for remembrance of the covenant (Exod. 24:8; 1 Cor. 11:23-26; Mk 14:22-24; Lk. 22:17-20) as in the example from the reign of Esarhaddon (672 BCE). Every citizen and vassal was entitled to participate in the ritual and swear their oath to the king: 'Thus you shall say in your heart: "Ishtar holds watch". But when you come home to your towns and eat bread in your areas, you will forget the oath you have sworn. Now, drink this water and you will remember and keep the covenant, I, Esarhaddon, have cut with you.'[20] Like Gilgamesh and Enkidu, mankind began in the worlds of gods and animals and eventually found its own place. In this place, humanity is free to eat or not to eat, but 'let the eater be wary, and look very carefully at this food on offer, and the one with the ready invitation. Recognize the symbiotic system, for the question is not only: to eat or not to eat, but where is Wisdom in this choice?' (McKinlay 1999: 83).

Bibliography

Aletti, J. N. (1977), 'Seduction et parole en Proverbes I–IX', *VT*, 27: 129–44.
Broberg, L. (2014), 'Asherah i Genesis 2–3?', Masters thesis, University of Copenhagen.
Camp, C. V. (2000), *Wise, Strange and Holy: The Strange Woman and the Making of the Bible*, Sheffield: Sheffield Academic Press.
Carstens, P. (1998), 'Asherah', in G. Hallbäck and H. J. Lundager Jensen (eds), *Gads Bibel Leksikon*, 51, Copenhagen: Gads Forlag.
Cavigneaux, A. and F. Al-Ravi (1993), 'New Sumerian Literary Texts from Tell Haddad (Ancient Meturan): A First Survey', *Iraq* 55: 91–105.
Clifford, R. J. (1999), *Proverbs: A Commentary*, Louisville, KY: John Knox Press.

---

20. The text is from Otto (1999: 82): 'Wasser aus einem *ṣarṣaru*-Krug hat sie ihnen zu trinken gegeben, ein Trinkgefäß hat sie zur Hälfte aus dem *ṣarṣaru*-Krug gefüllt und mit den Worten gegeben: In eurem Herzen werdet ihr sprechen: Istar hält Wacht! Und ihr werdet in eure Städte gehen und in eure Bezirke und euer Brot essen, und ihr werdet diesen Bund vergessen (tallaka…NINDA.MEŠ takkala tamaššia adê annûti). Wenn ihr aber von diesem Wasser trinkt, dann werdet ihr euch erinnern und diesen Bund halten, den ich Asarhaddon betreffend geschlossen habe' (K. 2401111:4-15).'

Crawford, S. W. (1998), 'Lady Wisdom and Dame Folly at Qumran', *DSD*, 5 (3): 355–66.
Elliger, K. and W. Rudolf (1990), *Biblia Hebraica Stuttgartensia*, 4th rev. ed., Stuttgart: Deutsche Bibelgesellschaft.
Fevell, D. N. and D. M. Gunn (1993), *Gender, Power & Promise: The Subject of the Bible's First Story*, Nashville: Abingdon Press.
Foster, B. R. (1997), 'The Adapa Story', in W. W. Hallo (ed.), *The Context of Scripture, Vol. I: Canonical Compositions from the Biblical World*, 449, Leiden: E. J. Brill.
Fox, M. V. (1997), 'Ideas of Wisdom in Proverbs 1–9', *JBL*, 116: 613–33.
Goethe, J. W. von. (1819), *West-östlicher Divan (Gedichte)*, Leipzig: Philip Rechlam. Repr. in E. Trunz (ed.), *J. W. von Goethe, Werke*, 2:49, Munich, 1998.
Greenfield, J. C. (1985), 'The Seven Pillars of Wisdom (Prov. 9:1) – A Mistranslation', *JQR*, 76: 13–20.
Gudme de Hemmer, A. K. and J. Høgenhaven (2009), 'Det Gamle Testamentes eksegese', *Fønix*, 3 (32), http://teol.ku.dk/formidling/teologi_derfor/.
Hjelm, I. (2015), 'Livets og dødens føde i GT og nærorientalske tekster', in F. Damgaard and A. K. De Hemmer Gudme, *Mad og drikke i bibelsk litteratur*, 8–25, FBE 19, Copenhagen: ANIS, http://teol.ku.dk/abe/publikationer/forum_for_bibelsk_eksegese/f19/Hjelm_FBE19.pdf.
Izre'el, S. (2001), *Adapa and the South Wind: Language Has the Power of Life and Death*, Mesopotamian Civilizations 10, Winona Lake, IN: Eisenbrauns.
Jacobson, T. (1976), *The Treasures of Darkness: A History of Mesopotamian Religion*. New Haven: Yale University Press.
Kvanvig, H. S. (2011), *Primeval History: Babylonian, Biblical and Enochic: An Intertextual Reading*, Leiden: E. J. Brill.
Liverani, M. (2004), 'Adapa, Guest of the Gods', in *Myth and Politics in Ancient Near Eastern Historiography*, 3–23, Ithaca, NY: Cornell University Press.
Loretz, O. (1990), *Ugarit und Die Bibel. Kanaanäische Götter und Religion im Alten Testament*, Darmstadt: Wissenschaftliche Buchgesellschaft.
Magonet, J. (1992), 'The Themes of Genesis 2–3', in P. Morris and D. Sawyer (eds), *A Walk in the Garden: Biblical, Iconographical and Literary Images of Eden*, 39–46, Sheffield: Sheffield Academic Press.
McKinlay, J. E. (1999), 'To Eat or Not to Eat: Where Is Wisdom in this Choice?', *Semeia*, 86: 73–83.
Mettinger, T. N. D. (2007), *The Eden Narrative: A Literary and Religion-historical Study of Genesis 2–3*, Winona Lake, IN: Eisenbrauns.
Otto, E. (1999), *Das Deuteronomium, Politische Theologie und Rechtsreform in Juda und Assyrien*, Berlin: de Gruyter.
Picchioni, S. A. (1981), *Il poemetto di Adapa*, Budapest: Eötvös Loránd Tudományegyetem.
Pritchard J. B., ed. (1969), *Ancient Near Eastern Texts Relating to the Old Testament: Third Edition with Supplement = ANET*, Princeton, NJ: Princeton University Press.
Schmid, H. H. (1997), 'Skabelse, retfærdighed og frelse', in P. Carstens and H. J. Lundager (eds), *Læsninger og tolkninger af Det Gamle Testamente*, 43–62, Tekst og teologi I, Copenhagen: Anis.
Speiser, E. A. (1969), 'Adapa', in *ANET*: 101–3.
Thompson, T. L. (2009), 'Imago Dei: A Problem in Pentateuchal Discourse', *SJOT*, 23 (1): 135–48. Danish trans.: 'Imago dei. Et problem i de fem Mosebøgers diskurs', *DTT* (2009): 81–98, http://danskteologisktidsskrift.dk/.
Wallace, H. N. (1985), *The Eden Narrative*, Atlanta: Scholars Press.

Westenholz, U. and A. Westenholz (1997), *Gilgamesh – Enuma Elish. Guder og mennesker i oldtidens Babylon*, Copenhagen: Spektrum.

Whitelam, K. W. (1996), *The Invention of Ancient Israel: The Silencing of Palestinian History*, London: Routledge.

Wilcke, C. (1991), 'Göttliche und menschliche Weisheit im Alten Orient', in A. Assman (ed.), *Weisheit: Archäologie der literarischen Kommunikation III*, 259–70, Munich: Wilhelm Fink.

Wyatt, N. (1995), 'Asherah', in K. van der Toorn, B. Becking and P. van der Horst (eds), *Dictionary of Deities and Demons in the Bible (DDD)*, 183–95, Leiden: E. J. Brill.

A Gate in Gaza:
An Essay on the Reception of Tall Tales*

Jack M. Sasson

Few who are aware of Tommy Thompson's work would want to tackle the historicity in the patriarchal narratives (or most biblical lore with historical contents, for that matter) without wishing to know more about the time, the circumstance and the setting for their origins. More, they might also want to ask why, how and when editors gave up further manipulations of these traditions, deciding that they have become too sacred (canonical may be another term) to mess with.

The Subject

In this paper, offered to a friend and colleague of several decades, I keep all these matters in mind, but actually deal with one narrow aspect of their reception: Were these narratives set as past events taken to be true accounts when read or heard by their earliest recipients? The issue is interesting because until the past couple of centuries, all but the fewest skeptics regularly relied on biblical narratives to chronicle the march of history. Even the occasional jolt to credulity – as in crossing a sea on foot, halting the sun in mid-course or surviving for days in a fish's innards – was accorded veracity through mumbo-jumbo science or via unverified survival-tales collected from far-off shores.

---

* I gratefully acknowledge the helpful comments on an earlier draft by colleagues Jennifer Williams (Linfield College) and Fook-Kong Wong (Hong Kong Theological Seminary).

My exploration of this matter focuses on one episode from many concerned with Samson of the tribe of Dan: his visit with a prostitute in Gaza.[1] I hardly need to annotate too deeply the few verses that retell this incident (16:1-3) and I will take it for granted that anyone inspecting this essay would be familiar with the tales about Samson as told in Judges 13–16. The Gaza excursion comes after several confrontations with Philistines that invariably ended painfully for them. Heretofore, the bouts had occurred in and around Naḥal Sorek, mostly between Samson's birthplace (ṣŏrʿâ, Zorah) in Danite territory and Philistine Timnah, a stone's throw away from home.[2] The Gaza whoring interlude, however, occurs miles from these familiar spots, giving many occasions for later moralists to condemn consorting beyond marriage, especially with foreign women. Its local prostitute is nameless, as are all women characters through this juncture of the cycle.[3] In fact, subsequent to this episode, Samson will experience his deepest emotional entanglement in neighboring Naḥal Sorek when he falls in love with Delilah, a named courtesan of fluid ethnicity.[4]

The passage in the received Hebrew is brief enough to warrant full citation:

---

1. Unless specified otherwise, all citations are from the book of Judges. This essay is adapted from the second volume of an *Anchor Yale Bible* commentary on that book now in preparation. (The first volume is available as Sasson 2014.) I reserve detailed philological comments to its pages.

2. Some incidents found him by Ashkelon (Judg. 14:19) and by other places (Etam, Lehi) that are difficult to pinpoint on a map. See Rainey and Notley (2006: 141) for a succinct presentation of the matter.

3. Exum (2016: 48) playfully wonders (I am not sure why) whether she was an Israelite plying her trade in a foreign land.

4. Delilah's name betrays nothing about her foreign origin, as it is plausibly Semitic, whether Hebrew (*dālal*, 'to dangle') or Akkadian (*dalālum*, 'to praise'). In the literature, Delilah is commonly a Philistine because Samson's fate was to engage the Philistines, because in Timnah and in Gaza, Philistine women seem to attract him because Philistines would more likely trust one of their own to deceive Samson, and because a Hebrew woman (God forbid) would not betray her kin. Plausible enough, each and every explanation, except for the fact that in the Samson tales, his kin from Judah seem quite willing to hand him over to the Philistines (Judg. 15). In Judges too, Jael, not likely a Hebrew, deceived her own kind (Judg. 4). Then there are always Joseph's brothers and Judas as betrayers of one's own kith as well as the dozen kings of Judah and Israel abandoned by their followers. Given her proximity to – if not location in – Danite territory, Delilah may well provide us with one more example of tribal disloyalty. We might consider her a Hebrew if we wish; but nothing in her pedigree would reveal a motivation to doom Samson other than greed.

> **16** ¹Samson went down to Gaza. He saw there a prostitute and slept with her. ²To the people of Gaza, it was said, 'Samson has come here'. They encircled him in ambush all night by the city gate, shushing each other all night by saying, 'Come daybreak, and we will kill him'. ³Samson slumbered until midnight. Rising at midnight, he gripped the door panels of the city gate as well as the two doorposts. Tearing them loose with the shaft still in place, he set them on his shoulders and hauled them up towards the peak of the hill, the one facing Hebron.⁵

> ¹וַיֵּלֶךְ שִׁמְשׁוֹן עַזָּתָה וַיַּרְא־שָׁם אִשָּׁה זוֹנָה וַיָּבֹא אֵלֶיהָ: ²לַעַזָּתִים לֵאמֹר בָּא שִׁמְשׁוֹן הֵנָּה וַיָּסֹבּוּ וַיֶּאֶרְבוּ־לוֹ כָל־הַלַּיְלָה בְּשַׁעַר הָעִיר וַיִּתְחָרְשׁוּ כָל־הַלַּיְלָה לֵאמֹר עַד־אוֹר הַבֹּקֶר וַהֲרַגְנֻהוּ: ³וַיִּשְׁכַּב שִׁמְשׁוֹן עַד־חֲצִי הַלַּיְלָה וַיָּקָם בַּחֲצִי הַלַּיְלָה וַיֶּאֱחֹז בְּדַלְתוֹת שַׁעַר־הָעִיר וּבִשְׁתֵּי הַמְּזוּזוֹת וַיִּסָּעֵם עִם־הַבְּרִיחַ וַיָּשֶׂם עַל־כְּתֵפָיו וַיַּעֲלֵם אֶל־רֹאשׁ הָהָר אֲשֶׁר עַל־פְּנֵי חֶבְרוֹן:

The Issue

By featuring a Samson who is alert to danger as well as highlighting Philistines who still hope to vanquish him by force of arm, this episode does contrast significantly from previous occurrences. Most glaring is the lack of obvious motivation for Samson's trek. While it is true that Samson will soon face his greatest challenge in Gaza, hard to fathom is why Samson would thread his way deeply into enemy territory just to sample carnally its local hookers. True too is that by moving to the antipodes of Philistine power, Samson (or God) has globalized his war against them. Still, aside from anticipating Samson's final days in Gaza, the incident seems neither to emerge from what had transpired nor to provide a fitting transition to what follows. In fact, no harm overtakes the overall architecture of the Samson cycle were it removed. Additionally, this narrator's relatively brief exploration of Samson's remarkable feat markedly contrasts with the expansive interest in events either around Timnah or in Delilah's boudoir. Striking in this instance, too, is Samson's bloodless confrontation with the Philistines when in previous (and ensuing) sequences, his opponents pay heavily at each conflict. Finally, in this encounter, there is no reference to

---

5. For the few grammatical and idiomatic oddities of the Hebrew text, see the annotations in my forthcoming Judges commentary. The two Greek renditions differ in minor ways from the Hebrew. They both (as well as Josephus) adopt a literal rendition of the euphemism *bō' 'el-* (a woman), by having Samson just stay there. They both also expand the ending to state that Samson sets the Gaza gates at the summit of a mountain facing Hebron, I suppose lest anyone imagine that he parked them only when he got to Delilah's gate.

any infusion of divine spirit (as at 14:6, 19; 15:4), when it at least equals previous displays of prowess. These observations lead to the following comments on the incident:

1. *Its Derivation*. Why among so many Samson exploits that test credulity, does the narrator invite disbelief by inserting this brief, yet gaudy, yarn? The answers in the literature are few. Most commentators simply ignore its distinction from the others, choosing to forge straight into the Delilah episode. Some propose that it is 'of the same character with the rest of the cycle, and doubtless of the same origin' (Moore 1895: 348). Others claim that it sharpens Samson's behavior as a clue in an allegory for Israel's compulsion to whore after foreign gods.[6] There is invariably the opinion that it comes from a different hand, period, school or the like.[7] Yet, if spliced into the series of Samson moves, the episode is by no means intrusive, as its language smoothly partakes from other components of the tales (Amit 1999: 283). To begin with, its opening phrase harks back to the moment Samson went to Timnah (see at 16:1). In setting this brief incident at Gaza, the narrator is also looking ahead to the cataclysm that will end Samson's life at the Gaza Temple. There is mention of ambushing Samson (forms of *'ārav*) here (16:2) and later (16:9, 12); of seizing (verb: *'āḥaz*) door panels (16:3) as well as Samson (at 16:21); and of pulling out (verb: *nāsaʿ*) components of the gate at one heave (at 16:3) and those of a loom similarly (at 16:14).[8] None by itself suggests a clear linkage; but their occurrence in such a compact narrative is worthy of attention.

2. *Its Oddity*. Neither Samson's morals – he was a Nazir, so consecrated to God – nor his perplexing movements are as curious as the deed attributed to him on awakening in a whore's house. He knows that he is under watch;

---

6. Wong (2006: 231–6) follows others in championing this fragile linkage.

7. Opinions and criteria are many but are all equally speculative; see Brettler 2002: 54–6. Some take the mention of Gaza, its carnal focus and its (arguable) temporal unity as clues of its connection with the remaining events in ch. 16. Others locate it among the episodic elements of the previous chapters, due to an integral construction that defies clear-cut chronology. Still others consider it a stray that originally may not have belonged to Samson stories. Startling is Guillaume's (2004: 186–8) severely historicizing take that also plays on Sun mythology: the episode sharpens the failure of Neo-Babylonian rulers to take Egypt, leaving Gaza bereft of power, as does Samson, 'little sun', on removing its gate.

8. Amit (1999: 283–4) argues that without Samson's heroics at the Gaza gate, the Philistines might not have offered Delilah such a large sum to capture him. I would imagine that their earlier loss of thousands at his hand might have been enough incentive.

but rather than luring Philistines to a thrashing, he opts to deny them future protection by turning their city gateless, so defenseless: a deserved turn of events for cowardly soldiers who egged each other into postponing a confrontation with their nemesis (see at 16:2).

The Gates. Several cities of Levant had multiple fortifications: Nineveh and Babylon were each circled by at least two sets of formidably high walls. Movement in and out of a city occurred through several of their gates. Nineveh's fifteen gates (Reade 2016) punctured a wall that stretched out for about 7 miles (12 km). Babylon's wall was one and halftime as long (12 miles) and in the first millennium had nine gates. The wall around Jerusalem at the end of the monarchic period was likely a fraction of that circumference; in modern times, it is about 2.5 miles (4 km). The Bible mentions almost two dozen gates for Jerusalem, although the likelihood is that over time the same gate may have held several names.

The city gates of most fortified cities were not just gaps in massive walls; rather, at both ends of the breach (*petaḥ*, 'opening'), they included towers that could reach – as they did at Tell Dan – 25 feet (8 m) in height.[9] Gaza's fortifications await a full archaeological review; our knowledge of its gate system is scant. The Gaza besieged by Sargon (late eighth century) may have had two gates, leading to separate directions. If a scene on Assyrian reliefs proves to represent one of Gaza's gates, entry into the city was through a narrow opening, an arch topped by a horizontal lintel. Tall towers flanked the opening, each with its own battlement from which soldiers can shoot arrows.[10]

The Portals. Access into a town had to be wide enough to allow the attended entry of carts, chariots, and other vehicles. Minimally, they would be almost 7 feet (over 2 m) broad. The main gateway at Lachish was 16 feet (5 m) broad; most other gates of the area were likely around 10-12 feet wide. Height differed; but while those of Assyria can be exceptionally tall, those of Canaan and Israel seem to equal the width of the two leaves. A gate had a door (*delet*, most often plural *daltôt*), normally consisting of a pair of foot-thick, heavily nailed timber panels (likely pine, acacia and/

---

9. The literature on fortification and city gates is enormous. A good overview of gates and their functions in the Levant is in May 2014. To annotate this passage, I have found most useful the very fine dissertation by Frese (2012; especially ch. 4, 'The Gatehouse Entrance', 73–99), as well as the detailed lexical comments of Otto 2006. For Mesopotamia and Anatolia, there is a series of brief notices in the *Reallexikon der Assyriologie,* 13: 86–96 (under 'Stadttor'). All three resources include exhaustive bibliographies.

10. Widely reproduced illustration, as in Frese 2012: 124.

or cypress). On their outer side, these panels were either sheathed with metal (most often bronze) or had several broad bands of the same. The process not only reinforced them, but also prevented (or at least slowed) torching by the enemy.[11] The panels were connected to massive doorposts (*mězûzâ*, most often plural *mězûzôt*) and rested on pivots (*'ammôt*) that were molded into a threshold of hard stone (*saf* and *miptān*, likely outer and inner sills). In allowing traffic, the panels swung to the inside of the gate. At night-time, the panels dovetailed shut into each other. One of several methods of locking them required sliding a beam or a metal bar (*běrîᵃḥ*) through brackets (metal usually) fastened to the inside face of the panels.

The Feat

The Heave. These details on Gaza's portal give us an inkling of Samson's herculean power. In one stroke, he was dealing with two panels (*daltôt*), two doorposts (*mězûzôt*), as well as the bar (*běrîᵃḥ*). In belonging neither to an ordinary home nor even to a compound, these elements made for a city gate of staggering width, length, girth and weight. Ordinarily, gates were shuttled on ox-pulled beds, given their weight and size; Samson's simply placed them on his shoulders (*vayyāśem ᶜal-kětēfāʸv*) to haul them away. This feat undoubtedly gave rise to a Talmudic notice about Samson enormous size: 'R. Simeon the Pious said: "The width between Samson's shoulders was sixty cubits (90 feet, 28 meters)"…and there is a tradition that the gates of Gaza were not less than sixty cubits [in width]' (*b. Sot.* 10a; *Num. Rab.* 14:9).[12]

---

11. On making door panels, we have this letter from a Mari administrator (ARM 13 7; see Sasson 2017: 304–5): 'My lord wrote to me about the panel of cedar to produce for placement to match the panel at the Uṣur-pi-šarrim's Gate… I have measured comprehensively the pivot of the panel at the Uṣurpi-šarrim Gate: 2 reeds, 4 cubits, 8 fingers [just over 8 meters] is its entire span. The frame is 2 reeds and 10 fingers [about 7 meters]. For the size of this panel with its double casing of 2 cubits (1 meter) each, I am taking one veneer casing […]. My lord should know this.'

12. In other lore, Samson could take two mountains and knock them against each other, as might ordinary humans knock stones. When infused with divine spirit, he could traverse with a single step the distance between towns (*Lev. Rab.* 8:2). Similar hyperboles developed about Gilgamesh in the Hittite version: 'The great gods [created] Gilgamesh: His body was eleven yards [in height]; his breast was nine [spans] in breadth; his…was three […] in length'; G. Beckman in Foster 2001: 158. Whereas the Old Babylonian Gilgamesh was just larger than most of his

The Haul. How far Samson took these panels is debated. He did haul them away (*vayyaʿălēm*) to the top of a specific mount (*hāhār*); but which hill was it? The Hebrew says ʿ*al-pĕnê*, a compound preposition that covers much ground: comparative – 'additional to', 'in preference over' (someone); spatial – 'opposite', 'over' something and the like. The targeted direction is Hebron, a town that will have its moment of glory by crowning David and hosting his first years of rule. The distance from Gaza to Hebron is about 37 miles (60 km); a bit farther is the hill that carries its name. Daunting must have been the climb necessary to reach that hill. Gaza's elevation is about 50 feet (so less than 15 m) above sea level; that of Hebron is close to 3,000 feet (900 m), with Mt Hebron over a thousand feet higher. Perhaps its mention implies 'Eastward', so away from the Mediterranean (Lagrange 1903: 243)? Whatever the favored interpretation, both Greek versions (as well as Josephus) felt the need to relieve Samson of his burden, adding 'and he set them down there'.

Given the syntax of the final clause, however, it is possible to argue that Samson took the gates to a nearby hill, one *that faced* distant Hebron. The highest point in the Gaza area is (Joz) Abu ʿAwdah, a hillock 350 feet (100 m) above sea level. Slightly less elevated is Muntar, to the Southeast of the town, favored by some Christian fathers as Samson's climbing goal. This approach would be the prudent understanding of what Samson did with the gates; yet given the other circumstances of Samson's behavior in Gaza, turning pragmatic here would be missing the drift of the anecdote.

---

contemporaries (as were other kings such as Eannatum of Lagash), within centuries he acquired the oversized stature of gods; see George 2007: 247–8. Modern exegetes are not too far behind when comparing Samson to Hercules, Cuhullin and other mythical heroes. More modestly, Gunkel (1913: 40–1) labels him a *Naturmensch* who depends on his hands to crush lions and enemies; a marked contrast to the Philistines, who wield the products of culture to achieve their goals.

Samson also caught the imagination of artists as they set mosaic for their patrons. Earliest are diverse scenes in the Roman catacombs (early fourth century), with Samson battling a lion and striking Philistines with a jawbone (Gass and Zisu 2005: 169–72). Fullest is a series of nine scenes in a fifth-century synagogue (or church) in Mopsuestia (Misis) in Cilicia, with Samson larger than other humans (Avi-Yonah 1981). From about the same period, the Tell Huqoq (Galilee) synagogue preserves fragments of two, albeit non-contiguous, scenes: Samson deploys foxes and hauls away Gaza's gate (Grey and Magness 2013: 30). A scene with Samson striking Philistines with a jawbone decorated a Wadi Hammam synagogue. Leibner and Miller (2010: 256–7) report on several Samson scenes in Byzantine codices and in a tenth-century Armenian church (Achtamar, Lake Van in Turkey).

The Reception

I take it for granted that, however we might feel about the historical value of any episode in the Bible, its narrators and first hearers hardly doubted that the featured ancestors once fulfilled all actions assigned to them. Patriarchs, matriarchs, kings and heroes all met and surmounted extraordinary challenges. If such events featured divine protagonists, the more the necessity to suspend disbelief. This must certainly have been how the faithful absorbed the truths of Creation, the Flood and the Exodus. Occasionally, the defeat of Israel's enemies occurs through supernatural means – among them opportune earthquakes, celestial fires or rocks, powerful winds, sea parting and arrest of luminaries. How could these challenges to nature be doubted when Almighty God had full control over the cosmos? The same suspension of disbelief likely applied to interactions between humans and the divine, directly or through surrogates. Among such examples are Lot and his visitors in Sodom and Jacob and his wrestling bout with a man, both proving to come from the beyond. These occasions and interactions, albeit touched by the supernatural, must have occurred if only because Heaven orchestrated them.

Embellished Tales. The matter is more complicated when it comes to evaluating narratives of contacts among individuals of flesh and blood. Here, one needs to distinguish between an embellished tale and a 'Tall Tale'. The former features embroidered versions of the realistic (indeed, historical) and we meet with it whenever we come across bloated numbers of felled enemies or read about individuals wielding implausible weapons when decimating foes (Samson and Shamgar ben Anat in the book of Judges). The stories about Samson and his bouts with foes partook of these characteristics. The encounters he has had with a lion, foxes and diverse phalanxes of Philistines are all examples of heightened violence that might strain credulity (of some readers anyway); but there is nothing at the core of their plausibility that a dash of salt would not help to lend them verisimilitude. In hearing or reading about them, the discerning mind automatically trims them down to their proper balance, permitting focus on the intended lesson. For example, in terms of credibility (never mind historicity), the story of Moses's spies in Canaan (Num. 13:17-33) need not have been discounted because the men retrieved enormous grape clusters or saw gargantuan foes. The main points there were the promise as well as the challenge of conquering a very fruitful yet heavily defended Promised Land.

Tall Tales. It is otherwise with 'Tall Tales' in which the exaggerations are themselves the focus of the story, giving them a 'fictionality' that encourages transposal into other forms of comprehension, such as a parable or a paradigm. In such accounts, narrators tend to sharpen implausibility by multiplying clues, their main intent being to promote the didactic via the entertaining. In antiquity, any Samson reader acquainted with fortified cities would know that city gates, not least because of their size, bulk and weight, were not transportable on the back of any one individual, however mighty. For such gates were neither graspable by one pair of arms nor easily balanced on a human back. This is certainly the reason why the rabbis, acquainted though they were with divine miracles, converted Samson into a giant, his shoulders spanning dozens of cubits.

Samson might have negotiated the gate by climbing or vaulting over it, thus managing to escape Gaza just the same. Yet, by alluding to Hebron, the narrator made certain to generate doubt on the realism of this particular episode. Hebron, as noted above, is uphill from Gaza and miles away. A good bit of the territory in between was infested with Philistines who might have welcomed launching javelins and arrows on a gate-burdened Samson. This potential problem may well have inspired Pseudo-Philo into converting one panel of the gate into a shield.[13] More telling, however, is the reticence of the narrator to involve God in this particular exploit. Had we read that God's spirit landed on Samson as he faced the gates of Gaza, such a notice might certainly have thwarted most ancient readers from doubting the validity of the exploit.

I have made much of this observation less to question the historical value of this particular tale about Samson than to suggest that on occasion Scripture consciously indulged in assigning its heroes acts that skirted historical likelihood. In the first volume of my Judges commentary, I have had occasion to alert to another episode with fanciful writing pitting Othniel against Cushan-rishatayim (Judg. 3:7-11). My clue there was how a patently moralistic name ('Doubly Wicked Cushan') rhymed with the name of the land he ruled, Aram-naharayim. Not surprisingly, since Josephus, traditional and modern commentators on that passage have twisted our knowledge of the past into pretzels, not just to thread Cushan-rishatayim's move from Upper Syria deep into southern Canaan, but also to keep him in power there for almost a decade. Elsewhere in Scripture, narrators also use diverse tactics to alert perceptive readers

---

13. Pseudo-Philo could hardly allow the Philistines to escape unscathed; his Samson considers them 'fleas' and uses the gates on his back to kill 25,000 of them; *LAB* 43.2-4; following Harrington 1985: 356–7.

or audiences on the fictionality of what lies before them by assigning moralistic or whimsical names to characters that no parents would wish on their children. Such a tactic is obvious in Genesis 14 with its series of the named kings of Sodom (Bera, 'In Evil'), Gomorrah (Birsha, 'In Wickedness') and one of their allies (Bela, 'Swallower', likely king of Zoar).[14]

The Lesson

Our particular segment of Samson hardly demands historical validation; yet it urges us to consider the probability that, on a few occasions, biblical traditions did strive to convey instruction that offered sharper lessons than those derived from history. Neither the circumstance surrounding Samson's birth nor his Nazirite status was exceptional to Scripture. Yet we may now ask, why insert a Tall Tale of pronounced whimsy among a series of yarns with obvious embellishments? I doubt that the intention was to invite wholesale skepticism about the whole cycle. I speculate that by positioning this particular episode within two distinctively phrased statements on Samson's tenure as judge (at 15:20 and 16:31), the narrator framed distinct panels for the Samson traditions. In the first of these (13:1 through 15:20), Samson is played like a 'comic dupe', a character (by no means hilarious) who serves as an instrument by which to carry out a divinely set agendum. This program opens on Samson seeking a bride among foreskinned Philistines, 'Now his father and mother had no idea that this was from the LORD, for he (Samson and/or God) was prodding a reaction from the Philistines'. It develops over a sequence of crucial clashes in which God manipulates Samson through measured infusion of divine spirit (rûᵂaḥ 'ĕlōhîm) with which to bludgeon beasts and enemies.

---

14. Other schemes include (1) promoting non-existent rulers from periods otherwise scripturally well-documented, for example, Darius the Mede of Dan. 6:1; (2) formulating bogus titles, such as 'King of Nineveh' (Jon. 3:6), Nebuchadnezzar of Assyria (Jdt. 11), or Belshazzar, son of Nebuchadnezzar (Dan. 5:1-2); and (3) inventing non-existent locales, among them Bethulia (many variant spellings) in Jdt. 4:9 and Jeremiah's Merathaim ('double rebellion [possibly, Babylon]' Jer. 50:21). Complicated is how to evaluate the many moments in which narrators challenge their audience by referring to material found in archives, for example to the 'Book of Jashar' (Josh. 10:13; 2 Sam. 1:18), to the 'Book of YHWH wars' (Num. 21:14) or to several 'annals' (divrēʸ hayyāmîm) of departed rulers of Israel and/or Judah. Certainly beyond likelihood is the invitation to inspect the records of foreign kings, such as those of 'Persia and Media' (Est. 6:1; 10:2; see also Ezra 6:2).

The second panel occupies ch. 16, enfolding over three distinct settings: a Gaza brothel, Delilah's boudoir and a Gaza building. Especially in the first two of these scenes, Samson is a 'comic hero', in literary exploration a character with a supersized ego, defiant, conflicted about authority, oscillating between hubris and humility, not always self-aware and certainly not servile to consistency but in full control of destiny.[15] Samson is nonchalant about danger and can compete with the gods for brute strength, his portraiture hardly aiming for verisimilitude or credibility. In my reading of the second scene, with Delilah, Samson is dangerously playful. Perversely misreading her intentions, he seeks repeatedly (and always unsuccessfully) to egg her on toward some erotic escapade by proposing successive realizations of ancient love charms in which binding, cutting, knotting and use of bodily elements such as sinews, hair, or nail clippings are essential ingredients.[16]

It is in the third setting that both aspects of Samson's character come together. In it, a blinded Samson gets set between pillars in a building, likely a Gaza temple for Dagon. Petitioning God for renewed strength, he brings it down over its myriad celebrants. An avenged Samson is among the many victims, thus losing none of his potential for shaping his own fate. Yet in doing so, he once again submits to being an instrument in the wider war that the God of Israel was waging. In Hebrew theosophy, that battle was non-ending. False though they may have been, these gods nonetheless remained pervasively (and perversely) dominant over their own worshipers. Worse, even as they experienced the might of their own god, Hebrews repeatedly turn to them without ever verifying their competence (Deut. 11:28; 13:3, 14 and elsewhere). As such moments, it was not enough for prophets to warn against foreign gods. Rather, false gods needed punishment directly, as was the case in many theomachies in which YHVH discomfited his many foes.[17]

---

15. The literature on this portrayal is large; but see Torrance 1978. I have commented on both the comic dupe and the comic hero in a study on Jonah; see Sasson 1990: 345–52.

16. I sustain, flesh out and defend these comments in my forthcoming *Anchor Yale Bible* commentary and, more succinctly, in a study of Judges 16 offered to a colleague.

17. Theomachy, the confrontation between and among gods, is a major component of cosmological mythmaking in antiquity. In its best-known variety, individual gods rise by supplanting others either violently or peacefully. In the process, successful deities confer primacy on their chosen people or city. This version of the combat is heavily featured in the Hebrew Bible (lastly, Miller 2018) and elsewhere (Heimpel 1997: 549, 561–2; Beckman 1997: 569–70). Since the nineteenth century, yet with

However, there were other manifestations of theomachy. In them, humans were facilitators or instruments in divine apotheoses. In the Hebrew Bible, a parade example is when Moses discomfits Pharaoh, hence also the gods of Egypt, or Elijah exterminates Baal priests, proving the impotence of their god (1 Kgs 18:20-46). Less directly, when aboard a storm-tossed ship, Jonah proves God's superiority over Sea (Jon. 1). Samson's final moments in Gaza belong to a variation of this trope, wherein the human instrument dies in the process. The fullest example of this manifestation from antiquity occurs in two variants of the Anatolian myth 'Illuyanka' (see Hoffner 1998: 10–14; Beckman 1982). Both feature a Storm God (Taru) conniving to regain power from Illuyanka (a serpent) that had defeated him. In one version, his daughter, (the goddess Inara) marries a mortal (Hupasiya) who trusses a drunken Illuyanka before the Storm God kills him. In the second and more relevant version, the son of the Storm God betrays Illuyanka into surrendering a powerful asset, and loses his own life as a result.

Little in this Anatolian tale matches what we find in the Samson account save for its outcome. Here, God is triumphant, Dagon is defeated (not for the last time, see 1 Sam. 5) and Samson perishes as a result. Both parties get to play a role in the Philistine debacle: Samson leaves Gaza defenseless by removing its gate and God empowers him to destroy its temple. True enough, neither Hebrew nor modern historiography corroborates this take on events at Gaza. Yet, with such a heady lesson to derive from the Gaza confrontations, readers past and new might absorb even the tallest tale in the cycle without unduly dismissing the whole. Some yarns need not be true to convey truths.

Bibliography

Amit, Yairah (1999), *The Book of Judges: The Art of Editing*, trans. J. Chipman, Leiden: E. J. Brill (Hebrew version, 1992).
Avi-Yonah, Michael (1981), 'The Mosaics of Mopsuestia – Church or Synagogue', in Lee I. Levine (eds), *Ancient Synagogues Revealed*, 186–90, Jerusalem: Israel Exploration Society.
Beckman, Gary (1982), 'The Anatolian Myth of Illuyanka', *JANES*, 14: 11–25.

elusive success, Samson has been portrayed as an avatar of alpha deities (from Mesopotamian Ninurta and Shamash to Greek Heracles) or of epic heroes (from Gilgamesh to Cúchulainn). There are overviews of these efforts in works from Palmer 1913 to Mobley 2006. A less direct application of the theme considers Samson tales as 'folklorization of mythological compositions aiming at emptying them of their power' (Guillaume 2004: 191).

Beckman, Gary (1997), 'Mythologie. A.II. Bei den Hethitern', *Reallexikon der Assyriologie* 8: 564–72.
Brettler, Marc Zvi (2002), *The Book of Judges*, New York: Routledge.
Exum, J. Cheryl (2016), *Fragmented Women: Feminist (Sub)versions of Biblical Narratives*, 2nd ed., London: Bloomsbury T&T Clark.
Foster, Benjamin R. (2001), *The Epic of Gilgamesh: A New Translation, Analogues, Criticism*, New York: W. W. Norton.
Frese, Daniel Allan (2012), 'The Civic Forum in Ancient Israel: The Form, Function, and Symbolism of City Gates', PhD dissertation, University of California, San Diego, https://escholarship.org/uc/item/8tp5j3ch#page-1.
Gass, Erasmus and Boaz Zissu (2005), 'The Monastery of Samson up the Rock of Etham in the Byzantine Period', *ZDPV*, 121: 168–83.
George, Andrew R. (2007), 'The Gilgameš Epic at Ugarit', *AuOr*, 25: 237–54.
Grey, Matthew J. and Jodi Magness (2013), 'Finding Samson in Byzantine Galilee: The 2011-2012 Archaeological Excavations at Huqoq', *Studies in the Bible and Antiquity* 5: 1–30.
Guillaume, Philippe (2004), *Waiting for Josiah: The Judges*, London: T&T Clark.
Gunkel, Hermann (1913), *Reden und Aufsätze*, Göttingen: Vandenhoeck & Ruprecht.
Harrington, Daniel J. (1985), 'Pseudo-Philo (First Century A.D.)', in J. P. Charlesworth (ed.), *The Old Testament Pseudepigrapha. Vol. 2, Expansions of the 'Old Testament' and Legends, Wisdom and Philosophical Literature, Prayers, Psalms, and Odes, Fragments of Lost Judeo-Hellenistic Works*, 297–377, New York: Doubleday.
Heimpel, Wolfgang (1997), 'Mythologie (mythology). A.I. in Mesopotamien', *Reallexikon der Assyriologie*, 8: 537–64.
Hoffner, Harry A., Jr. (1998), *Hittite Myths*, 2nd ed., SBL Writings from the Ancient World Series, Atlanta, GA: Scholars Press.
Lagrange, Marie-Joseph (1903), *Le livre des Juges*, Études bibliques, Paris: V. Lecoffre.
Leibner, Uzi and Shulamit Miller (2010), 'A Figural Mosaic in the Synagogue at Khirbet Wadi Hamam', *JRA*, 23: 238–64.
May, Natalie N. (2014), 'Gates and their Functions in Mesopotamia and Ancient Israel', in N. N. May and U. Steinert (eds), *The Fabric of Cities: Aspects of Urbanism, Urban Topography and Society in Mesopotamia, Greece and Rome*, 77–121, Leiden: E. J. Brill.
Miller, Robert D. II (2018), *The Dragon, the Mountain, and the Nations: An Old Testament Myth, its Origins, and its Afterlives*, University Park, PA: Eisenbrauns.
Mobley, Gregory (2006), *Samson and the Liminal Hero in the Ancient Near East*, LHBOTS 453, New York: T&T Clark.
Moore, George F. (1895), *A Critical and Exegetical Commentary on Judges*, The International Critical Commentary, New York: Charles Scribner's Sons.
Otto, E. (2006), 'ša'ar', in H. Ringgren and H. Fabrey (eds), *Theological Dictionary of the Old Testament, vol. 15*, 359–405, Grand Rapids: Eerdmans.
Palmer, Abram Smythe (1913), *The Samson-saga and Its Place in Comparative Religion*, London: I. Pitman.
Rainey, Anson F. and R. Steven Notley (2006), *The Sacred Bridge*, Carta's Atlas of the Biblical World, Jerusalem: Carta.
Reade, Julian Edgeworth (2016), 'The Gates of Nineveh', *State Archives of Assyria, Bulletin*, 22: 39–93.
Sasson, Jack M. (1990), *Jonah: A New Translation with Introduction, Commentary and Interpretations*, The Anchor Bible 24b, Garden City: Doubleday.

Sasson, Jack M. (2014), *Judges 1–12: A New Translation, With Introduction and Commentary*, The Anchor Yale Bible, New Haven: Yale University Press.

Sasson, Jack M. (2017), *From the Mari Archives: An Anthology of Old Babylonian Letters*, University Park, PA: Eisenbrauns (paperback reprint, with Additions and Corrections).

Torrance, R. M. (1978), *The Comic Hero*, Cambridge, MA: Harvard University Press.

Wong, Gregory T. K. (2006), *Compositional Strategy of the Book of Judges: An Inductive, Rhetorical Study*, Leiden: E. J. Brill.

DEBORAH'S TOPICAL SONG:
REMARKS ON THE *GATTUNG* OF JUDGES 5

Bob Becking

When I first met Thomas L. Thompson in Dublin 1996, he stressed the view that before even thinking about drawing historical conclusions from a text, one should first and foremost try to understand the *Genre* of that text. His argument ran as follows: the way in which a text is moulded into its form is informative about the message a writer wanted to communicate at the time of his/her writing. The story of the past is often so mutilated by the fabrics of a specific *Gattung* that no historical conclusions can be drawn (see Thompson 1999).

The Song of Deborah: A Few Remarks on Recent
(and not so Recent) Scholarship

The Song of Deborah is to be found in ch. 5 of the book of Judges. Judges 4 contains a narrative on the clash between the Canaanite king Jabin and his army-commander Sisera on the one hand, and the Israelite Barak who was summoned on divine command by the prophetess-judge Deborah on the other. Barak leads the Israelites into victory, but the final blow is delivered by the cruel act of Jael. She kills Sisera by driving a tent peg into his temple.

Judges 5 describes the same theme in a hymnic form. In view of its poetical form and the at times archaic type of Hebrew the Song of Deborah has traditionally been construed as one of the oldest remaining pieces of Hebrew literature (see, e.g., Wellhausen 1963: 218; Weiser 1959; Boling 1975: 105–20; de Moor 1993: 484; Cross and Freedman 1995; Schniedewind 2004: 52–6).[1] This consensus, however, has been

---

1. This view is almost a consensus among scholars and is – in conservative circles – construed as a hard scientific fact.

challenged along two lines of argumentation – which are often combined. Firstly, the archaeological record from the Late Bronze/Early Iron Age would not support an extensive presence of Israelites as is assumed by the Song of Deborah. Secondly, the supposed archaic character of the Hebrew in Judges 5 is more and more seen as a scholarly construct with no hard evidence to support it. On the winds of change caused by the breakdown of the traditional view on the emergence of the Pentateuch and the Deuteronomistic History, the Song of Deborah was relocated in time. Some scholars see the Song of Deborah as a product of the literary activity during the early monarchy (Soggin 1981: 80–1; Lindars 1995: 213–15). Other scholars construe the Song of Deborah to have been composed in the late monarchic period (e.g., Bechmann 1989: 198–213; Görg 1993: 31; Baker 2017 [Assyrian period]). Frolov (2011) is of the opinion – based on an analysis of the grammar, syntax, vocabulary, intertextual links, outlook and agenda – that the Song of Deborah was an integral part of Dtr and hence composed in or around the period of the Babylonian exile. Diebner (1995) dates the composition as late as the Roman period.

As a result of this later dating of the Song of Deborah, the traditional view that the text would contain trustworthy historical information is slowly fading away. It is interesting to note that in this debate on dating, the element of the *Gattung* of the Song of Deborah only plays a marginal role. The text is generally seen as a victory hymn or a heroic song (see the standard commentaries and Blenkinsopp 1961; Hauser 1987: 268; Echols 2008).

The Concept of a Topical Song

In the realm of folk music, the *Gattung* of a topical song is well known (see, e.g., Donaldson 2014; Peddie 2017). A topical song is a hymn that focuses on what for the composer is a recent and important event. A topical song could be seen as a newspaper in hymnic form. In pre-literate societies the communicative aim of a topical song was twofold: to inform and to convince. Like a newspaper message, such a song informed hearers about what had happened. A choice of facts communicated the fabric of the event as it was seen by the composer. At the same time, a topical song is never without an evaluation. The lyrics also communicated a view on the event and had as their purpose to convince the audience of that specific view on reality. In other words, like a newspaper message, a topical song is never without ideology.

Bethwel Allan Ogot, a historian from Kenya, used oral sources, among them traditional topical songs, for the writing of the history of his country. These traditional songs contained elements that were often silenced by the official – read British – sources (for instance: Ogot 2009). Many more examples could be given. The *Genre* survived the threshold of literacy and continued, especially in folk music and similar styles. Famous examples are Tom Waits's 'Road to Peace', Peter Gabriel's 'Biko' and Bob Dylan's 'The Lonesome Death of Hattie Carroll' (see Dylan 2004: 275-87).

Although topical songs generally refer to recent events, they sometimes persist long after the event narrated. In that case a topical song is part of the cultural memory of a community referring to a shared historical memory. A case in point is the hymn 'Jerusalem', the lyrics of which were written by William Blake. They were partly based on the legend that Joseph of Arimathea accompanied Jesus to Glastonbury, and also inspired by the atrocities of the 'dark satanic mills' of the Industrial Revolution. During WWI, Hubert Perry set the text to music, turning it into a song of consolation for those in the trenches and those at home (see Ferber 2000; Whittaker forthcoming). This example is also an indication that topical songs can meaningfully be transferred to new contexts.

In my opinion, the Hebrew Bible contains a variety of topical songs, that is, hymns that are the written sediments of a cultural memory that earlier on would have been transmitted in oral form. Elsewhere, I have argued that Psalm 137 can be characterized as such (Becking 2012). In this contribution, I would like to propose that the Song of Deborah too can be construed as such a hymn.

Deborah's Topical Song

The Song of Deborah contains narrative and commentary that are interwoven. As in a topical song, the news is transmitted together with a view on the event. The 'facts'[2] that the song communicates are partly of a very general but mostly of a very specific nature.

---

2. I put 'facts' in inverted commas here, indicating that the propositions mentioned are pieces of information than could or could not be historically trustworthy. Further on, when using the word fact, I omit the commas for convenience, but they are always implied. In view of the limited space, I will only sparsely refer to the secondary literature, but the reader could consult the standard commentaries as well as Echols (2008).

Facts as Information

The first piece of information is given in vv. 6-8. In poetic language the dreadful situation in the era of Shamgar and Jael is depicted. Traveling through the land was dangerous. The traditional trade routes were no longer safe. The idea is evoked that travellers would fall in the hands of bandits and robbers. Those who had to make a journey are advised to take ארחות עקלקלות, 'winding by-routes'.[3] The despair is deepened by the remarks on the depopulation of the countryside. The words of vv. 6-7a can be read as an implied hymnic variant to one of the refrains in the book of Judges: 'there was no ruler in the land'. The other refrain 'everybody did what was right in his eyes', is referred to in v. 8. The continuous theme in the book of Judges of the betrayal of the relationship with YHWH is here formulated in the way that the veneration of 'other deities' was the cause of the presence of the enemy at the gates of Israel, which had a sizeable but poorly equipped army.

In the midst of all this misery, Deborah stood up (קום), not as a warrior but as an אם בישראל, 'mother in Israel' (see, e.g., Exum 1985; Lindars 1995: 239). She comes to the scene in an encompassing role, looking for the best for her children, which will turn out to be liberation from the Canaanite suppressor.

A further group of facts is narrated in vv. 11b-18. In lyrical language the Israelite army marching to battles is depicted. The section is moulded by internal contrasts. It is composed around a list of the ten Northern tribes. Some of them participated in the battle and can be qualified as righteous Israelites: Ephraim, Machir, Zebulon, Benjamin and Naphtali. Some other tribes did not join the league, but continued about their business and gave no sign of solidarity: Gilead did not cross the Jordan, Dan is mockingly asked why it remained with its ships[4] and Aser remained at the shores of the sea. These lines are written with restrained indignation. A middle position is taken by Ruben. This tribe is accused of entering into some sort of Polish sejm: endlessly deliberating without coming to a decision and hence not showing up at the crucial moment. The image is communicated of a lack of solidarity between the various tribes.

---

3. Note that in Isa. 27:2, the Leviathan is presented as a 'winding (עקלתון) serpent', which gives the impression that the 'secondary routes' of Judges 5 were monstrously dangerous.

4. Within the narrative of the book of Judges, the tribe of Dan is still living on the coast before the migration to the North as narrated in Judges 17–18. I will not dwell on a discussion of the historicity of this migration; I only note that the narrator's view on the Danites is consistent. On the Danites see Niemann 1985; Guillaume 2004: 129–42.

A third set of facts informs about the enemy, the kings and rulers of Canaan who battled near Taanakh and Megiddo. Despite their powers, they were unable to gain victory. In almost mythic language, their downfall is depicted. In mentioning the forces of nature as devastating powers to the Canaanites, the narrative becomes entwined with the author's commentary.

Intriguing is the section in which the inhabitants of Meroz are cursed for not having participated in the battle (see Brettler 2002: 72). מרוז, 'Meroz', was situated on the northern slopes of the valley of Jezreel. The inhabitants of this place were probably a community originating from the vicinity of Barak's home in Kedes and would in all likelihood have been expected to help Barak in the fight against Sisera, which would explain the mention of this relatively unimportant village. According to Brettler, the curse on them later became the 'model example of a curse' (Brettler 2002: 72).

Very detailed is the information on Jael's killing of Sisera. In Judges 4 the scene is described in almost matter-of-fact clauses (Judg. 4:21). This short report is extended into three lines of poetry in the Song of Deborah (Judg. 5:26-27).

The hymn shows a delight in details. This graphic presentation of the death of Sisera provokes – in my view – a much stronger image in the mind of the audience. This section in the biblical hymn communicates a subtle ambivalence between inhuman cruelty and laudable female heroism. The reader must be aware of the fact that while praising Jael for her act, an act of violence is sanctioned that otherwise would have been disapproved of (see Niditch 1995). This delicate balance gave rise to an ever-continuing series of illustrations and paintings of the scene. In the famous painting by Artemisia Gentileschi (1593–1656), Jael is represented as a very attractive woman even in the act of killing, thus echoing the biblical ambiguity in a slightly different way (see the essays in Bal 2006).

A final piece of information is given in vv. 28-30 (on this section see Baker 2017). This section contains a description from the point of view of Sisera's mother. It is full of ambiguity. At first sight, Sisera's mother and her wise female advisor are introduced as if the author is willing to look at the whole scene from the perspective of the other party. The questions they ask are full of hope. Sisera's mother is waiting at the window eager to hear the rattling of her son's chariot. The delay to the hoped-for return is explained by her advisor, who assumes that dividing the spoil might take more time than expected. The hymn ends in a cynical description – with sexual overtones – of the beauty of Sisera's spoil. His mother's questions remain unanswered. At this point the Song of Deborah is open-ended. The fact that the audience is well aware of the outcome of the battle makes this scene bitter, giving it an element of mocking.

Moulded in Ideology

The commentary on the battle in the Song of Deborah is clear and straightforward. The author wants to convince the audience of the view that it had been YHWH who had given Israel the victory. Although human obedience and craftiness were of importance, it was the deity whose presence was decisive. It is YHWH who should be praised and honored. This commentary comes to the fore at various instances and often in mythic language.

Verses 4-5 contain the language of theophany. Theophany is an ancient Near Eastern literary pattern to describe the appearance of the deity on the stage of history. This coming – mostly from a remote place – is accompanied with dramatic events in the realm of nature, underscoring the power of the deity and his/her firm determination to set things straight. In ancient Near Eastern texts, the deity appears to bring justice and righteousness, sometimes in the form of doom and sometimes as liberation from oppressing forces (e.g., Jeremias 1977).

The theophany in the Song of Deborah is reified in the victory of YHWH over the oppressing forces. This theme is always part of a summons to praise (Judg. 5:9-11). Next to that the divine victory is the basis for an *argumentum ad deum* (see Sanders 2007), a ground for a prayer to God to act again in the same way in moments of despair and destruction for Israel. Judges 5:31 reads:

> So may all your enemies perish, YHWH!
> But may all who love you be like the sun when it rises in its strength.

This double message summarizes Deborah's topical song. In later crises, its recognition of trouble and hope for liberation was grounds for its preservation over time.

The Ongoing Enigma of Date and Historicity

I do not dare to date the composition of Judges 5. An evaluation of the historical claims made in the narrative part of the song commands a study on its own in which the evidence is debated within a discourse that is drenched in historical methodology. I can only assume that Deborah's topical song was a source of consolation during troubled times in ancient Israel.

Bibliography

Baker, R. (2017), 'A Mother's Refrain: Judges 5:28-30 in Cultural Context', *VT*, 67: 505–18.
Bal, M., ed. (2006) *The Artemisia Files: Artemisia Gentileschi for Feminists and Other Thinking People*, Chicago: University of Chicago Press.
Bechmann, U. (1989), *Das Deboralied zwischen Geschichte und Fiktion. Eine exegetische Untersuchung zu Richter 5*, Dissertationen: Theologische Reihe 33, St. Ottilien: EOS.
Becking, B. (2012), 'Memory and Forgetting in and on the Exile: Remarks on Psalm 137', in E. Ben Zvi and C. Levin (eds), *Memory and Forgetting in Early Second Temple Judah*, 279–99, FAT 85, Tübingen: Mohr Siebeck.
Blenkinsopp, J. (1961), 'Ballad Style and Psalm Style in the Song of Deborah: A Discussion', *Bib*, 42: 61–76.
Boling, R. G. (1975), *Judges*, Anchor Bible 6A, Garden City, NY: Doubleday.
Brettler, M. Z. (2002), *The Book of Judges*, OTR, London: Routledge.
Cross, F. M. and D. N. Freedman (1995), *Studies in Ancient Yahwistic Poetry*, Biblical Resource Series, Grand Rapids, MI: Eerdmans.
de Moor, J. C. (1993), 'The Twelve Tribes in the Song of Deborah', *VT*, 42: 483–94.
Diebner, B.-J. (1995), 'Wann sang Deborah ihr Lied? Überlegungen zu zwei der ältesten Texte des TNK (Ri 4 und 5)', *Amsterdamse Cahiers voor Exegese en Bijbelse Theologie* 14: 106–30.
Donaldson, R. C. (2014), *'I Hear America Singing': Folk Music and National Identity*, Philadelphia: Temple University Press.
Dylan, B. (2004), *Chronicles. Vol. 1*, New York: Simon & Schuster.
Echols, C. F. (2008), *Tell Me, O Muse: The Song of Deborah (Judges 5) in the Light of Heroic Poetry*, LHBOTS 487, London: T&T Clark.
Exum, J. C. (1985), '"Mother in Israel": A Familiar Figure Reconsidered', in L. M. Russell (ed.), *Women in the Bible: Feminist Interpretation of the Bible*, 73–85, Oxford: Blackwell.
Ferber, M. (2000), 'Blake's "Jerusalem" as a Hymn', *Blake: An Illustrated Quarterly*, 34: 82–94.
Frolov, S. (2011), 'How Old is the Song of Deborah?', *JSOT*, 36: 163–84.
Görg, M. (1993), *Richter*, NEB. Würzburg: Echter Verlag.
Guillaume, P. (2004), *Waiting for Josiah: The Judges*, JSOTSup 385, London: T&T Clark.
Hauser, A. J. (1987), 'Two Songs of Victory: A Comparison of Exodus 15 and Judges 5', in E. R. Follis (ed.), *Directions in Biblical Hebrew Poetry*, 265–81, JSOTSup 40, Sheffield: Sheffield Academic Press.
Jeremias, J. (1977), *Theophanie: Die Geschichte einer alttestamentlichen Gattung*, WMANT 10, Neukirchen-Vluyn: Neukirchener Verlag.
Lindars, B. (1995), *Judges 1–5: A New Translation and Commentary*, Edinburgh: T. & T. Clark.
Niditch, S. (1995), *War in the Hebrew Bible: A Study in the Ethics of Violence*, Oxford: Oxford University Press.
Niemann, H. M. (1985), *Die Daniten: Studien zur Geschichte eines altisraelitischen Stammes*, FRLANT 135, Göttingen: Vandenhoeck & Ruprecht.
Ogot, B. A. (2009) *A History of the Luo-Speaking Peoples of East Africa*, Kisumu: Anyange Press.
Peddie I., ed. (2017), *The Resisting Muse: Popular Music and Social Protest*, London: Routledge.

Sanders, P. (2007), '*Argumenta ad Deum* in the Plague Prayers of Mursili II and in the Book of Psalms', in B. Becking and E. Peels (eds), *Psalms and Prayers: Papers Read at the Joint Meeting of SOTS and OTW*, 181–217, OTS 55, Leiden: E. J. Brill.

Schniedewind, W. M. (2004), *How the Bible Became a Book: The Textualization of Ancient Israel*, Cambridge: Cambridge University Press.

Soggin, J. A. (1981), *Judges*, OTL, London: SCM Press.

Thompson, T. L. (1999), *The Bible in History: How Writers Create a Past*, London: Jonathan Cape.

Weiser, A. (1959), 'Das Deboralied. Eine gattungs- und traditionsgeschichtliche Studie', *ZAW*, 71: 67–97.

Wellhausen, J. (1963), *Die Composition des Hexateuchs und der historischen Bücher des Alten Testaments*, Berlin: de Gruyter.

Whittaker, J. (forthcoming), 'Blake and the New Jerusalem: A Very English Form of Modernism', in *Visual Culture in Britain*.

How Jerusalem's Temple Was Aligned to Moses' Tabernacle: About the Historical Power of an Invented Myth

Rainer Albertz

Thomas Thompson, whom I warmly congratulate on the occasion of his 80th birthday, is a pioneer in questioning more or less weak historical reconstructions done by Old Testament scholars, reconstructions that were mainly based on biblical texts and only sometimes supported by a few arbitrarily selected extra-biblical data. I still remember how his Tübinger Dissertation on the historicity of the patriarchal narratives (Thompson 1974) struck like a bomb in Heidelberg during the preparation stage of the second volume of Westermann's commentary on Genesis. Claus Westermann – after Wellhausen's influential scepticism – had always been inclined to follow the reconstructions of a 'Patriarchal Period' put forward by William Foxwell Albright and several other American scholars on the basis of comparison with terms and customs in the Mari and Nuzi texts from the second millennium BCE. He now, however, felt compelled by the strong arguments of Thomas Thompson and others,[1] who referred to similar customs in much later texts of the first millennium, thus declaring the dating of the 'Patriarchal Period' an open question (see Westermann 1981: 52–5, 73–90; the more detailed discussion in Westermann 1975: 69–93, in which I was involved as his assistant), although he did not give up the concept completely. In my book, *A History of Israelite Religion*, I myself felt obliged to define the religion shown by the patriarchal narratives 'not as a preliminary stage but as a substratum of Yahweh religion' (Albertz 1994: 1:29). Thus, Thomas Thompson belongs to the few scholars in our field whose dissertation already had a considerable influence on Old Testament research.

1. Besides Thompson, Westermann was also impressed by Van Seters (1975).

Later on Thompson extended and radicalized his historical scepticism with regard to the Hebrew Bible. According to him, all the texts from Genesis to 2 Kings constitute a 'mythic past' composed by redactors of the Persian and Hellenistic periods from many traditions (Thompson 1999). They show no historiographical interest, but are intended to construct a Judean or Samarian identity and to enfold a theological and philosophical worldview (Thompson 1992: 353–423). I think Thompson is right as far as those biblical texts are not historiographical in the modern sense (similar Blum 2015: 31–54), but I think that their relation to a possible historical background can be very different and that – read against the grain – some historical and sociological information can be detected from many of them. We had detailed discussions about these questions over the years when participating in the 'European Seminar on Methodology in Israel's History' led by Lester L. Grabbe. In order to continue those discussions I would like to present to Thomas Thompson a little case study, which shows that a clearly unhistorical passage of the 'mythic past' became nevertheless historically powerful, shaping not only the literary history of other texts but also changing the historical reality of some details: I refer to the priestly tabernacle texts of Exodus 25–31; 35–40. I hope this study will be to his enjoyment.

1. *The Priestly Tabernacle Texts – An Invented Myth*

Up to the eighteenth century, the priestly tabernacle texts were regarded as historical, serving as a model for Solomon's temple in Jerusalem. In the nineteenth century, however, serious doubt was cast on their historicity.[2] According to Wilhelm Martin Leberecht de Wette, it is highly improbable that the liberated Israelite slaves would have possessed such large quantities of precious metals, luxurious textiles and exotic perfumes, which these texts deemed to be necessary for construction of the tabernacle (Exod. 25:1-7; 30:22-38; 35:5-35), let alone the significant technical skills needed for it (de Wette 1806/7 [1971]: 1:259; 2:265–70).[3] The expensive purple wool must have been imported from Phoenicia, pure gold from south Arabia or east Africa and cinnamon from Ceylon or the Moluccas, none of which would have been attainable for the Israelites in the desert without any state-run trade. Moreover, the wooden planks, beams and pillars alone needed for the substructure of the tent would have

---

2. For a history of research see Houtman (1993–2002: 3:325-35).
3. He called the reports about Moses' tabernacle a 'holy fairy tale' (de Wette 1806/7 [1971]: 1:259) belonging to the 'realm of myth' (2:269).

been too heavy to be carried through the mountainous wilderness (26:15-37). Depending on their thickness, the 56 Acacia wood planks alone would have weighed between 12.3 and 72.8 tons, far too much for those four wagons with eight oxen from Num. 7:8 to be able to move.[4] You would need two or three lorries! Thus, Julius Wellhausen, after having ascribed the tabernacle text to the early post-exilic P source, rightly understood Moses' tabernacle not as an early prototype, but as a late copy or a back projection of Solomon's temple (see Wellhausen 1927 [2001]: 36–7). Considering the conceptual and material differences between the two, however, it would perhaps be better to speak of an ideal counter model to the pre-exilic Jerusalem temple now fallen into ruins, which was implanted into the foundation history of Israel.[5] Thus, Moses' tabernacle is clearly an element of the mythic past in Thompson's terms, but it was nevertheless conceptualized to exert some influence on the future.

2. *The Reports on Solomon's Temple – Secondarily Connected to the Tabernacle*

The reports on the building and inauguration of Solomon's temple in 1 Kings 6–8 are literarily disputed and in some respects difficult to understand. They cannot be discussed here in detail. However, whatever the date of their original composition,[6] this must have been earlier than the tabernacle texts in the book of Exodus, because in spite of some similarities concerning the structure (holy and holy of the holies) and several furnishings (ark, incense altar, table), the described Jerusalem temple shows important differences to Moses' tabernacle: it possesses a huge cherub throne for the deity in the holy of the holies (1 Kgs 6:23-28) instead of two small cherubs installed on the top of the ark, called *kapporet* (Exod. 25:17-22). Its inner rooms are enclosed by walls with wooden doors (1 Kgs 6:31-35), while the tabernacle uses an inner (*pāroket*) and an outer curtain (*māsāk*) for the same purpose (Exod. 26:31-37).[7] Its holy main room is illuminated by ten lamp stands (1 Kgs 7:49), while the tabernacle has one big lamp stand with seven arms (*mĕnôrah*)

---

4. See for this calculation Albertz (2012/15: 2:176–7). The thickness of the planks is not indicated, but one cubit seems to be assumed. Josephus reckons with four fingers (*Ant.* 3.116, 119).

5. For such an appraisal see Albertz (2012/15: 2:24, 142–85).

6. The proposed dates vary between the time of Solomon, such as Noth (1968: 106), and the period of exile, such as van Seters (1997: 56–7).

7. There is no reason for the supposition that the word *pāroket* in 1 Kgs 6:21 should be added, *pace* Rudolph (1955: 204–5) and others.

instead (Exod. 25:31-39). Apart from the outer altar,[8] Solomon's temple has many more bronze objects in the courtyard, not just one water basin like the tabernacle (Exod. 30:17-21), but a decorated sea of cast metal (1 Kgs 7:23-26) and ten ornamented trolleys of bronze (vv. 27-39), which are later partly deconstructed (2 Kgs 16:17).

Although Solomon's temple and Moses' tabernacle differ in so many respects, some later priestly scribes seemed to be obliged to bring them closer together literarily. They introduced into 1 Kings 8 that somewhat strange idea that not only the ark, on which the Dtr inauguration report was focussed (vv. 1, 3-4, 5-9), but also the tabernacle, the tent of meeting and all its holy devices, were brought up into Solomon's temple. Verse 4a$\alpha_2\beta$b, however, is clearly secondarily intruded.[9] The practical difficulties – where to appropriately store all these planks, beams, stands and rolls of textiles from the tabernacle in the rooms of Solomon's temple without disrupting its own service – remain unsolved.[10] It is not just by chance that the tabernacle is never mentioned again in the book of Kings. Those priestly scribes, however, inserted some other additions in order to bring the inauguration of Solomon's temple in contact with the mythic past told in the Pentateuch: interpreting the term 'elders of Israel' in v. 1 they record the fact that 'all the heads of tribes and the chiefs of the families of the Israelites' were present at the inauguration of the temple, a description similar to that used for the tabernacle's inauguration (Num. 7:2).[11] For similar reasons they changed the term 'all Israel' (כל־ישראל) in 1 Kgs 8:5, often used in the DtrH (cf. 4:1, 7; 5:27; 8:62, 65), to 'the whole congregation of Israel' (כל־עדת ישראל) in order to be reminiscent of the people of the foundation period in its priestly perspective (cf. Exod. 12:3, 47; Lev. 4:13). Therefore, it is highly probable that the additional

---

8. The outer bronze altar is missing in the building report for reasons unknown; nevertheless, it is presupposed in 1 Kgs 8:64; cf. 2 Kgs 16:14, 15.

9. In 1 Kgs 8:3 only the priests are regarded as carriers of the ark, while in v. 4b the Levites are mentioned next to the priests as carriers of all the holy equipment, because the former were commissioned to do so in Num 4. Without the intrusion in v. 4* (from 'and the tent of meeting' onwards) the plot becomes clear: gathered by the king, the elders of Israel came, and the priests picked up the ark (v. 3) and brought up the ark together (beginning of v. 4), while Solomon and the assembled people offered sacrifices in front of it (v. 5).

10. Although Friedman (1980: 241–8) tried hard to find a technical solution, Hurowitz (1995) made a compelling case for rejecting it.

11. The terminology used in 1 Kgs 8:1 does not exactly agree with the typical priestly terms of the Pentateuch; the closest parallels can be found in its late priestly layers (Num. 30:2; 36:1).

dating of Solomon's temple building from 1 Kgs 6:1* in the 480th year after the exodus of the Israelites from Egypt does not come from the Deuteronomistic historian as often thought (see, e.g., Noth 1968: 110; Fritz 1996: 68–9), but from the same late priestly scribes, who intend to connect the Jerusalem temple with the mythic past of the Pentateuch.[12] To this past belongs a short theophany event, where YHWH entered the erected tabernacle in the form of a cloud and filled it with his glory (Exod. 40:34-35). Thus the late priestly scribes included a similar event in their revision of the inauguration report a (1 Kgs 8:10-11), doubling the divine promises for Solomon's temple of 9:1-3 already given in the DtrH:[13] after the priests had left the temple, it was filled by a cloud and divine glory so that they could not carry out their service. Thus Solomon's temple received the same visible confirmation of God's presence as had been given to Moses' tabernacle.[14]

What is the reason for this rather strange combination and parallelization of two sanctuary passages of the Hebrew Bible? What is the force behind it? It has nothing to do with a mutual adaptation. Only the tabernacle texts from the Pentateuch show an impact on the report on Solomon's temple building, not vice versa. Although invented they seem to have become powerful, probably a result of the authorization and implementation of the Pentateuch in the early fourth century BCE. Moses' tabernacle, as one of the most important institutions of Israel's foundation period, became so authoritative that some late Jerusalem priests felt compelled to connect their temple to it in some way. The relation to Moses, which the Dtr historian had already established via the Decalogue tablets of the ark (1 Kgs 8:9; Deut. 10:1-5), was no longer sufficient for them to defend the legitimacy and reputation of the Jerusalem temple.[15]

---

12. The dating follows stylistically exactly those priestly dating formulas of the books of Exodus and Numbers, cf. Exod. 19:1; Num. 33:38, cf. Exod. 16:1; Num. 1:1; 9:1. Thus, Achenbach (2007: 252) has appropriately assigned it to his theocratic editions.

13. To create a frame together with 1 Kgs 9:1-3 a divine promise was inserted in 6:11-13 by an editor, who uses Dtr language, but who refers to the priestly topic that YHWH will dwell among the Israelites (cf. Exod. 25:8; 29:45-46). The passage is still missing in Chronicles and LXX, but presupposed by Josephus (*Ant*. 8.125–26). Thus, it must be very late.

14. Since the shorter report of the LXX in 3 Kgdms 8:1–11 presupposes the main late priestly additions in vv. 4, 10-11, it cannot represent an older text tradition as sometimes thought; for details see Van der Keulen (2005: 151–63).

15. A similar late priestly alignment to the canonized Pentateuch can be found in the book of Joshua; see Albertz (2007). It also mentions the tent of meeting in Josh.

3. The Jerusalem Temple in Chronicles – as a Right Follower of the Tabernacle

The authors of the books of Chronicles already presuppose the late priestly revisions in the books of Kings (cf. 2 Chron. 5:2, 5, 11-14),[16] but they were dissatisfied with them: How could the tabernacle be brought convincingly into the Jerusalem temple, if it had never been mentioned and honoured before?[17] Thus, in their new work the Chroniclers first constructed an unbroken historical continuity between Moses' tabernacle and Solomon's temple. From its beginning onwards they made clear that there was a regular cult at the tabernacle on the high place of Gibeon – besides a smaller cult at David's tent for the ark in Jerusalem (1 Chron. 16:1-38; 2 Chron. 1:4) – before Solomon built the temple (1 Chron. 6:17; 16:39-41; 21:29; 2 Chron. 1:3–6). Thus, it became logical that Moses' tabernacle was integrated into this temple together with the ark (5:5). Secondly, the Chroniclers adjusted the preparations for the temple building to those of the tabernacle: the inspired David presented a model (*tabnît*) of the temple to his son (1 Chron. 28:11) as God had shown it to Moses for the tabernacle (Exod. 25:9, 40). The temple was no longer financed only by the state as in 1 Kings 5–7 (cf. 1 Chron. 29:2), but also by private donations from David (29:3-5a) and the representatives of the people (vv. 6-9). Typical for the tabernacle texts is the call for donations (Exod. 25:2-8; 35:4-19) enthusiastically followed by all the people (35:20–36:7). Such a call is imitated in 1 Chron. 29:5b. Thus, the Chroniclers' account of 1 Chronicles 29 looks like an adjustment to the wilderness scenario under the conditions of statehood.

18:1; 19:51, erected in Shilo. Since this Joshua revision is more interested in the High Priest Eleazar as guarantor of a just land distribution than in the tabernacle and differs from the terminology of the people's leaders used in 1 Kgs 8:1 (see Josh. 14:1; 19:51; 21:1; cf. Num. 32:28), it does not seem to come from the same authors as the late priestly revision of 1 Kings 6–8. In any case, the different late priestly groups did not intend the edition of an Enneateuch; likewise Achenbach (2007: 253), although he did not distinguish between them.

16. Only the reference to the exodus in 1 Kgs 6:1 is missing in 2 Chron. 3:2, because the Chroniclers generally neglected this date of Israel's foundation myth in order to emphasize the crucial importance of the David and Solomon period; see Kegler (1989). Instead, they refer in 2 Chron. 3:1 to another element of Israel's mythic past: Abrahams offering at Moriah in Gen. 22:2.

17. In the priestly revised DtrH the tabernacle is forgotten after Josh. 19:51. The mention of it in 1 Sam. 2:22bβ is still missing in the LXX and 4QSam^a and seems to be a very late addition.

The authors of the books of Chronicles surpassed their priestly forerunners in adjusting thirdly Solomon's temple to the tabernacle even in terminological and architectural concerns. Thus, in 1 Chron. 28:11 they called the holiest inner part of the temple the 'shrine of expiation' (*bêt hak-kapporet*), using the technical term from Exod. 25:17-22, as if the cult symbol for divine presence and expiating power conceptualized here and in Lev. 16:2 had really been present there.[18] Moreover, they introduced an inner curtain into Solomon's temple (2 Chron. 3:14) to separate the holy of the holiest from the holy main room. Not only did they use the same term *pāroket* for this, as in the tabernacle text (Exod. 26:31, 33, 35), but they also described it as having been made from identical luxurious materials. In preparation for this innovation they broadened the skills of the craftsman Hiram from Tyre – called Huram-Abi here – a famous expert of bronze work in 1 Kgs 7:13-47, to all kinds of handicraft, including working with precious textile materials (2 Chron. 2:6, 13), thus putting him on a par with Bezalel, the leading craftsman and artist of the tabernacle (Exod. 31:1-5; 35:30-33; cf. 2 Chron. 1:5). We are not sure whether in the time of Chroniclers during the last half of the fourth or the early third century BCE the Jerusalem temple was actually provided with an inner curtain[19] as evidenced in later times.[20] But taking into consideration that the authors explicitly mention doors between the two inner rooms (4:22b), where 1 Kgs 7:50 only speaks of door-hinges, the idea of an additional curtain inspired by the example of the tabernacle would seem to be rather a new architectural concept to be realized later. Finally the Chroniclers further extended the inauguration of the temple in accordance with the tabernacle scenario, when they described not only how the completed temple was accepted by God (2 Chron. 5:11-14; cf. 1 Kgs 8:10-11), but also how the first prayers and offerings were answered by him through a further theophany (2 Chron. 7:1-3): the offerings were consumed by a heavenly fire as in Lev. 9:24a and the temple was so impressively filled with God's glory (cf. v. 23) that all people fell down and praised YHWH (cf. v. 24b).

Thus, the authors of the books of Chronicles invested a lot of energy not only in relating but to almost identifying the Jerusalem temple with the sanctuary of Israel's famous mythic past. In order to bring the two together as closely as possible, they added to the former specific items

18. In their description of the holy of the holiest (2 Chron. 3:8-13), however, the Chroniclers did not follow the concept of Exod. 25:17-22 but that of the *Vorlage* 1 Kgs 6:23-28.

19. This was supposed by Rudolph (1955: 204–5) and Japhet (2003: 53).

20. Cf. 1 Macc. 4:51; Josephus, *B.J.* 5.219; Heb. 6:19; 9:3; 10:20.

from the latter, such as the inner curtain, or largely removed from the former what was missing from the latter, such as the bronze trolleys (2 Chron. 4:6, 14). Even in those cases where the number of devices differs, such as the ten lamp stands in Solomon's temple (4:7), the Chroniclers assured that they would accord to the law (vv. 7, 20). There can be no doubt that, for the Chroniclers, the tabernacle texts of the Pentateuch constituted the decisive norm to which they felt obliged to align their report of the foundation and inauguration of Jerusalem's temple. But why were they so eager? An answer may be given by 2 Chron. 29:6, where the Chroniclers once more took up one of the two old terms for the tabernacle, *miškān*, to denote the temple of Jerusalem just at the time, when King Hezekiah reopened it and invited all Israel, including the population of the former Northern Kingdom, to participate in the cult of Jerusalem. Thus, in aligning Jerusalem's temple as closely as possible with Moses' tabernacle, the Chroniclers intended to bestow upon their sanctuary the highest degree of legitimacy and authority in the eyes of the Samarians. We know that the Samarians had also accepted the Pentateuch as their Holy Scripture; and if we trust a much later note from Josephus (*Ant.* 18.85), the Samarians likewise legitimated their own sanctuary on Mount Gerizim by referring to vessels from Moses' tabernacle that were buried next to it. Thus, there were competing claims to the mythic past making this even more powerful. Therefore, the Chroniclers worked hard to prove that their temple in Jerusalem was the rightful successor to the normative tabernacle of Moses, that is, the only legitimate sanctuary of YHWH.

4. *The Appearance of Jerusalem Temples –*
Changed by the Tabernacle

As time passed the tabernacle texts of the Pentateuch not only influenced increasingly other literary concepts of the Jerusalem temple, but also changed the real appearance of later temple buildings in Jerusalem. The most impressive change was the installation of a coloured outer curtain at the entrance to the sanctuary. The tabernacle texts envision such a curtain (*māsāk*) at the entrance to the main holy room, made 'from finely woven linen, embroidered with violet, purple, and scarlet' and hung on five columns (Exod. 26:36-37). It is less artistic than the inner curtain (*pāroket*) dividing the main room from the holy of the holies (vv. 31-35), but still provides the tabernacle with an impressive appearance in spite of its mobile construction. An even more impressive outer curtain of tremendous size (55 times 16 cubits) is certainly testified for the Herodian temple of Jerusalem, installed within the vestibule before the golden doors of the main hall. Josephus describes it as 'a Babylonian curtain, embroidered with blue, and fine linen, and scarlet, and purple, and of a texture that was truly wonderful' (*B.J.* 5.211-112), which is clearly reminiscent of the tabernacle texts. Josephus describes such an installation of wooden doors covered by a curtain already existing at Solomon's temple (*Ant.* 8.75), but this seems to be clearly an anachronism; according to its oldest description Solomon's building only had decorated wooden doors and no curtains at all (1 Kgs 6:31-35). Even in the Chronistic description an outer curtain is still missing. The references that the entrance of the Second Temple was covered with a curtain come from the second century BCE (Sir. 50:5;[21] 1 Macc. 1:22; 4:51; *Ant.* 12.318) and later (*Let. Arist.* § 85; *Ant.* 14.107) (cf. Légasse 1980). A possible hint that an outer curtain for the temple obtained more importance already during the second half of the third century BCE may be given by the Septuagint. While their translators generally use the term καταπέτασμα for both curtains[22] of the tabernacle (Exod. 26:31, 33-35, 37 etc.),[23] they speak once of an ἐπίσπαστρον, where the outer curtain is introduced (v. 36). This term, used in one of the Greek inscriptions from Delos, denotes '"un article comprenant un système à cordon de tirage", du type qui ornait l'entrée des sanctuaires grecs' (see Légasse 1980: 571). Thus, the Greek translators – by interpreting the normative tabernacle texts – seem to intend the authorization of a bigger curtain installation for their contemporary temple.[24]

---

21. Since the High Priest Simon becomes visible to the congregation, the curtain of the temple, by which he leaves, can only be the outer one, although the Hebrew text uses the expression *bêt hap-pāroket* 'house of the curtain', the term for the inner one. The Hebrew expression shows that curtains are regarded as distinct features of the Jerusalem temple at the beginning of the second century BCE.

22. The term means verbatim 'a piece of hanging material serving to conceal what is behind it'.

23. The Vaticanus even mentions a καταπέτασμα of the inner temple court in 3 Kgdms 6:36a, while Exod. 27:16 uses the term κάλυμμα for this type of curtain. The text, however, seems to be defective; see Van der Keulen 2005: 134-5.

24. This is one of the few examples where a Pentateuchal sanctuary text is changed to suit contemporary interests. Another example is the description of the tabernacle by Josephus, where he adds a fine linen veil to be drawn over the entrance in order to protect the outer curtain from bad weather. From this Josephus even deduces a later custom for the period after the temple was built (*Ant.* 3.128-129), but as far as I see he never came back to this topic.

References to the inner curtain are fewer, probably because this one could not be seen from outside. Josephus already presupposed it inside the Solomonic temple, where it separated – along with a wooden door – the most holy chamber from the rest (*Ant.* 8.71–72). This is, however, a back projection. After being conceptually introduced by the Chroniclers as an innovation (2 Chron. 3:14), the inner curtain also seems to have been installed in the Second Temple during the second century BCE (1 Macc. 4:51; *Ant.* 12.318; cf. 14.107). The best piece of evidence comes from the Herodian temple, where Josephus no longer mentions any wooden wall or doors next to it (*B.J.* 5.219).[25] This indicated that an important relic of Solomonic architecture was completely removed in favour of the textile structure of the tabernacle. Thus, it took 300–500 years for an invented text, which had become part of the mythic past, to obtain so much power that it even changed parts of the existing reality.

5. *Concluding Remarks*

This short case study has shown that literary passages of the Hebrew Bible, which are evidently unhistorical, can develop an astonishing power that shapes not only the further literary history of other biblical passages but also elements of the historical reality. The priestly tabernacle texts from the book of Exodus are a good example of this. The dynamic power has to do with the decision made in the Judean and Samarian communities of the fourth century BCE to accept a bigger part of their literary tradition, the *tôrat Mošeh*, as authoritative. By doing so, they did not only concede that the concepts and rules of the Pentateuch should have more or less influence on their lifestyle, but they also obtained a powerful basis, on which they could found their theological claims and the legitimacy of their cultic institutions. Because of this authoritative textual corpus priests and other responsible persons felt obliged to change the appearance of the Jerusalem temple in order to align it with aspects of Moses' famous tabernacle. Thus, we should perhaps not classify all texts from Genesis to 2 Kings as 'mythic past' on the same level because of their common contrast to modern historiography. Some of them, especially those of the

---

25. The juxtaposition of the wooden doors and the inner curtain, which might have been a compromise between the older Jerusalem temple architecture and the structure of the tabernacle found in the Second Temple during the Hellenistic period, stands possible behind later Rabbinic disputes, whether the sanctuary had one or two veils for separating the holy of the holiest from the rest (see *Yom.* 5:1 and Légasse 1980: 580–2).

Pentateuch, possess more 'mythical dynamic' than others. I agree with the statement Thomas Thompson made in his dissertation: 'In fact, we can say that the faith of Israel is not an historical faith, in the sense of a faith based on historical event; it is rather a faith within history' (see Thompson 1974: 328–9). I would like just to emphasize that this faith – expressed by biblical texts – cannot only change the mind and behaviour of people, but is also able in some way to change historical reality.

Bibliography

Achenbach, R. (2007), 'Der Pentateuch: Seine theokratischen Bearbeitungen und Josua – 2 Könige', in T. Römer and K. Schmid (eds), *Les dernières rédactions du Pentateuque, de l'Hexateuque et de l'Enneateuque*, 225–53, BEThL 203, Leuven: University Press and Peeters.
Albertz, R. (1994), *A History of Israelite Religion in the Old Testament Period*, 2 vols, Louisville, KY: Westminster John Knox Press.
Albertz, R. (2007), 'The Canonical Alignment of the Book of Joshua', in O. Lipschits, G. N. Knoppers and R. Albertz (eds), *Judah and the Judeans in the Fourth Century BCE*, 287–303, Winona Lake, IN: Eisenbrauns.
Albertz, R. (2012/2015), *Exodus*, 2 vols, Zürich: Theologischer Verlag Zürich.
Blum, E. (2015), 'Historiographie oder Dichtung? Zur Eigenart alttestamentlicher Geschichtsüberlieferung', (repr.) in *Grundfragen der historischen Exegese*, 31–54, FAT 95, Tübingen: Mohr Siebeck.
Friedman, R. E. (1980), 'The Tabernacle in the Temple', *BA*, 43: 241–8.
Fritz, V. (1996), *Das erste Buch der Könige*, ZBK.AT 10/1, Zürich: Theologischer Verlag Zürich.
Houtman, C. (1993–2002), *Exodus*, 4 vols, Kampen: KOK; Leuven: Peeters.
Hurowitz, V. A. (1995), 'The Form and Fate of the Tabernacle: Reflections on a Recent Proposal', *JQR*, 86: 127–51.
Japhet, S. (2003), *2 Chronik*, HThKAT, Freiburg: Herder.
Kegler, J. (1989), 'Das Zurücktreten der Exodustradition in den Chronikbüchern', in R. Albertz, F. W. Golka and J. Kegler (eds), *Schöpfung und Befreiung: Für Claus Westermann zum 80. Geburtstag*, 54–66, Stuttgart: Calwer.
Légasse, S. (1980), 'Les voiles du temple de Jérusalem: essai de parcours historique', *RB*, 87: 560–89.
Noth, M. (1968), *Könige: 1. Teilband: 1. Könige 1–16*, BK IX/1, Neukirchen-Vluyn: Neukirchener.
Rudolph, W. (1955), *Chronikbücher*, HAT I/21, Tübingen: Mohr Siebeck.
Thompson, T. L. (1974), *The Historicity of the Patriarchal Narratives: The Quest for the Historical Abraham*, BZAW 133, Berlin: de Gruyter.
Thompson, T. L. (1992), *Early History of the Israelite People: From the Written and Archaeological Sources*, SHANE 4, Leiden: E. J. Brill.
Thompson, T. L. (1999), *The Mythic Past. Biblical Archaeology and the Myth of Israel*, New York: Basic Books.
Van der Keulen, P. S. F. (2005), *The Versions of Solomon Narrative: An Inquiry into the Relationship between MT 1 Kgs. 2–11 and LXX 3 Reg. 2–11*, VTSup 104, Leiden: E. J. Brill.

Van Seters, J. (1975), *Abraham in History and Tradition* (New Haven: Yale University Press.
Van Seters, J. (1997), 'Solomon's Temple: Fact and Ideology in Biblical History and Near Eastern Historiography', *CBQ* 59: 45–57.
Wellhausen, J. (1927), *Prolegomena zur Geschichte Israels*, 6th ed., Berlin: Reimer (repr. Berlin: de Gruyter, 2001).
Westermann, C. (1975), *Genesis 12–50*, EdF 48, Darmstadt: Wissenschaftliche Buchgesellschaft.
Westermann, C. (1981), *Genesis. 2. Teilband, Genesis 12–36*, BK I/2, Neukirchen-Vluyn: Neukirchener.
Wette, W. M. L. de (1806/7), *Beiträge zur Einleitung in das Alte Testament*, 2 vols, Halle: Schimmelpfennig (repr.: Darmstadt: Wissenschaftliche Buchgesellschaft, 1971).

CAN THE BOOK OF NEHEMIAH BE USED AS AN HISTORICAL SOURCE, AND IF SO, OF WHAT?

Lisbeth S. Fried

I am happy to dedicate this essay to my dear friend Professor Thomas Thompson in honor of him, our friendship, and in honor of the sea-change that he created in the field of biblical studies with his 1974 book, *The Historicity of the Patriarchal Narratives: The Quest for the Historical Abraham.* Thompson taught the importance of looking beyond the situation in which the biblical story is set to the situation in which the book may have been written. Following in that path, we recognize that while the biblical book Ezra-Nehemiah is set in the Persian period, it was written over a long period of time. Much of it is definitely Hellenistic (Fried 2015a: 4–5; Finkelstein 2018); some of it may be Persian, however, and may be used as an historical source if used cautiously and if confirmed by corroborating documents. I test this hypothesis by examining the portrayal of Nehemiah as the Persian governor of Judea during the reign of Artaxerxes I. Is Nehemiah's portrayal historical, i.e., does his portrayal match what we know in general about provincial governors under Achaemenid rule?

The Persian Governor and the Temple Priesthood

I begin with vv. 63-65 of Nehemiah 7 (= Ezra 2:61-63), which describe a curious relationship between the Persian governor and the local temple priesthood:

וּמִן־הַכֹּהֲנִים... ⁶⁴ אֵלֶּה בִּקְשׁוּ כְתָבָם הַמִּתְיַחְשִׂים וְלֹא נִמְצָא וַיְגֹאֲלוּ מִן־הַכְּהֻנָּה: ⁶⁵ וַיֹּאמֶר הַתִּרְשָׁתָא לָהֶם אֲשֶׁר לֹא־יֹאכְלוּ מִקֹּדֶשׁ הַקֳּדָשִׁים עַד עֲמֹד הַכֹּהֵן לְאוּרִים וְתֻמִּים:

> And among the priests…these [men] sought the registry of their genealogies but it was not found, so they were deemed unfit for the priesthood. 'Attiršata' told them that they may not eat from the most holy food until a priest arises having Urim and Thummim.

Who or what is ''Attiršata'? The word *hattiršātā'* is often translated into English as 'the governor'. Unfortunately, this translation is based on an outdated etymology. *Tarsa* means 'to fear' in Old Persian (Kent 1953: 186), and it had been assumed that in *hattiršātā'* we find *'tarsa'*, 'frightened', or 'trembling in fear', so that the term had been believed to refer to 'the one feared', that is, 'Excellency'. Because Nehemiah, the governor, is called this in the book of Nehemiah (Neh. 8:9; 10:2), it had been routinely translated into English as 'the governor' (e.g., Fried 2015a: 90, 131–2). The difficulty with this translation is that *tarsa* never refers to the one feared, but always to the one who is frightened (Skjaervo 1994: 501). Moreover, there is no Iranian, Persian, Elamite or Akkadian title remotely similar to *hattiršātā'* or even *tiršātā'* (Tavernier 2015).

Rather than assuming that the initial *hat* is the Hebrew definite article 'the', thus indicating some sort of title, the prefix *hattir* is more likely a corruption of Attar, and refers either to Atar, the Persian fire [god] (Benveniste 1966: 120; Zadok 2012: 160–1; Tuplin 2013: 615 n. 3; Jan Tavernier, personal communication, 18 February 2016), or to the West-Semitic goddess Attar, associated with the planet Venus (Lemaire 2015). The second element, *š(y)ata*, is a common component of Iranian personal names and means 'prosperous', 'happy' or 'blissful' (Kent 1953: 210–11). The word is now considered simply to be a personal name meaning 'Prosperous or Happy through Atar/Attar', that is, 'through, or by means of, the god/goddess Atar/Attar'. Thus, Nehemiah seems to have had two names like many American Jews today, an 'outer' Persian (or English/American) name and an 'inner' Hebrew one, as is explicitly stated in both Neh. 8:9 and 10:2:

וַיֹּאמֶר נְחֶמְיָה הוּא הַתִּרְשָׁתָא

And Nehemiah, that is 'Attiršata, said… (Neh. 8:9)

וְעַל הַחֲתוּמִים נְחֶמְיָה הַתִּרְשָׁתָא בֶּן־חֲכַלְיָה

And on the sealings is [that of] Nehemiah 'Attiršata ben Ḥakalia (Neh. 10:2)

Thus, in Neh. 7:63-65 (= Ezra 2:61-63) we read that it was *Attiršātā'*, that is, Nehemiah, the Persian governor (Neh. 5:14), who controlled admittance to the priesthood. It was not Jeshua the High Priest who decided on priests' eligibility, nor was it any other priest. Rather, it was Nehemiah the Persian governor himself.

This intrusion of Persian officials into the organization of Jerusalem's temple priesthood is consistent with what we read from contemporaneous Persian-period documents, both Babylonian and Egyptian. Indeed, Persian approval was required for appointment to temple offices throughout the Achaemenid Empire. The Achaemenids subverted local temple structures for their own purposes, and in Persian times a kind of tax was introduced requiring candidates for priestly offices to pay for the privilege (Waerzeggers and Jursa 2008). Babylonian records (e.g., BM 79293 and VS 4 85) reveal the required payments of silver to the palace official 'in charge of temples' (*ša-muḫḫi bītāni*) for the consecration of priests. This was also true in Egypt, indicating an empire-wide practice. The following text records, for example, a fee of 2 *deben* of silver to Parnu, the Persian governor of the southern province of Syene and Elephantine, paid by Paibes for the appointment of his son Djedhor to the rank of 'second priest of Khnum':

> Year 35, Pharmouthi, of Pharaoh Darius.
>
> Payment received for making second priest of Khnum, the Great, Lord of Elephantine, Djedhor son of Paibes, 1 silver *deben-ḥr*, makes…in accordance with the…, (which) Paibes son of Petiese, his father, brought to the collection-box of Parnu, [he of Tshet]res, to whom the fortress of Syene is entrusted, amounting to 2 silver *deben-ḥr*, in accordance with the…(to) the collection-box of Parnu, he of Tshetres, to [whom the] fortress of Syene is entrusted. They were received; they were delivered; their payment which was made for him before was in them. (P.Berlin 13582, 21 July–19 August 487 BCE)

Paibes son of Petiese had to pay Parnu, the Persian governor, in order to secure the appointment of his son, Djedhor. It was not the high priest whom he paid, but the Persian provincial governor. Other texts from Elephantine show the temple of Khnum having to procure the Persian satrap's stamp of approval of their candidate for the Lesonis priest, the chief priest of Khnum. The satrap rejected the first two of their nominees, approving only the third (see references in Fried 2004: 80–6).

The Persian Governor and Temple Lodging

A revealing peek into the relationship between the local temple hierarchy and the Persian governor is also visible in Nehemiah 13. Verses 7-9 describe Nehemiah throwing Tobiah, a relative of the priest Eliashib, out of the rooms in the temple where he had been staying.

⁷[When I] returned to Jerusalem…I discovered the wrong that [the priest] Eliashib had done on behalf of Tobiah, preparing a room for him in the courts of the house of God. ⁸And I was very angry, and I threw all the household furniture of Tobiah out of the room. ⁹Then I gave orders and they cleansed the chambers, and I brought back the vessels of the house of God, with the grain offering and the frankincense [which had previously been stored there]. (Neh. 13:7-9)

This text shows that the temple priesthood had no control over who could lodge in the rooms of their own temple. Lodging in the temple was evidently not decided by the priests but by the Persian governor. Commentators assume that Tobiah's staying in the temple was a sacrilege because he was not Jewish, and that Nehemiah was offended by this breach of religious norms (e.g., Batten 1913: 290; Rudolph 1949: 204; Blenkinsopp 1988: 355). This could not have been the reason for his ouster, however. Although governor of Ammon, Tobiah very likely was of Judean ancestry, and a Yahwist. His name, Tobiah, means 'YHWH is good'. If it is the same Tobiah who was Nehemiah's nemesis, then he was married to the daughter of Shecaniah son of Arah of Jerusalem, a Judean. They named their son Johohanan, and this son married the daughter of Meshullam son of Berechiah also of Jerusalem (Neh. 6:18). These relationships suggest a Judean identity and ancestry. He was also related (either by blood or by marriage) to the priest Eliashib who supervised the temple rooms (Neh. 13:4).

The fact of Tobiah being a Yahwist and of Judean descent was not relevant to Nehemiah though, nor was the fact that the temple priesthood had approved of his staying in the temple. All that was relevant was that Nehemiah, as governor of Judah, had the final say on who could lodge where. Nehemiah's ejection of Tobiah and his things 'points unmistakably to gubernatiorial jurisdiction over the temple and its operations' (Blenkinsopp 1988: 355). Indeed, we find a parallel to this in the inscription of Udjaḥorresnet:

I made a petition to the majesty of the King of Upper and Lower Egypt, Cambyses, about all the foreigners who dwelled in the temple of Neith, in order to have them expelled from it, so as to let the temple of Neith be in all its splendor, as it had been before. His majesty commanded to expel all the foreigners [who] dwelt in the temple of Neith, to demolish all their houses and all their unclean things that were in this temple.

When they had carried [all their] personal [belongings] outside the wall of the temple, his majesty commanded to cleanse the temple of Neith and to return all its personnel to it, the…and the hour-priests of the temple. His majesty did this because I had let his majesty know the greatness of Sais, that it is the city of all the gods, who dwell there on their seats forever. (*The Statue Inscription of Udjaḥorresnet*, Lichtheim 1980: 36-41, lines 18-23)

Even though Udjaḥorresnet was high priest of the temple of Neith in Sais, Egypt, he had no say over who could live in his temple and who could not. He had to appeal to Cambyses, king of Persia, for relief from the presence of foreigners dwelling in his temple.

The Persian Governor and Temple Funds

The book of Nehemiah also illustrates the role of the Persian governor in controlling temple funds. We read that it was Nehemiah, the Persian governor, and not the high priest, who selected officials to monitor and disburse these funds:

> And I appointed over the temple treasuries the priest Shelemiah, the scribe Zadok, and Pedaiah of the Levites, and as their assistant Hanan son of Zaccur son of Mattaniah, for they were considered loyal (נֶאֱמָנִים נֶחְשָׁבוּ). (Neh. 13:13)

As this passage shows, Nehemiah chose men who were 'loyal' or 'reliable', but reliable to whom, loyal to whom? I suggest it would have been to him, of course, to Nehemiah himself, and therefore to the Persian administration. Prior to Persian domination, native kings routinely donated to local temples in order to obtain the favor of the god who dwelled within them. After the Persian conquest, however, funds went the other way, not from the king to the temple, but from the temple to the king (San Nicolò 1949; Schaper 1995, 1997; Fried 2004; Jursa 2007).

As with every temple in the Achaemenid Empire, a portion of the funds of the Jerusalem temple went directly to satrap and king (see Fried 2004 and references cited there), and as with every temple in the Achaemenid Empire, the Jerusalem temple kept a careful record in order to give a precise annual accounting to the satrap. The necessity of this accounting process is visible in a letter from the head accountant of the Egyptian satrapy to the high priest of the temple of Khnum.

> Khnemibre greets the priests of Khnum of Elephantine (Yeb), the Lesonis priest, [and] the temple scribes: Oh may Neith make your life long! I have earlier written to you what they wrote in my name, namely in the name of

the satrapal accountant, to wit: Let them bring the priests of Khnum – the Lesonis Priest, and the temple scribe – to the house where I am staying, on a day within about ten days, about the 16th of Mechir of the 24th year. But until today you have not arrived in the house where I am staying, the house of the satrapal accountant.

When this letter reaches you, come to the house where I am staying, and bring the temple audit that is written in your hand, [namely] three books and the invoice of the wealth of the temple of Khnum from the years 22, 23, and 24 [of Darius]. And go to the house in which the satrapal accountant is. Let the date not go by, about which I, the satrapal accountant, am writing to you. (498 BCE; P.Berlin 13536; Zauzich 1993; Fried 2004: 80–1)

According to this letter, Khenmibre, the chief accountant for all of Egypt, required the current Lesonis priest, that is, the current high priest of the Temple of Khnum in Elephantine, to report to him, and to bring with him his scribe, and the temple account books for the current and the previous two years. The Lesonis priest apparently was supposed to have brought his account book to the satrapal accountant every year, but he had been delinquent, perhaps in an attempt to resist Persian control. The only purpose for which the satrapy would be interested in the account books of an individual temple in far off Elephantine would be to collect taxes and tribute from it. This text makes clear how temples served as local collection centers for the Empire, and how the Persians dominated the local landscape. It also makes clear why the satrap had to approve of each candidate for the temple's Lesonis priest, since he was the one who brought the account books. He would need someone loyal and trustworthy to keep the books, as did Nehemiah.

In addition to Jerusalem and Egypt, the same occurred in Anatolia. It was the Persian Megabyzus at the temple of Artemis at Ephesus, not a native Lydian priest, who, as *neokoros*, oversaw deposits, expenditures and other financial matters at the temple (Xen., *Anabasis* 5.3.6; Dusinberre 2013: 218).

The Nobles of Judah

Other texts in Nehemiah equally illustrate the control that the Persian governor had over provincial elites. According to Neh. 13:17, Nehemiah chastised the 'nobles of Judah' for allowing Sabbath customs to be neglected:

> In those days I saw in Judah people treading wine on the Sabbath and bringing piles [of wheat] and loading them on donkeys, and even wine, grapes, and figs and every burden, and bringing [them] into Jerusalem on the Sabbath (…). And I remonstrated against the nobles of Judah חֹרֵי יְהוּדָה, and I said to them, 'What is this evil thing you are doing, to profane the Sabbath day?' (Neh. 13:15, 17)

The phrase 'in those days' evidently refers to the time when Nehemiah had just returned from being with the king (Neh. 13:6). The sacrilege had apparently begun while he was away. But why blame the nobles? Were they the ones who spearheaded business on the sabbath (so Batten 1913: 290)? Or had Nehemiah simply left these nobles in charge of the province while he was away and they had been derelict in their duties? If so, who were these 'nobles', and why would he have left them in charge and not the High Priest?

Xenophon explains exactly who the nobles were within the various satrapies of the Persian Empire. They were those who received land and palaces from king, satrap or governor in the various provinces (Briant 1985; Sekunda 1988; Dusinberre 2013: 76–8; Fried 2013, 2015b, 2018):

> He [Cyrus the Great] gave orders to all the satraps he sent out to imitate him in everything that they saw him do: they were, in the first place, to organize companies of cavalry and charioteers from among the Persians who went with them and from the allies; *to require as many as received lands and palaces to attend at the satrap's court* and exercising proper self-restraint to put themselves at his disposal in whatever he demanded; to have the boys that were born to them educated at the local court, just as was done at the royal court; and to take the retinue at his gates out hunting and to exercise himself and them in the arts of war. (Xen., *Cyropaedia* VIII 6: 10)

The Greek authors, the Elephantine and Bactrian papyri, the Murašu documents and the Stele of Mnesimachus all testify that conquered land was royal land (Fried 2013, 2015b). Plots of this now royal land were allocated as revocable grants to friends and relatives of the king or satrap as well as to foreign military and non-military colonists. Briant has described this process of replacing a hereditary nobility with a court-appointed nobility (e.g., Briant 2002: 326; Sekunda 1988). Land was no longer received by individuals by virtue of their belonging to a hereditary caste. Rather, conquered land throughout the empire was obtained due to one's relationship with and support of king or satrap. Since land in Judah had been depopulated as a result of the Babylonian conquest (Fried 2015a: 32–45), Achaemenid kings and satraps were able to freely distribute land in Judah to members of the Persian royal family, to their retainers and to their friends (Jursa 2010: 406). This landed aristocracy now formed the nobles of Judah. Except for a few known collaborators (cf. the *Stele of Mnesimachus, TAD* A6.13), they would not have been ethnic Judeans, but ethnic Persians (Sekunda 1988; Dusinberre 2013: 77). Some of these wealthy Persians were absentee landlords, while others may have lived on the estates they received, but both types would have rented out their farmland to the Judean returnees. The Judeans who worked it would then have paid rent to their Persian landlords (Fried 2015b). That the Judeans were only renting the land they lived on is illustrated in Nehemiah 5:

> Now there was a great outcry of the people and of their wives to their brothers, the Judeans. ²For there are those who say, 'With our sons and with our daughters, we are many; let us get grain, so that we may eat and stay alive'. ³There are also those who say, 'We are mortgaging our fields and our vineyards and our houses so that we may get grain in the famine. ⁴And there are those who say, 'We have had to borrow silver for the royal rent (*middat hammelek*) [due on] our fields and vineyards. ⁵Now, as the flesh of our brothers is, so is our flesh; as their children are, so are our children; but see! we are having to force our sons and daughters to be slaves, and some of our daughters have been violated; we are powerless, and our fields and vineyards belong to others. (Neh. 5:1-5)

Verse 5 stresses that their fields and vineyards belonged to others, that is, to the Persian nobility who now owned the land. The nobles left in charge of Judah while Nehemiah was away with the king were not hereditary Judean landowners who had received their estates from their fathers or grandfathers. Rather, they were the Persian aristocracy, relatives or friends of king or satrap, who received land in Judah as rewards for services rendered – and they were Persian (Sekunda 1988; Fried 2015b). Grave goods all across the empire indicate a common elite culture, and one separate from that of the locals (Dusinberre 2013: 262; Miller 2010; Fried 2018). The silver and gold dishes and utensils shown being brought to the king on the Apadana reliefs are the same items that appear as valued heirlooms among grave goods of the elites in excavations throughout the empire (Sancisi-Weerdenburg 1989; Lewis 1987; Miller 2010).

That members of the Persian aristocracy were routinely put in charge of satrapies while the satrap was away is visible in the letters from the Arsames archive, such as the following letter from Arsames to the Persian Artavant (late fifth century BCE):

> From Arsames to Artavant. I send you abundant (greetings of) welfare and strength. And [now], (one) named Psamshek son of Aḥḥapi, my servant, complained [to me] here. He says thus, 'When I was coming to my lord [in Babylon], slaves of Aḥḥapi my father whom I...after me to my lord... PN1-PN8, all told 8 persons – took my property and fled from me. Now if it please my lord, let word be sent to Artavant [that those slaves whom] I shall present before him: the flogging for which I shall issue an order, let it be done to them.'

Now Arsames says thus: PN1 and his colleagues, the slaves of Aḥḥapi, whom Psamshek will present before you there, you issue an order: the flogging that Psamshek says shall be done to them, let that be done to them (*TAD* A6.3).

Arsames, the satrap of Egypt, did not put local Egyptians in control of Egypt when he went away to the king. It was to Artavant, a Persian noble, that Arsames directed his letters of instruction. Of the sixteen letters in the Arsames archive found in Egypt, six are between Arsames and Artavant, dealing with issues confronting the satrapy. The ten others are to the Egyptian who was only in charge of Arsames's personal estates in Egypt. These personal estates, by the way, were estates that had been confiscated from the Egyptian nobles.

This letter illustrates Achaemenid satrapal management. When the Egyptian Psamshek left Egypt to go to Arsames in Babylon, eight of Psamshek's slaves escaped, taking some of Psamshek's property with them. According to the command of Arsames, when Psamshek returns to Egypt he must find and capture the runaways and present them before Artavant, proving that these were the ones who had run away. Then Artavant, on order of Arsames, will have them flogged. It is only Artavant, a Persian noble, who administered justice in Egypt while Arsames was away, not an Egyptian.

The nobles whom Nehemiah left in charge of Yehud while he was away with the king would have been, like those whom Arsames left behind in Egypt, not native, but Persian. They would have been the same nobles that ate daily at Nehemiah's table (Neh. 5:17; see further below; Fried 2018). Nehemiah fulminated against them, not because they were Judean leaders conducting business on the Sabbath (as commentators assume), but because he had left them in charge of the province while he was gone and they had been derelict in their duties. Presumably he had commanded that Judean religious customs be maintained.

The Governor Controls Religious Customs

Gubernatorial control over provincial religious customs is also seen in the following passage:

> And it happened when the gates of Jerusalem began to cast shadows before the Sabbath that I ordered the doors closed, and I said that they should not be opened until after the Sabbath, and I positioned some of my boys at the gates so that a burden would not enter on the Sabbath day. So the peddlers and the sellers of all kinds of merchandise spent the night once or twice outside of Jerusalem. I warned them, and said to them, 'Why are you spending the night against the wall? If you do it again, I will send my hand against you. From now on, do not come in on the Sabbath.' (Neh. 13:15-21)

Using the sabbath as a pretext, and the soldiers at his command as enforcers, Nehemiah, and not the high priest, determined which religious customs must be followed and when. It was Nehemiah, and not the high priest, who ordered the city gates closed before the sabbath and opened only when the sabbath was over. When the governor ordered merchants to spend the night out of doors, to avoid desecrating the sabbath, they were forced to do so.

It was not only in Judah, but we see the Persian governor controlling religious practices in far-off Sardis as well (c. 369 BCE):

> In the thirty-ninth year of Artaxerxes' being king, Droaphernes son of Barakes, hyparch of Lydia, [is donating] a statue to Baradates Zeus. (leaf) He commands the ones entering into the Holy of Holies, the temple wardens, as well as the ones tending the god and crowning him, not to partake of the mysteries of Sabazios, of the ones carrying the burnt offering, of Angdistis, or of Ma. They [also] command Dorates, the temple warden, to keep apart from those mysteries. (leaf). (Robert 1975; see also Fried 2004: 129–37)

According to this inscription, Droaphernes, the Persian governor of Lydia, has forbidden the priests of the temple of Zeus in Sardis from participating in the mystery cults of the gods Sabazios, Angdistis and Ma, the gods of nearby Phrygia and Cappadocia. The Achaemenid governor determined which gods local residents might worship, which religious practices they could pursue and which they must avoid.

The Governor Tells People Whom They May Marry

Besides determining who could eat the 'most holy' food of the priesthood, who could lodge in the local temple, how temple funds may be allocated, or who could enter the city and when, Nehemiah, the Persian governor, apparently had a say in whom a Judean could marry. We see Nehemiah fulminating against Judeans who married people from outside the province of Judah:

> [23]Also in those days I saw [that] Judeans had taken as wives Ashdodian, Ammonite and Moabite women. [24]And of their children, half speak Ashdodite, and they do not know how to speak Judean but only the language of the various peoples. (Neh. 23:23-24)

As we all know, there is nothing in the Torah that outlaws intermarriage, and indeed Moses himself married both a Midianite (Exod. 2:15-22) and an Ethiopian (Num. 12:1) woman. It was not because of Torah law that Nehemiah objected to marriage with non-Judeans, but it was out of his role as Persian governor of Judah. The primary concern of the king in appointing satraps and provincial governors was to maintain himself as the source of power and authority, and to keep those satraps and governors he appointed from forming alliances against him. Bans on intermarriage were commonly used in empires not only to control the population, but to prevent alliances that might exert a centrifugal force that might counteract imperial control (Eisenstadt 1963; Dusinberre 2013: 43). Nehemiah's goal, like that of other servants of autocratic rulers, was to prevent this centrifugal force and so to divide and conquer, *divide et impera*. There is a long history of examples: Lucius Aemilius Paullus, a Roman general, in 168 BCE divided Macedonia into four separate provinces and forbade intermarriage and land-ownership across the boundaries (Livy XLV.29; Shallit 1975: 41). The deified Augustus established a code of rules for the administration of the Privy Purse (BGU 210), a code maintained for 200 years. This code consisted of over a hundred laws that greatly prevented interaction among the various ethnic groups, restricting interactions even with the higher-caste Greeks (Lewis 1983: 32–3; Bagnall and Frier 1994: 28–9). Akbar, one of the descendants of Genghis Kahn, established a military occupation in China and forbade intermarriage among the various ethnic groups there (Duverger 1980: 12). As is well known, a similar ban on intermarriage was enacted in fifth-century Athens under Pericles (Fried 2009, and references cited there).

To punish Judeans engaged in intermarriage we read that Nehemiah physically pulled out hair from the head and beard of the offenders:

> I fulminated against them and cursed them and beat some of the men and pulled out the hairs of their head and beard and I made them swear by God, 'Do not give your daughters to their sons, or take their daughters for your sons or for yourselves!' (Neh. 13:25)

This is not metaphorical. Nor was it a result of a spur-of-the-moment pique (*pace* Williamson 1985: 398–9). Second Isaiah, in a text usually dated to the Persian period, refers to this same type of purposeful punishment, apparently for insubordination to a Persian official. He states that 'I gave my back to those who struck me, and my cheeks to those who pulled out the beard; I did not hide my face from insult and spitting'. Indeed, a text from the Murashu archive, dated to 420 BCE, refers to the threat of this same type of punishment:

> ...If they have not completed the groundbreaking by the first day of the fifth month they shall be beaten one hundred times with a *nitpu*, their beards and hair (of the head) shall be plucked out, and Ribat son of Bel-iriba, servant of Rimut-Ninurta, shall keep them in the workhouse. (420 BCE; *CBS* 5213; Heltzer 1995–6)

Persian opposition to marriages across the artificial boundaries of the provinces of the Levant is also exhibited in Nehemiah's reaction to the presence of the grandson of the high priest Eliashib because he had married the daughter of Sanballat, governor of Samaria. Nehemiah records that 'Among the sons of Yehoiada ben Eliashib, the high priest, was a son-in-law to Sanballat the Horonite. I drove him away from me.'

Nehemiah claims he 'drove him away', but it is not clear what that means, or what exactly the problem was that Nehemiah had with him. It could not have been because he was not a Yahwist. Numerous engravings at the temple at Har Gerizim in Samaria indicate that the Persian period temple there was dedicated to YHWH (Knoppers 2006, 2007; Magen 2007). Ostraca and papyri found throughout Persian period Samaria also attest to a majority of Yahwistic names. It was therefore not because a member of the high priestly family had married into a non-Yahwistic family that upset Nehemiah, but only because the marriage was across provincial boundaries. Again, the fear was of political alliances that would exert a centrifugal force against the Persian rulers.

Conclusions – Persian Officials and Local Elites

It must be concluded that some aspects, at least, of the book of Ezra-Nehemiah reflect actual practices of governors in the Achaemenid Empire. As was true elsewhere during the Persian period, the priesthood had no control over who could enter its ranks and eat of their most holy food or who could lodge in the temple's rooms. Only the Persian governor could decide this. Nor was it the high priest who could choose a temple's accountants, but rather it was the Persian governor. It was the Persian governor, not the local hereditary nobility, who decided when to close the city's gates and when to open them. Nor was it the high priest who ruled on marriages across provincial boundaries, but the Persian governor. Extra-biblical data overwhelmingly support these disturbing observations derived from the biblical text.

Bibliography

Bagnall, R. S. and B. W. Frier (1994), *The Demography of Roman Egypt*, Cambridge: Cambridge University Press.

Batten, L. W. (1913), *The Books of Ezra and Nehemiah: A Critical and Exegetical Commentary*, The International Critical Commentary, Edinburgh: T. & T. Clark.

Benveniste, É. (1966), *Titres et Noms Propres en Iranien Ancien*m, Paris: C. Klincksieck.

Blenkinsopp, J. (1988), *Ezra-Nehemiah: A Commentary*, OTL, Philadelphia: Westminster Press.

Briant, P. (1985), 'Dons de terres et de villes: L'Asie mineure dans le contexte achéménide', *REA*, 87 (1-2): 53–71.

Briant, P. (2002 [1996]), *From Cyrus to Alexander: A History of the Persian Empire*, trans. P. T. Daniels, Winona Lake, IN: Eisenbrauns.

Dusinberre, E. R. M. (2013), *Empire, Authority, and Autonomy in Achaemenid Anatolia*, Cambridge: Cambridge University Press.

Duverger, M. (1980), 'Le concept d'empire', in M. Duverger (ed.), *Le concept d'empire*, 5–23, Paris: Presses Universitaires de France.

Eisenstadt, S. (1963), *The Political Systems of Empires*, New York: Free Press of Glencoe.

Finkelstein, I. (2018), *Hasmonean Realities Behind Ezra, Nehemiah, and Chronicles*, Atlanta: SBL Press.

Fried, L. S. (2004), *The Priest and the Great King: Temple–Palace Relations in the Persian Empire*, BJSUCSD 10, Winona Lake, IN: Eisenbrauns.

Fried, L. S. (2009), 'The Concept of "Impure Birth" in Fifth Century Athens and Judea', in S. Holloway, J. A. Scurlock and R. Beal (eds), *In the Wake of Tikva Frymer-Kensky: Tikva Frymer-Kensky Memorial Volume*, 121–41, Piscataway, NJ: Gorgias Press.

Fried, L. S. (2013), 'The Role of the Governor in Persian Imperial Administration', in A. F. Botta (ed.), *In the Shadow of Bezalel: Aramaic, Biblical, and Ancient Near Eastern Studies in Honor of Bezalel Porten*, 319–31, Leiden: E. J. Brill.

Fried, L. S. (2015a), *Ezra: A Commentary*, Sheffield Phoenix Critical Commentary Series, Sheffield: Sheffield Phoenix Press.

Fried, L. S. (2015b), 'The Exploitation of Depopulated Land in Achaemenid Judah', in M. L. Miller, E. Ben Zvi and G. N. Knoppers (eds), *The Economy of Ancient Judah in Its Historical Contex*t, 149–62, Winona Lake, IN: Eisenbrauns.

Fried, L. S. (2018), '150 Men at Nehemiah's Table: The Role of the Governor's Meals in the Achaemenid Provincial Economy', *JBL*, 137: 821–31.

Heltzer, M. (1995–6), 'The Flogging and Plucking of Beards in the Achaemenid Empire and the Chronology of Nehemiah', *AMI*, 28: 305–7.

Jursa, M. (2007), 'The Transition of Babylonia from the Neo-Babylonian Empire to Achaemenid Rule', *Proceedings of the British Academy*, 136: 73–94.

Jursa, M. (2010), *Aspects of the Economic History of Babylonia in the First Millennium BC*, AOAT 377, Münster: Ugarit-Verlag.

Kent, R. G. (1953), *Old Persian: Grammar, Texts, Lexicon*, New Haven: American Oriental Society.

Knoppers, G. N. (2006), 'Revisiting the Samarian Question in the Persian Period', in O. Lipschits and M. Oeming (eds), *Judah and the Judeans in the Persian Period*, 265–89, Winona Lake, IN: Eisenbrauns.

Knoppers, G. N. (2007), 'Nehemiah and Sanballat: The Enemy Without or Within?', in O. Lipschits, G. N. Knoppers and R. Albertz (eds), *Judah and the Judeans in the Fourth Century B.C.E.*, 305–31, Winona Lake, IN: Eisenbrauns.

Lemaire, A. (2015), 'Atarshamain', in E. Orlin et al. (eds), *The Routledge Encyclopedia of Ancient Mediterranean Religions*, 104–5, New York: Routledge.

Lewis, D. M. (1987), 'The King's Dinner (Polyaenus IV 3, 32)', in H. Sancisi-Weerdenburg and A. Kuhrt (eds), *Achemenid History 2: The Greek Sources*, 79–87, Leiden: Nederlands Instituut voor het Nabije Oosten.

Lewis, N. (1983), *Life in Egypt Under Roman Rule*, Oxford: Clarendon Press.

Lichtheim, M. (1980), 'Statue Inscription of Udjahorrensne', in M. Lichtheim (ed.), *Ancient Egyptian Literature, III: The Late Period*, 36–41, Berkeley: University of California Press.

Magen, Y. (2007), 'The Dating of the First Phase of the Samaritan Temple on Mount Gerizim in Light of the Archaeological Evidence', in O. Lipschits, G. N. Knoppers and R. Albertz (eds), *Judah and the Judeans in the Fourth Century B.C.E.*, 157–211, Winona Lake, IN: Eisenbrauns.

Miller, M. C. (2010), 'Luxury Toreutic in the Western Satrapies: Court-Inspired Gift-Exchange Diffusion', in B. Jacobs and R. Rollinger (eds), *Der Achämenidenhof / The Achaemenid Court*, 853–97, Classica et Orientalia 2, Wiesbaden: Harrassowitz Verlag.

Robert, L. (1975), 'Une nouvelle inscription grèque de Sardes: Réglement de l'autorité relative à un culte de Zeus', *CRAIBL*, 119 (2): 306–30.

Rudolph, W. (1949), *Esra und Nehemia Samt 3. Esra*, Tübingen: Mohr Siebeck.

San Nicolò, M. (1949), 'Zur Verproviantierung des Kgl. Hoflagers in Abanu durch den Eanna-Tempel in Uruk', *ArOr*, 17: 323–30.

Sancisi-Weerdenburg, H. (1989), 'The Personality of Xerxes, King of Kings', in L. Van den Berghe (ed.), *Archaeologia Iranica et Orientalis. Miscellanea in honorem Louis vanden Berghe*, 549–61, Gent: Peeters Press.

Schaper, J. (1995), 'The Jerusalem Temple as an Instrument of the Achaemenid Fiscal Administration', *VT*, 45 (4): 529–39.

Schaper, J. (1997), 'The Temple Treasury Committee in the Times of Nehemiah and Ezra', *VT*, 47 (2): 200–206.

Sekunda, N. V. (1988), 'Persian Settlement in Hellespontine Phrygia', in A. Kuhrt and H. Sancisi-Weerdenburg (eds), *Achaemenid History 3: Method and Theory*, 175–96, Leiden: Nederlands Instituut voor het Nabije Oosten.

Shallit, A. (1975), 'The End of the Hasmonean Dynasty and the Rise of Herod', in M. Avi-Yonah (ed.), *WHJP*, vol. 7, 44–70, New Brunswick, NJ: Rutgers University Press.

Skjaervo, P. O. (1994), 'Review of Edwin M. Yamauchi, *Persia and the Bible*', *JAOS*, 114: 499–504.

Tavernier, J. (2015), 'Review of Manfred Hutter, *Iranische Personennamen in der Hebräischen Bibel*', *AfO*, 53: 472–4.

Thompson, T. L. (1974), *The Historicity of the Patriarchal Narratives: The Quest for the Historical Abraham*, BZAW 133, Berlin: de Gruyter.

Tuplin, Ch. (2013), 'Serving the Satrap: Lower Rank Officials Viewed Through Greek and Aramaic Sources', in B. Jacobs, W. F. M. Henkelman and M. Stolper (eds), *Die Verwaltung Im Achämenidenreich / Administration in the Achaemenid Empire*, 613–76, Classica et Orientalia 17, Wiesbaden: Harrassowitz Verlag.

Waerzeggers, C. and M. Jursa (2008), 'On the Initiation of Babylonian Priests', *ZAR*, 14: 1–38.

Williamson, H. G. M. (1985), *Ezra, Nehemiah*, WBC 16, Waco, TX: Word Books.

Zadok, R. (2012), 'Some Issues in Ezra–Nehemiah', in I. Kalimi (ed.), *New Perspectives on Ezra–Nehemiah: History and Historiography, Text, Literature and Interpretation*, 151–81, Winona Lake, IN: Eisenbrauns.

Zauzich, K.-T. (1993), *Papyri von der Insel Elephantine*, [Monographie] Demotische Papyri aus den Staatlichen Museen zu Berlin, Preussischer Kulturbesitz, Berlin: Akad.-Verlag.

Chronicles' Reshaping of Memories of Ancestors Populating Genesis

Ehud Ben Zvi

Since texts are read in ways strongly informed by the world of knowledge of the readers, including all the other texts that they know, the introduction of a new text into a socially accepted, core repertoire has an impact on the way in which in-group members read all the other texts, and *vice versa*, that is, the ways in which they read the other texts influence the ways in which they read the new one.[1] Of course, not all texts carry the same impact in the world of knowledge of the group: some carry more weight than others, but still each carries, at least, *some* weight. The Pentateuchal collection carried more cultural and ideological capital than Chronicles; however, readers of Genesis informed by Chronicles would be wearing 'lenses' that 'allowed' them to 'see' certain things, but turn others less 'visible' to them, and to draw attention to or away from some matters.

Reading Chronicles, like reading Genesis for that matter, involved the construction of memories about the past. This being the case, one may be certain that reading and rereading Chronicles could not but make some impact on the social construction of memories held by the readers about the ancestors mentioned in Genesis. Reading Chronicles and identifying with the message conveyed by the Chronicler[2] led, *inter alia*, to processes of drawing attention to or away from some events, characters or some of their features, and led to a reshaping and re-signifying of implicit or explicit mnemonic narratives.

To be sure, each reading community reads the text differently depending on their world of 'knowledge', which included all their texts as they read

---

1. This point has been advanced numerous times by Umberto Eco.
2. By 'Chronicler' I refer to the author that the readers construed (and imagined) when they read the book. From the perspective of the reading community, this is the 'author' whose work/message they are reading.

them (or the 'encyclopedic knowledge' that the group possesses, to use Eco's terminology). Their world of 'knowledge', in turn, is strongly influenced by social location and historical circumstances. Thus, one must specify the historically contingent group who does the reading and thus construes itself and their memories through it. In this essay, I will focus on the Yehudite literati of the late Persian or early Hellenistic period, among whom and for whom the book of Chronicles emerged.[3]

In what follows I will explore the contribution made by the literati's reading and rereading of Chronicles to their socially shared memories of (what they believed to be) their ancestors, and related matters. I will do this by focusing on some aspects of a number of substantially different cases: some of them dealing with 'obvious' matters the significance of which (for the present purposes) is far less than 'obvious', and others whose significance is perceived only or mainly when seen in the light of other texts, basic assumptions and other components of the literati's world of knowledge.

Exploring Specific Cases

Some Observations about Jacob/Israel

As it is well-known,[4] there is strong preference in Chronicles to refer to the patriarch 'Jacob' as 'Israel' (see 1 Chron. 1:34; 2:1; 5:1, 3; 6:23; 7:29; 16:13, 17; 29:10, 18; 2 Chron. 30:6). Thus, whereas the triad for the male ancestors in the Pentateuch is consistently 'Abraham, Isaac and Jacob' (see Gen. 50:24; Exod. 2:24; 3:6, 15, 16; 4:5; 6:3, 8; 32:13 (LXX and Samaritan);[5] 33:1; Num. 32:11; Deut. 1:8; 6:10; 9:5, 27; 29:12; 30:20; 34:4 (cf. 2 Kgs 13:23), it is 'Abraham, Isaac and Israel' in Chronicles (1 Chron. 1:34; 29:18; 30:6; cf. 1 Kgs 18:36, the latter within an Elijah narrative). In fact, the triad in the form 'Abraham, Isaac and Jacob' occurs nowhere in Chronicles. Likewise, the fraternal dyad 'Esau-Jacob' is explicitly referred to as such in Genesis (24 times) and the very same preference is attested in Josh. 24:4; Obad. 18; Mal. 1:2, whereas in Chronicles, the brothers are Esau and Israel (1 Chron. 1:34).[6]

---

3. To be sure, theoretically, it is always possible to read the text against its grain, but pragmatically this was a very unlikely option for the literati mentioned here.

4. See, e.g., Williamson 1977: 62 and cited bibliography.

5. The triad in MT Exod. 32:13 is 'Abraham, Isaac and Israel'. If the reading is 'original', it would be the only attestation of this triad in the Pentateuch.

6. The LXX has 'Iakob' here, but most likely this is a 'correction' towards the anticipated brotherly dyad.

To be sure, 'Jacob' appears twice in Chronicles, in 1 Chron. 16:13, 17. The text of 1 Chron. 16:8-22 follows that of Ps. 105:1-15 with minor changes. This is not the place to study these texts in any detail. For the present purposes, it is sufficient to note that, of the two relevant verses, the text of one, namely v. 17, is identical to that of Ps. 105:10. In this case, replacing 'Jacob' with 'Israel' in Chronicles would have been an extremely poor stylistic choice, for it would have resulted in a text reading ויעמידה לישראל לחק לישראל ברית עולם* instead of the much better and actually attested ויעמידה ליעקב לחק לישראל ברית עולם. In any event, the parallelism between 'Jacob' and 'Israel' clearly communicates that 'Jacob' is 'Israel'.

As for the other verse, namely v. 13, here the term 'Jacob' occurs within the expression בני יעקב. The text here follows Ps. 105:6, but with a significant change, namely זרע אברהם עבדו בני יעקב בחיריו in Ps. 105:6 becomes in Chronicles זרע ישראל עבדו בני יעקב בחיריו. Replacing Abraham with Israel shapes a new parallelism between זרע ישראל עבדו and בני יעקב בחיריו that actually underscores the point that 'Jacob' is 'Israel'.

Of course, that Jacob is Israel is not an innovation of Chronicles. It is a 'fact' agreed upon within the community and well represented in its textual repertoire. But this does not mean that the consistent choice of one term over the other carries no meaning. The consistency in referring to the ancestor as 'Israel' not Jacob was likely a way of countering an important perceived anomaly in Genesis and the memories it evoked.

According to Genesis and within the memory world of the literati, Abram became Abraham and the divine proclamation ולא יקרא עוד את שמך אברם, 'no longer shall your name be Abram' (Gen. 17:5), was clearly fulfilled. The ancestor's name appears as Abram from Gen. 11:26–17:5, but not after 17:5.[7] Thus, they have every reason to anticipate that when the divinely caused name change from Jacob to Israel takes place, the same will hold true. In fact, the precise language used in the two stories that they remember (and vicariously experience as readers of the text) clearly recalls that of Gen. 17:5, namely לא יעקב יאמר עוד שמך כי אם

---

7. The reference to 'Abram' in Neh. 9:7 is due to the fact that speaker recalls the figure of the ancestor at a time in which he was still called Abram. The only other case of 'Abram' is in 1 Chron. 1:27 ('Abram, who is Abraham'). The Chronicler here selected 'Abram' because it was in the context of the list of the descendants of Shem and such is the name of the son born to Terah, but they immediately explain that this person is Abraham, and then refer to him as Abraham when it comes to his descendants, since Isaac was born to Abraham. (We shall return to this text later, in a different context.)

ישראל, 'Your name shall no longer be called "Jacob" but Israel' (Gen. 32:29) and שמך יעקב לא יקרא שמך עוד יעקב כי אם ישראל יהיה שמך, 'as for your name Jacob, your name shall no longer be called "Jacob" but Israel will be your name' (Gen. 35:10).[8] But clearly this is not the case in Genesis. The ancestor is at times called 'Israel' after these events (e.g., Gen. 35:21, 22; 37:3, 13; 43:6, 8, 10), but also and very often 'Jacob' (e.g. Gen. 46:6; 49:33, passim). In fact, the literati read and remember that YHWH himself called him Jacob, even when the narrator of the story tells them that he is 'Israel' (see Gen. 46:2).

The literati's reading and rereading Chronicles activated their socially-agreed upon memory that Israel was Jacob, just like the memory that Abraham was Abram. However, more importantly, they were, by implication, reminded that 'Jacob' should be remembered as 'Israel'. Chronicles 'normalized' the memories evoked by reading Genesis and addressed a lingering question about a potential anomaly that emerged out of the literati's reading (and remembering the text) of Genesis.

To be sure, the preference for Israel over Jacob as the name of the ancestor in Chronicles, like many other preferences, served multiple purposes and shaped additional messages to the literati. For one, Israel in Chronicles stands for the Israel construed by the Chronicler and those identifying with him. In other words, it is and can only be a Jerusalem-centered Israel. Consistently remembering the patriarch Jacob as Israel within the context of the world evoked in Chronicles connoted and performed a partial reshaping of the memory of the patriarch.

The bracketing out of the Jacob stories – which tend to associate him with territories in 'Northern Israel', not Judah – except for a reference to the brotherhood of Israel and Esau in Chronicles also played a role in this partial reshaping. It is in this context that one may notice a subtle message in the choice to highlight Edom far more than all other nations other than Israel in the genealogies (see 1 Chron. 1:35-54). Highlighting Edom, the brother of Jacob/Israel, conveys an indirect highlighting of Israel's southern character and thereby draws attention away from Jacob's northern associations.

The outcome of all these subtle memory shifts affecting the relative social mindshare of various features associated with the site of memory 'Jacob/Israel' was a partial, and subtle reshaping of this site in a way that

---

8. The anticipation that an authoritative name change be observed is also clear from another case: Hoshea bin Nun, whom Moses renames Joshua bin Nun, and as such is recalled in the book of Joshua. This expectation is based on the idea that such name changes involved a change in status and of 'essence' in the nature of the individual.

stressed the permanent, uni-directional, essential change from 'Jacob' to 'Israel' and contributed to the appropriation of the figure of 'Israel' (/Jacob) for the ideological discourse of Yehud and its memory-scape.

It is worth noting that, although achieved through different means, this outcome is basically comparable to that achieved by the Chronicler's reshaping and appropriation of the memory of Abraham for the Jerusalem-centred literati of Yehud through the association of Moriah with Jerusalem (2 Chron. 3:1) – an association that again runs contrary to claims advanced in Samaria.[9]

Some Observations about Keturah

Reading Gen. 25:1 clearly invited the literati to imagine Keturah as Abraham's wife. The language itself, ויקח אשה ושמה קטורה, is reminiscent of that used in, e.g., Gen. 26:34 (cf. Gen. 38:26) and 1 Kgs 16:31, ויקח אשה את איזבל בת אתבעל מלך צידנים, 'he (Ahab) took as his wife Jezebel daughter of King Ethbaal of the Sidonians,' who clearly was not Ahab's *pileges* (see also 1 Chron. 11:18). Moreover, the point that the 'unmarked' expression used here seems to communicate the status of wife for the woman is implicitly conveyed by the fact that when a similar phrase is used for a *pileges*, the phrase does not occur unmarked anymore. Instead, it carries, and seems to need to carry, an additional, explicit marker (see Judg. 19:1, ויקח לו אשה פילגש, 'he took to himself a wife, a *pileges*').[10]

Further, the textual proximity of Gen. 24:67b to Gen. 25:1 in the Genesis story suggested to the readers that Abraham took Keturah as a wife following the death of Sarah, and that to some extent his action was a kind of counterpart to the action of his son Isaac, as reported in the immediately preceding verse.

---

9. Samaritan tradition associates Mt. Moriah with Mt. Gerizim rather than with Jerusalem. There is no reason why generative grammars of appropriation would be at work in only one book or genre, see, e.g., the case of Salem/Shalem which in Samarian discourse was most likely already identified as Shechem, as they probably read the text of Gen. 33:18 ויבא יעקב שלם עיר שכם אשר בארץ כנען בבאו מפדן ארם ויחן את פני העיר as reporting that 'Jacob arrived to Salem, the/a city of Shechem which is in the land of Canaan – when he came from Paddan-aram – and he encamped before the city' (cf. *Jub.* 30:1; but see Pss. 76:3; 110:2-4).

10. Further, the very case that the readers of Chronicles notice that their Chronicler rewrote the text in 2 Sam. 5:13 from ויקח דוד עוד פלגשים ונשים to יקח דוד עוד נשים (1 Chron. 14:3) and that this rewriting was meant to contribute to the way in which they imagined David suggests that they and their Chronicler thought that the term אשה alone in this context was not conveying a sense of a *pileges* but wife.

Genesis 25:2 continues the story of the (seeming?) marriage between Abraham and Keturah with a notice of the children that 'she bore *him*'. A short list of descendants follows, but by v. 4b, in the summary note, the descendants explicitly become 'the children of Keturah' (not of Abraham) and they disappear from the narrative.[11] Is this one of these 'minority reports' present from time to time in past-shaping texts within the repertoire of the community that are at odds with its main narratives and, therefore, carries only a minor social mindshare?

Clearly in this case, there is no doubt that the main mnemonic narrative shared by the community was about Abraham, Sarah and Hagar, about two children – Ishmael and Isaac, and about the choice of the latter over the former, not about multiple wives and multiple children. In fact, this main mnemonic narrative reasserts itself in the text from v. 5 on (see Gen. 25:5-11), and perhaps indirectly already in v. 4b that refers to the children as the sons of Keturah (not Abraham).[12] In fact, the language and context of Gen. 25:6 seems to suggest to the readers that contrary to what they just read, Keturah was a *pilegeš* and her children were the children of a *pilegeš*.

But should Gen. 25:5-11 alone govern the readers' understanding of the reference to Keturah as Abraham's wife, thus transforming her into a *pilegeš*, even if she is never called so, reshaping her status to be not only lower than that of Sarah, but also clearly inferior to the servant Hagar, the mother of Ishmael?

Certainly, doing so would simplify matters and diminish the cognitive and ideological cost of remembering a story that stood at odds with the main narrative about these important sites of memory. Clearly, doing so would 'normalize' the story of Genesis 25, as understood by the readers, by aligning it with the main memory-world of the group. Moreover, this could have been easily achieved by merely adding the word *pilegeš*.[13] The literati reading Genesis 25 were well aware that the author of Genesis 25,

---

11. Or become unnamed and subsumed under the taxonomic category of 'children of a *pilegeš*' in Gen 25:6; see below.

12. This said, the text in v. 4b could still be interpreted as a reference to the houses of the various mothers as subunits within the house of the father, as in the case of Gen. 46:8-24 (and note the language of vv. 15, 18, 19, 22) and cf. Gen. 35:22b-26 (in both cases, there are references to sub-houses of the mother within the house of the mother); and Gen. 36:1-18 (see esp. vv. 12, 13, 16, 17, 18).

13. The 'problem' could have been easily resolved by adding *pilegeš* to the text of Gen. 25:1; see Judg. 19:1. *Tg. Pseudo-Jonathan* and *Gen. R.* 61:4 solve 'the problem' differently: Keturah becomes Hagar. Of course, 'solving' the problem implies awareness of it.

as they imagined this personage to be, could have followed that easy path and 'solved the problem'. But they were also well aware that this author did not follow that path, and that Gen. 25:2 read as it read and thus shaped not only a text that remained open, but one that asked them to entertain a memory of Keturah as Abraham's wife.[14]

As they read Chronicles, however, they cannot but notice Keturah is explicitly referred to as פילגש אברהם (1 Chron. 1:32). Moreover, the ותלד לו, 'she bore to him (i.e., Abraham)', of Gen. 25:2 was now replaced with just ילדה, 'she gave birth'. Reading Gen. 25:1-4 in a way informed by Chronicles meant disambiguating the account in Genesis and remembering Keturah as only a *pilegeš*, and her children, the ones who 'she bore Abraham', as of less status than even Ishmael – a point reinforced explicitly in 1 Chron. 1:28, בני אברהם יצחק וישמעאל, 'the sons of Abraham were Isaac and Ishmael'.

This case illustrates how Chronicles contributed to the social selection of a particular reading of Genesis 25 and to the 'normalization' of the text. Despite the fact that neither the Chronicler nor the readers of the book seem to have a problem in principle with ambiguities and logical tensions,[15] the text here clearly and explicitly disambiguates and reduces these tensions, and, by doing so, 'controls' (or attempts to control) the 'preferred' reading of the relevant text in Genesis and social memories evoked by it.

A Particular Observation about the Supreme Patriarch

A perhaps less straightforward example concerns a particular facet of the memories about another patriarchal figure of shared memory evoked by reading Chronicles, even this figure was conceived as substantially different from the others populating the book, namely the supreme patriarch YHWH. To be sure, within the world of memory and the world in general of the relevant literati, YHWH was present everywhere and his 'hands' were in all. But none of this makes meaningless the way in which texts select what is to be explicitly mentioned and thus particularly remembered, and what is not. For instance, the beginning of narrative plots and the first action explicitly associated with the main character, by

---

14. It is worth noting that although Keturah's children contribute to the list of nations in the lineage of Abraham, the father of many nations (Gen. 17:4-6), and specifically, Midian, Keturah does not have to be Abraham's wife to do so, as the case of Hagar shows. In fact, the line from Sarah leads only to two nations (Edom and Israel).

15. See, e.g., Ben Zvi 2006: 44–77. In fact, a tendency towards 'fuzziness' was widely attested in the core repertoire of the literati. See Ben Zvi (2019), passim.

name, tend to carry particular significance. Thus, it would be very unlikely that the readers of Genesis (as well as the Pentateuch and the Primary History) would have thought that it was just the outcome of random choice that the first explicit reference to both *elohim* and YHWH had to do with creation (Gen. 1:1; 2:4), or, for that matter, that the first explicit reference to YHWH in Deuteronomy (and the Deuteronomistic historical collection as a whole) was in relation to 'all that YHWH had commanded him concerning them (i.e., the Israelites)' (see Deut. 1:3), or even that Moses' speech begins with a reference to YHWH, our god (Deut. 1:6).[16] Similarly, the first explicit reference to YHWH, by name, in Proverbs is in Prov. 1:7 ('the fear of YHWH is the beginning of knowledge'); in Psalms, Ps. 1:2 ('their delight is in YHWH's torah').[17]

This being so, it is worth noting that the first time that the deity is explicitly mentioned in Chronicles is in ויהי ער בכור יהודה רע בעיני יהוה וימיתהו (1 Chron. 2:3a), 'Er, Judah's firstborn, was wicked in YHWH's sight so he killed him', which is not, incidentally, the first story about the line of Judah. Given that the literati read Chronicles in the late Persian/ Early Hellenistic period, the reference to YHWH and Er served them as a reminder of the precariousness of Judah, the Davidic line and of 'Israel', since at times 'David' stood not only for the Davidic king but also for 'Israel'. This precariousness was balanced by the knowledge of the 'fact' that, although 'Er' was executed, the line of Judah did continue.

Similarly, it is worth noting, and particularly against this context of precariousness, that the first explicit reference to אלהים and to אלהי ישראל in Chronicles is in 1 Chron. 4:10, also within the genealogy of Judah. The text states 'Jabez called on the God of Israel, saying, "Oh that you would bless me and enlarge my border, and that your hand might be with me, and that you would keep me from hurt and harm!" And God granted what he asked.' This reference complements and balances the first explicit reference to YHWH.

With regards to Er, reading Chronicles serves as commentary about what the literati should consider most worth remembering from the story of Er, Onan, Judah and Tamar in Genesis, and that what is most worth remembering has nothing to do with the memorable details of the story, but with the message of precariousness and hope for Judah (i.e., Israel, as the literati understood it to be) and the dangers of sinful behaviour.

---

16. See also Prov. 1:7, in which the first explicit reference to YHWH.
17. To be sure, all these books/collections had a long redactional history. My point here is only that the readers of the present texts would have assigned meaning to these first references.

Moreover, in Chronicles there is a clear tendency to draw less attention to images of YHWH as a creator, and far more to YHWH as a deity engaged with and acting upon Israel, even if often through intermediaries.[18] This tendency and the shift mentioned above converge and support each other. Again, one may think/say that this is to be expected in a 'national' (albeit clearly segmented) 'history';[19] however, this would still be another way of saying that Chronicles reshaped the significance of the reported events, appropriated them for its own ideological narrative and constructed sites of memory that were part and parcel of a shared memory-scape in a slightly different way.

Some Observations about Remembering the Beginning of the Beginning
The way a book begins is important. It introduces the book (or text, for that matter) to the readers and shapes a set of expectations about what the book is about.[20] Chronicles begins with genealogies and these genealogies begin with the ancestors born before the flood: 'Adam, Seth, Enosh, Kenan, Mahalalel, Jared, Enoch, Methuselah, Lamech, Noah'. This is a linear genealogy and thus the אדם, *adam*, whose memory is evoked at the very beginning of the book is that of a male (Adam) who has fathered a son, and is, by necessity, conceptually unlike the אדם, *adam*, that stands for 'humanity' in general, including both male and female in Gen. 1:26-31 or the, at least somewhat ambiguous, אדם, *adam* of Gen. 2:4-20 who is a human being that existed before human gender differentiation.

---

18. Of course, Chronicles does not ask its readers to 'forget' that YHWH created the world. Similar to all literature of the time, it participates in a discourse and mnemonic system in which this is either stated or implied. See ברוך יהוה אלהי ישראל אשר עשה את השמים ואת הארץ in 2 Chron. 2:11 (most ET 2:12; the reference to creation is not included in Hiram's words in the version in 1 Kgs 5:21) and cf. Gen. 2:4; Exod. 20:11; 31:17; 2 Kgs 19:15; Isa. 37:16; Pss. 115:15; 121:2; 124:8; 134:3. Instead, the claim here is that reading Chronicles involves allocating more social mindscape to the interactions between YHWH and David/Judah/Israel and both the seemingly precariousness of the latter and its continuous survival, even through less than 'predictable' agents. On constructions and images of YHWH in Chronicles, see also Japhet 1989: 53–136.

19. On Chronicles as 'segmented history' see Ben Zvi 2016.

20. To be sure, in the case of the repertoire of the literati of late Persian/early Hellenistic Yehud/Judah, readers were rereaders and thus the opening of a book and its associated, conveyed expectations opened an implied 'conversation' with what they knew already about the book and its contents. The interaction between the two, in turn, facilitated the explorations of core attributes of the book or its subject matter.

In other words, reading Chronicles contributed to an increase in the social mindshare of some aspects of אדם, *adam*, namely his being male and his reproduction capabilities, both from a biological and social perspective. After all, אדם, *adam*, like the other ancestors mentioned in the list, stands for and as a site of memory which embodies the father himself and the entire house of the father.

Thus, when the literati read Genesis, or for that matter, the socially and ideologically complementary, even if substantially different, account of creation in Prov. 8:22-31, they activate images of a beginning that go back to the start of the cosmos, or the beginning of Wisdom and the start of the cosmos, or some world unlike any actual human world (e.g., the Garden of Eden). Reading Chronicles, however, balanced this tendency by suggesting that when thinking of beginnings, they may also think in terms of the beginning of 'human society' and its main structure (the house of the father), and as they do so, they may also internalize (a) a sense of basic continuity concerning human existence and (b) the resilience of humanity/ the male 'seed' implied in this continuity.[21] Both matters, however, had also to be balanced by other considerations (see the section on discontinuity below).

Some Observations about the First Ten Ancestors

As mentioned above, Chronicles begins with a list ten ancestors, 'Adam, Seth, Enosh, Kenan, Mahalalel, Jared, Enoch, Methuselah, Lamech, Noah' (1 Chron. 1:1-4).[22] An asyndetic list, with no comments of any

---

21. To be sure, the difference between the focus of Chronicles on the beginning and those of Genesis and Prov. 8:22–31 may well be rooted in literary genre matters. Unlike these texts, Chronicles begins with a male, linear genealogy and such a genre is not conducive for extensive narratives of cosmic beginnings. But even if one were to explain the reason for the difference only in these formal terms and bracket out the question of why Chronicles opens with such a genealogy, this would not have any substantial bearing on the issue of the social impact of reading Chronicles and its beginning in terms of shaping social memory and exploring ideological issues. Pointing at the 'reason' of something is not tantamount to exploring its social effect.

22. MT 1 Chron. 1:1-4 actually has a list of thirteen names, as it includes 'Shem, Ham and Japhet' immediately following the name 'Noah'. The LXX[AB] versions read '...Noah. The sons of Noah were Shem, Ham and Japhet'. The LXX[AB] may well reflect a tendency to clarify and simplify the text, but in any case attests to an understanding that there is an organizational break between the asyndetic list of the first ten ('Adam...Noah'), which they knew well to be structured exclusively under the one father–one son linear principle, and the following 'Shem, Ham, and Japhet', for they knew that Ham was not the son of Shem, nor Japhet of Ham (notice also the

kind, attests to the fact that processes of formation of social memory involve remembering as much as bracketing out that which was evaluated as carrying less importance, all matters considered. To be sure, a linear, asyndetic genealogy does not leave room for the addition of much information about the characters, but again reading such a list and the fact that Chronicles begins with it is not without meaning and social effect on the readers and their ways of construing and remembering their ten most ancient ancestors.

Further, one may take into account that there was no genre requirement to shape the opening genealogy as an asyndetic list of names, as obviously demonstrated by the presence of other genealogies in the book. Moreover, Chronicles includes instances of informative notes about characters, groups or even about instances related to them that readers were asked to consider relevant or worth remembering, even in the genealogies, as, e.g., נמרוד הוא החל להיות גבור בארץ, 'Nimrod; he was the first heroic warrior on the earth' (1 Chron. 1:10);[23] כסלחים אשר יצאו משם פלשתים ואת כפתרים, 'the Casluhites from whom the Philistines came and the Caphtorites' (1 Chron. 1:12)[24] and פלג כי בימיו נפלגה הארץ, 'Peleg, because in his days the land was divided' (1 Chron. 1:19). To be sure, in these three instances, Chronicles follows its source texts literally (Gen. 10:8, 14, 25 respectively), but as the case of קטורה פילגש אברהם in 1 Chron. 1:32 demonstrates, that does not have to be case (cf. Gen. 25:1), and see also, *inter alia*, 1 Chron. 7:24. In sum, from the perspective of the literati, the Chronicler could have chosen to include additional information about 'Adam, Seth, Enosh, Kenan, Mahalalel, Jared, Enoch, Methuselah, Lamech, Noah' but did not.

It is clear then that the list of the ten antediluvian patriarchs shaped and communicated a sense that much of the community's knowledge about these figures (see Genesis) could be bracketed out. This includes the interplay between the lineages of Seth and Cain (see Gen. 4:17-24)[25]

'and' before Japhet). In any event, 1 Chron. 1:5-23 informed the readers that there are actually two groups of characters, one consisting of ten and another of three individuals and their descendants. On the text of 1 Chron. 1:4, and from different perspectives, see, e.g., Braun 2006 [1984]: 14; Klein 2006: 53; Knoppers 2003: 267; Boda 2010: 34, and relevant bibliography.

23. This translation follows Boda 2010: 32.

24. The text is often emended to 'Casluhites, Caphtorites, from whom the Philistines came', because of Jer. 47:4; Amos 9:7 (cf. Deut. 2:23). This issue has no bearing on the matters discussed here.

25. See e.g., Sasson 1978.

and the potential messages that such interplay communicated, including negotiations involving porousness of boundaries, fuzziness and the like, but much more than that. It includes cosmogony, the story of Eden, the origins of life-as-is, that is, outside Eden, the first murder, Enoch's relationship with YHWH, a main story of human violence and sin, YHWH's regret of creation and the flood. All of them were considered not worthy of explicit mention, despite that at least some of them would have provided Chronicles with outstanding didactic examples for some of the ideological motifs addressed in the book. Thus, for instance, the story of Adam and Eve could have provided Chronicles with an excellent example for sin and punishment, and for testing and resilience. The flood story could have also served as an excellent didactic example for sin, punishment and new beginnings. The ejection from Eden could have provided a type for exile, with Eden standing for Jerusalem or its temple.[26] Significantly, these images and memories already existed among the literati. There was a (potential) grammar of preference for including references to these matters in Chronicles, but obviously, it was overcome by another grammar whose preferences were grounded, for the Chronicler, in weightier considerations.

For instance, it is well-known that pacing is an important narrative tool that allows for controlling the story being narrated,[27] whether within a literary work or in socially accepted memories of a group about itself, which are most often framed as narratives. A linear asyndetic genealogy devoid of any comments is the best device available to speed up, as much as possible, the literary tempo of the narrative, while still maintaining two social/mnemonic conventions: (a) the ten generation scheme, which also occurs in close textual proximity in the linear genealogy from Shem to Abraham and is attested elsewhere in the discourse of the community,[28] and (b) the allocation of the seventh position (in this case, Enoch) to someone important, which again is well attested in the discourse of the

---

26. On Jerusalem and/as Eden within the discourse of the Yehudite literati, see, e.g., Stordalen 2008.

27. Cf. Genette 1988: 33–7, and see, in relation to our particular field, Thomas 2011: 87–8.

28. Cf. the ten generations between Shem and Abraham, which is also covered with a very high narrative tempo in 1 Chron. 1:24-27. See below. The motif of the ten generations in Chronicles also appears in relation to Jesse (1 Chron. 2:10-12; cf. Ruth 4:18-22) and Zadok (on the latter, see Klein 2006: 495). On the place 'seven' in Chronicles, see, e.g., 1 Chron. 2:15. The importance of the seventh place was noticed also later in *Lev. Rab.* 29:11. Needless to say, these conventions point at preferred, but not mandatory patterns.

community.²⁹ In any event, in just ten words, the narrative manages to cover the span of time between father Adam and Noah.

Fast pacing is not a goal in itself. It is a literary technique that draws attention to certain matters and away from others, and in doing so, it serves ideological and narrative goals. Fast pacing draws much attention to the point at which it stops, which is thus construed as a salient discontinuity point. In the case of the ten ancestors, such a point is achieved immediately after the last of them, Noah. His children represent, from the perspective of the literati and within their world of knowledge, the beginning of a world in which humanity does not consist or can be remembered as consisting essentially of one single father's house(hold); instead they stand for the beginning of the existing world of multiple peoples, 'nations' and perceived 'families of nations'. The discontinuity between the world up to Noah and the one whose point of departure are his children was marked in the world portrayed in Genesis by the flood, which separates the antediluvian and the postdiluvian worlds.³⁰

To be sure, the flood is not explicitly mentioned in 1 Chronicles 1, or anywhere in Chronicles, but the demarcation between the first ten ancestors, i.e., up until Noah, and humanity from the sons of Noah and on is clear. This is the case not only because the genealogies stop being linear, asyndetic and from a single father to a single son, but also because the textual space allocated to multiple descendants and peoples emerging out of the sons of Noah in 1 Chron. 1:4b–23 stands in sharp contrast with that of the ten ancestors in 1 Chron. 1:1-4a. Of course, genealogies are mainly a way to classify people and/or peoples. The monolithic world construed and communicated by 1 Chron. 1:1-4a gives way to peoples in 1 Chron. 4b-23 and thus raises the need for a classification of them. But a second linear, asyndetic list of ten ancestors appears in 1 Chron. 1:24-27, to be followed again by the list of the children of the tenth ancestor (i.e., Abram who is Abraham) and their offspring.

The first ten ancestors lead to Noah, and the second ten to Abraham. The fast-pacing list shapes an implied trajectory that moves from Adam (the first male) to Noah and then via Shem (who now occupies the slot of Adam) to Abram/Abraham (1 Chron. 1:27), who points to the beginning

---

29. Both conventions were present and at work in the world of Chronicles (see above), in Genesis (see, e.g., Sasson 1978) and other works included in the repertoire of the literati of the period. They were part and parcel, most likely, of a set of common cultural conventions widely shared within the community.

30. A separation between ante- and postdiluvian times is explicitly and implicitly marked already in the Sumerian King List and the motif has a very long history in the ancient Near East.

of a path that eventually leads towards Israel and to Israel's relationship with YHWH – the explanatory note in 1 Chron. 1:27 '(Abram) who is Abraham' (cf. Gen. 17:5) hints at and activates the memory of the divine promise to Abraham. Thus a central trajectory drawing attention to itself shapes a sense of 'launching and re-launching' the world, and links Adam, Noah and Abraham.[31]

Needless to say, the mentioned trajectory carries a strong ideological message to the literati about their place in the world they imagined. In addition, and in a complementary manner, a strong message about social memory priorities is conveyed. First, the trajectory leading to Abraham is to be remembered as a central issue, not only standing on its own, but also standing for its world structuring (and periodization) role. Further, the simple single father to single son formation, with no references to other matters, shapes the message that the most essential role of this trajectory was to lead to Abraham (and Israel), and that this principle should be guiding in terms of social memory.

As important as readers were to find the details of the story of Adam and Eve or Cain and Abel, or the flood and the like, it becomes clear that the 'historical' essential role of the twenty ancestors was to beget another one, so that eventually Abraham (and Israel) would emerge. Likewise, characters that do not contribute to this line (e.g., Abel) are at the very end, not 'historically' crucial and may be bracketed out in the narrative. To be sure, to convey this message (and to keep the distinctive character of the two lists of ten ancestors), the text had to avoid mentioning these past events and characters whose actions and deeds were not considered of ultimate importance. The result is, of course, that the construction of the ancestral past remembered by the literati who read both Chronicles and Genesis would have been different than the one advanced by the literati, if they would have had and read only Genesis.

In fact, Chronicles in this section communicates a much-heightened sense of retro-causality as a guiding grammatical principle for constructing social memories in comparison to Genesis. In this section of Chronicles, (a) a great descendant at some point in the lineage grants honour and remembrance to a much earlier ancestor, (b) when an individual dies without having progeny or a group disappears from the (construed) 'historical scene', the act erases/brackets out the remembrance of all previous generations of that group or person, unless another branch that

---

31. Significantly, and especially given the hints at divine promises, the trajectory to David is not marked this way in the genealogies. The matter requires a separate discussion that goes well beyond the scope of this contribution.

evolved out of the mentioned group or person continues to exist,[32] and (c) lateral branches (e.g., the children of Keturah, or Edomite kings) are remembered regardless of their deeds – which in any case are often considered not worth remembering – due to their connection to an earlier ancestor, whose memory carried a very substantial social mindshare among members of the group, because of a later great descendant.

These principles are reflected and embodied well in various genealogies and particularly in branched or horizontal genealogies. Although these principles are at work in the genealogical sections of both Genesis and Chronicles, they are far more prominent in the latter, in part because Chronicles does not include the narratives found in Genesis. In this context, it is worthwhile to note that the ideological worldview communicated by these principles took precedence in this section of Chronicles over the potential to explore some of the narratives in Genesis for didactic purposes. This precedence, in this section, was possible (or at the very least strongly facilitated) by the fact that Chronicles as a book includes more than genealogies. To be sure, the readers of Chronicles were asked to notice who is worthy of being included and thus remembered in the genealogical lists, but they were also asked to remember and consider multiple cases in which there was a coherence between deeds and rewards or punishment *as well as* multiple cases in which there was no such coherence, thus exploring in an extensive and balanced way[33] some of the issues that the narratives about the earlier ancestors in Genesis (but not in Chronicles) raised.

An Observation on the Generation of Discontinuity and Change against the Background of a Continuous World

Genealogies are, in part, a rhetorical strategy to use seemingly biological images and languages to communicate social structures. A father fathers a son, who in turn fathers another and so on. Images and language, however, carry some 'baggage' and thus raise questions. The most common image of biological reproduction in ancient Israel and the ancient Near East in general involved one (main?) 'seed' provided by the male and inserted into a fertile womb for incubation and the like.[34] In any event, within this

32. Cf. the worldview implied in e.g., Ps. 83:5 and passim in the HB.
33. I have discussed this feature of Chronicles in several publications. See Ben Zvi 2006: 21–6 and passim, and 2019.
34. In other words, and as per a widely attested and influential viewpoint, the role of the woman in biological reproduction was construed as akin to that of the field, and that of the man to the bull/farmer who ploughs/penetrates the field and thus leaves the seed in a fertile receptacle. Cf. Biggs 2000; Leick 2003: 91; Stol 2000: 5–7. For

social, gendered discourse, it was the male seed that usually provided the main socially acknowledged classification (and potential) of the person,[35] e.g., kings in Judah/Israel had to be ('literally') from the 'seed' of David; priests from that of Aaron and so on. In other words, within this discourse something essential about the male to be born was in a 'nutshell' in that seed and his vital and most characterizing attributes were at least, at the potential level, present and communicated by that seed.[36]

Since within this discourse women do not produce seeds – or if they do their seeds do not affect the 'essential' character of the male seed (see above) – the seed carried within a male lineage cannot mix with any other seed, and thus remains stable generation after generation. In other words,

the antiquity of this view, see Cooper 1986: 34. See also Levine 2002; cf. Num. 5:28. This said, there might be some evidence for female seed in ancient Mesopotamia (see, e.g., Stol 2000: 8, 200). There is also potential evidence for a notion of a female seed in ancient Israel. MT Lev. 12:2 (but not the Samaritan or the LXX versions) may be understood as a reference to the production of a female seed. See, e.g., the discussion in Milgrom 1991: 743–4, and Stol 2000: 7–8, but as Milgrom acknowledges and elaborates, the text does not require such an interpretation. Milgrom tends, however, to accept the idea that 'the probability rests with the literal translation, "produces seed"' (743), but partially on the basis of rabbinic time ideas about the female production of seed. To be sure, later rabbinical sources attest to the idea of a female seed (e.g., *b. B. Qam.* 92a; *b. Nid.* 31a) and even contain a claim that if the woman releases her seed before the man does, the result will be a son (see *b. Ber.* 60a), and it is clear that the rabbis read Lev. 12:2 as referring to the release of the female seed (see *b. Ber.* 60a). On all these matters, see also Grohmann 2010.

35. As even the most cursory transcultural, historical analysis shows, the concept that the male seed carries as it were an 'essence' that effects nobility (including, often, nobility of character), rights, ability to perform particular tasks and the like has informed multiple, and probably even most human societies across time and space. It is a key feature of most patriarchal discourses through history.

36. For heuristic purposes one may compare this construction of social cohesion and identity through seed with later constructions of 'blood', as carrying/embodying seemingly essential features that characterize an inner-group and sets it apart from others. For the concept in the Greek world, see, e.g., 'there is the fact of our Greek identity, our sharing the same blood and the same language, and having temples of the gods and sacrifices in common...', Herodotus, *Hist.* 8.144; cf. Aristagoras's speech to Cleomenes, 'rescue the Ionians – men with whom you share the same blood – from slavery!' (*Hist.* 5.49); cf. the reference to the Lesbians enslaved by their kinfolk in *Hist.* 1.151. See Baragwanath 2008: 161–202 (cited texts translations from pp. 162 and 168). (Of course, there is a long history of the use of 'blood' for such purposes, and at times, with very tragic results, as easily demonstrated by relatively recent history, and the same holds true for prescribed social organization forms based on an essentialist notion of 'seed' or 'birth'.)

the male lineage was construed as physically carrying and embodying the same 'seed' of their crucial ancestor. For instance, within this discourse, the seed of David was carried by his descendants, and so is the seed of Abraham, and so is the seed of Aaron.[37]

The internal logic of this way of understanding social/biological reproduction leads to a system of social classification based on the characterization of differences as innate, essentialist and essentializing. No one could be a Davide, unless born a Davide; no one could be an Aaronide except the children of Aaron.[38]

This approach supported and legitimized a construction of a social world whose 'order' was construed as not only stable, but static, and in which continuity was (supposed to be) omnipresent. But then the question arises, how did this discourse address new beginnings and points of discontinuity? How could this ideological, conceptual frame explain key points of 'discontinuity' within lineages that were crucial within the memory-scape and ideological discourse of the community and which served as new beginnings? How, for instance, out of the seed of Adam, could that of Abraham emerge, and out of the latter, particular seeds such as those of 'Israel', 'David' and 'Aaron' and so on?

Within the imaginative (and socially legitimizing), seemingly biological framework, there had to be room for the addition of some new 'essential features' to the male seed at crucial points. Given their general discourses of the ancient near East, such additional features to the seed were the result of divine choice/selection/adoption, which affected and enhanced one male and thus all his progeny afterwards.

Reading Genesis (and, e.g., Samuel) meant that narratives about these past instances of divine choice and essential change were recalled and activated among the literati. Despite the fact that Chronicles and Genesis and the literati reading them at the time all partook in the same basic discourse, the texts of Chronicles and Genesis differed and had to differ in this respect in so far as they concern the early ancestral figures. Matters of genre, i.e., the genealogical character of the relevant section in Chronicles, the type of genealogies used for the ancestral figures and

---

37. In an ironic inversion, one may compare their discourse with our current, biological knowledge about mitochondrial DNA. Since mitochondria are inherited only from mothers, one entire maternal line is supposed to have the same mtDNA.

38. Of course, 'prescribed reality' may be and often is substantially different from 'reality'. In addition, all these societies accepted the concept of 'adoption' and dealt with it at the conceptual level in various ways. Significantly, this holds as true of the ancient Near Eastern societies as of much later societies, cf. Luhmann 2013: 56–7 and passim.

the related pacing mentioned above, all contributed to the shaping of a different emphases on what could or had to be made explicit in Chronicles.

In any event, the very same literati who read Chronicles also read Genesis, and their comprehensive social memory was informed by their readings of both texts (and others, of course). In fact, it is precisely because the readers of Chronicles had some idea about who Adam was, and why Noah is important or the like that they could 'fill in the gaps' to make 1 Chron. 1:1-4 pragmatically intelligible and thus allow for the fast pacing mentioned above. Incidentally, the same holds true for the omission of important explicit narratives about pre-David Israel. Chronicles could be a segmented history with no reference, for instance, to Moses and *torah* in Sinai, precisely because its readers could easily fill in the gap. Otherwise, its own references elsewhere to Moses and torah (e.g. 2 Chron. 23:18; 25:4; 30:16; 34:14) would have been unintelligible.[39]

In other words, the fact that the literati reading Chronicles were aware of Genesis and that references to the relevant names in Chronicles activated their knowledge of them was a necessary pre-condition for the development of this section of Chronicles in the form that it emerged. Moreover, at times, even within the constraints in which the literati imagined their Chronicler working, they noticed that their (construed/ implied) author still managed to hint via textually inscribed markers at the transforming event in ancestral times that begins the 'story of Israel' and 'Abram who is Abraham' in 1 Chron. 1:27 (cf. Gen. 17:5) that within their world of knowledge signals at and activates the memory of the divine promise to Abraham (see above).

Observations on Father Adam in the Context of Overall Historical Narratives

Father Adam was remembered as the 'universal man'; his seed encompassed all humanity. The fact that the literati partook in a long tradition about the shared origin of human beings is not surprising, for this was a very common concept in the ancient Near East.

Moreover, within the world of the literati, Adam had to be the first man. This was a non-malleable fact agreed upon by the community, about which there could not have been any dispute. But socially agreed upon 'facts' tend to appear in narratives, and the way in which they are interwoven in these narratives provides much of the 'significance' assigned to the 'shared fact'.

---

39. The full interplay between the implicit, explicit and just hinted at in Chronicles or Genesis, or the general repertoire of the community requires a separate essay. I discussed the concept of Chronicles as a segmented history in Ben Zvi 2016.

The narrative in Genesis that begins with the universal world and the universal man concludes with the death of Joseph in Egypt and the promise of return. If we think in terms of the Pentateuch rather than of Genesis alone, the narrative would conclude then with the death of Moses and the promise of the land.[40] In Chronicles, however, the book that opens directly with the 'universal man' concludes with Cyrus, the one to whom 'all the kingdoms of the earth' were given by YHWH, that is, the 'universal K/king'. Significantly, from the perspective of the literati, Cyrus, the universal human king, is to be remembered above all as the individual who was charged by YHWH, the universal King (and King of Judah/Israel, see 1 Chron. 17:14), to rebuild YHWH's Temple in Jerusalem, which is in Judah (2 Chron. 36:23). For them, remembering both the universal man and the universal human king meant exploring how and why remembering the 'universal', including the universal King, leads to remembering Judah/Israel and the Jerusalemite Temple, and the promise of restoration.[41] It might be argued that perhaps, on some level, the end of the Pentateuch is not so far on this matter from Chronicles, even if implicitly. But even if this were the case, there would still be a difference, and this difference retroactively informs the way in which Adam was construed and remembered by the readership of Chronicles.

To be sure, this shift from an original 'universal' background towards Israel in a 'national' history is only to be expected, even if the opening and conclusion of Chronicles provide the readers with some flavor of 'world history'. The reason is that ancient and not so ancient 'national' histories (and genealogies) are often projects that aim at and reinforce a particular sense of group social identity and self-understanding via a social memory narrative.

This said, it is still important to note that in Chronicles, including the genealogies, the nations do not stand and draw attention to themselves only for the sake of Israel, and that conversely, Israel's Temple, which stands at the center of Chronicles' world, does not stand only for the sake of Israel (see 2 Chron. 6:32-33; and cf. 2 Kgs 8:41-43).

---

40. Of course, we may think also of the narrative concluding with the end of 2 Kings. See Wilson 2014 for a study of the ending of the Primary History in general and particularly in comparison to that of Chronicles and the significance of their similarities and differences.

41. When Chronicles is read within its *Sitz im Diskurs*, this promise of restoration may be understood, though not necessarily so or only so, as leading not only to a rebuilt temple, but to YHWH's utopian world empire, with its center in Jerusalem. Cf. the book of Isaiah in which the shift from the Davide to Cyrus is to be followed by the utopian world empire. Cf. Willi 2001.

Balancing Trends within one Memory-Scape

Of course, more examples can be brought to bear, but those discussed here suggest a general tendency governing the re-shaping of memories of the ancestors, big and small, in Chronicles. Chronicles neither stood against nor attempted to displace the memories evoked by Genesis and which were part of the world of knowledge of the literati who read and reread Chronicles. To put it simply, a book attempting to do so would not have emerged among these literati.

Instead Chronicles co-opted, partially reconfigured and partially re-signified memories about the early ancestors evoked by reading Genesis, and thus, to the extent that Chronicles could influence the general discourse of the literati,[42] it impacted not only how and why these ancestors were to be remembered, but also to an extent how Genesis was read. Reading Genesis, in a way strongly informed by Chronicles, for instance, leaves no doubt that Keturah was Abraham's *pilegeš*, not his wife. Likewise, reading Genesis wearing the 'lenses' of Chronicles draws attention to a seeming tension between the divine renaming of Jacob and the continuous use of this name after the renaming, and so on.

Conversely, Genesis also informed readings of Chronicles and provided context to them, and memories of the ancestors in Genesis informed the memories of them evoked by reading Chronicles within the very same social circle of Jerusalem-centered literati. This goes beyond 'simply' filling in the gaps. For instance, reading Chronicles in a way informed by Genesis and by Genesis in the context of the Pentateuchal collection could not help but draw attention to the 'strange' case of the renaming of Jacob/Israel, or complement the memory trajectories that begin with Adam. After all, even in Chronicles, the temple in Jerusalem is grounded in YHWH's *torah* and not *vice versa*.

Further, a memorized list of fathers, in which the only feature connecting them is that each was the father of the other and which brackets out as less important whatever else each may have done, served as an embodiment of the message that the continuation of the male line was the foremost contribution they could have made, and as such the most worthy of being remembered (and celebrated). It meant also embodying and communicating a sense of teleological retro-causality; that is, the line that continues is the one most worth remembering. But as expected in any 'national history', segmented or not, the main character whose

---

42. One is to keep in mind that the Pentateuchal collection carried more social mindshare than the book of Chronicles among the literati.

continuity is to be reaffirmed is that of the 'nation' (not Seth, Noah or even Abraham). From this perspective, what is very much worth remembering for the community of literati is that beyond the vicissitudes of individual characters and of its 'history' as a whole, there existed a line of continuity spanning from the foundational first man to those who settled back after the exile (1 Chron. 9), and then continuing to they themselves, i.e., the very literati who read this book, and future Israel.[43] Reading Chronicles in this way was actually an act of constructing and remembering a story of the past that embodied the promises to Israel's ancestors portrayed in Genesis; and *vice versa*, such a reading could not but impact the way in which the same readers read Genesis.

Of course, the reading of texts among the literati served social functions. One of the main social roles of reading past-shaping texts, such as Genesis and Chronicles, was to construe and evoke a socially shared memory among the readers. The literati read one text they evoked, recalled and re-shaped memories evoked, recalled and re-shaped by the act of reading the other and *vice versa*. Thus the memories construed and activated via the literati's reading of these texts not only informed one another, but were part and parcel one comprehensive mnemonic system. This does not mean, however, that there are no differences. For instance, when, through reading and imagination, the literati vicariously encountered and experienced[44] the events associated with the ancestors in Genesis, they developed memorable memories, and when reading Chronicles they thought about their significance in terms of the larger scheme advanced by the Chronicler, with whom they also identified. Conversely, when reading Chronicles, they could not but activate their memories of characters such

---

43. This is consistent and complementary with an important ideological aspect of Chronicles' utopianism, if one may call it that: namely, that of Israel's long-term, continuous existence in Judah/Jerusalem, despite sin, punishment and the like.

44. Empathy plays an important, transcultural role in reading texts. If one understands empathy as 'the ability to put oneself into the position of some other person...and imagine the sensation of being in that situation' or 'visualizing what the world looks like from another's vantage point', one has to assume that the readers vicariously experience what the character in the story, as construed by the reader, experiences. Not only that readers share vicariously that experience, but also share the experience of having vicariously experienced it through their readings. Of course, these readings shape memories.

The literature on empathy and reading/literature is quite large. See, e.g., Hammond and Kim 2014 and literature cited there. The citations above are common definitions of empathy; see Hammond and Kim 2014: 7–8.

as Adam, Noah, Abraham and related figures not even mentioned in Chronicles, such as Eve, Cain, Abel and so on. All in all, however, the readings and memories informed and balanced each other.

To be sure much more may be said (and written) on these matters, but I hope that the present contribution is sufficient to encourage further studies on these issues. May it serve also as a proper token of my appreciation for Thomas and as my birthday present to him. Happy 80th birthday, Thomas!

Bibliography

Baragwanath, E. (2008), *Motivation and Narrative in Herodotus*, Oxford: Oxford University Press.

Ben Zvi, E. (2006), *History, Literature and Theology in the Book of Chronicles*, London: Equinox.

Ben Zvi, E. (2016), 'Late Historical Books and Rewritten History', in S. B. Chapman and M. A. Sweeney (eds), *The Cambridge Companion to the Hebrew Bible-Old Testament*, 292–313, Cambridge: Cambridge University Press.

Ben Zvi, E. (2019), *Social Memory among the Literati of Yehud*, BZAW 509, Berlin: de Gruyter.

Biggs, R. D. (2000), 'Conception, Contraception and Abortion in Ancient Mesopotamia', in W. G. Lambert, A. R. George and I. L. Finkel (eds), *Wisdom, Gods and Literature: Studies in Assyriology in Honour of W. G. Lambert*, 1–13, Winona Lake, IN: Eisenbrauns.

Boda, M. J. (2010), *1–2 Chronicles*, Cornerstone Biblical Commentary, Carol Stream, IL: Tyndale House.

Braun, R. (2006 [1984]), *1 Chronicles*, WCB 14, Dallas: Word Books.

Cooper, J. S. (1986), *Presargonic Inscriptions*, New Haven: American Oriental Society.

Genette, G. (1988), *Narrative Discourse Revisited*, Ithaca, NY: Cornell University Press.

Grohmann, M. (2010), 'Biblical and Rabbinic Ideas of Female Semen? An Intertextual Reading of Lev 12,2', *SJOT*, 24: 39–52.

Hammond, M. M. and S. J. Kim, eds. (2014), *Rethinking Empathy through Literature*, Routledge Interdisciplinary Perspectives on Literature 31, London/New York: Routledge.

Japhet, S. (1989), *The Ideology of the Book of Chronicles and its Place in Biblical Thought*, BEATAJ 9, Frankfurt am Main: Peter Lang.

Klein, R. W. (2006), *1 Chronicles: A Commentary*, Hermeneia, Minneapolis: Fortress Press.

Knoppers, G. N. (2003), *1 Chronicles 1–9*, Anchor Bible 12, New York: Doubleday.

Leick, G. (2003), *Sex and Eroticism in Mesopotamian Literature*, London/New York: Routledge.

Levine, B. A. (2002), '"Seed" versus "Womb": Expressions of Male Dominance in Biblical Israel', in S. Parpola (ed.), *Sex and Gender in the Ancient Near East*, 337–43, Helsinki: The Neo-Assyrian Text Corpus Project.

Luhmann, N. (2013), *Theory of Society. Vol. 2*, Stanford: Stanford University Press.

Milgrom, J. (1991), *Leviticus 1–16*, Anchor Bible 3, New York: Doubleday.

Sasson, J. M. (1978), 'A Genealogical "Convention" in Biblical Chronography', *ZAW*, 90: 171–85.

Stol, M. (2000), *Birth in Mesopotamia and the Bible: Its Mediterranean Setting*, Groningen: Styx.

Stordalen, T. (2008), 'Heaven on Earth – Or not? Jerusalem as Eden in Biblical Literature', in K. Schmid and C. Riedweg (eds), *Beyond Eden: The Biblical Story of Paradise (Genesis 2–3) and Its Reception History*, 28–57, FAT 2/34, Tübingen: Mohr Siebeck.

Thomas, M. A. (2011), *These Are the Generations: Identity, Covenant, and the Toledot Formula*, LHBOTS 551, London/New York: T&T Clark.

Willi, T. (2001), 'Der Weltreichsgedanke im Frühjudentum. Israel, Menschheit und Weltherrschaft in den biblischen Chronikbüchern', in C. Maier, R. Liwak and K.-P. Jörns (eds), *Exegese vor Ort: Festschrift für Peter Welten zum 65. Geburtstag*, 389–409, Leipzig: Evangelische Verlanganstalt.

Williamson, H. G. M. (1977), *Israel in the Book of Chronicles*, Cambridge: Cambridge University Press.

Wilson, I. D. (2014), 'Joseph, Jehoiachin, and Cyrus: On Book Endings, Exoduses and Exiles, and Yehudite/Judean Social Remembering', *ZAW*, 126: 521–34.

THE BOOK OF PROVERBS AND HESIOD'S
WORKS AND DAYS

Philippe Wajdenbaum

T. L. Thompson (1992, 1999, 2001) and N. P. Lemche (2001 [1993]) have raised the possibility that the Hebrew Bible was produced in the Hellenistic era. There is no physical evidence for the Hebrew Bible before the Dead Sea Scrolls, and the spread of Hellenism in the Levant after Alexander's conquest provides the best context for its creation. Thompson's vision has elicited a paradigm shift in biblical studies, inspiring several scholars to posit a direct influence upon the redaction of several Hebrew Bible books of such Greek classical authors as Homer (Brodie 2001: 447–94; Louden 2011: 324; Kupitz 2014), Herodotus (Nielsen 1997; Wesselius 2002) and Plato (Wajdenbaum 2011; Gmirkin 2017). The *Copenhagen International Seminar* series has been a home for scholars defending this challenging perspective. Some of these scholars' opinions were gathered in a volume which I had the pleasure to edit with T. L. Thompson (Thompson and Wajdenbaum 2014a, reviewed by Lang [2015] and Tobolowski [2017]). R. Gmirkin (2016; 2017: 264) has convincingly demonstrated that the authors of the Hebrew Bible were inspired by Plato's model for the creation of a national literature in the *Laws* and emulated the various Greek literary genres represented in Alexandria's Library. Within this perspective, I would like to discuss in the present contribution the possible influence of Hesiod's *Works and Days* upon the book of Proverbs.

The majority of scholars consider the book of Proverbs as composed of various collections of sayings written over several centuries, and place its final redaction during the late Persian period or the early Hellenistic era (Toy 1899: xxx; Oesterley 1929: xxvi; Perdue 2000: xiii; Sandoval 2006: 42; Lucas 2015: 8). Proverbs has been compared to ancient Near Eastern wisdom texts such as the *Instructions of Shurrupak* or the *Counsels of Wisdom* (Kitchen 1977), and Prov. 22:17–24:22 appears to be an adaptation of the Egyptian *Teaching of Amenemope* (Snell 1993: 3; Westerman 1995: 155; Overland 1996; West 1997: 94; Shupak 2005; Laisney 2007: 245–6; Thompson 2007: 15; 2013 [1998]: 140; Lemche 2008: 241–2; see Ruffle [1977] and Whybray [1994: 134; 1995: 156] for a differing opinion).

The kinship between *Works and Days* and Proverbs is thought to derive from a common origin in the genre of ancient Near Eastern wisdom teachings (Brown 1995: 292–303; West 1997: 325–33; Byrne and Houlden 2003 [1995]: 11; Armitage 2016: 143; Powell 2017: 104). Hesiod's succession myth in *Theogony* seems derived from Hurrian and Hittite traditions known as the *Kingship in Heaven Cycle*, witnessed notably in the *Song of Kumarbi* (Walcot 1962b: 13; West 1997: 285–6; Rutherford 2009: 10; Lazaridis 2016: 189). While an influence on *Works and Days* from oriental wisdom texts or traditions is probable (Lazaridis 2016: 200), P. Walcot (1962a: 215; 1962b: 36; cf. Lazaridis 2007: 41 n. 135; Rutherford 2009: 18, 20) has argued that Hesiod's works may have in turn influenced later Egyptian wisdom texts, such as the *Instruction of Onchshechonqy*.

Such a possible Hesiodic influence on oriental texts may have extended to biblical texts as well. Genesis 1–11 shows an inspiration from Mesopotamian myths, probably mediated through Berossus's *Babyloniaca*, written in Greek in the late fourth century BCE (Gmirkin 2006: 89–139). However, it seems that Genesis' author blended these Mesopotamian motifs with elements borrowed from Hesiod's works (Lemche 2016: 67–71). For instance, the creation of Eve and the deceitful Serpent in Genesis 3 seem derived from Hesiod's story of Prometheus stealing the fire from Zeus and offering it to men, after which the gods created the first woman, Pandora (*Theog.* 507-616; *Op.* 42-105; cf. Taylor 2007: 31; Louden 2011: 232; Wajdenbaum 2011: 99–101; Gnuse 2017: 136–7). The name of Japheth as the ancestor of the Greeks in Gen. 10:2-5 seems evidence of direct knowledge of Hesiod's Titan Iapetos (Wajdenbaum 2011: 75; Louden 2013; Thompson and Wajdenbaum 2014b: 15). P. Guillaume (2014) has compared Hesiod's age of the Heroes with the biblical period of the Judges. Nebuchadnezzar's dream of successive kingdoms in Dan. 2:31-45 and Hesiod's myth of the five ages (*Op.* 109-201) are both structured on the motif of metals of declining value (Feldman 1966: 16–17; Brown 1995: 302; West 1997: 313). P. Niskanen (2004: 30) argues that since Daniel was written in the second century BCE, its author might have directly drawn this theme from Hesiod. Therefore, if Hesiod's works were possibly used for Genesis, Judges and Daniel, we might contemplate Hesiod's influence upon Proverbs. Moreover, Genesis' apparent blending of Mesopotamian and Greek literary traditions would present an analogy to Proverbs' possible use of both the Egyptian *Amenemope* and the Greek *Works and Days*.

The majority of the biblical Proverbs are ascribed to Solomon (Prov. 1:1; 10:1), some of which are said to have been collected by the people of Hezekiah (25:1). In the MT, ch. 30 is said to be the sentences of Agur, and ch. 31 those of Lemuel. The other biblical texts traditionally attributed to Solomon are dated by most scholars to the Hellenistic era and are thought to reflect influences from Greek literature. Song of Songs seems to imitate the works of Alexandrian poets Theocritus and Callimachus (Hagedorn 2003; Burton 2005; Loprieno 2005). Ecclesiastes' Hellenistic dating is widely accepted (Crenshaw 1987: 44; Whybray 1977 [1989]: 19–12; Collins 1998: 14; Bartholomew 2009: 39, 46), and H. Ranston (1918) has convincingly demonstrated that Ecclesiastes borrowed from the collection of *Sentences* attributed to sixth century BCE elegiac poet Theognis, which presents significant parallels with Proverbs too.

Parallels with *Works and Days* are found in all parts of Proverbs, regardless of the traditional divisions of the book into various units. In the next sections, similarities of vocabulary between Hesiod and the Septuagint text of Proverbs will be signalled, even though the latter greatly differs from the original Hebrew. These common terms might be due to the Septuagint translators, who were probably versed in Greek literature, having noticed semantic similarities between the Hebrew text of Proverbs and *Works and Days*, and therefore incorporating Hesiodic vocabulary into their Greek adaptation. Still, I would argue that the original Hebrew text itself may have been influenced by Hesiod.

For Prov. 1:7, the fear of the Lord is the foundation of knowledge. Hesiod reproaches those who do not fear the anger of the gods (*Op.* 251; cf. Louden 2011: 247). Proverbs 1:18-19 (cf. 26:27) and *Op.* 265 share the idea that plotting or causing evil towards another is like hurting oneself (Plaut 1961: 272). The metaphor of the path is encountered in both Proverbs and Hesiod. Proverbs 2:8 speaks of guarding the ways of righteous deeds (LXX ὁδοὺς δικαιωμάτων) and Hesiod says that the better path (ὁδός) is the one leading to justice (δίκαια, *Op.* 217). Proverbs 2:20 evokes the smooth (LXX λείους, an addition in the Greek text of Proverbs [Cook 1997: 143–4]) paths of righteousness. Hesiod writes that the road to badness is smooth (λείη μὲν ὁδός, *Op.* 287). Proverbs 3:17 speaks of the paths of wisdom that are pleasant and peaceful. Proverbs 15:19 distinguishes between the path of the lazy, which is overgrown with thorns, and the path of the upright, which is a level highway. For Hesiod, the path leading to goodness is long and steep, and rough at first, but becomes easy when one has reached the top (*Op.* 289-94).

Proverbs 3:9-10 suggests to honour the Lord by offering the first fruits, so that one's barns will be filled (LXX πίμπληται) with plenty (πλησμονῆς). Hesiod instructs Perses to remember working, so that Hunger may hate him, and that Demeter may fill (πιμπλῇσι) his barn with food. If he works properly, in the right season, Perses's barns will be full (πλήθωσι, *Op.* 298-307) of victuals. Proverbs 3:27-8 orders not to delay the giving of what is due, and Hesiod says to let a wage promised to a friend be fixed (*Op.* 370).

Proverbs 5:3-6, 6:23-6 warns against seduction by the foreign woman, whose lips drip of honey. Her speech is smooth but leads to Sheol. Hesiod warns his brother not to let a flaunting woman deceive him, for she is after his barn (*Op.* 372-4; West 1997: 326). Proverbs 6:29 warns not to sleep with one's neighbour's wife, an act that will be punished. Hesiod enumerates a list of wrong-doings (*Op.* 327-34) including sleeping with one's brother's wife, which will be punished by Zeus (West 1997: 325 n. 135; Tan [2008: 36)] finds this parallel loose). While Prov. 5:20 warns against adultery with a foreign woman, Hesiod teaches to marry a woman that lives near (*Op.* 699-701).

Both texts speak of the ant (whom Hesiod calls 'the industrious one'), who gathers (ἀμήτῳ, LXX Prov. 6:8; ἀμᾶται, *Op.* 778) her food. Proverbs specifies that the ant gathers her food during summer and warns against idleness which leads to poverty and hunger, which recalls Aesop's fable of the *Ant and the Grasshopper* (Niditch 2015: 50). LXX Prov. 6:8a-c adds a praise of the bee, not found in the MT (Cook 1997: 154; Forti 2008: 106). According to J. Cook (1997: 166–8, 172, 318–19), the translator of Proverbs directly borrowed this motif from Aristotle's *History of the Animals*, where the ant and the bee are discussed in the same order (622b). Both texts call the bee industrious (ἐργάτις, LXX Prov. 6:8a; ἐργάτιδες, *Hist. An.* 627a).

Proverbs 6:9-11 (cf. 24:33-34) states that with a little sleep, one will be surprised by poverty. Hesiod counsels his foolish brother to work, otherwise he will have to beg from his neighbours (*Op.* 397-404). Proverbs 6:11 personifies Poverty (LXX πενία) and Want, whereas Hesiod personifies Helplessness and Poverty (πενίη, *Op.* 496; West 1997: 327). LXX Prov. 6:11a states that if one is diligent (ἄοκνος), harvest shall arrive as a fountain. Hesiod writes that the industrious (ἄοκνος, *Op.* 495) man will greatly prosper in his house. MT Prov. 10:5 says that a son who gathers during summer is prudent, but a son who sleeps during harvest brings shame. LXX Prov. 10:5 says that the intelligent son is rescued from the heat (καύματος) of the day, and a transgressing son is blasted by the wind during harvest time (ἐν ἀμήτῳ). Hesiod tells his brother to avoid sleeping until dawn during the harvest season (ἐν ἀμήτου), but rather to be busy gathering fruits and getting up early (*Op.* 574-7). Hesiod further speaks of the burning heat (καύματος, *Op.* 588) of summer.

Proverbs 6:19 (cf. 12:17; 14:5, 25; 19:5, 9, 28; 21:28; 24:28; 25:18) condemns the unjust witness (LXX μάρτυς ἄδικος) who kindles falsehood (ψεύδη), like Hesiod condemns he who lies (ψεύσεται) in his witness (μαρτυρίῃσι, *Op.* 282-85). Proverbs 10:20 asserts that the tongue (LXX γλῶσσα) of the righteous is choice silver; and in 13:3, those who guard their mouths preserve their lives. Hesiod writes that the best treasure a man can have is a sparing tongue (γλώσσης, *Op.* 720). Both Prov. 11:10-11 and Hesiod (*Op.* 225-42) state that a city prospers because of righteous men and may be overthrown by the faults of the wicked (cf. Theognis 43; Brown 1995: 293). For Prov. 11:24-6, those who give freely grow richer, and those who withhold what is due suffer want. The one who holds back grain is cursed, but blessed is he who sells it. For Hesiod, one should give to the one who gives, as they give to the free-handed, and not to the close-fisted. The man who gives willingly rejoices in his gift and is glad in his heart, but the one who takes something himself freezes his heart (*Op.* 354-63).

Proverbs 12:4 claims that a good wife is the crown of her husband, but she who brings shame is like the rottenness in his bones (MT) or like a worm eating up wood (LXX). Hesiod also uses an antithesis in writing that a man wins nothing better than a good wife and nothing worse than a bad one, a greedy soul who roasts her man without fire and brings him to a raw old age (*Op.* 702-6). MT Prov. 12:27 claims that the lazy do not roast their game, but the diligent obtain precious wealth. In 13:4, the appetite of the lazy (LXX ἀεργός) craves and gets nothing, while the appetite of the diligent is richly supplied. Hesiod tells Perses that Hunger is the comrade of the sluggard (ἀεργὸς, *Op.* 302-306). Gods and men are angry with the idle man, who is like a stingless drone who wastes the labours of the bees, eating without working. Further, Hesiod writes that the sluggish worker does not fill his barn, while industry makes work go well (*Op.* 409-413). MT Prov. 13:10 affirms that wisdom is with those who take advice, and Hesiod declares that he is good who listens to an adviser. The one who does not think for himself nor keeps in mind what another tells him is an unprofitable man (*Op.* 295-298). Proverbs 13:11 suggests that wealth hastily gained will dwindle, but those who gather little by little will increase it. Hesiod writes that if one adds little to a little, soon that little will become great (*Op.* 361-362; cf. West 1997: 326).

Proverbs 17:5 warns against mocking the poor, which is like insulting the Creator. Hesiod cautions never to taunt a man with deadly poverty, for it is sent by the deathless gods (*Op.* 717-19; cf. Theognis 155-58; Brown 1995; West 1997: 327). Proverbs 17:23 reproaches the wicked who accept a concealed bribe to pervert the way of justice. Hesiod writes that there is a noise when Justice is dragged by those who devour bribes and give crooked judgments (*Op.* 220-221, 263-264; cf. Hagedorn 2004: 124–5). Proverbs 19:15 declares that an idle person (LXX ἀεργοῦ) will suffer hunger. One should not love sleep, or else will come poverty. With open eyes, one will have plenty of bread (20:13). Hesiod enjoins Perses to remember working, so that Hunger may hate him, for Hunger is the comrade of the sluggard (ἀεργῷ, *Op.* 299-301).

Proverbs 19:26 claims that one who wastes his father and chases away his mother is a son who causes shame and brings reproach. Hesiod writes that he who abuses his old father at the threshold of old age and attacks him with harsh words makes Zeus angry, and the latter will lay heavy requital on him for his evil doing (*Op.* 331-334). MT Prov. 20:4 states that the lazy person does not plough because of winter; when harvest comes, there is nothing to be found. Hesiod tells his brother that if he ploughs the ground at the winter solstice, that is, too late, he will reap sitting, grasping a thin crop in his hand, so that he will bring all home in a basket (*Op.* 479-482). Proverbs 27:10 tells not to forsake a friend, and not to go the house of one's brother on a day of calamity for 'Better is a neighbour who is nearby (LXX ἐγγὺς) than a brother who is far away'. Hesiod counsels Perses to call his friend to a feast, and especially the one who lives near (ἐγγύθι) him, for if any mischief happens, neighbours come without girting themselves, whereas kinsmen need to girt themselves (*Op.* 342-346; cf. West 1997: 325).

LXX Prov. 27:16 mentions the North Wind (βορέας...ἄνεμος), like Hesiod does (ἀνέμου βορέου, *Op.* 517, cf. 506, 546, 551). LXX Prov. 27:25 enjoins to gather fodder (χόρτον) from the hills, like Hesiod advises to bring in fodder (χόρτον, *Op.* 606) and litter for oxen and mules. Proverbs 27:26 says that the lambs will provide clothing. Hesiod teaches Perses, when comes the season of frost, to stitch together skins of firstling kids with ox-sinew, to have his back covered from the rain (*Op.* 543-6). MT Prov. 27:27 says that one should have the milk of goats as food, like Hesiod advises his brother to drink milk drained from goats (*Op.* 590).

While these similarities might not be sufficient to assert the dependence of Proverbs upon Hesiod, we may note that Proverbs also presents several parallels with Theognis's *Sentences* (Brown 1995: 293–303; West 1997: 518–21), a text which seems to have been the main source of Ecclesiastes

(Ranston 1918). Proverbs 5:15-18 and Theognis 959-62 both refer to drinking from one's own source of water as a metaphor for one's wife's fidelity. Proverbs 11:17, 25 and Theognis 573-74 both enjoin to do good to others, from which one will benefit. Both texts say that the rich has many friends (φίλοι δὲ πλουσίων πολλοί, LXX Prov. 14:20; πλουτῇις πολλοὶ φίλοι, Theognis 927-930), but not the poor. Proverbs 17:3 and Theognis 499-502 both speak of testing gold and silver as an analogy for testing one's heart. While Prov. 17:17 states that a friend loves at all times and is like a brother in hardship, Theognis 97-99 writes that he wants a friend who would support him like a brother. Both MT Prov. 19:7 and Theognis 857-60 claim that one will be abandoned by their friends when poverty or hardship hits them. Proverbs 20:6 says that it is difficult to find (LXX εὑρεῖν) a faithful (πιστὸν) man, much like Theognis 79-81 (cf. 645-46) writes that he will not find (εὑρήσεις) faithful (πιστοὺς) companions. Both Prov. 27:2 and Theognis 611-14 claim that it is better to be praised by someone else than by oneself.

Although Proverbs and Ecclesiastes differ in content and purpose, they may have, after all, been penned by the same author(s), who would have distributed elements borrowed from various Greek and Near Eastern texts into the biblical wisdom books. These authors probably worked at the Great Library of Alexandria, and seem to have dismantled the works of Hesiod by using his mythical narratives about the gods and early humans in order to create the first chapters of Genesis on the one hand, and to have incorporated his wisdom sentences from *Works and Days* in their selection of sayings on the other hand. The new paradigm initiated by Thompson and Lemche of the Hebrew Bible having being composed in the Hellenistic era, as well as the recent studies it has fostered, invite us to consider a possible direct Greek influence over the redaction of these books.

Bibliography

Armitage, David J. (2016), *Theories of Poverty in the World of the New Testament*, WUNT 2/423, Tübingen: Mohr Siebeck.

Bartholomew, Craig G. (2009), *Ecclesiastes*, The Baker Academic Commentary on Wisdom and Psalms, Grand Rapids, MI: Baker Academic.

Brodie, Thomas L. (2001), *Genesis as Dialogue: A Literary, Historical and Theological Commentary*, Oxford: Oxford University Press.

Brown, John P. (1995), *Israel and Hellas, Vol. 3: The Legacy of Iranian Imperialism and the Individual*, Berlin: de Gruyter.

Burton, Joan B. (2005), 'Themes of Female Desire and Self-Assertion in the Song of Songs and Hellenistic Poetry', in A. C. Hagedorn (ed.), *Perspectives on Song of Songs*, 180–205, BZAW 346, Berlin: de Gruyter.

Byrne, Peter and Leslie Houlden, eds (2003 [1995]), *Companion Encyclopedia of Theology*, London: Routledge.
Collins, John J. (1998), *Jewish Wisdom in the Hellenistic Age*, Louisville, KY: Westminster John Knox Press.
Cook, Johann (1997), *The Septuagint of Proverbs: Jewish and/or Hellenistic Proverbs? Concerning the Hellenistic Colouring of LXX Proverbs*, Leiden: E. J. Brill.
Crenshaw, James L. (1987), *Ecclesiastes: A Commentary*, Cambridge: Cambridge University Press.
Feldman, Louis H. (1996), *Jew and Gentile in the Ancient World: Attitudes and Interactions from Alexander to Justinian*, Princeton: Princeton University Press.
Forti, Tova (2008), *Animal Imagery in the Book of Proverbs*, Leiden: E. J. Brill.
Gmirkin, Russell E. (2006), *Berossus and Genesis, Manetho and Exodus: Hellenistic Histories and the Date of the Pentateuch*, LHBOTS 433 / CIS 15, New York: T&T Clark.
Gmirkin, Russell E. (2016), 'Greek Genres and the Hebrew Bible', in I. Hjelm and T. L. Thompson (eds), *Biblical Interpretation Beyond Historicity: Changing Perspectives 7*, 92–101, CIS, London: Routledge.
Gmirkin, Russell E. (2017), *Plato and the Creation of the Hebrew Bible*, CIS, London: Routledge.
Gnuse, Robert K. (2017), 'Greek Connections: Genesis 1–11 and the Poetry of Hesiod', *BTB*, 47 (3): 131–43.
Guillaume, Philippe (2014), 'Hesiod's Heroic Age and the Biblical Period of the Judges', in T. L. Thompson and P. Wajdenbaum (eds), *The Bible and Hellenism: Greek Influence on Jewish and Early Christian Literature*, 146–64, CIS, London: Routledge.
Hagedorn, Anselm C. (2003), 'Of Foxes and Vineyards: Greek Perspectives on the Song of Songs', *VT*, 53 (3): 337–52.
Hagedorn, Anselm C. (2004), *Between Moses and Plato: Individuals and Society in Deuteronomy and Ancient Greek Law*, FRLANT 204, Göttingen: Vandenhoeck & Ruprecht.
Kitchen, Kenneth A. (1977), 'Proverbs and Wisdom Books of the Ancient Near East: The Factual History of a Literary Form', *Tyndale Bulletin*, 28: 69–114.
Kupitz, Yaakov S. (2014), 'Stranger and City Girl: An Isomorphism between Genesis 24 and Homer's *Odyssey* 6-13', in T. L. Thompson and P. Wajdenbaum (eds), *The Bible and Hellenism: Greek Influence on Jewish and Early Christian Literature*, 117–45, CIS, London: Routledge.
Laisney, Vincent P.-M. (2007), *L'Enseignement d'Aménémopé*, Studia POHL: Series Maior 19, Rome: Editrice Pontificio Istituto Biblico.
Lang, Bernhard (2015), 'Review of *The Bible and Hellenism: Greek Influence on Jewish and Early Christian Literature*, edited by Thomas L. Thompson and Philippe Wajdenbaum', *Semitica et Classica*, 8: 275–9.
Lazaridis, Nikolaos (2007), *Wisdom in Loose Form: The Language of Egyptian and Greek Proverbs in Collections of the Hellenistic and Roman Periods*, Leiden: E. J. Brill.
Lazaridis, Nikolaos (2016), 'Different Parallels, Different Interpretations: Reading Parallels between Ancient Egyptian and Greek Works of Literature', in I. Rutherford (ed.), *Greco-Egyptian Interactions: Literature, Translation, and Culture, 500 BC–AD 300*, 187–208, Oxford: Oxford University Press.

Lemche, Niels Peter (2001 [1993]), 'The Old Testament – a Hellenistic Book?', in L. L. Grabbe (ed.), *Did Moses Speak Attic? Jewish Historiography and Scripture in the Hellenistic Period*, 287–318, JSOTSup 317 / ESHM 3, Sheffield: Sheffield Academic Press.

Lemche, Niels Peter (2008), *The Old Testament between Theology and History: A Critical Survey*, LAI, Louisville, KY: Westminster John Knox Press.

Lemche, Niels Peter (2016), 'Is the Old Testament still a Hellenistic Book?', in I. Hjelm and T. L. Thompson (eds), *Biblical Interpretation Beyond Historicity: Changing Perspectives 7*, 61–75, CIS, London: Routledge.

Loprieno, Antonio (2005), 'Searching for a Common Background: Egyptian Poetry and the Biblical Song of Songs', in A. C. Hagedorn (ed.), *Perspectives on Song of Songs*, 105–35, BZAW 346, Berlin: de Gruyter.

Louden, Bruce (2011), *Homer's Odyssey and the Near East*, Cambridge: Cambridge University Press.

Louden, Bruce (2013), 'Iapetus and Japheth: Hesiod's *Theogony*, *Iliad* 15.187-93, and Genesis 9-10', *Illinois Classical Studies*, 38: 1–22.

Lucas, Ernest (2015), *Proverbs*, Grand Rapids, MI: Eerdmans.

Niditch, Susan (2015), *The Responsive Self: Personal Religion in Biblical Literature of the Neo-Babylonian and Persian Periods*, ABRL, New Haven, CT: Yale University Press.

Nielsen, Flemming A. J. (1997), *The Tragedy in History: Herodotus and the Deuteronomistic History*, JSOTSup 251 / CIS 4, Sheffield: Sheffield Academic Press.

Niskanen, Paul (2004), *The Human and the Divine in History: Herodotus and the Book of Daniel*, JSOTSup 396, London: T&T Clark.

Oesterley, Oscar E. (1929), *The Book of Proverbs*, London: Taylor & Francis.

Overland, Paul (1996), 'Structure in the Wisdom of Amenemope and Proverbs', in J. E. Coleson and V. H. Matthews (eds), *Go to the Land I Will Show You: Studies in Honor of Dwight W. Young*, 275–92, Winona Lake, IN: Eisenbrauns.

Perdue, Leo (2000), *Proverbs*, Interpretation: A Bible Commentary for Teaching and Preaching, Louisville, KY: Westminster John Knox Press.

Plaut, W. Gunther (1961), *Book of Proverbs: A Commentary*. New York: Union of American Hebrew Congregations.

Powell, Barry B. (2017), *The Poems of Hesiod:* Theogony, Works and Days, *and* The Shield of Herakles, trans. B. B. Powell, Oakland: University of California Press.

Ranston, Harry (1918), 'Ecclesiastes and Theognis', *The American Journal of Semitic Languages and Literatures*, 34: 99–122.

Ruffle, John (1977), 'The Teaching of Amenemope and its Connection with the Book of Proverbs', *Tyndale Bulletin*, 28: 29–68.

Rutherford, Ian (2009), 'Hesiod and the Literary Traditions of the Near East', in F. Montanari, C. Tsagalis and A. Rengakos (eds), *Brill's Companion to Hesiod*, 9–36, Leiden: E. J. Brill.

Sandoval, Timothy J. (2006), *The Discourse of Wealth and Poverty in the Book of Proverbs*, Leiden: E. J. Brill.

Shupak, Nili (2005), 'The Instruction of Amenemope and Prov. 22:17–24:22', in R. L. Troxel, K. G. Friebel and D. R. Magary (eds), *Seeking Out the Wisdom of the Ancients: Essays Offered to Honor Michael V. Fox on the Occasion of His Sixty-fifth Birthday*, 203–20, Winona Lake, IN: Eisenbrauns.

Snell, Daniel C. (1993), *Twice-told Proverbs and the Composition of the Book of Proverbs*, Winona Lake, IN: Eisenbrauns.

Tan, Nancy N. H. (2008), *The 'Foreignness' of the Foreign Woman in Proverbs 1–9: A Study of the Origin and Development of a Biblical Motif*, Berlin: de Gruyter.

Taylor, John (2007), *Classics and the Bible: Hospitality and Recognition*, Classical Literature and Society Series, London: Duckworth.

Thompson, Thomas L. (1992), *The Early History of the Israelite People from the Written and Archaeological Sources*, SHANE 4, Leiden: E. J. Brill.

Thompson, Thomas L. (1999), *The Mythic Past: Biblical Archaeology and the Myth of Israel* (New York: Basic Books) = *The Bible in History: How Writers Create a Past*, London: Jonathan Cape.

Thompson, Thomas L. (2001), 'The Bible and Hellenism: A Response', in L. L. Grabbe (ed.), *Did Moses Speak Attic? Jewish Historiography and Scripture in the Hellenistic Period*, 274–86, JSOTSup 317, Sheffield: Sheffield Academic Press.

Thompson, Thomas L. (2007), *The Messiah Myth: The Near Eastern Roots Jesus and David*, London: Pimlico.

Thompson, Thomas L. (2013 [1998]), '*4Q Testimonia* and Bible Composition', in T. L. Thompson (ed.), *Biblical Narratives and Palestine's History: Changing Perspectives 2*, 133–46, CIS, Sheffield: Equinox.

Thompson, Thomas L. and Philippe Wajdenbaum, eds (2014a), *The Bible and Hellenism: Greek Influence on Jewish and Early Christian Literature*, CIS, London: Routledge.

Thompson, Thomas L. and Philippe Wajdenbaum (2014b), 'Introduction: Making Room for Japheth', in T. L. Thompson and P. Wajdenbaum (eds), *The Bible and Hellenism: Greek Influence on Jewish and Early Christian Literature*, 1–15, CIS, London: Routledge.

Tobolowsky, Andrew (2017), 'Review of *The Bible and Hellenism: Greek Influence on Jewish and Early Christian Literature*, edited by Thomas L. Thompson and Philippe Wajdenbaum', *Journal of Hebrew Scriptures*, 17, http://www.jhsonline.org/reviews/reviews_new/review781.htm.

Toy, Crawford H. (1899), *A Critical and Exegetical Commentary on the Book of Proverbs*, The International Critical Commentary, Edinburgh: T. & T. Clark.

Wajdenbaum, Philippe (2011), *Argonauts of the Desert: Structural Analysis of the Hebrew Bible*, CIS, Sheffield: Equinox.

Walcot, Peter (1962a), 'Hesiod and the Instructions of 'Onchsheshonqy', *JNES*, 21 (3): 215–19.

Walcot, Peter (1962b), 'Hesiod and the Didactic Literature of the Near East', *Revue des Études Grecques*, 75: 13–36.

Wesselius, Jan-Wim (2002), *The Origin of the History of Israel: Herodotus' Histories as Blueprint for the First Books of the Bible*, JSOTSup 345, Sheffield: Sheffield Academic Press.

West, Martin L. (1997), *The East Face of Helicon: West Asiatic Elements in Greek Poetry and Myth*, Oxford: Clarendon.

Westermann, Claus (1995), *Roots of Wisdom: The Oldest Proverbs of Israel and Other Peoples*, trans. J. D. Charles, Louisville, KY: Westminster John Knox Press.

Whybray, Roger N. (1994), *Composition of the Book of Proverbs*, JSOTSup 168, Sheffield: Sheffield Academic Press.

Whybray, Roger N. (1995), *The Book of the Proverbs: A Survey of Modern Study*, Leiden: E. J. Brill.

Whybray, Roger N. (1997 [1989]), *Ecclesiastes*, Sheffield: Sheffield Academic Press.

The Villain 'Samaritan':
The Sāmirī as the Other Moses
in Qur'anic Exegesis

Joshua Sabih

I will open my mouth in a parable; I will utter riddles concerning ancient times. (Ps. 78:2)

Prelude:
The Qur'an as a Restorative Text-scripture

Is the Qur'an a historical document? Does the Qur'an claim to be a historical document? The answer to both questions is no. The Qur'an, in its canonised recension-vulgate (Ar. *mushaf*),[1] testifies to its own historicity, and as such it considers itself as a *restorative* text-scripture in relation to the other text-scriptures preceding it. Although a new text-scripture, according to this restorative approach, the Qur'an, while it perceives itself as being in the same family as the Jewish and the Christian Bibles, presents itself in this genealogy as an 'orphan book' (Khatibi 2009; Reeck 2017; Sabih 2015). From this vantage point, the Qur'an's reading approach begins from this premise: recognising Torah, Prophets, Psalms (*zabūr*) and Gospel (*ingīl*) – in addition to other scriptures alluded to, through engaging them – in their present recensions together with the conflicting perceptions of them – into this restorative reading approach. On the basis of Halbertal's definition of the restorative approach, I argue that the Qur'an's restorative reading approach 'presents positions on all of the components needed for a theoretical basis for a divine scripture – 'revelation, interpretation, truth, authority' (Halbertal 2014: 102). In this context, the Qur'an's relationship with its cognate scriptural texts and their exegetical traditions

---

1. On the Qur'an's two faces see Neuwirth (2010).

is articulated textually through the lens of Q 2:106: 'Any message which, We (Allah) annul or consign to oblivion, We replace with a better or a similar one. Do not you know that God has the power to will anything?' Through notions of revelation, interpretation, truth and authority, the Qur'an's restorative approach follows a reading modality that stratifies its palimpsestic relationship through the grids of intra-textuality. Biblical material as a reference becomes, in the Qur'an-as-a-critical-reading, a site of negotiation the strategy of which is for the Qur'anic message to position itself in the chain of affiliation and filiation with the existing holy scriptures as an ur-text (protected tablet and mother-book) and an orphan book by which Khatibi means Mohammed's prophecy as 'the orphanage of the lost book through which the Prophet sacrifices his signature. He gives it as an offering to Allah' (Khatibi 2009: 692). The Janus-faced nature of the Qur'an as an open-closed text challenges both the view that the Qur'an is self-sufficient and the opposite view that dismisses the Qur'an text as non-relevant for Biblical Studies.

The dialectics between being a novelty in time and space and being a restorative text-scripture is not a dialectics between an old scripture and a new one but a dialectics *within* the ur-text, which is the quintessential modus operandi of the Qur'an's self-perception (1) as being articulated by two separate voices: Allah, the addresser and Mohammed's the addressee and (2) whose restorative function is cathartic. It restores the ur-text by purifying it from the Jewish and Christian accretions. Although the Qur'an is replete with biblical materials and allusions it subjects these to its own intra-textuality: at the end of the day, the Qur'an cites itself as a meta-scripture, according to which the biblical material is made to stand as an object of scrutiny. It is now up to the Qur'an to decide whether the biblical material is conforming with the Ur-text or not, not the other way around. By critical reading, I mean critique as *mise en crise* of the biblical text. Equally interesting is Khatibi's concept of the 'orphan book', according to which God, as the One, is the founding signature of Qur'an as an 'orphan book'. The palimpsestic relations that the Qur'an might entertain is restricted by the translational at the level of its content (Sabih 2015). The Qur'an as a meta-scripture challenges (Fr. *mise en crise*) the claim that the Bible is a historical document and parent-origin by (1) re-defining the relationship between divine scripture and history, and (2) cutting the umbilical cord of the biblical parent.

One of the features that the attentive reader of the Qur'anic text may notice is that the Qur'an's reception of biblical material – in particular narratives of the biblical patriarchs – represents a 'hermeneutical act in which heavenly revelation, [of which the Qur'an is its Arabic articulation], becomes a living reality' (Hamel 1975: 275) Qur'anic narratives are literary sites within which the reader experiences how the textually oriented past shapes the present and is shaped by his/her own perception intertwined with the present's perceptions! Biblical material – including biblical stories – as past is fashioned by the Qur'an's mythological language that resists any attempt to turn these stories into history by blurring all forms of time markers and space fixations. These literary sites operate through the grids of remembering/forgetting, inclusion/exclusion, and the different modes of elision, abrogation and addition. One thing that is certain is that the way the Qur'an remembers and relates story and history expresses their modus vivendi for the sake of the authority of the text as *the* word of God: *a miracle*. God's enunciated word's linguistic, discursive and literary embodiment of a text-as-an exception does not exclude its self-claimed teleology: restoring the credibility of scriptures that has been tarnished by positive history. Instead memory is called upon in Qur'anic narratives through the fictionalisation of hi-story. In dealing with the Sāmirī figure in the Qur'anic Moses narrative, some scholars – Muslims and non-Muslims – have been debating about the Qur'an and history, or, to put it correctly, the truthfulness of the Qur'an's claim to be the Word of God.

Literary Identities of al-Sāmirī

In his English translation of and commentary on the Qur'an, Yusuf Ali re-iterates the classical question that presupposes the Qur'an is a 'historical document' or that the Qur'an answers historical questions: Who is this Sāmirī that the Qur'an mentions in Q 20:83-97 (Ali 1934)? Who is this figure that the Qur'an blames for creating a calf-god and introducing calf-worship into the monotheistic religion of the Qur'anic Moses? Before answering these questions, what we should remember here is that the Sāmirī as a figure in the Qur'anic Moses narrative *is an exclusive Qur'anic literary figure*, and that there is no such figure in the corresponding biblical Moses narrative. At first glance, the Sāmirī figure appears as a Qur'anic innovation/addition despite the fact that all encyclopaedic entries consider him a *historical figure identical with the biblical Samaritans/Samarians* or a stranger – non-Israelite – figure. In *Encyclopaedia Judaica*, Hirschberg (2007: 738) seems to be so puzzled that he confesses that 'in the Koran [*sic*] al-Sāmirī is a *strange figure*... The name al-Sāmirī is difficult to explain and usually is *interpreted* as an allusion to the Samaritans'. Despite the lack of any historical evidence as to the connection between the Qur'anic *Sāmirī* and the biblical Samaritans, Stenhouse does not hesitate to state, in his entry on the Samaritans, that 'the only *unequivocal reference* to the

Samaritans in the Qur'an is al-Sāmirī' (Stenhouse 2004: 524). Although I agree with Neuwirth that the Sāmirī's story in Q 20:83-99 is 'an edifying narrative', I find her claim that in the Sāmirī's story 'no blame, let alone any lasting guilt, is laid upon the Israelites, since it is not the people but a *stranger, al-Sāmirī*, who is charged with initiating the act of idolatry' to be baseless (Neuwirth 2014: 10).

Scholars and non-scholars still premise the 'historicity' of the Qur'anic Sāmirī figure – or the lack of it – on the taken-for-granted belief that the Bible is a historical document, including the accounts on the origin of the Samaritans and their 'non-Jewish' ethnicity as well as the cult of calf worship in the Northern Kingdom of Israel and its rejection of Jerusalem's political and religious dominance (2 Kgs 17:7-41; 1 Kgs 12:28-33). On the issues of origin and identity, it is clear that Scriptures have construed the biblical Samaritan and the Qur'anic Sāmirī through the lens of theology: 'privileging of one sign or element above others is fundamentally, or rather structurally *theological*' (Anidjar 2008: 13–14). Apologetic Muslim literature keeps claiming the historicity of the Sāmirī figure by accusing the Bible's redactors of *taḥrīf* (falsification). The Sāmirī figure has been, however, construed, inter alia, in polemical literature – Jewish, Christian and Islamic – and Qur'an exegesis as a historical figure. It is also construed as the patronym for the current religious and ethnic group, the Samaritans in Israel/Palestine.[2] If one should find a plausible biblical reference for the origin of the Qur'anic Sāmirī I would choose one of these two biblical figures: Shomer/Shamer son of Heber son of Beria son of Asher son of Jacob/Israel (1 Chron. 7:30-34) or Shimron son of Issachar son of Jacob/Israel and the Shomroni clan (Gen. 46:13; Num. 26:23-25).[3] Biblical references for the Israelite origin of the Qur'anic Sāmirī are not lacking, but Qur'an's investment in the evil

---

2. Since the post-Qur'anic period Muslims have not ceased to believe that the Sāmirī's story in Q 20:83-97 applies to the Samaritans as we know them today. They are still viewed through this 'heretical heritage', despite recognizing them as a people of the book. Muslims, however, do agree with the Samaritan historiography with regard to their Israelite ancestry when the Q 20:83-97 places them at the time of Moses (*pace* 2 Kgs 17:7-41). Actually, Muslims have no problem considering them authentic natives of Palestine. It looks as if Qur'anic exegesis about al-Sāmirī (Q 20:83-97) and Islamic historiography accommodate both Jewish and Samaritan narratives about the Samaritans.

3. It is worth mentioning that one may find in 1 Chron. 7:30-34 and Num. 26:23-25 two plausible biblical references to the Qur'anic Sāmirī: 1 Chron. 7:30-34: '30. The sons of Asher: Imnah, Ishvah, Ishvi and Beriah. Their sister was Serah. 31. The sons of Beriah: Heber and Malkiel, who was the father of Birzaith. 32. Heber

agency of the Sāmirī – a Satan-like figure – transcends tribal politics in the ur-text restorative modus operandi. The theological implications of such a narrative have nothing to do with the historicity of the Sāmirī figure. This, in my opinion, is the reason why the Qur'an mentions the calf-worship incident in four places; one with the Sāmirī and three without. And as we shall see later, the Sāmirī's story should be read in relation to these other Qur'anic places first and to the Qur'an restorative approach second. I must confess, however, the perception that there is a correspondence between the Jewish representations of Samaritans and the Qur'anic Sāmirī has become the dominant interpretation of the Qur'anic Sāmirī figure.

In this article, I consider the Sāmirī's story a hapax-narrative, i.e., a micro-narrative that is mentioned only once in the Qur'an in general and in the Qur'anic Moses narrative. It functions both as a literary element – a micro-narrative – in the Qur'anic Moses narrative[4] and as a discursive output of Qur'anic iconoclastic theology and the prophet's two bodies: natural and political. The latter constitutes, together with the doctrine of the 'Oneness of God', the foundation of Qur'anic political theology (Sabih 2019), in addition, of course, to the Qur'an's restorative approach to the aforementioned notions: revelation, interpretation, truth and authority.

By 'literary identity', I mean identities that are enunciated through the lens of palimpsestic trans-textuality, the very premise of what Derrida suggests: 'there is no outside-text'. Literary identities as no-outside-text do not bother erasing their literary and textual genealogy in the dynamic process of engendering-engendered narrative form. The way Qur'anic texts construe literary identities – including that of the Sāmirī – is different from the way Qur'anic exegesis does.

was the father of Japhlet, *Shomer* and Hotham and of their sister Shua. 33. The sons of Japhlet: Pasak, Bimhal and Ashvath. These were Japhlet's sons. 34. The sons of Shomer: Ahi, Rohgah, Hubbah and Aram'; Num. 26:23-25: '23. The descendants of Issachar by their clans were: through Tola, the Tolaite clan; through Puah, the Puite clan; through Jashub, the Jashubite clan; through *Shimron*, the *Shimronite clan.* These were the clans of Issachar; those numbered were 64,300.'

Personally, I am not saying that the Qur'an passage for sure refers to one of these two biblical patronyms. I simply use these two references as an argument against the claim that there is no biblical text that confirms the existence of such a figure at the time of Moses. The Qur'anic passage is about one single person/character – Sāmirī – and not a whole tribe, or a stranger.

4. The Qur'anic Moses narrative consists of the following micro-narratives that are textually included in thirteen Suras (chapters) which I list according to their arrangement in the Qur'an: Q 2:47-71; Q 5:20-26; Q 7:103-156, 159-166; Q 10:75-93; Q 17:4-7, 101-104; Q 20:9-97; Q 26:10-66; Q 27:7-14; Q 28:2-46; Q 40:23-46; Q 43:46-55; Q 44:17-33; Q 79:15-25.

Unlike the good Samaritan figure in Jesus' parable (Lk. 10:25-37), I argue that the Qur'anic Sāmirī figure is a villain (Jn 8:48),[5] and for the reasons mentioned above, Qur'anic exegesis construes this figure as, inter alia, the Other Moses. I consider the Sāmirī's hapax-narrative an example of how identities can be fashioned textually and articulated literarily. Therefore, any 'similarities' or 'differences' between the Qur'anic Sāmirī story in Qur'anic exegesis and the biblical – and extra-biblical – stories about calf worship as well as the Samaritans are simply the result of textual-literary-discursive reconstruction of the *Samaritan trope* on the one hand, and a clear articulation of the Qur'an's political theology – iconoclastic theology and the prophet's two bodies – on the other (Sabih 2019). The Samaritan trope, I should add, operates politically in the economy of salvation in Jewish–Christian polemics: Jesus as the heretic Samaritan (Jn 8:48) versus Christ Jesus as the ideal Samaritan (Lk. 10:25-37), whereas in Qur'anic exegesis, the Sāmirī functions literarily as a narrative of iconoclasm theology: narrating and remembering as two intertwined modes of Islam's iconoclastic genealogy (Q 20:98-99).

The many figures of the 'Samaritan', their contradictory representations, together with the Samaritan trope in biblical Scriptures are enticed by and through Qur'anic exegesis into a game of detection in order to 'unveil' the identity of the Qur'anic Sāmirī. The novelty in Qur'an exegesis is the story of the two Moses-figures: *Mūsā ibn ʿimrān* and *Mūsā ibn Ẓafar*.

The Qur'anic Hapax-Narrative about the Sāmirī in Q 20:83-99[6]

Methodologically, I deal with the Qur'anic Moses narrative as one single narrative despite the fact that textually speaking it is made up of thirteen micro-narratives, and each narrative is enunciated through webbed

---

5. As a matter of fact, the Gospels representations of the Samaritan (Luke and John) is the product of the Jewish–Christian Schism rather than Samaritan–Jewish schism and identity politics. The fact that Jesus' parable about the good Samaritan does not fit with the Qur'anic Sāmirī figure has nothing to do with who is Jewish and who is not, but rather with a pre-Samaritan or non-Samaritan figure. As far as the expression *villain Samaritan* is concerned, it is inspired by the title of Chang's book: *Bad Samaritans: The Myth of Free Trade and the Secret History of Capitalism* (2008)

6. As we know, the arrangement of the Suras in the codified Qur'an (Ar. *muṣḥaf*) is different from the chronology of revelation (Ar. *waḥy; tanzīl*). Most modern scholars follow the German scholar Theodor Nöldeke's chronology and periodisation that consists of four periods: three Meccan periods and one Medinan period. Both periods cover Mohammed's prophetic mission 610-632). According to Nöldeke's chronology

textual relations: as narrative units these micro-narratives are integral elements – textually and functionally – of its immediate text on the one hand, and constitute a pre-formed literary material re-constructible into other potential autonomous text-narratives on the other. The latter feature is known as the stories of the prophets (*qaṣaṣ al-'abiyā'*) – a literary genre that emerged within Qur'anic exegesis. So instead of considering the Sāmirī's hapax-narrative in Q 20:83-99 as an anomaly within the Qur'anic Moses narrative, I consider it a cohesive literary element within the Qur'anic Moses' narrative. The interplay between these elements can clearly be seen in the way the divine voice – the addresser – uses and identifies the Sāmirī figure – a literary figure – as *the creator* of a 'living' calf, *the instigator* of calf-worship, and like Moses he is in possession of supernatural powers: magic and miracle working. In the Qur'anic text the Sāmirī functions as *the opponent* to God's authority and Moses' political and religious leadership,[7] but in Qur'anic exegesis he shares with Moses many biographical features. The encounter between the Sāmirī and Moses reveals the nature of their literary and theological agency. This is the reason why I propose that the extra-textual reading (Qur'an/biblical material) should be read intra-textually. Restoratively the intra-textual reading generates an ur-text and interprets the biblical text according to what the Qur'an as an authority-text takes as the true veridical meaning. This is why Q 20:83-99 should be read in the light of Q 7:148-154 and vice versa. While Q 7:148-154 re-iterates Exodus 32, Q 20:83-99 interprets Q 7:148-154 intra-textually in a restored text. Q 20:83-99 represents a sort of 'embedded midrash' or 'embedded tafsīr'.

The Sāmirī's[8] hapax-narrative in Q 20:83-99 consists of three subunits: prelude, story and conclusion:

the four Suras in which the calf-worship is mentioned would be arranged thus: (1) Q 20 (55), (2) Q 7 (87), (3) Q2 (91) and (4) Q 4 (100). Following al-Azhar's chronology, however, the arrangement of these four Suras would be different: (1) Q 7 (39), (2) Q 20 (45), (3) Q 2 (87) and (4) Q 4 (92). As we know, the total number of Suras in the Qur'an is 114. Since the discursive nature of Q 20:83-97 and Q 7:148-154 is not juridical, but literary, the significance of order of revelation is zero (Reynolds 2011).

7. It is worth mentioning that in both the Jewish Bible (Old Testament) and the Greek Christian Scriptures (New Testament) the Samaritan/Samarian trope has engendered several contradictory literary representations: from the impostor Jew to good Samaritan. Although the Qur'anic Sāmirī figure has one literary and theological function, it has engendered several representations in Qur'anic exegesis.

8. In these three instances the term Sāmirī appears morphologically as what looks like an active particle of the first form: *samar*, *with* a final *yī* (masculine: *iyy*; feminine: *iyyah*) called *yā' al-nisbah* (a suffix *yī* as marker of adjectivization).

Prelude:

83. [When Moses was up on the Mount, God said:] 'What made you hasten in advance of your people O Moses?' **84.** He replied: 'Behold, they are close on my footsteps: I hastened to You. O my Lord, to please You.' **85.** [God] said: 'We have tested (Ar. *fatannā*) your people in your absence and **al-Sāmirī** has led them astray (Ar. *'aḍalla-hum*).'

Story:

86. So, Moses returned to his people in a state of indignation (Ar. *ġaḍbāna*) and disappointment (Ar. *'āsifanan*). He said: 'O my people! Did not your Lord make a handsome (Ar. *ḥasanan*) promise (Ar. *wa'dan*) to you? Or did you desire that wrath should descend from your Lord on you, and so you broke your promise to me?' **87.** They said: 'We broke not the promise to you as far as lay in our power, but we were made to carry the weight of the ornaments of the (whole) people, and we threw (Ar. *qadafnā*) [into the fire], and *that was what **al-Sāmirī** suggested* (Ar. *'alqā*), **88.** *then he brought out* (Ar. *'aḫraja*) *[of the fire] before the [people] a calf*[9] (Ar. *'ijlan*), *a body* (Ar. *jasadan*) *with a low* (Ar. *lahu ḫuwārun*); so they said: 'This is your god, and the god of Moses, but he forgot (Ar. *fa-nasiya*)!' **89.** Could they not see (Ar. *'a-fa-lā yarawna*) that it could not answer them, nor could it harm them or do them good? **90.** Aaron had certainly told them earlier: 'O my people! You are being tested by it, for verily your Lord is the All-beneficent, so follow me and obey my command!' **91.** They had said: 'We will not abandon clinging (Ar. *'ākifīna*) to it until Moses returns to us'. **92.** He [Moses] said: 'O Aaron! What kept you, when you saw them going astray, **93.** from following me? Did you disobey my command?' **94.** [Aaron] replied: 'O son of my mother! Seize me not by my beard nor by my head! Truly I feared lest you should say: "You have caused a rift among the Children of Israel and did not heed my word"'. **95.** *[Moses] said: 'What is the matter with you, O **Sāmirī**?'* **96.** *[al-Sāmirī] replied: 'I saw* [or *I know*] (Ar. *baṣurtu bi-*) *what you did not see* [or you did not know] *(Ar. mā lam tabṣirū bi-hi)*[10]. *I took a handful [of dust] from the messenger's trail* (Ar. *'aṯari al-rasūl*) *and threw it. That is how my soul prompted me.'* **97.** *[Moses] said: 'Begone! It shall be your [lot] throughout life to say: "lā masās" indeed there is a promise that you will not fail! Now look at your god to whom you went on clinging. We will burn it down and then scatter it[s ashes] into the sea.'*

---

9. Al-Hasan al-Basri: 'the name of the calf is *behemoth*!' Ibn Khathir; see Job 40:15-24.
10. Another reading: 'I saw (Ar. *baṣurtu bi-*) what they were not able to see (Ar. *mā lam yubṣirū bi-hi*)'.

Conclusion:

98. Indeed, your God is Allah: *There is no god except Him*. He embraces all things in [His] knowledge. Thus, do We [Allah] *narrate* (Ar. *naquṣṣu*) to you [Mohammed] some stories (Ar. *min 'anbā'i*) of what had happened before. **99**. Certainly, We, Ourselves, have told you a story for *to tell/to remember* (Ar. *ḏikrā*).

The Calf-worship in Q 7:148-154 consists of a synopsis, a story consisting of four sections and a conclusion.

A synopsis:

148. And the people of Moses made, after [his departure], from their ornaments a calf – an image having a lowing sound. Did they not see that it could neither speak to them nor guide them to a way? They took it [for worship], and they were wrongdoers. **149**. And when regret overcame them, and they saw that they had gone astray, they said, 'If our Lord does not have mercy upon us and forgive us, we will surely be among the losers'.

Story:

Section I: [Moses returns in a state of indignation and sorrow]

150a. And when Moses returned to his people, in indignation (Ar. *ġaḍbāna*) and disappointment (Ar. *'āsifanan*), he said, 'Vile is the course which you have followed in my absence. Were you impatient over the matter of your Lord?'

Section II:

150b. And he threw down the tablets and seized his brother by [the hair of] his head, pulling him toward him. [Aaron] said, 'O son of my mother, indeed the people oppressed me and were about to kill me, so let not the enemies rejoice over me and do not place me among the wrongdoing people.'

Section III: [Moses prayer]

151. [Moses] said, 'My Lord, forgive me and my brother and admit us into Your mercy, for You are the most merciful of the merciful'.

Section IV: [God's answer]

152. indeed, those who took the calf [for worship] will obtain anger from their Lord and humiliation in the life of this world, and thus do We recompense the inventors [of falsehood]. **153**. But those who committed misdeeds and then repented after them and believed – indeed your Lord, thereafter, is Forgiving and Merciful.

[Conclusion]

154. And when the anger subsided in Moses, he took up the tablets; and in their inscription was guidance and mercy for those who are fearful of their Lord.

As mentioned earlier, Moses' narrative is told in thirteen Suras; the issue of calf worship, however, figures in four Suras only: Q 2:51-54, 92-93, Q 4:153, Q 7:148-154, Q 20:83-99. As a literary character in the Qur'anic Moses narrative, the Sāmirī appears exclusively in Q 20:83-97. While Q 7:148-154 reiterates in its synopsis that calf-worship is a collective sin for which people asked God for forgiveness after they realised that the calf was not Moses' God. As the Sāmirī's hapax-narrative shows, Q 20:83-97 answers three crucial questions: (1) the identity of the creator of the living calf, (2) the nature of the Sāmirī's agency and (3) Aaron's responsibility. The synopsis is narrated by an omniscient narrator in the third person singular. In Q 20:83-99, the hapax-narrative begins with a prelude that has the form of a conversation with God, who informs Moses about the calf-worship problem and names the two agents behind it: God who is doing the testing and God who is doing the misleading. The complementarity of Q 20:83-99 and Q 7:148-154 with regard to the above-mentioned questions can be seen from these two texts' focalisation points and narration forms. In Q 7:148-154 Moses, in his state of indignation and disappointment, points to his people for replacing him. The Arabic term *khalaftumūnī* used in Q 7:150a could mean: 'you have become/have done after me' and 'you have replaced me with'; in the latter meaning the replacement can be an object, a practice and a person. Q 20:83-99 seems to render explicit what the replacement consists of: the competing Sāmirī and his calf-worship. Moses' behaviour towards and conversation with his brother Aaron indicate that Aaron's sin was not simply the calf-worship but Aaron's failure to be a good replacement, a good leader during Moses' absence. In Q 20:83-99, God declares Aaron to be innocent and confirms Aaron's justification in Q 7:150b: 'O son of my mother, indeed the people oppressed me and were about to kill me, so let not the enemies rejoice over me and do not place me among the wrongdoing people'. God puts the blame squarely on the Sāmirī for his abuse of the power that God has given, a fact that justifies God's blaming tone against Moses in the prelude of Q 20:83-99. Aaron's explanation cuts straight into the heart of Qur'anic political theology, i.e., the relationship between the political/politics and religion: God's unity in the iconoclastic sense and the people's unity in the political sense. In this connection, the Arabic term *fitnah* ('test') in the theological sense gets its political meaning *to cause a rift* and *heed not* in Q 20:94: 'Truly I feared lest you should say: "You have caused a *rift* among the Children of Israel and did not heed my word"'. Aaron's response shows the impossibility of doing both.

The prelude consists of two parts in the form of a brief dialogue between God and Moses. In God's question (Q 20:83), God seems to disapprove of Moses' presence before Him and blames him for leaving the Israelite leaderless. In the second part Q 20:85, God gives Moses the reason for his disapproval: '*We* have tested your people in your absence' and '*al-Sāmirī* has led them astray'. The Sāmirī becomes the instrument by which God tests the son of Israel. It seems that the Sāmirī is God's agent and a necessary evil. The theological implications of such a statement are representative of the Qur'an's theodicy: God is the creator of good and evil, but some of his creations can be vehicles by which good or evil are carried out. It is in the absence of Moses that God's testing and *the Sāmirī's* misleading take place. The Sāmirī figure is introduced in the story with ease, which suggests that Moses might have been familiar with him.

The story unit (Q 20:86-97) begins with a brief but eloquent description of Moses's reaction in Q 20:86a: indignation or anger mixed with sorrow. Implicitly, it shows the state in which his meeting with God ended and the nature of his return to his people. In a condensed diegetic commentary, the extradiegetic homodiegetic narrator shows the urgency of the matter at hand and the psychological situation of Moses: anger and sorrow. The narration of Moses' return to his people in Q 20:86b-97) is to find out and to deal with what God has told him happened during his absence – *fitnah* ('test') and *ḍalālah* ('going astray'). The narration's events are structured thus: first, Moses's conversation with the people, second with his brother Aaron, then with the Sāmirī, who seems to be in possession of supernatural powers that enabled him to create a calf from inanimate metals. This event is reminiscent of Moses being accused of being a magician in Q 7:109 and his later confrontation with the Egyptian magicians that ended with defeat and conversion to Moses's faith in Q 7:111-126. In the encounter between Moses (the good) and the Sāmirī (the evil), Moses does not inquire about the identity of the Sāmirī (who are you?), but he inquires about the nature of the Sāmirī act of creating the calf: 'What is the matter with you, O Sāmirī?'. Like Moses, the Sāmirī is also a miracle worker.[11]

---

11. On man's ability to create, see, for instance. *Sanh.* 65b in the Talmud: 'Rava says: If the righteous wish to do so, they can create a world, as it is stated: "But your iniquities have separated between you and your God". In other words, there is no

Moses's confrontation with the *Sāmirī* in Q 20:95-97 ends with the destruction of the calf by burning and throwing its ashes in the sea: a symbolic drowning of the calf in the sea reminiscent of the drowning of the Egyptians in the sea. The Sāmirī *is condemned to repeat a mysterious formula: lā masās* ('no touching') for the rest of his life. Unlike the people who sinned by worshiping the calf, the punishment of the Sāmirī is as follows: In addition to him being unmasked as a fraudulent 'prophet', his created calf-god has not only been found a false god, but the whole idea of making an image of the true God is condemned and rejected by the iconoclastic theology. As a final blow, the Sāmirī is ostracized and stripped of his social identity according to the Qur'an's politics of friendship. The latter punishment of the Sāmirī reminds us of another punishment: Satan's. In earlier conversations between God and Satan in Q 7:11-18, God expelled him from his presence because he refused to obey God when He ordered him to bow down to Adam.

Q 20:83-99 and Q 7:148-154 conclude with a restoration of the true worship through the authority of God's law (Q 7:154) and divine history as remembrance of an iconoclastic theology (Q 20:98-99). Moses restores the tablets of God's law and as the true inheritor of Moses's prophethood Mohammed does and should remember to do the same: restore the true revelation and the true worship.

In and through indirect speech, the narrator's voice operates bi-directionally: backwards and forwards, past and present. The direct speech functions as both the enunciating and the enunciation of the iconoclastic ideology of the Qur'an. According to this ideology the Bible's monotheisms are deemed not iconoclastic enough, whence the Qur'an's cathartic modus operandi: it works in texts as well as in reality. The past here is narrated both as and through the present: total suspension of disbelief. The extradiegetic homodiegetic narrator, as an omnipresent voice, introduces the Sāmirī figure as a *flat* and *symbolic* figure that plays the role of the

distinction between God and a righteous person who has no sins, and just as God created the world, so can the righteous. Indeed, Rava created a man, a golem, using forces of sanctity. Rava sent his creation before Rabbi Zeira. Rabbi Zeira would speak to him but he would not reply. Rabbi Zeira said to him: You were created by one of the members of the group, one of the Sages. Return to your dust.'

In the same tractate, one can also find the creation of animals such as the calf: 'The Gemara relates another fact substantiating the statement that the righteous could create a world if they so desired: *Rav Ḥanina and Rav Oshaya would sit every Shabbat eve and engage in the study of Sefer Yetzira, and a third-born calf [igla tilta] would be created for them, and they would eat it in honor of Shabbat.*'

indispensable metaphysical villain, who is similar to Satan, the *Other*, who is narrated in the Qur'anic radical monotheistic discourse as the instigator of calf worship.[12]

The Sāmirī as the Other Moses Qur'an Tafsīr

While the Qur'anic text portrays the Sāmirī according to the above-mentioned functions, Qur'anic exegesis is haunted by a hermeneutical conflict due to preconceived theological perceptions, biblical representations of the 'Samaritan', and the legal and religious status of the Samaritan community within the Islamic territories. This hermeneutical conflict is caught up in a mythical understanding of history. As far as the first point is concerned, the doctrine of the infallibility of the prophets, Muslim exegetes seem to find in Q 20:83-97 their textual argument for the innocence of Aaron from the sin of associating other gods with Allah.[13] Judging from the high numbers of anecdotes relating to the Sāmirī's identity, and the presence of biblical and extra-biblical materials in these exegetical anecdotes, the Samaritan option has been considered by Muslim exegetes as well. For Muslim jurists, the question of who should be included in *Ahl al-kitāb* (people of the book) has played a major role in adopting the Jewish narrative vis-à-vis the Samaritan community. The Qur'anic Sāmirī figure has been used as an argument for considering the Samaritans as an aberrant Jewish sect.

Muslim exegetes' hermeneutical conflict has been articulated in two ways: (1) literary-form: an assemblage of different, disconnected and

---

12. Calf worship in the Bible are of two kinds: (1) unauthorized: Exodus 32; Deut. 9:7-21; cf. Neh. 9:18; Ps. 106:19-20; Acts 7:39-40 (Shepherd 2011), and (2) authorized: authorized calf-worship in Northern Israel is mentioned in 2 Kgs 12:28-33; 10:29; 17:16; Hos. 8:5-6; 10:5-6; 13:2; 2 Chron. 11:15; 13:8.

13. I find Neuwirth's interpretation of the Qur'anic expression *rabbuka* ('your Lord') in Q 20:9-15 – 'When he came to it a voice cried, "Moses, I am your Lord (*rabbuka*). Put off thy shoes; thou art in the holy valley Ṭuwā. I myself have chosen thee; therefore, give your ear to this revelation! Verily I am God. There is no god but I (*lā ilāha illā anā*)! Therefore, serve me and perform the prayer (*ṣalāh*) of My remembrance!"' – as a 'usual rendering of the Tetragrammaton' far-fetched. The Tetragrammaton is never expressed as 'your Jahweh' in the Hebrew Jewish Bible. One can find expressions such as 'Jahweh your God'. Regarding God's name in the Qur'an see my forthcoming paper: 'Dieu, il est et il n'est pas: Surat 112 comme cas d'étude'. This paper is written in dialogue with Angelika Neuwirth's and Thomas Thompson's works on this issue (Neuwirth 2010; Thompson 2013: 119–32).

uniform stories (*aiṣaṣ, hagadot*) and (2) trans-textual: a chain of commentaries, in which a story can play different roles: being the core-text of commentary(/ies) and/or being a commentary itself. One single and short story has always kindred relatives somewhere as in the case of the Sāmirī's story. In Qur'anic exegesis and stories of the prophets (*qiṣaṣ al-'abiyā'*), the Sāmirī's hapax-narrative is enunciated textually and discursively through the lens of identity politics: who is this villain Sāmirī whose theological and political agency have been perverted by inter-religious polemics?

Sāmirī's 'family romance' in Qur'anic exegesis has a literary form of the hadith genre. It consists of a chain of transmitters/authorities marked by a repetitive phrase 'X has told us, and he said', and a content/story. The literary sources/stories of Sāmirī's family romance at the disposal of the exegete are fragmentary and concise. Here I present some of these stories that deal with name(s), birth, clan(s), religion and so on.

The Sāmirī's birth and infancy: The Sāmirī is reported to have been born in the most tragic conditions similar to those under which the biblical Moses is born. The survival of both is described as miraculous. While Moses is rescued by and raised in the palace of Pharaoh, the Sāmirī's survival narrative is significantly different. As a matter of fact, the Sāmirī's infancy has not been corrupted by the urban life of the Egyptian elite. He has been raised under the caring, nourishing hands of the chief-angel Gabriel:

> On the authority of al-Qāsim he told this on the authority of al-Ḥusayn, on the authority of Ḥajjāj on the authority of Jurayḥ who said: 'When Pharaoh slew male infants the Sāmirī's mother said [to herself, when she gave birth to him]: "What if I hid him somewhere so that I would see him nor I would witness him being slain?" Then she took him him to a cave [and left him there]. At that moment [Angel] Gabriel came to him and he put the fingers of his palm hand in his mouth. He fed him [out of his fingers] milk and honey. He continued to visit him until [the enfant] grew up to know him. This the meaning of "I took a handful [of dust] from the messenger's trail" (Q 20:96) because when the Sāmirī saw Gabriel [on his horse] he recognized him.' (Tabari 2010: 16:254)

The Sāmirī's name(s) and tribal status: As mentioned earlier, Muslim exegetes have been – and still are – obsessed with the historicity of the figure of the Sāmirī. For instance, Ibn Khatir, in his commentary, lists a number of contradicting accounts (hadiths) pertaining to his identity. What is striking is the name of this Sāmirī:

> Muhammad bin Ishaq reported from Ibn ʿAbbas that he said, 'The Sāmirī was a man from the people of Bajarma, a people who worshipped cows. He still had the love of cow worshipping in his soul. However, he acted as though he had accepted Islam with the Children of Israel. His name was *Mūsā ibn Ẓafar* (Moses son of Zafar).'[14] (Ibn Kathir 2001: 219)

The novelty in Islamic Qur'anic exegesis is not how these biographical accounts came about, but how the identities are constructed and construed literarily. In the minds of the exegete the ambiguity of the Sāmirī figure's Qur'anic identity left him with no option but to venture into the realm of mythologized understanding of history according to which the Qur'an is both the eternal word of God and his message of salvation to mankind. The invention of such a figure with all the theological elements of iconoclastic theology and literary anatomy of mythology was construed as history. Exegetes had to invent another Moses whose biography is a mimicry of the biblical and Qur'anic Moses. In their trying to solve the ambiguity of the Sāmirī's story and his culpability, exegetes failed to see the Qur'an's restorative approach to Scriptures as well as to humans' fragile relations to God.

Bibliography

Ali, Abdullah Yusuf (1934), *The Holy Qur'ān: English Translation & Commentary*, Lahore: Shaik Muhammad Ashraf.

Anidjar, Gil (2008), *Semites: Race, Religion, Literature*, Cultural Memory in the Present, Stanford: Stanford University Press.

Chang, Ha-Joon (2008), *Bad Samaritans: The Myth of Free Trade and The Secret History of Capitalism*. New York: Bloomsbury.

Halbertal, Moshe (2014), *Maimonides: Life and Thought*, Princeton: Princeton University Press.

Hamel, E. (1975), 'La théologie morale entre l'Écriture et la raison', *Gregorianum*, 56 (2): 273–320.

Hirschberg, Haïm Z'ew (2007), 'Samaritans in Islam'. *EncJud* 17: 738.

Ibn Kathir, Isma'il (2001), *Tafsīr Al-Qur'ān Al-ʿAẓīm, Vol. 2*, 6th ed., Beirut: Mu'assasat al-Rayyān.

Khatibi, Abdelkebir (2009), 'Frontiers: Between Psychoanalysis and Islam', *Third Text*, 23 (6): 689–96.

Neuwirth, Angelika (2010), 'Two Faces of the Qur'ān: Qur'ān and Muṣḥaf', *Oral Tradition*, 25 (1), https://muse.jhu.edu/article/402427.

Neuwirth, Angelika (2014), 'Qur'anic Studies and Historical-Critical Philology: The Qur'an's Staging, Penetrating and Eclipsing of Biblical Tradition', in *IQSA*, http://www.almuslih.com/Library/Neuwirth,%20A%20-%20Historical-Critical.pdf.

---

14. In his commentary on Q 20:5 Ibn Kathir mentions that name of the Sāmirī is Aaron in the Israelite sources (Ibn Kathir 2001: 217).

Reeck, Matt (2017), 'The Poetics of the Orphan in Abdelkébir Khatibi's Early Work', *Journal of French and Francophone Philosophy*, 25: 132–49.
Reynolds, Gabriel S. (2011), 'Le Problème de La Chronologie Du Coran', *Arabica*, 58: 477–502.
Sabih, Joshua (2015), 'Under the Gaze of Double Critique: De-Colonisation, De-Sacralisation and the Orphan Book', *Tidsskrift for Islamforskning*, 9 (1): 79–108.
Sabih, Joshua (2019), 'Qur'anic Political Theology: God's Law, Jews and the Politics of Friendship', in R. Rosario Rodriguez (ed.), *T&T Clark Handbook of Political Theology*, T&T Clark Handbooks, London: Bloomsbury.
Schmitt, Carl (2005), *Political Theology: Four Chapters on the Concept of Sovereignty*, trans. George Schwab, Chicago: University of Chicago Press.
Shepherd, Michael B. (2011), *The Twelve Prophets in the New Testament*, Studies in Biblical Literature, Bern: Peter Lang.
Stenhouse, Paul (2004), 'The Samaritans', in J. Dammen McAuliffe (eds), *Encyclopedia of the Qur'an*, Leiden: E. J. Brill.
Tabari, Ibn Jarir (2010), *Jāmiʿ Al-Bayān*. Vol. 16. Cairo: Dar Hajar lil-Tibaraa wa-Nashr.
Thompson, Thomas L. (2013), *Biblical Narrative and Palestine's History: Changing Perspectives 2*, CIS, Sheffield: Equinox.

Index of References

Hebrew Bible/ Old Testament		15:10-17	110	32:29	228
		17	108	32:55-26	230
Genesis		17:4-6	231	33:1-3	56
1–11	87, 161, 249	17:5	227, 242	33:4	56
		17:7-8	108	33:18	229
1–3	160	17:18	52	35:10	228
1:1	232	18	108	35:21	228
1:26-31	233	21:8-21	52	35:22	228
1:26	171	21:9-11	52	36	108
2–4	172	21:10-11	54	36:1-18	230
2–3	113, 160, 163, 164, 166	21:20	52	36:12	108, 230
		22	108	36:13	230
		22:1-13	51	36:16	230
2:4-20	233	22:2	203	36:17	230
2:4	232, 233	22:10	110	36:18	230
2:9	165	22:11-12	110	37	55
2:16-17	165	24:67	229	37:3	228
3	164, 168, 249	25	230, 231	37:13	228
		25:1-4	51, 231	38:26	229
3:5	165	25:1	229, 230, 235	41:37-57	55
3:6	165			43:6	228
3:20	172	25:2	230, 231	43:8	228
3:22	165, 172	25:4	230	43:10	228
4:17-24	235	25:5-11	230	46:2	228
6	108	25:5	230	46:6	228
7–8	108	25:6	230	46:13	261
9	108	25:9	52	49	108
9:1	109	25:15	230	49:3-9	109
9:27	109	25:18	230	49:10	109
10:2-5	249	25:19	230	49:33	228
10:8	235	25:22	230	50:24	226
10:14	235	25:23	54		
10:25	235	25:28	54	*Exodus*	
11	108	26:34	229	2:1-10	52
11:26–17:5	227	28	108	2:15-22	220
14	185	28:3-4	110	2:24	226
15	108	32–33	170	3:6	226

3:12	106	35:5-35	199	29:12	226
3:15	226	35:20–36:7	203	30:15-20	167
3:16	226	35:30-33	204	30:20	226
4:5	226			32:9	57
6:3-7	108	*Leviticus*		33:10	57
6:3	107, 226	4:13	201	34:4	226
6:8	226	9:24	204		
12:3	201	12:2	240	*Joshua*	
12:47	201	16:2	204	10:13	185
16:1	202			14:1	203
19:1	202	*Numbers*		18:1	203
20:11	233	1:1	202	19:51	203
24	106, 107	5:28	240	21:1	203
24:4-6	106	7:2	201	24:4	226
24:4	106	7:8	200		
24:8	106, 173	9:1	202	*Judges*	
25–31	199	12:1	220	3:7-11	184
25:1-7	199	13:17-33	183	4	177, 190, 194
25:2-5	203	21:8-9	164	4:21	194
25:8	202	21:14	185	5	190, 191, 193, 195
25:9	203	26:23-25	261, 262	5:4-5	195
25:17-22	200, 204, 205	30:2	201	5:6-8	193
		32:11	226	5:6-7	193
25:31-39	201	32:28	203	5:8	193
25:40	203	33:38	202	5:9-11	195
26:15-37	200	36:1	201	5:11-18	193
26:31-37	200			5:26-27	194
26:31-35	205	*Deuteronomy*		5:28-30	194
26:31	204, 206	1:3	232	5:31	195
26:33-35	206	1:6	232	6:15	55
26:33	204	1:8	226	6:27	55
26:35	204	2:23	235	8:22-26	55
26:36-37	205	6:10	226	13–16	177
26:36	206	7:3-4	96	13:1	185
26:37	206	9:5	226	13:2-24	52
27:16	206	9:7-21	270	14:6	179
29:45-46	202	9:27	226	14:19	177, 179
30:17-21	201	10:1-5	202	15	177
30:22-38	199	11:28	186	15:4	179
31:1-5	204	12:4	99	15:20	185
31:17	233	13:3	186	16	179, 185, 186
32	270	13:14	186		
32:13	226	23:3-6	58	16:1-3	178
33:1	226	23:3-5	96	16:1	179
35–40	199	23:7	58		
35:4-19	203	25:19	109		

Judges (cont.)		25:33	169, 170	6:11-13	88
16:2	179, 180	25:36-38	171	6:14-38	84
16:3	179	25:40-42	171	6:15-38	86
16:9	179	25:41	171	6:23-28	200, 205
16:12	179	26	169	6:31-35	200, 206
16:14	179	26:11	169	6:36 LXX	206
16:21	179	26:23	169	6:37	97
16:31	185	26:25	169	7:1-51	84
17–18	193			7:1-12	86
19:1	230	*2 Samuel*		7:6-8	86
		1:18	185	7:12	86
Ruth		5:13	229	7:13-47	204
4:18-22	236	6	4	7:13-14	86
		7	88	7:21	86
1 Samuel		8	84, 88	7:23-26	201
2:22	203	10	84, 88	7:25	86
5	187	21:19	149	7:27-39	201
5:11-12	97			7:27	86
14:47	57	*1 Kings*		7:36	86
14:48	109	3–11	83, 84	7:43	86
15:1-9	109	3	88	7:49	200
16:4-13	55	4:1-6	88	7:50	204
17	149	4:1	201	7:63-65	86
18:3-4	169	4:7-19	84	8	88, 201
20:12-17	169	4:7	201	8:1-11 LXX	202
23:16-18	169	4:20-28	84	8:1	201, 203
24	169	4:26-28	84	8:3-4	201
24:7	169	5–8	85	8:3	201
24:21	169	5–7	203	8:4	201
24:25	169	5:1-12	88	8:4 LXX	202
25	160, 169, 172	5:6	86	8:5-9	201
		5:9	86	8:5	201
25:3	169, 170	5:13–7:51	85	8:9	202
25:7	170	5:13-18	84	8:10-11	202, 204
25:10-11	170	5:14	86	8:11 LXX	202
25:13	170	5:15	86, 97	8:62	201
25:17	170	5:17-18	86	8:64	201
25:22	170	5:18	86	8:65	201
25:24	171	5:21	233	9:1-14	88
25:25	170, 171	5:27	201	9:1-3	202
25:26-27	170	6–8	200, 203	9:15-24	84
25:27	171	6–7	4	9:15-19	85
25:28-31	170	6:1-10	84	9:25	88
25:28	170, 171	6:1	97, 202, 203	9:26-28	84
25:29	170			10:1-27	84
25:31	170, 171	6:2-9	86	10:18-20	86
25:32-35	170	6:3	86	10:28-29	84

11:1-13	88	19:15	233	5:1	226
11:14-25	84	19:19	78	5:3	226
11:15-16	57	19:35-37	79	6:3-15	95
11:26-43	88	21–25	82	6:17	203
11:41	83	21:1–22:1	83	6:23	226
12:1-31	88	21:3	83	7:24	235
12:1	97	21:7	172	7:29	226
12:19	97	21:20	83	7:30-34	261
12:28-33	261	22:2	83	9	245
14	170	22:3-10	83	11:18	229
16:24	81	22:11	83	14:3	229
16:31	79, 229	22:12-17	83	16:1-38	203
16:34	81	22:18-20	83	16:8-22	227
18:19	172	23:1-25	83	16:13	226, 227
18:20-46	187	23:4-7	172	16:17	226, 227
18:36	226	23:22	99	16:39-41	203
22:39	81	23:26–25:26	83	17:14	243
		23:32	83	20:5	149
2 Kings		23:37	83	21:29	203
3:1-27	78	24:9	83	28:11	203, 204
8:41-43	243	24:10-16	78	29	203
9	170	24:19	83	29:2	203
9:2	80	25:27	78	29:3-5	203
10:29	270			29:5	203
12:28-33	270	1 Chronicles		29:6-9	203
13:23	226	1	237	29:10	226
15:19-20	78	1:1-4 MT	234	29:18	226
15:29-30	78	1:1-4	234, 237, 242	30:6	226
16:7-10	78	1:4-23	237	2 Chronicles	
16:14	201	1:4	235	1:3-6	203
16:15	201	1:5-23	235	1:4	203
16:17	201	1:10	235	1:5	204
17	93, 99	1:12	235	2:6	204
17:3–18:10	78	1:19	235	2:11	233
17:7-41	261	1:24-27	236, 237	2:12 ET	233
17:16	270	1:27	227, 237, 238, 242	2:13	204
17:21	97			3:1	203, 229
17:24-34	87	1:28	231	3:2	203
17:24-28	91	1:32	231, 235	3:8-13	205
17:29-33	91, 94	1:34	226	3:14	204, 207
17:34-41	91	1:35-54	228	4:6	205
17:34	92, 94	2:1	226	4:7	205
17:35-39	92	2:3	232	4:14	205
17:40	92, 94	2:10-12	236	4:20	205
17:41	92, 94	2:15	236	4:22	204
18:11-12	98	4:10	232	5:2	203
18:13	78				

2 Chronicles (cont.)		13:6	216	2:16	166
5:5	203	13:7-9	212, 213	2:18	167
5:11-14	203, 204	13:13	214	2:20	250
6:32-33	243	13:15-22	96	3:9-10	251
7:1-3	204	13:15-21	219	3:13	166
11:15	270	13:15	216	3:14-17	166
13:8	270	13:17	215, 216	3:16	169
23:18	242	13:25	221	3:17	250
25:4	242	23:23-24	220	3:18	166, 167
29:6	205			3:27-28	251
30:6	226	*Esther*		4:8	167
30:16	242	6:1	185	4:10	167
34:14	242	10:2	185	4:13	167
36:23	243			5:1-23	166
		Job		5:3-6	251
Ezra		28	172	5:3	167
6:1-12	96	40:15-24	265	5:5	167, 168
6:2	185			5:15-19	166
7:1	95	*Psalms*		5:15-18	254
7:11-26	95, 96	1:1	166	5:15	168
10:18-44	95	1:2	232	5:19	167
40:34-35	202	14:7	57	5:20	167, 251
		76:3	229	6:8	251
Ezra		78	57	6:9-11	251
2:61-63	210, 211	78:2	258	6:11	251
		83:5	239	6:19	252
Nehemiah		105:1-15	227	6:20-35	166
1:9	99	105:6	227	6:23-26	251
2:11-19	95	105:10	227	6:24	166
3:1-32	95	106:19-20	270	6:26	166
5:1-5	217	110:2-4	229	6:29	251
5:5	217	115:15	233	6:32	166
5:14	211	121:2	233	7:1-17	166
5:17	218	124:8	233	7:5	166
6:15–7:4	96	134:3	233	7:11-12	167
6:18	213	137	191	7:13	167
7:63-65	210, 211			7:18	167
8:1-8	95	*Proverbs*		7:21	167
8:9	211	1–9	166, 167,	7:27	167
8:17	99		172	8:1-4	166
9:7	227	1:1	250	8:5	166
9:18	270	1:7	232, 250	8:6-13	167
10:2	211	1:18-19	250	8:22-31	234
13	212	1:20-21	167	8:30	167
13:1-3	96	1:22	166	8:35	167
13:4	213	2:8	250	9	167

9:1	167	27:10	253	*Jonah*	
9:4-6	167	27:16	253	1	187
9:6	168	27:25	253	3:6	185
9:7-12	168	27:26	253		
9:11	167	27:27	253	*Malachi*	
9:13-18	168	30	250	1:2	226
9:13	166			1:4	57
9:18	168	*Isaiah*			
10:1	250	2	160	NEW TESTAMENT	
10:5	251	9:7	57	*Matthew*	
10:20	252	27:2	193	2:1-16	52
11:10-11	252	34:9-13	57	26:28	173
11:17	254	37:16	233		
11:24-26	252	60	160	*Mark*	
11:25	254	66	160	14:22-24	173
12:4	252				
12:17	252	*Jeremiah*		*Luke*	
12:27	252	31:31	160	10:25-37	263
13:3	252	47:4	235	22:17-20	173
13:4	252	50:21	185		
13:10	252			*John*	
13:11	252	*Lamentations*		6	153
14:5	252	4:21-22	58	8:48	263
14:20	254			20:31	148
14:25	252	*Ezekiel*			
15:19	250	44:15	103	*Acts*	
17:3	254			7:39-40	270
17:5	253	*Daniel*			
17:17	254	2:31-45	249	*1 Corinthians*	
17:23	253	5:1-2	185	10:4	149
19:5	252	6:1	185	11:23-26	173
19:7	254				
19:9	252	*Hosea*		*Hebrews*	
19:15	253	8:5-6	270	6:19	205
19:26	253	10:5-6	270	9:3	205
19:28	252	10:14	84	10:20	205
20:4	253	12:13	57		
20:6	254	13:2	270	APOCRYPHA	
20:13	253			*Judith*	
21:28	252	*Amos*		4:9	185
22:17–24:22	248	9:7	235	11	185
24:28	252				
24:33-34	251	*Obadiah*		*Ecclesiasticus*	
25:1	250	18	226	15:1	172
25:18	252			24:23	172
27:2	254			49:11-13	97
				50:5	206

Baruch
4:1	172

1 Maccabees
1:22	206
2:29-41	97
4:51	205–7

2 Maccabees
1:1-9	98
2:13	96
5:22	94

PSEUDEPIGRAPHA
1 Enoch
42	172

Jubilees
30:1	229
38:10	56
38:12-14	56

Letter of Aristeas
§85	206

Liber Antiquitatum Biblicarum
10:7	149
43:2-4	185

Josephus
Jewish Antiquities
3.116	200
3.119	200
3.128-129	206
8.71-72	207
8.75	206, 206
8.125-26	202
9	93
9.277-789	93
9.290	93, 94
9.291	94
10.20-21	79
11.179	96
11.302-311	94
11.302	94
11.306-312	96
12.138-146	95
12.257	94
12.318	206, 207
13.66-270	131
13.66-135	132
13.74-79	98
13.189-270	132
13.255-258	98
13.257-258	59
13.282-283	120
14.107	206
14.145-148	131
14.150-155	131
14.163	125
14.190-264	131
14.192-195	124
14.195	125
15.14-15	124, 133
15.14	135
15.15	132
15.23-28	128
15.30	127
15.31-32	128
15.42	127
15.51	123
15.72-73	129
15.72	128
15.73	128
15.75	128
15.79	128
15.80	129
15.92	127
15.96	127
15.108	126
15.112-120	126
15.118-119	133
15.160	127
15.164	129
15.165-182	130
15.165-179	125
15.167-173	133
15.172	127
15.174-178	132, 133
15.174	133
15.176	129
15.178	132
15.182	133
15.183	132
15.243	130
15.255-257	128
15.266	134
15.341	126
15.380	126
16.136	126
17.149	132
17.207-208	132
17.339	132
18.3-4	132
18.23-26	132
18.85	205
18.89-122	131
18.114-115	125
18.116-119	121, 129
18.117-119	119
18.117-118	130
18.117	130
18.118-119	129
18.118	129
18.119	130
18.310-379	131
20.248	129, 130, 132

Against Apion
1.106-27	79

Jewish War
1.401	126
1.433-434	128
1.437	129
1.438	123
1.439-444	129
2.129	122
2.137-139	122
2.150	122
5.211-112	206
5.219	205, 207
7.300	128

DEAD SEA SCROLLS
1QS
3.6-12	122
5.13-14	122

4Q158
frag. 4,
  ll. 1-7   106
  ll. 1-2   106
  ll. 6-7   107

4Q179
frag. 1, col. I,
  ll. 1-15   114

4Q252
5 iv 5   108
col. III,
  ll. 1-6   110
col. IV   108
col. VI   109
cols. I-III   108
frag. 2, col. ii,
  ll. 10-12   111
frags. 1 and 3, col. ii,
  ll. 7-8   110
frags. 1, 3-5, col. iii,
  ll. 12-13   110

4Q501
ll. 1-3   115

4Q504
frag. 1-2 ii
  9-10   112
  11   112
  12-13   112
  15-16   112
frag. 1-2 iv
  2   112
  3-6   112
  5-8   112
  14   112
frag. 1-2 v
  6-14   113
frag. 1-2 vi
  2-10   113
frag. 3 ii
  7-17   112
frag. 4
  5-8   112

frag. 6
  6   114
  10   112
  12   112
frag. 8 4   112

CD
1–8   102
1.1-6   102
1.2   102
1.7-8   102
2.11   103
2.17-18   103
3.2   103
3.3-4   103
3.19   103
3.21–4.1   103
MS A
  3.18-21   103
  4.1-4   103, 104

MISHNAH
Yoma
5:1   207

BABYLONIAN TALMUD
Baba Qama
92a   240

Berakhot
60a   240

Niddah
31a   240

Sanhedrin
21b   92
65b   268

Sotah
10a   181

TOSEFTA TALMUD
Pesahim
1:15   93

MIDRASH
Genesis Rabbah
61:4   230

Leviticus Rabbah
8.2   181
29.11   236

Numbers Rabbah
14:9   181

CLASSICAL AND ANCIENT
CHRISTIAN LITERATURE
Aristotle
History of the Animals
622b   251
627a   251

Poetics
ch. 9   147

Herodotus
Histories
1.151   240
5.49   240
8.144   240

Hesiod
Work and Days
42-105   249
109-201   249
217   250
220-221   253
225-242   252
251   250
263-264   253
265   250
282-285   252
287   250
289-294   251
295-298   252
298-307   251
299-301   253
302-306   252
327-334   251
331-334   253
342-346   253

Work and Days (cont.)		Cyropaedia		TAD	
354-363	252	VIII 6: 10	216	A6.13	217
361-362	252			A6.3	218
370	251	Ostraca, Papyri			
372-374	251	and Tablets		VS	
397-404	251	P.Berlin		4 85	212
409-413	252	13536	215		
479-482	253	13582	212	Qur'an	
495	251			2	264
496	251	BM		2.47-71	262
506	253	79293	212	2.51-54	267
517	253			2.87	151, 152
518-521	253	Inscriptions		2.92-93	267
543-546	253	Adapa		2.106	259
545	253	A, l. 1-21	161	2.136	151
551	253	A, l. 4	161	2.253	151, 152
574-577	252	A, l. 6	164	3.35-37	148
590	253	B, l. 57	164	3.48-49	151
699-701	251	D, ll. 9-10	164	3.52-53	152
702-706	252	D, ll. 10-11	163	3.59	154
717-719	253			3.84	151
720	252	ARM		4	264
778	251	13 7	181	4.153	267
				4.157-159	153
Theogony		CBS		4.163	151
507-616	249	5213	221	4.171-172	154
				5	152
Livy		Chronicle		5.20-26	262
XLV.2	220	1, i.28	78	5.46-47	152
		5, r. 11-13	78	5.72-75	154
Theognis				5.75	154
Sentences		Gilgamesh		5.110-111	152
79–81	254	tabl. I,		5.112-115	152
97–99	254	l. 183-89	168	5.116-118	154
155-58	253			6.85	151
499-502	254	Mesha Stele		7	264
573-574	254	4–11	78	7.11-18	269
611-614	254	17–18	81	7.103-156	262
645-646	254	18–19	78	7.109	268
857-860	254			7.111-126	268
927-930	254	OB Penn		7.148-154	264, 266, 267, 269
959-962	254	tablet II,			
		ll. 55-67	168	7.150	267
Xenophon				7.154	269
Anabasis		Statue Inscription of		7.159-166	262
5.3.6	215	Udjahorresnet		9.30-31	154
		ll. 18-23	214	10.75-93	262

11	150	20.83-97	260, 261, 264, 267, 270	28.2-46	262
12	149, 151			33.7	151
17.4-7	262			33.40	150
17.101-104	262	20.83	268	40.23-46	262
19.28	148	20.85	268	42.13	151
20	264	20.86-97	268	43.46-55	262
20.5	272	20.86	268	43.57-59	154
20.9-15	270	20.94	268	43.63	152
20.9-97	262	20.95-97	269	44.17-33	262
20.83-99	261, 263, 264, 267, 269	20.98-99	263, 269	57.27	151–3
		21.51-70	149	66.12	148
		26.10-66	262	79.15-25	262
		27.7-14	262		

Index of Authors

Abdel Haleem, M. A. S. 151, 155
Abu el-Haj, N. 39, 43
Achenbach, R. 202, 203, 208
Aharoni, Y. 16, 17
Al-Ravi, F. 161, 173
Albertz, R. 198, 200, 202, 208
Aletti, J. N. 167, 173
Ali, A. Y. 260, 272
Allegro, J. M. 105, 108, 115, 117
Alper, B. S. 10, 11, 17
Alt, A. 43
Amit, Y. 179, 187
Ammons, L. L. 66, 73
Anderson, B. 53, 60
Anidjar, G. 261, 272
Ariel, D. T. 4, 8
Armitage, D. J. 249, 254
Arnold, B. T. 25, 33
Ash, P. S. 84, 89
Atkinson, K. 134, 136
Attridge, H. 111, 117
Avalos, H. 25, 33, 36, 43
Averett, E. W. 13, 17
Avi-Yonah, M. 182, 187

Bagnall, R. S. 220, 222
Bahrani, Z. 37, 43, 44
Baillet, M. 117
Baker, D. W. 24, 34, 191, 194
Baker, R. 196
Bal, M. 194, 196
Baragwanath, E. 240, 246
Barr, D. 11, 17, 24, 30
Barr, J. 33
Barth, F. 15, 17, 29, 33
Bartholomew, C. G. 250, 254
Bates, M. J. 14, 17
Batten, L. W. 213, 216, 222
Baumgarten, J. M. 104, 117

Bechmann, U. 191, 196
Becking, B. 196
Beckman, G. 186–8
Ben Zvi, E. 38, 44, 58, 60, 231, 233, 239, 242, 246
Benardou, A. 11, 15, 18
Benveniste, E. 211, 222
Berger, P. 38, 44
Berlin, A. 115–17, 134
Bernbeck, R. 44
Bernick-Greenberg, H. 4, 6, 9, 38
Bernstein, M. J. 105, 109, 117
Bienkowski, P. 80, 89
Biggs, R. D. 239, 246
Blair, A. 10, 18
Blenkinsopp, J. 191, 196, 213, 222
Blevins, C. 13, 18
Bliss, F. J. 3, 8
Blum, E. 199, 208
Boaretto, E. 9
Boda, M. J. 235, 246
Böhl, F. M. T. 64, 73
Boling, R. G. 190, 196
Borchardt, E. A. 13, 18
Bourdieu, P. 35, 44
Braun, R. 235, 246
Brettler, M. Z. 179, 188, 194, 196
Briant, P. 216, 222
Broberg, L. 169, 171–3
Brodie, T. L. 248, 254
Bronson, B. 16, 18
Bronstein, J. 13, 20
Brooke, G. J. 105, 108, 109, 117
Brown, J. P. 249, 252–4
Bruneau, P. 94, 100
Buhl, P. 150, 155
Bultmann, R. 140, 144
Bunimovitz, S. 16, 18
Burton, J. B. 250, 254

Bush, K. H. 10, 18
Byrne, P. 249, 255

Camp, C. V. 166, 173
Campbell, E. F. 65, 67, 74
Carroll, R. P. 39, 44
Carstens, P. 171, 173
Cavigneaux, A. 161, 173
Chang, H.-J. 263, 272
Charnigo, L. 10–12, 18
Claessen, H. J. M. 15, 16, 18
Clark, D. 11, 19
Clifford, R. J. 167, 173
Clivaz, C. 13, 18
Collins, J. J. 250, 255
Cook, J. 250, 251, 255
Cooper, J. S. 240, 246
Corbishley, T. 126, 132, 136
Counts, D. B. 13, 17
Crenshaw, J. L. 250, 255
Cross, F. M. 190, 196
Crowfoot, J. W. 3, 8
Crown, A. D. 10, 18
Cryer, F. H. 39, 44
Cullis, J. 11, 18

Dalton, M. S. 10–12, 18
Davies, P. R. 39, 44, 102, 117
Davis, P. 12, 18
Dearman, A. 80, 89
Deeb, L. 37, 44
Dever, W. G. 16, 18, 26–9, 33, 40, 44, 89
Dickie, A. C. 3, 8
Diebner, B.-J. 191, 196
Donaldson, R. C. 191, 196
Drinkard, J. 79, 84, 89
Duncan, J. G. 3, 6, 9
Dušek, J. 94, 100
Dusinberre, E. R. M. 215–17, 220, 222
Duverger, M. 220, 222
Dylan, B. 192, 196

Echols, C. F. 191, 192, 196
Edmunds, A. 10, 11, 18
Edwards, S. 21
Egger, R. 94, 100
Eilers, C. 131, 136
Eisenstadt, S. 220, 222
Elliger, K. 165, 174

Ellis, D. 11, 18
Eshel, I. 4, 9
Exum, J. C. 177, 188, 193, 196

Faust, A. 41, 42, 44
Feldman, L. H. 249, 255
Ferber, M. 196
Fewell, D. N. 171, 174
Filson, F. V. 66, 75
Finkelstein, I. 5, 8, 28, 29, 33, 44, 80, 81, 85, 89, 98, 100, 210, 222
Fitzgerald, G. M. 3, 8
Ford, M. 11, 18
Forti, T. 251, 255
Foster, B. R. 161, 163, 164, 174, 181, 188
Fox, M. V. 168, 174
Franken, H. J. 3, 6, 8
Freedman, D. N. 190, 196
Frei, H. W. 147, 155
Frese, D. A. 180, 188
Fried, L. S. 210–12, 214, 215, 217–19, 222, 223
Fried, M. H. 15, 18, 216
Friedman, R. E. 201, 208
Frier, B. W. 220, 222
Fritz, V. 202, 208
Frolov, S. 191, 196

Gadot, Y. 4, 8
Galil, G. 77, 89
García Martínez, F. 113, 115, 117
Garfinkel, Y. 81, 85, 89
Gass, E. 182, 188
Gatto, J. T. 31, 33
Gellner, E. 15, 18
Genette, G. 236, 246
George, A. R. 182, 188
Gmirkin, R. 83, 87, 89, 248, 249, 255
Gnuse, R. K. 249, 255
Goethe, J. W. von 159, 174
Goodblatt, D. 131, 136
Gordon, J. M. 13, 17
Görg, M. 191, 196
Gottwald, N. K. 29, 33
Grabbe, L. L. 39, 44
Green, H. 15, 18
Greenberg, R. 44
Greenfield, J. C. 167, 174

Gregory, A. 13, 18
Grey, M. J. 182, 188
Griffith, S. H. 149, 156
Grohmann, M. 240, 246
de Groot, A. 4, 6, 8, 9
Gudme de Hemmer, A. K. 160, 174
Guillaume, P. 179, 187, 188, 193, 196, 249, 255
Gunkel, H. 182, 188
Gunn, D. M. 174
Gunn, L. 119, 136, 171

Haapoja, J. 11, 18
Haber, S. 122, 135, 136
Hachlili, R. 123, 136
Hagedorn, A. C. 250, 255
Halbertal, M. 258, 272
Hamel, E. 259, 272
Hammond, M. M. 245, 246
Harrington, D. J. 184, 188
Hauser, A. J. 191, 196
Heger, P. 52, 60
Heimpel, W. 186, 188
Heltzer, M. 221, 223
Hendin, D. 123, 136, 137
Herzog, Z. 8
Hess, R. S. 25, 33
Hirschberg, H. Z. 260, 272
Hjelm, I. 174
Hoffmeier, J. K. 35, 44, 120, 137
Hoffner, H. A., Jr 187, 188
Høgenhaven, J. 104, 108, 111, 115, 117, 118, 160, 174
Holden, C. 12, 13, 19
Holloway, S. W. 40, 44
Holst, S. 105, 107, 108, 117
Horgan, M. 115, 118
Houlden, L. 249, 255
Houtman, C. 199, 208
Hurowitz, V. 85, 89, 201, 208
Huvila, I. 13, 19

Ibn Kathir, I. 272
Ilan, T. 123, 137
Ivakhiv, A. 14, 19
Izre'el, S. 161, 162, 164, 174

Jacobsen, T. 42, 44, 163
Jacobson, T. 174
Jamali, H. R. 14, 19

Japhet, S. 204, 208, 233, 246
Jaroš, K. 67, 74
Jeremias, J. 195, 196
Jursa, M. 214, 217, 223

Keestra, M. 13, 14, 19
Kegler, J. 203, 208
Kelle, B. 77, 80, 89
Kent, R. G. 211, 223
Khalidi, T. 153, 156
Khatibi, A. 258, 259, 272
Kim, S. J. 245, 246
King, D. W. 10, 12, 21, 37
King, P. J. 44
Kirby, P. 120, 137
Kitchen, K. A. 24, 33, 248, 255
Klawans, J. 122, 137
Klein, J. T. 14, 19, 235, 236
Klein, R. W. 246
Kletter, R. 15, 16, 19, 38, 39, 42, 44, 45
Knoppers, G. N. 221, 223, 235, 246
Kofoed, J. B. 24, 33, 68, 74
Kooij, G. van der 71, 72, 74, 98, 100
Kupitz, Y. S. 248, 255
Kvanvig, H. S. 167, 174

Lagrange, M.-J. 132, 137, 182, 188
Laisney, V. P.-M. 249, 255
Landhuis, E. 11, 15, 19
Lang, B. 248, 255
Lapp, N. L. 66, 74
Lazaridis, N. 249, 255
Leibner, U. 182, 188
Légasse, S. 206–8
Leick, G. 239, 246
Lemaire, A. 211, 223
Lemche, N. P. 24, 28, 31, 33, 34, 39, 40, 42, 45, 49, 60, 68, 74, 248, 249, 256
Levin, Y. 87, 89
Levine, B. A. 40, 45, 240, 246
Levy, T. E. 35, 45
Lewis, N. 217, 220, 223
Lichtheim, M. 214, 223
Lindars, B. 191, 193, 196
Linde, S. J. van der 69, 72, 75
Lindhardt, P. G. 23, 34
Lively, L. 11, 19
Liverani, M. 161, 163, 164, 174
Lockman, Z. 37, 45
Long, B. O. 27, 34, 39, 45

Long, V. P. 24, 34, 68, 74
Longman, T. 24, 34
Lönnqvist, H. 13, 19
Loprieno, A. 250, 256
Loretz, O. 167, 174
Louden, B. 248–50, 256
Lucas, E. 248, 256
Luckenbill, D. D. 89
Luckmann, T. 38, 44
Luhmann, N. 241, 246
Lyall, C. 14, 19

Mabe, M. 10, 21
Macalister, R. A. S. 3, 6, 9
Macchi, J.-D. 98, 100
Magen, Y. 94, 100, 221, 223
Magness, J. 134, 136, 182, 188
Magonet, J. 171, 174
May, N. N. 188
Mays, R. 10, 12, 21
Mazar, E. 5, 9
McKinlay, J. E. 165, 169–74
Meho, L. I. 11, 19
Mendels, D. 56, 60
Mendenhall, G. E. 29, 34
Menken, S. 13, 14, 19
Meshel, Z. 80-2, 89
Mettinger, T. N. D. 161-3, 174
Milgrom, J. 240, 246
Millard, A. 35, 44, 77, 80, 89
Miller, M. C. 217, 223
Miller, R. D. 188
Miller, S. 182, 186, 188
Mobley, G. 187, 188
de Moor, J. C. 190, 196
Moore, G. E. 179, 188
Moorey, P. S. 37, 45
Morgan, C. L. 11, 19
Morris, A. 10, 11, 18
Müller, M. 34, 147, 151, 156
Mumcuoglu, M. 81, 85, 89

Na'aman, N. 80, 88, 89
Neuwirth, A. 150, 156, 258, 261, 270, 272
Nicholas, D. 11, 14, 19
Niditch, S. 194, 196, 251, 256
Nielsen, F. A. J. 248, 256
Niemann, H. M. 193, 196
Niesiołowski-Spanò, L. 50, 51, 53, 59, 60

Nir, R. 120, 137
Niskanen, P. 249, 256
Noam, V. 120, 137
Nodet, E. 96, 100, 122, 131, 137
Noth, M. 200, 202, 208
Notley, R. S. 177, 188

Oesterley, P. 248, 256
Ogot, B. A. 196
Olsson, M. 13, 19
Otto, E. 173, 174, 180, 188
Overland, P. 249, 256

Paine, E. 11, 12, 19
Palmer, A. S. 187, 188
Palmer, C. L. 11, 12, 14, 20
Parrinder, G. 151, 156
Peddie, I. 191, 196
Perdue, L. 248, 256
Pfoh, E. 38, 39, 45
Picchioni, S. A. 161, 174
Pijpers, A. 10, 20
Pirmann, C. M. 11, 20
Plaut, W. G. 250, 256
Plume, A. 10, 15, 20
Pollock, S. 37, 44
Pontis, S. 10, 11, 17, 20
Popovič, M. 87, 89
Powell, B. B. 249, 256
Power, C. D. 13, 20
Prag, K. 4, 9
Pritchard, J. B. 161, 174
Provan, I. 24, 34, 40
Provan, I. W. 45
Pucci Ben Zeev, M. 124, 137
Puech, E. 99, 100, 109, 118
Pummer, R. 94, 98, 100
de Pury, A. 52, 60

Rainey, A. F. 177, 188
Räisänen, H. 151, 156
Ranston, H. 250, 254, 256
Reade, J. E. 180, 188
Reeck, M. 258, 273
Regev, J. 6, 9
Reinhartz, A. 122, 135, 136
Renear, A. H. 11, 12, 20
Reynolds, G. S. 264, 273
Rhoads, J. 132, 137
Robert, L. 219, 223

Robinson, E. 63, 74, 151
Robinson, N. 156
Rowton, M. B. 29, 34
Rudolf, W. 165, 174
Rudolph, W. 200, 204, 208, 213, 223
Ruffle, J. 249, 256
Runnels, C. 11, 20
Russell, J. 86, 90
Rutherford, I. 249, 256

Sabih, J. 258, 259, 263, 273
Sahas, D. J. 149, 156
San Nicolò, M. 214, 223
Sancisi-Weerdenburg, H. 217, 223
Sanders, E. P. 122, 137
Sanders, P. 195, 197
Sandoval, T. J. 248, 256
Sasson, J. 39, 45, 177, 181, 186, 235, 237, 246
Sasson, J. M. 188, 189
Schaper, J. 214, 223
Schenker, A. 99, 100
Schloen, J. D. 16, 20
Schmid, H. H. 172, 174
Schmitt, C. 273
Schniedewind, W. M. 190, 197
Schwartz, D. R. 104, 117, 120, 131, 137
Segal, M. 105, 118
Sekunda, N. V. 216, 217, 224
Sellin, E. 64, 74
Service, E. R. 15, 20
Shachar, I. 137
Shallit, A. 220, 224
Sharon, N. 123–5, 137
Shepherd, M. B. 270, 273
Sherrard, B. 66, 74
Shiloh, Y. 4, 6, 9
Shupak, N. 249, 256
Silberman, N. A. 81, 85, 89
Singer-Avitz, L. 8
Skalnik, P. 15, 18
Skjaervo, P. O. 211, 224
Skjeggestad, M. 15, 20
Smith, A. D. 15, 20
Snell, D. C. 249, 256
Soggin, J. A. 191, 197
Solomon, Y. 13, 20
Spanner, D. 14, 20
Speiser, E. A. 161, 174
Stager, L. 16, 20, 67, 74

Steiner, M. L. 3, 5, 6, 8, 9
Stenhouse, P. 261, 273
Stol, M. 239, 240, 247
Stone, S. 11, 15, 20
Stordalen, T. 236, 247
Sufian, A. 13, 20
Szanton, N. 9

Tabari, I. J. 271, 273
Tadmor, H. 84, 90
Taha, H. 68, 71, 72, 74
Tan, N. N. H. 251, 257
Tavernier, J. 211, 224
Taylor, J. E. 98, 100, 249, 257
Teffeau, L. C. 11, 20
Tenopir, C. 10, 12, 21
Thomas, M. A. 236, 247
Thompson, T. L. 27, 34, 35, 39, 45, 46, 49, 60, 61, 67, 74, 90, 101, 105, 118, 141, 142, 144, 165, 174, 197–9, 208, 224, 248, 249, 257, 270, 273
Thomsen, P. 64, 74
Tibbo, H. R. 11, 19
Tigchelaar, E. J. C. 113, 117
Tindale, T. J. 10, 21
Tobolowsky, A. 248, 257
Torrance, R. M. 186, 189
Tov, E. 105, 118
Toy, C. H. 248, 257
Trafton, J. L. 108, 118
Tudhope, D. 13, 21
Tuplin, C. 211, 224
Tushingham, A. D. 3, 9
Tyrell, G. 138, 144
Tzoref, S. 109, 111, 118

Ussishkin, D. 8, 81, 86, 90
Uziel, J. 4, 8, 9

Van den Dries, M. H. 69, 72, 75
Van der Keulen, P. S. F. 202, 206, 208
Van Seters, J. 49, 61, 198, 200, 209
van Wijlick, H. 126, 127, 137
Vermes, G. 146, 156
Vincent, L.-H. 6, 9
Vlachidis, A. 13, 21
Volentine, R. 10, 12, 21

Waerzeggers, H. G. M. 224
Wajdenbaum, P. 51, 61, 248, 249, 257

Walcot, P. 249, 257
Wallace, H. N. 172, 174
Ware, M. 10, 21
Warren, Ch. E. 3, 9
Webster, A. C. 11, 18
Weijen, D. van 10, 15, 20
Weill, R. 4, 9
Weiser, A. 190, 197
Wellhausen, J. 190, 197, 200, 209
Wenham, G. J. 24, 34
Wesselius, J.-W. 248, 257
West, M. L. 249, 251–3, 257
Westenholz, A. 164, 168, 175
Westenholz, U. 164, 168, 175
Westermann, C. 198, 209, 249, 257
Wette, W. M. L. de 199, 209
White, H. D. 14, 21
White, M. 94, 100
White Crawford, S. 105, 118, 172–4
Whitelam, K. W. 39–41, 46, 160, 175
Whittaker, J. 197
Whybray, R. N. 249, 250, 257
Wightman, G. J. 81, 90
Wilcke, C. 161, 175

Willi, T. 243, 247
Williamson, H. G. M. 221, 224, 226, 247
Wilson, I. D. 243, 247
Wilson, P. 11, 14, 15, 21
Winegar, J. 37, 44
Wintermute, O. S. 56, 61
Winters, J. 11, 19
Wise, M. 134, 137
Wong, G. T. K. 179, 189
Wright, G. E. 65, 71, 75
Wright, G. R. H. 67, 70, 75
Wu, L. 10, 12, 21
Wyatt, N. 171, 175

Yoffee, N. 15, 21

Zadok, R. 95, 100, 211, 224
Zahn, M. 105, 107, 118
Zauzich, K.-T. 215, 224
Ze'evi, D. 52, 61
Zevit, Z. 37, 46
Zissu, B. 182, 188
Zwelling, J. 68, 75

www.ingramcontent.com/pod-product-compliance
Lightning Source LLC
Chambersburg PA
CBHW070015010526
44117CB00011B/1588